**Wisdom**

# Wisdom
## Its nature, origins, and development

*Edited by*

ROBERT J. STERNBERG
*Yale University*

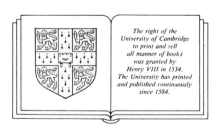

CAMBRIDGE UNIVERSITY PRESS
*Cambridge*
*New York   Port Chester   Melbourne   Sydney*

Published by the Press Syndicate of the University of Cambridge
The Pitt Building, Trumpington Street, Cambridge CB2 1RP
40 West 20th Street, New York, NY 10011, USA
10 Stamford Road, Oakleigh, Melbourne 3166, Australia

First published 1990

Printed in the United States of America

*Library of Congress Cataloging-in-Publication Data*
Wisdom : its nature, origins, and development /
edited by Robert J. Sternberg.

   p.   cm.

ISBN 0-521-36453-1. – ISBN 0-521-36718-2 (pbk.)

1. Wisdom.   I. Sternberg, Robert J.
BF431.W575   1990
153–dc20   89–13901


*British Library Cataloguing-in-Publication Data*
Wisdom : its nature, origins, and development.

1. Knowledge. Philosophical perspectives
I. Sternberg, Robert J.
121


ISBN 0-521-36453-1 (hardback)
ISBN 0-521-36718-2 (paperback)

# Contents

# Contributors

Patricia Kennedy Arlin
School of Education
University of British Columbia
Vancouver, BC V6T 1V7
Canada

Paul B. Baltes
Max Planck Institute for Human
  Development and Education
Lentzeallee 94
D–1000 Berlin 33
Federal Republic of Germany

James E. Birren
Borun Center
University of California—Los Angeles
UCLA School of Medicine
10833 LeConte Avenue (CHS32-144)
Los Angeles, CA 90024–1687

Helene G. Brenner
School of Education
University of Denver
University Park
Denver, CO 80208–0181

Michael J. Chandler
Department of Psychology
University of British Columbia
2136 West Mall
Vancouver, BC V6T 1Y7
Canada

Mihaly Csikszentmihalyi
Department of Behavioral Sciences
University of Chicago
5848 S. University Avenue
Chicago, IL 60637

Laurel M. Fisher
Department of Psychology, MC1061
University of Southern California
Los Angeles, CA 90089–1061

Stephen Holliday
Riverview Hospital
2136 West Mall
Vancouver, BC V6T 1Y7
Canada

Karen Strohm Kitchener
School of Education
University of Denver
University Park
Denver, CO 80208–0181

Deirdre A. Kramer
Department of Psychology
Rutgers University
Tillett Hall, Kilmer Campus
New Brunswick, NY 08903

Gisela Labouvie-Vief
Department of Psychology
Wayne State University
71 W. Warren Avenue
Detroit, MI 48202

John A. Meacham
Department of Psychology
SUNY at Buffalo, Park Hall
Buffalo, NY 14260

Lucinda Orwoll
Department of Psychology
University of Michigan
300 North Ingalls
Ann Arbor, MI 48109

Juan Pascual-Leone
Department of Psychology
York University
4700 Keele Street
North York, Ontario M3J 1P3
Canada

Marion Perlmutter
Institute of Gerontology
University of Michigan
300 North Ingalls
Ann Arbor, MI 48109

Kevin Rathunde
Department of Psychology
University of Chicago
5848 S. University Avenue
Chicago, IL 60637

Daniel N. Robinson
Department of Psychology
Georgetown University
Washington, DC 20057

Jacqui Smith
Max Planck Institute for Human
    Development and Education
Lentzeallee 94
D–1000 Berlin 33
Federal Republic of Germany

Robert J. Sternberg
Department of Psychology
Yale University
New Haven, CT 06520

# Preface

Wisdom is about as elusive as psychological constructs get. It is perhaps for this reason that it is one of the least studied such constructs. Indeed, few people even view wisdom as defining a field of inquiry, in the way that, say, perception, learning, thinking, intelligence, or creativity would be viewed as defining fields of inquiry. But within the past few years, a field that came close to being a nonentity has burgeoned, and the present book is an attempt to document the progress that has been made – mostly during the 1980s – toward understanding wisdom and to point the way for future theory and research.

Fields of knowledge go through a series of overlapping periods, which might roughly be characterized in terms of four stages:

1. an initial stage in which people become interested in a phenomenon and start thinking about how to study it;
2. an early developmental stage in which theory and research really get going and people try to set paradigms and convince others of the worth of their paradigms;
3. a mature stage in which one or more of a small number of paradigms become prominent while others wither on the vine, and a bevy of researchers further develop those paradigms that have passed the early stages;
4. and a postmature stage in which researchers become frustrated with inconsistencies in experimental results and with the inability of the going paradigm or paradigms to answer the questions they really want to answer.

During the postmature stage, people are searching around for new paradigms. If they succeed, they enter the first stage, which merges almost imperceptibly with the last. If they do not succeed, the field usually becomes dormant until one or more investigators with some new ideas reinitiate the first stage.

I believe that the ideal time to edit a book on a topic is during the second stage of development. During the first stage of development, there is not enough research and often not enough well-formulated ideas to support a substantial book. By the third stage, the going paradigms are already established, so that an edited book serves less to guide a field than to review what has already been done. This latter is a valuable function but I believe results in a book that is less influential because the ways of the field have already been set. Of course, by this third stage there is more to review and less likelihood that the leads provided in the book will be viewed as false. But not to worry, because by the end of the fourth stage, all of the leads will be viewed as false anyway – as having led to a dead-end or down a garden path with no clear end.

It was a combination of my interest in the topic of wisdom with my perception of the field as being in the second stage of development that encouraged me to initiate the present project. I came to believe that after years of being moribund, the field was experiencing a rebirth, and that the time to nurture the field in its growing years had come. I hope, of course, that readers of this book will view it as serving that function.

This book is intended for advanced undergraduates, graduate students, and professionals interested in understanding the nature of wisdom. Although the authors of the book are all psychologists, many of them draw heavily upon the philosophical literature, and hence I believe the book will be of interest to philosophers as well as psychologists. Within psychology, the authors draw upon the theories and methods of developmental, cognitive, social, personality, differential, and educational psychology, and hence I believe that the book will be readable by individuals in many areas of specialization. To my knowledge, it is the only book of its kind, and hence I believe that it will be indispensable reading for those wishing a broad review of current psychological thinking about wisdom.

As usual, there are several people to thank for helping this book come to be. Most important are the authors: This was that rare edited book where everyone asked to contribute agreed to do so and then actually came through with a chapter. I am particularly grateful to Paul Baltes: It was while listening to him lecture about the results of his program of research on wisdom, probably the most comprehensive such program in the field, that I became convinced that this book could become a reality. I am also grateful to Susan Milmoe, my acquisitions editor at Cambridge University Press, for supporting this project, as she has supported many others. Finally, I wish to thank my children, Seth and Sara, whose entrance into the world probably taught me more about wisdom and the need for it than has any other single event in my life. We all hope that the current children of the world will grow up to have more wisdom than we have had: If they don't, there may not be a world in which their children can have the chance to have more wisdom than their parents.

RJS

September 1989

*Part I*

# Approaches to the study of wisdom

# 1    Understanding wisdom

*Robert J. Sternberg*

To understand wisdom fully and correctly probably requires more wisdom than any of us have. Thus, we cannot quite comprehend the nature of wisdom because of our own lack of it. But if scientists were to demand total understanding, they would quickly be out of their jobs, because total understanding is something we can fancy we are approaching, but it is almost certainly not something we can ever achieve. And if we are to believe the authors of the chapters in this book, the recognition that total understanding will always elude us is itself a sign of wisdom.

The chapter authors take a number of different approaches to understanding wisdom. Any attempt to classify these approaches is bound to be an oversimplification, and a rather gross one at that. Yet, in order to give readers at least a rough lay of the land, I have sought to divide the book into five parts, the middle three of which represent three distinctive, although overlapping, approaches to understanding wisdom and the first and last of which respectively serve to introduce and to integrate the three approaches. The three approaches draw on philosophical, folk, and psychodevelopmental views of wisdom, respectively.

Part I, Approaches to the Study of Wisdom, comprises just the present chapter, chapter 1, which sets the stage for "understanding wisdom." This chapter describes the three main approaches used by authors of this book in understanding wisdom and briefly summarizes the main contents of each chapter.

Part II of the book describes work drawing primarily on philosophical conceptions of wisdom. This part comprises three chapters.

Chapter 2, "Wisdom through the Ages," by Daniel N. Robinson, is the only chapter in the book where an author was given an explicit "assignment," in this case, to provide a brief history of philosophical views on wisdom. Robinson begins with Socrates in the 5th century B.C. and ends with the interpreters of Kant in the 19th century A.D. Robinson notes that the Platonic *Dialogues* provide the first comprehensive analysis of wisdom. Wisdom is here viewed as taking three forms: as a special gift of the philosopher and those who pursue truth; as the practical gift of statesmen and lawgivers; and as the

3

gift of those who pursue scientific knowledge of the nature of things. These three aspects of wisdom continue to be seen in present-day accounts of the nature of the construct.

Chapter 3, by Mihaly Csikszentmihalyi and Kevin Rathunde, also views wisdom in terms of three aspects, although the three aspects do not directly correspond to Plato's. In "The Psychology of Wisdom: An Evolutionary Interpretation," the authors suggest an approach to the study of wisdom that they refer to as "evolutionary hermeneutics." This approach is based on the idea that historically used concepts relating to the evaluation of human behavior, including wisdom, are likely to have adaptive value for humankind. The goal of the authors, then, is to understand how wisdom has been understood through the ages, particularly in the philosophical literature but also in psychology and elsewhere. First, wisdom can be understood as a cognitive process used in attempts to understand the world in a disinterested way, seeking the ultimate causes and consequences of events while preserving the integration of knowledge. Wisdom can also be understood as a virtue providing a compelling guide to action. Through wisdom, it becomes possible to improve our lives by understanding how better to order our actions so as to achieve closer harmony with the laws of the physical universe. Third, wisdom can be understood as a personal good, that is, as an intrinsically rewarding experience that provides high enjoyment and happiness when a person reflects on the connection between events in a disinterested way. Through these three aspects, wisdom provides a major mechanism of cultural evolution and an alternative to extrinsic rewards based on pleasure and materialism.

In chapter 4, "Wisdom as Integrated Thought: Historical and Developmental Perspectives," Gisela Labouvie-Vief draws heavily on two modes of thought suggested by the ancient Greeks: *mythos* and *logos*. In the former mode, *mythos*, experience is holistic and based on a bond of close identification between the self and the object of thought. Thought and the thinker, knower and the known, merge into a single, indivisible unit. The meaning of experience derives from this integration. Thus, integration plays an important role in Labouvie-Vief's conception of wisdom, as it does in Csikszentmihalyi and Rathunde's. In the latter mode, *logos*, meaning is disembedded from a reality of flux and change and is related instead to stable systems of categorization. It is embedded in that part of knowledge that is arguable and that can be demonstrated and defined with precision and agreement. In *logos*, knowledge can be rendered in a way that is mechanistic and computable. Labouvie-Vief suggests that wisdom is grounded in *mythos*, whereas much of our society is grounded in *logos*, the mode of thought that has come to be associated with scientific thinking. Labouvie-Vief believes her notion of wisdom to be closely related to Plato's in asserting the essential compatibility of the abstract with the concrete and the theoretical with the practical. We cannot find wisdom in a disembedded theory of abstract or hypotheticodeductive thought.

Part IV of the book contains four chapters drawing heavily upon folk conceptions of wisdom. None of these chapters rely exclusively upon such conceptions. Rather, they use these conceptions in the way they should be used: to serve as a basis for the formulation of explicit psychological theories. Folk conceptions are thus a springboard for theory rather than the final theory in and of themselves.

Chapter 5, by Paul B. Baltes and Jacqui Smith, draws upon the large program of theory and research instigated some years back by Baltes to understand intellectual functioning and its development. In their chapter, "Toward a Psychology of Wisdom and Its Ontogenesis," Baltes and Smith draw upon Baltes's dual process framework of intelligence, according to which intelligence is understood in terms of basic mechanics of information processing and in terms of knowledge-rich pragmatics. The former is largely content free, universal and biological, and susceptible to genetic differences. The latter is largely content rich, culture dependent, and experience based. They view the latter, pragmatic aspect of intelligence as most relevant to wisdom, which they define as expertise in the domain of fundamental life pragmatics, such as life planning, management, and review. Wise persons are viewed as having exceptional insight into human development and life matters and as having exceptionally good judgment, advice, and commentary about difficult life problems. Five criteria for assessing wisdom are rich factual knowledge about matters of life, rich procedural knowledge about life problems, knowledge about the contexts of life and their relationships, knowledge about differences in values and priorities, and knowledge about the relative indeterminacy and unpredictability of life. They describe a series of studies supporting their view, particularly studies of people's folk conceptions of wisdom done in their laboratory and others'. They pool the data from various folk studies in support of their view. Two of the supporting folk-conceptual data sets are those of Chandler and Holliday and of Sternberg, whose contributions form the next two chapters.

Chapter 6, by Michael J. Chandler with Stephen Holliday, reviews a number of conceptions of wisdom, including Baltes's. Chandler and Holliday do not interpret their data in the same way as do Baltes and Smith, and indeed, the former authors are critical of the conception of Baltes and Smith, believing it too much to emphasize expertise, which they believe can narrow rather than broaden people's visions of what is wise, and too much to emphasize an abstract good that may not work in real-life contexts. Drawing on their own data on folk conceptions of wisdom, Chandler and Holliday suggest as key elements of wisdom exceptional understanding, judgment and communication skills, and general competence.

Chapter 7, by Robert J. Sternberg, also draws upon a study of folk conceptions of wisdom. The chapter, "Wisdom and Its Relations to Intelligence and Creativity," describes a study rather different from other studies in that it compares conceptions of wisdom with those of intelligence and creativity and also draws upon subjects not only from the lay population but also from a population of professors of art, business, philosophy, and physics. Multidimensional scaling of the lay data revealed six basic elements in folk conceptions of wisdom: reasoning ability, sagacity, learning from ideas and environment, judgment, expeditious use of information, and perspicacity. Wisdom was most distinguished from intelligence in the dimension of sagacity. These data form the backdrop for a theory of wisdom that involves multiple elements, including aspects of knowledge, information processing, intellectual style, personality, motivation, and environmental context. It is argued that these elements can be used to distinguish behavior that is prototypically wise from behavior that is prototypically intelligent or prototypically creative.

Chapter 8, by Lucinda Orwoll and Marion Perlmutter, deals with wisdom and the study of wise persons. These authors suggest that wisdom is relatively rare because it entails exceptional personality development as well as exceptional cognitive functioning. Thus, for these authors, advanced cognitive development is necessary but not sufficient for wisdom to be displayed. The wise individual is not only smart, but also has a personality structure that enables him or her to transcend personal needs, thoughts, and feelings. These investigators propose an empirical approach to studying wisdom that involves an intensive study of adults who are considered wise. Such adults are selected on the basis of nominations, which in turn depend upon folk conceptions of wisdom and who is nominated on the basis of these conceptions. The authors also compare results of three studies of folk conceptions of wisdom – those of Clayton and Birren, Sternberg, and Holliday and Chandler, which they view as supporting their dual cognitive–personality conception of wisdom.

Part IV of the book contains chapters that emphasize psychodevelopmental approaches to understanding wisdom. The five chapters in this part draw upon a diversity of developmental theories.

Chapter 9, by John A. Meacham, is an outlier by any standard. In his chapter, "The Loss of Wisdom," Meacham suggests that wisdom may decrease, rather than increase, with age – a position taken, at least explicitly, by none of the other contributors to the book. Meacham views wisdom in terms of one's knowledge that one doesn't know. The wise person is one who appreciates the fallibility of knowledge. He or she balances knowledge, on the one hand, with doubting, on the other, thereby avoiding the extremes of too-confident knowing and of too-cautious doubting. Wisdom lies not in what a person knows, but rather in how the person uses the knowledge he or she has. It is an attitude toward knowledge as well as toward beliefs, values, and skills. Meacham believes that in addition to this attitude, wisdom involves varying degrees of profundity. One can be wise in a relatively simple domain, but such wisdom is ultimately less impressive than wisdom in a more profound domain.

Chapter 10, by Karen Strohm Kitchener and Helene G. Brenner, draws upon Kitchener's Reflective Judgment model, a model of adult cognitive development. The chapter, "Wisdom and Reflective Judgment: Knowing in the Face of Uncertainty," views wisdom as an advanced stage of intellectual development. Wisdom, according to the proposed model, comprises four aspects:

1. a recognition of the presence of unavoidably difficult and inherently thorny problems that confront all adults;
2. a comprehensive grasp of knowledge that is characterized by both breadth and depth of understanding;
3. a recognition that knowledge is uncertain and that it is not possible for truth to be absolutely knowable at any given time; and
4. a willingness and exceptional ability to formulate sound, executable judgments in the face of life's uncertainties.

All of these aspects are present in other models, but the present model is a unique integration of the four particular aspects. Kitchener's work is unusual in that it involves a measurement scale – the Reflective Judgment Interview – that can measure levels of thought and particularly the highest level, which Kitchener and Brenner see as prerequisite for wisdom.

Chapter 11, by Patricia Kennedy Arlin, is similar to chapter 10 in its drawing upon a stage model of the development of thought. But whereas Kitchener has postulated reflective judgment as the final stage, Arlin has postulated problem finding as the final stage in her model. Arlin suggests that wisdom is a function not of the answers one reaches but of the questions one poses. In "Wisdom: The Art of Problem Finding," Arlin suggests that wisdom and problem finding, although not identical, are highly related. Shared between them are

1. preoccupation with questions rather than answers,
2. the search for complementarity among points of view,
3. the detection of asymmetry in the face of evidence implying symmetry and equilibrium,
4. openness to change, pushing of the limits and possible redefinition of those limits,
5. a sense of taste for problems that are of fundamental importance, and
6. preference for certain conceptual directions.

In chapter 12, "An Essay on Wisdom: Toward Organismic Processes that Make It Possible," Juan Pascual-Leone takes what he refers to as a dialectical-constructivist perspective on wisdom, in particular, and on cognitive development, in general. He views wisdom as a complex state category of a domain he calls vital reasoning. Wisdom is the state reached by an individual when the interrelations and dialectical integrations (i.e., resolutions of contradictions) across all and any of the vital domains of that person's life have attained a critical mass wherein new qualitative principles of integration across various domains have emerged. What might some examples of these qualitative principles be? Pascual-Leone suggests three principles:

1. Wisdom causes the expert counselor to adopt a paradoxical attitude that fosters freedom while stressing the authority of reason and reasonable tradition.
2. Wisdom involves restricting one's interventions on others and on the world to those needed to restore harmonious relations among others and among elements of the world.
3. Wisdom involves dialectical integration of one's soul with one's agency in the world.

Here, as in the other chapters in this part of the book, wisdom is viewed as part of the unfolding of a developmental process, in this case, one in which a dialectical view of the world and one's role in it is finally reached.

Chapter 13, by Deirdre Kramer, sets a framework for conceptualizing wisdom based on the primacy of affect–cognition relations. Like Orwoll and Perlmutter, Kramer views the integration of affect and cognition as central to wisdom. Kramer suggests that there are five key wisdom-related processes:

1. recognition of individuality,
2. recognition of context,
3. ability to interact effectively,
4. understanding of change and growth, and
5. attention to affect and cognition.

Wisdom enables an individual to adapt to the tasks of adult life, such as choosing a career, developing an intimate relationship, raising children, and in general, adjusting to the stressors of adult life. In particular, it allows individuals to solve problems confronting themselves, to advise others, to manage social institutions, to review their own lives, and to introspect spiritually.

Part V contains a single chapter, chapter 14, by James E. Birren and Laurel M. Fisher, which serves to integrate the other chapters in this book. This chapter points out common as well as unique features of the various accounts of wisdom and suggests directions in which future theory and research might lead us.

I believe that readers of this book will find themselves well-educated regarding both contemporary and historical views of the nature of wisdom. I also believe they have another treat in store for them. Many edited books contain sets of independent chapters by authors who are unaware of (or unwilling to cite) each other's work, and of the relations of their work to that of other investigators in the field. This book represents an effort pretty close to the opposite end of the spectrum: Authors are obviously well-acquainted with each other's work and cite each other extensively. Moreover, they point out the interrelations of their views, so that interweaving of the contributions is not left for the final, integrative chapter. Some editors might have been inclined to edit out the extensive intercitation to conserve space and reduce redundancy. I have maintained it, because I believe that whatever redundancy may result is more than compensated for by the cross-fertilization of ideas that occurs precisely because authors have been so generous and assiduous in analyzing how their own ideas relate to those of others.

*Part II*

**Approaches informed by philosophical conceptions of wisdom**

**Wisdom through the ages**

*Daniel N. Robinson*

In this brief historical review of the topic of wisdom, selectivity is not only unavoidable but also unavoidably arbitrary. The subject forms perhaps the major chapter in the history of philosophy where it is often inextricably joined to political, moral, and jural matters. It is also both the aim and the target of various literary genres, of scripture, meditation, and the saintly ways of life. Most of this falls beyond the editor's expectations, not to mention the author's gifts. A manageable alternative, and the one adopted here, calls for a summary of the teachings of the major philosophers and their disciples or schools and the extent to which these teachings have found or might have found a place within that "mental science" of the 19th century that has now matured into "cognitive science."

### Socrates (469?–399 B.C.)

Long before the advent of genuinely philosophical modes of analysis and inquiry there was a prosperous folk philosophy contained in the epic poems attributed to Homer, epics that imposed a discernible pattern on the thoughts and perspectives of the more influential teachers in Hellenic and Hellenistic Greece. I have dealt with this at greater length elsewhere (Robinson, 1989), but the main points should be noted.

It is a feature of epic literature to teach lessons and to explain the causes of things through the medium of a story. Homer's *Odyssey* and *Iliad* are, of course, not merely tales of adventure. They are punctuated with folk theories of motivation, personality, the role and the limits of reason, and the power of the gods and of the fates in relation to human affairs. The early Greeks, like even the most primitive communities, had a conception of soul or spirit. Unlike most primitive communities – unlike even the advanced civilizations that preceded them – these same Greeks externalized their conceptions and made them topics first of epic poems, then of dramatic literature, and finally of philosophical analysis.

In the matter of wisdom, Homeric psychology is at once dualistic and exclusionary. Animals are endowed with souls but not with *noos* (later to be

13

*nous),* that special type of mental prowess at the foundation of plans and strategies. As Jan Bremmer notes, in Homer, "the *noos* is always located in the chest ... but is never conceived of as something material" (Bremmer, 1987, p. 57). Similarly, *menos* is the nonmaterial source of significant and coordinated but impulsive conduct typically performed in combat or under conditions of great duress. Beset by *lyssa,* the "wolf's rage," the warrior will even defy the gods as he visits punishment on those who have caused him grief or dishonor. It is, however, *noos* that is unique to human psychology, and thus as early as the Homeric epics, Greek teaching took rationality as humanity's defining mark.

The Platonic dialogues[1] offer the earliest record of a sustained analysis of the concept of wisdom. The analysis proceeds from the recognition that the term itself is not univocal but customarily refers to quite different aspects of intellectual, moral, and ordinary life. There is wisdom as *sophia,* the special gift of the philosopher and of those in general who have devoted themselves to a contemplative life in pursuit of truth. There is wisdom as *phronesis,* the "practical wisdom" of the statesman and lawgiver, the wisdom that locates the prudent course of action and resists the urgings of the passions and the deceptions of the senses. And there is wisdom as *episteme,* a form of scientific knowledge developed in those who know the nature of things and the principles governing their behavior.

Wisdom for the Socratics, either in the broader sense of *sophia* or in the prudential sense of *phronesis,* is one of the cardinal virtues and thus transcends the realm of the merely cognitive. Indeed, it is the first among the virtues *(Laws,* 688) and the only one that is innate *(Republic,* 518). But a corrupted form of wisdom is also the source of what is hurtful because wisdom

... more than anything else contains a divine element. ... Did you never observe the narrow intelligence flashing from the keen eye of a clever rogue? *(Republic,* 518)

As is made clear by the Athenian in Plato's *Laws,* wisdom must be the source of all political rule, its dictates imposed on what is often a reluctant and very unwise population. The citizen who resists the counsel of wisdom

... ought never to have any kind of authority entrusted to him: he must be stigmatized as ignorant, even though he be versed in calculation, and skilled in all sorts of accomplishments, and feats of mental dexterity; and the opposite are to be called wise, even although, in the words of the proverb, they know neither how to read nor how to swim. *(Laws,* 689)

Here, then, a clear dichotomy is introduced between specific mental abilities or skills and *wisdom,* which includes not only rationality but the will to conform one's life to its dictates. Wise men *(daimones)* may be illiterate, and the utterly unwise may be adept and accomplished. The two classes are separated by a difference in character, by a principle of self-control, by their ability to subordinate passion and desire to the authority of reason. To be wise is not, therefore, to possess a high IQ or to be a chess master or a theoretical physicist. It is to be a certain kind of person, temperamentally and morally won over to a love of harmony, beauty, and truth. This conception of wisdom is at the foundation of the well-known Socratic notion of evil as ignorance. As no one would intentionally do that which is injurious to oneself and incompatible with one's own flourishing, evil actions must proceed from that most devastating form of ignorance, the kind that rebels against the mandates of reason itself.

The Socratic conception of wisdom is also at the foundation of Socrates' well-known distrust of perceptual forms of knowledge and empirical modes of inquiry. The wisdom-loving person – the *philos-sophia* – is one who searches for the timeless and unchanging truths, never content with the shifting phenomena of the material world. The senses, equipped as they are to record only events in the realm of ceaseless fluxes, cannot be the light of truth. Like the emotions and other bodily distractions, the senses distort and deceive and otherwise hinge one's attention to the ephemeral and inconsequential. Thus are those hidden truths the *psyche* innately possesses rendered utterly inaccessible. Thus, also, is the *psyche* prevented from exercising and refining itself and becoming more fit for its subsequent incarnations. The play on the words *soma* (body) and *sema* (a grave) illustrates Socrates' conviction that the soul is entombed in the physical body, the latter being no more than a prison *(desmoterion)* that prevents the free flight of spirit toward wisdom. As he explains to Cebes in the *Phaedo*, the soul, after abandoning the spinning world of the senses and returning into herself,

...passes into the other world, the region of purity, and eternity, and immortality, and unchangeableness, which are her kindred, and with them she ever lives, when she is by herself and is not let or hindered; then she ceases from her erring ways, and being in communion with the unchanging is unchanging. And this state of the soul is called wisdom. *(Phaedo,* 79)


## Aristotle (384–322 B.C.)

Aristotle, whose anthropological studies ranged far beyond anything attempted by his celebrated teachers in the Academy, came to provide history's first integrated and systematic psychology. His treatises include detailed comparisons of numerous species as regards psychological attributes; careful delineations of the salient types of virtuous and vicious personalities; full discussions of the genetic, biological, cultural, and contextual factors influencing the formation of the human character from childhood to old age; and a taxonomy of the sensory, cognitive, and emotional dispositions and faculties and the various interactions occurring between and among them. Examined on the whole, his works yield a psychology that is naturalistic in spirit, empiricistic in method, and commonsensical in its theoretical biases. In the matter

16 DANIEL N. ROBINSON

of perception, emotion, motivation, and learning and memory, most of Aristotle's psychology identifies processes and principles common to nearly all animals, man included. It is only when he confronts both the fact of human rationality and its creations that his psychology becomes unequivocally dualistic. At this point, the naturalistic perspective is modified to accommodate the special powers of *human* nature. It is at this same point that his psychology becomes most vividly indebted to Socratic teaching.

Unlike Plato, Aristotle neither distrusts nor depreciates the material side of life and the material side of human psychology. A great biologist and ethologist, Aristotle appreciated the part taken by perception and emotion in the affairs of animal life. Survival depends on these conditions of the body, and senses that routinely deceive must finally make survival impossible. Thus, in his ethological and psychobiological treatises, Aristotle tends toward a commonsense realism, a nearly Jamesian pragmatism. He rejects older views that would attempt to separate souls from bodies, insisting instead that " ... each art must use its tools, each soul its body" *(On the Soul,* 407[b] 19–26).[2]

But as the very founder of comparative psychology, Aristotle was as cognizant of differences as of similarities. There are some attributes (e.g., sensation) that all animals have in common. There is at least one attribute (rationality; *epistemonikon)* that distinguishes human from nonhuman forms of animal life. Moreover, the identifying attributes of a creature signal the very particular task or mission – the *idion ergon* – that attaches to the life of that creature.

For man, the *idion ergon* is a life lived in conformity to the dictates of right reason *(orthos logos),* a life that thereby embodies *eudaimonia,* that condition of flourishing and completeness that constitutes true and enduring joy. To attain *eudaimonia,* one must, alas, possess wisdom and be ruled by it, for *eudaimonia* is not merely a set of pleasures or creature comforts or Epicurean delights. It is life lived in a certain way, where life here refers to life-on-the-whole, not some number of moments strung together. Progress toward this end calls for the recognition that the better course of action is not the one that invariably satisfies a current desire or even an abiding desire:

... [T]here is no necessity that because it is better it should also be more desirable: at least to be a philosopher is better than to make money, but it is not more desirable for the man who lacks the necessities of life. *(Topics,* 118[a] 8–15)

The mark of wisdom for Aristotle is the very character of the person as this character is revealed in that person's deliberated choices *(prohaireseis)* and dispositions *(hexeis).* The emotion of anger may be used illustratively. Anger is an entirely natural feeling, one expressed by all of the developed species and one on which survival often depends. The character of a person is assessed, then, not by determining *if* there is anger, but by noting that toward which the actor is disposed to be angry. One who is angered by injustice has a well-disposed anger – a "good *hexis*" for anger. One who is angered by the good fortune of another is beset by the vice of envy. What distinguishes the two is not the emotion *(pathos)* but the disposition *(hexis)*. To be wise is, among other considerations, to have passions and desires that are rightly disposed, such that one's deliberated choice *(prohairesis)* is always of that which promotes the flourishing of one's human and humanizing attributes. Lacking the power of rationality, animals (and children, too) cannot ground their choices in reasoned deliberation and are thus at passion's beck and call. In such a state, one is a slave, for a life of freedom is life as one *chooses* it to be.

To this point, the focus has been on the *practical wisdom (phronesis)* that stands at the foundation of action. Aristotle makes distinctions between this and the abstract or theoretical wisdom that stands at the foundation of philosophy itself. Theoretical knowledge *(theoretikes)* is devoted to truth, he says in the *Metaphysics,* whereas the object of practical knowledge *(praktikes)* is activity *(ergon),* though in both cases one must understand the causes of things *(Metaphysics,* 993$^b$ 20–24). Thus, Aristotle's famous theory of causation is inextricably tied up with his conception of wisdom. The wise man knows more than the material or efficient or formal causes behind events. He knows, too, the Final Cause, the *that for the sake of which* the other causal modalities are engaged. Given the close connection between Aristotle's conception of the Final Cause and of the *idion ergon* of something, it becomes clear why he finally votes for the contemplative rather than the practical life as the only path to *eudaimonia.* The latter is " . . . activity in accordance with excellence. . . . [T]his activity is contemplative *(theoretikos).* . . . And this activity alone would seem to be loved for its own sake" *(Nicomachean Ethics,* 1177$^a$ 11, 1177$^b$ 2). To be wise is to know thyself, to know the special sort of creature one is and to proceed to develop that unique power that sets one apart from all else that lives. To be wise is to strive for a condition of moral perfection or virtue *(arete)* by which the "golden mean" is found and adopted in all of the significant affairs of life.

The various powers and faculties of the *psyche* that so occupied Aristotle in his natural science are not neglected in the contemplative life. Note that *theoretikos* is rooted in meanings that include observation as well as speculation. Moreover, the contemplative life itself is a species of activity, indeed the most elevating. The wise man who is devoted to the development of his mind and the perfection of virtue may also find himself a statesman, a lawgiver, a leader of the people. Accordingly, the contemplative life has its public manifestations and its real-world challenges. Wisdom, however, requires this sort of life quite apart from any *other* good consequences. To recognize finally that one is essentially a rational being is to commit oneself to *theoretikos* for its own sake. Included in this commitment is an interest in the natural and social and political worlds and a lifelong attempt to understand the principles on which they rest.

## Stoic and Epicurean conceptions

There are points of agreement and disagreement in Stoic and Epicurean philosophy, the disagreements becoming more pronounced during the later histories of the two schools (Robinson, 1981, pp. 97–104). Epicurus (341–270 B.C.) advanced a materialistic psychology that emphasized the hedonistic and survivalistic impulses to action. In Fragment XXXVII he teaches that "Nature is weak towards evil, not towards good; because it is saved by pleasures, but destroyed by pains" (Oates, 1940, p. 42). The wise man comes to grips with his mortality and recognizes that the prudent life is one that will spare him such pain as might reasonably be avoided. What is to be sought is a secure serenity. By removing oneself from the arenas of competition and envy and by disciplining one's wants and needs, it is possible to minimize suffering. Wisdom is knowing how to achieve this end. The serenity *(apatheia)* is not one of indifference but one yielded by self-control and prudence: "Let nothing be done in your life, which will cause you fear if it becomes known to your neighbor" (Fragment, LXX).

In these and other fragments, as well as in the extraordinary *De Rerum Natura* of Lucretius (99–55 B.C.), which provides a poetic summary of the Epicurean system, there are obvious debts to portions of the older Greek philosophies of Plato and Aristotle. Epicurus accepts the biological and naturalistic psychology of Aristotle and then goes beyond Aristotle in reducing *psyche* – including the human *psyche* – to atomic elements. In the circumstance, the most that can be hoped for is to preserve the integrity of body and soul as long as possible and with as little pain and grief. The inevitable is, alas, inevitable. As Lucretius says in Book III (822–71), "Death therefore to us is nothing, concerns us not a jot, since the nature of the mind is proved to be mortal" (Oates, 1940, p. 131).

After Zeno of Citium (336–265 B.C.) founded Stoicism, the major figures in the school would retreat from Zeno's own generally materialistic orientation. Gradually, the naturalistic and biological features of the system were absorbed into a broader *physicalistic* system that then evolved into a fatalistic cosmology. "How do events happen?" asks Epictetus in his *Discourses:* "They happen as the Disposer of events has ordained them" (Book I, Ch. XIII; Oates, 1940, p. 248). Wisdom on the Stoic account is coming to grips with and fully reconciling oneself to the law-governed events of the world and the cosmos. "That which rules within," says Marcus Aurelius, "when it is according to nature, is so affected with respect to the events which happen, that it always easily adapts itself to that which is possible" *(Meditations, IV;*

Oates, 1940, p. 508). In Book IX, Marcus Aurelius adds to Aristotle's naturalism not only Stoic fatalism but a religious outlook that will become authoritative once Christianity takes root:

> He who acts unjustly acts impiously. For since the universal nature has made rational animals for the sake of one another to help one another according to their deserts, but in no way to injure one another, he who transgresses her will, is clearly guilty of impiety towards the highest divinity. (Oates, 1940, p. 553)

Wisdom now is less the result of deep study and reflection than a surrendering of the self to the nomic necessities of the world as these have been imposed by the fates and the gods. Where Aristotle would require of the wise man that he know the causes of things, the latter-day Stoic – in anticipation of the early Christian Fathers – confers wisdom on those who have reconciled themselves to the inevitable. Wisdom on this construal is at once a state of pious resignation and a cognitive recognition that Nature is but a face of Law *(nomos)*.

## Wisdom and Christian teaching

The traditional Christian perspective is a complex amalgam of Hebraic and Hellenic thought blended into the teachings of the New Testament. From the Hebrews the early Christians derived that sense of awe before the deep mysteries of the cosmos as well as a sturdy obedience to conscience and the willingness to accept God's love of man as the only remedy for what is otherwise an irremediable ignorance. Hebraism prepared the Christian mind for *revealed* truth. Hellenism, at least in its developed philosophical idiom, does not speak of revelation and does not even invest its gods with an omniscience that could be shared through revelation. The Hellenic canon is rich with analysis, observation, fallibilism, and naturalism. The aim is perfection through harmony. Thus, the Hellenic goal is a state of being, not a place. It is reached, if at all, through discipline, experience, study, good genes, good teachers, some luck, and much effort. A faith in the gods *(pistis theon)* is always prudent, but no one attains *sophia* through *pistis!*

Given the mixture of worldviews introduced at the very founding of Christianity, it is not surprising that it has had something of a divided history. One line of development has been self-consciously Aristotelian and has been rich in analysis, logic, formal argument, and attention to the facts of the world and the observable order of things. A parallel development has included more "eastern" Platonist themes enriched by prophesy and revelation. Within the corpus of Christian teaching, therefore, one finds life in the world either as real, natural, and consequential or as a largely symbolic and transitory proving ground from which the soul can only long for liberation. In light of these quite different outlooks, Christian conceptions of wisdom are understandably varied, ranging from wisdom as a nearly blind obedience to the teachings of

Jesus Christ to Thomistic conceptions that are often scarcely distinguishable from Aristotle's.

There is, however, a constant even amid these variations. As with the Socratics, Christian teachers have agreed that the truth is absolute and universal and that next to truth all else pales. To be wise is to be touched by the divine wisdom that conveys timeless and boundless verities. As Thomas Aquinas observes in the *Summa Theologica,*

For God the whole fullness of intellectual knowledge is contained in one object, namely the divine essence, in which he knows all things. Rational creatures achieve a lower and less simple completeness. What he knows in single simplicity they know in many forms. How a less exalted mind needs more ideas is partly illustrated by the fact that people of lower intelligence need to have things explained to them point by point in detail, while those of stronger mind can grasp more from a few hints. (Ia lv.3; Gilby, 1967)

This passage is revealing in several respects. First, it shows the general tendency of the Scholastics to examine the psychological dimensions of human cognition as a way of illustrating – in however so diminished a form – the mind of the divine. Second, it records the judgment that wisdom traffics in universals, not in details. Finally, it transmits the conviction that simplicity is at the foundation of all wisdom. There can be, then, a profound wisdom in a "simple faith" that recognizes the goodness of God to be the cause of all things. Whereas scientific understandings vary with the topics under consideration, " . . . wisdom is single" *(Summa Theologica,* la–2ae, lvii.2). Moreover,

Wisdom differs from mere science in looking at things from a greater height. The same holds true in practical matters. Sometimes a decision has to be taken that cannot follow the common rules of procedure. . . . Consequently a higher judging virtue is called for, that kind of prudence called *gnome,* or the ability of seeing through things. *(Summa Theologica,* 2a–2ae li.4)

It is worth noting that even at the dawn of the modern scientific age the essence of wisdom was still regarded as a "seeing through things," a discovery of the simple principle that explains the myriad. This view is implicit in the works of any number of savants and is explicit in the most technical of Isaac Newton's treatises. Galileo would successfully challenge several important features of Aristotle's physics but in the process would record allegiance to that larger Aristotelian perspective that equates both *episteme* and the mission of science itself with the discovery of general laws.

Of course, not everyone is able to "see through things." The Socratics, with such "convenient fictions" as men of gold, silver, brass, and iron, looked to eugenics as a way of increasing the stock of wise and prudent men *(Republic,* III, 415; V, 459–60). Aristotle, though fully aware of the importance of early discipline and lifelong exposure to the civilizing force of law, still produced a psychology that includes "slaves by nature" and that explains genius as a divine gift. From remote antiquity until the dawn of what is taken to be modern philosophy, wisdom, like genius, was explicated in terms of providential gods, muses, astrological forces, a sixth sense, genetic bounty, or accidents of nature. This long-standing attitude received its first sustained challenge in the 17th and 18th centuries when the nature of truth itself was exposed to such relentless scrutiny.

## The authority of experience

The secularization of knowledge and of scholarship began in the Renaissance and was nurtured by the evolution of urban centers of commerce and of patronage. Note that it was the Medici family and not the Church that established the new "Academy" in quattrocento Florence. The leaders of thought in this period looked not to revelation but to the Athens and Rome of classical times for inspiration (Robinson, 1981, Ch. 6). Their overall perspective is perhaps most directly expressed by the greatest genius of the period, Leonardo da Vinci (1452–1519), in his *Book on Painting:*

Many will think they may reasonably blame me by alleging that my proofs are opposed to the authority of certain men held in the highest reverence . . . not considering that my works are the issue of pure and simple experience, who is the one true mistress. (Richter, 1970)

This is a perspective that continuously gained in authority over the next two centuries. It is instructive to place in apposition to Leonardo's statement one made in 1776 by Sir Joshua Reynolds addressing students of the Royal Academy of Art:

We will allow a poet to express his meaning, when his meaning is not well known to himself, with a certain degree of obscurity. . . . But when, in plain prose, we gravely talk of courting the Muse in shady bowers; waiting the call and inspiration of Genius, finding out where he inhabits, and where he is to be invoked with the greatest success; of attending to the times and seasons when the imagination shoots with the greatest vigour, whether at the summer solstice or the vernal equinox . . . when we talk such language, or entertain such sentiments as these, we generally rest contented with mere words, or at best entertain notions not only groundless but pernicious. (Gay, 1973, p. 432)

The philosophical writings of Francis Bacon (1561–1626), John Locke (1632–1704), and David Hume (1711–76) had made empiricism the more or less official epistemology of the English-speaking world. On the Continent, René Descartes (1596–1650) had helped to usher in the New Age with his critical philosophy, his "method of doubt," his willingness to challenge all received scientific claims and to test them in the court of perception, reason, and common sense.

The success of empiricism in the epistemological domain carried any number of social and political implications. If, indeed, there is nothing in the intellect – no "furniture" of the mind – save that which arrives by way of the senses, then the ultimate *knowable* reality is *observable* reality. Each person, therefore, has the same access to the facts as any other, at least in principle; and those who claim to possess some special "wisdom" must verify the claim in that court of public experience that is the ultimate source of all epistemic authority (Robinson, 1981, Ch. 7). The integration of this perspective into a more general social and political philosophy was achieved in the 19th century by John Stuart Mill (1806–73), who would deny intuitive modes of knowledge even in mathematics (Robinson, 1982, Ch. 2).

The concept of wisdom is perforce dependent upon a prior metaphysical commitment, taking metaphysics to be composed of ontological and episte-mological elements. To regard one as *wise*, after all, is to ascribe a deeper understanding of reality, but this assumes that a more or less settled (onto-logical) position has been reached on the question of what is *real*. And this very position can be reached only after taking a stand (epistemologically) on the question of *how one can know anything*. Thus, to regard one as "wise" for knowing an absolute, universal, and nonempirical ("transcendent") truth is at once to accept that there is such a truth and that it *can* be known through, for example, contemplation, revelation, logic, intuition, or genius. If, instead, the official ontology leaves room only for the reality of physical things, then "wisdom" can be nothing but a scientific understanding of the laws governing matter in motion. The greater the inclination toward a materialistic ontology, therefore, the greater will be the degree of synonymy among *sophia, phro-nesis,* and *episteme.* In the end, "wisdom" would then refer to no more than a technical knowledge of how things work, its claims exhausted by purely pragmatic modes of evaluation.

### Scientism and Romanticism

The lines of conflict were clearly drawn in the 19th century when the leaders of scientific thought found it impossible to accept the metaphysical claims of the traditional philosopher-scientist. The immensely influential *Critique of Pure Reason* by Immanuel Kant (1724–1804) had erected what seemed to be a permanent barrier between the *phenomenal* world accessible to the senses (and, therefore, to experimental science) and that *noumenal* world of things *as in themselves they really are.* The disciples and interpreters of Kant and those who would "complete his system" – Herbart, Fichte, Schelling, Hegel – all dealt with the *phenomenal–noumenal* conflict differently. In time, however, and chiefly through the influence of Hegelian philosophy, a posi-tion was taken against empirical science. It was dismissed as limited, one-sided, grounded in (mere) *phaenomena,* incapable of liberating itself from the Kantian forms of perception and knowledge (Robinson, 1982; Ch. 2, 3).

The alternative to conventional science would come to have several names: romantic idealism, romanticism, transcendentalism, intuitionism. It migrated from the literary and intellectual centers of Weimar Germany to the England of the Lake Poets and then to the aesthetes and ethicists of Oxford. It took root in America, William James fighting it at Harvard with only marginal success. At the heart of the matter was the issue of reality. There is surely more to it than meets the eye, but science is confined to the sorts of things that meet the eye. Hadn't John Stuart Mill declared matter itself to be no more than "the permanent possibilities of sensation"?

If experience is limited to *phenomena,* then the great sages and geniuses of history must have had a more effective source of wisdom; a nonempirical source that *transcends* the domain of perception and reaches that of universal truth. Hegel had argued that this is the domain reached only through philosophy, religion, and art, these disciplines having the power to instantiate what is universal in the form of particulars. In dialectical fashion, the *particular* painting is the emblem of the *universal,* beauty; the tortured and dead Jesus is the *particular* man resurrected as the deathless and timeless Christ. Thus does the logic of negations yield noumenal reality.

Under the influence of such teaching, it was chiefly the aesthetes and artists of the 19th century who preserved the prescientific conception of wisdom: a divine gift, discovered through an introspective process and manifested in words or works of transcendent truth and beauty. Such a conception not only resisted scientific methods of analysis but stridently denied their validity. Accordingly, as psychology searched for scientific standing in the 19th century, its founders and leaders recognized that any number of ageless issues would have to be ignored, lest the new "science" be corrupted by the older "metaphysics." *Wisdom* was but one of these issues, though time has come to question the wisdom of this decision.

## Notes

1 All references to Plato's *Dialogues* are from Jowett (1942).
2 Aristotle passages are from the edition by Barnes (1984).

## References

Barnes, J. (Ed.) (1984). *The complete works of Aristotle* (2 vols.). Princeton, NJ: Princeton University Press.

Bremmer, J. (1987). *The early Greek concept of the soul.* Princeton, NJ: Princeton University Press.

Gay, P. (Ed.) (1973). *The Enlightenment: a comprehensive anthology.* New York: Simon & Schuster.

Gilby, T. (Trans.) (1967). *St. Thomas Aquinas: philosophical texts.* New York: Oxford University Press.

Jowett, B. (Trans.) (1942). *The Dialogues of Plato* (2 vols). New York: Random House.

Oates, W. (Ed.) (1940). *The Stoic and Epicurean philosophers.* New York: Random House.
Richter, J. P. (Ed.) (1970). *The literary works of Leonardo Da Vinci* (Vol. 1, pp. 116–117). London: Phaidon Press.
Robinson, D. N. (1981). *An intellectual history of psychology* (rev. ed.). New York: Macmillan.
Robinson, D. N. (1982). *Toward a science of human nature: essays on the psychologies of Hegel, Mill, Wundt and James.* New York: Columbia University Press.
Robinson, D. N. (1989). *Aristotle's psychology.* New York: Columbia University Press.

# 3  The psychology of wisdom:
## an evolutionary interpretation

*Mihaly Csikszentmihalyi and Kevin Rathunde*

In the attempt to illuminate what wisdom is about, we shall adopt a method that, for lack of a better term, we might call "evolutionary hermeneutics." This method is based on the assumption that concepts relating to the evaluation of human behavior – such as virtue, courage, freedom, or wisdom – and that have been used for many centuries under very different social and historical conditions are likely to have adaptive value for humankind. The method is based on the further assumption that to understand the significance of such concepts, it is advantageous to compare their meanings across time, in order to identify invariant components as well as possible variations in response to differing conditions in the surrounding cultural environment.

To find out what we mean by wisdom at the end of the 20th century is important, but it is not sufficient. No matter how advanced we think we are in terms of understanding the human psyche compared to former times, we still only have access to a limited cross section of the growing branch of knowledge. To ignore the hard-won insights of the past about issues that are vital for survival is like blinding ourselves on purpose out of false pride.

A simple example may help illustrate this point. Up to a few generations ago, children in our culture were warned against promiscuous sexuality, especially of a homosexual kind. Such behavior was labeled wrong, sinful, or immoral. In the last half-century, scientific knowledge discredited many of the assumptions and explanations on which these prohibitions were based. This led to the conclusion that sexual restraint was backed only by obsolete superstitions, and hence everyone should feel free to satisfy his or her sexual urges ad libitum. The medical and biological sciences, partly because they lacked hard "data," partly because they did not want to appear reactionary and spoil the fun, tacitly endorsed this position. What followed is history: a rampant increase in all forms of venereal diseases and the AIDS (acquired immune deficiency syndrome) epidemic.

Evolutionary hermeneutics is a corrective against the naïve assumption that present knowledge is in all respects superior to that of the past and that it is safe to ignore the cultural adaptations that were positively selected over time. It suggests, for instance, that the ancient and universal warnings against promiscuous sexuality might have been based on valid past experience. At the same time, it also suggests that the explanations for why such behavior is dangerous are likely to be given in terms of reasons that have lost their relevance. To say that promiscuity is "sinful" no longer means anything to a great number of people. Nevertheless, the meaning contained in the concept of "sin" may still be extremely relevant – indeed, a matter of life and death. Therefore the task of an evolutionary hermeneutics is to try uncovering the meanings of concepts discovered in the past that have stood the test of time; to translate these meanings in the relatively timeless categories of evolutionary theory; and finally, to translate them back into current concepts applicable to the present state of knowledge and to contemporary problems.

Evolutionary hermeneutics is a method that logically follows from evolutionary epistemology. Donald Campbell has been one of the first psychologists to observe that changes in knowledge systems – including "hardware" as well as "software" – obey the evolutionary laws of variation, selection, and transmission (Campbell, 1965, 1975, 1976; Csikszentmihalyi, 1988; Simon, 1969; Simonton, 1988). According to Campbell, for instance, scientific experimentation is functionally equivalent to sensory organs such as touch or sight in that it allows us to know what goes on around us and to test the environment vicariously. There is an unbroken line of gradual change from the physiological development of the senses all the way to cultural knowledge systems culminating (temporarily) in science – a line of development shaped by selective pressures favoring the ability to obtain objective information about the environment at the least cost to the organism.

The notion of evolution on which our perspective is based is not limited to biochemical instructions mediated by genetic selection and transmission. We believe, instead, that it is useful to expand the evolutionary model to include within its compass instructions for behavior that are mediated by cultural learning. Tools, weapons, as well as ideas, to the extent that they influence adaptation, can be seen as *memes* that are selected and transmitted across generations and that carry instructions that affect the survival of the human phenotype (Boyd & Richerson, 1985; Csikszentmihalyi & Massimini, 1985; Lumsden & Wilson, 1981, 1983). The meme of "wisdom," for instance, contains a nucleus of meaning that has been transmitted relatively unchanged for at least 80 generations, providing directions for human thought and behavior.

Cultural selection, as opposed to genetic selection, does not necessarily favor the selective fitness of the individual who is the carrier of positive variations (Burhoe, 1976; Csikszentmihalyi, 1988). Wise, creative, or intelligent persons are not likely to produce more numerous offspring – in fact, they may very well have fewer children than other people. Yet wise, creative, and intelligent behavior is likely to be noted, appreciated, and preserved by the community, and the people who display such behaviors will be remembered. They may or may not pass on more of their genes to posterity, but they will pass on their memes – that is, the memory of their thoughts, actions, and works. In Burhoe's terms, genetic and cultural traits evolve together in a coadaptive symbiosis; and commonly shared values provide the bonds that keep people working together who otherwise might compete to maximize their genetic progeny at each others' expense (Burhoe, 1976).

The folk conception of knowledge assumes a "progress" very similar to that which underlies evolutionary epistemology. However, everyday attitudes to what is known are usually influenced by a misperception that is not inherent in the theoretical model. We usually tend to assume that if a method for getting at knowledge comes after another, the latter is more credible, and it must displace the former. Because scientific knowledge is more recent than philosophy and religion, for instance, it is thought to be a more reliable symbolic system for representing reality, one that makes all previous ones obsolete. There are two problems with this assumption. In the first place, most variations in the evolutionary record are not advantageous and do not survive. Thus just because an organ of knowledge is more recent, it does not mean it is better; in fact, the presumption is that it will be worse. Second, even if the new organ is more sensitive or more powerful in some respects, it does not mean that it must displace earlier ones. Just as sight and smell present different pictures of the world, myth, religion, philosophy, and science provide complementary yet discrete windows on experience. Science may be a more evolved eye, but it does not compensate for being blind. It does not make sense to say that science, as a more evolved organ for providing information, is a substitute for the ability to see. For the same reason science may not be a substitute for earlier epistemologies such as religion or wisdom.

Evolutionary hermeneutics is simply the name we have given to the attempt at reconciling what has been said in the past about certain important concepts with what is being said about them now within the framework of current psychological knowledge informed by evolutionary theory. The aim is to integrate the experience of previous generations with our own, trying to understand the adaptive value of former responses, thereby providing a deeper and richer context for present understanding. In practice, the method consists in reviewing what has been said about a concept by previous writers as distant from us in time and cultural background as possible. The next step consists in identifying whether there are common meanings attributed to the concept and whether these change over time. Then the following questions are put to the data: What is the adaptive significance of this concept? For instance, what did the ancient Israelites mean when they wrote: "Wisdom is the principal thing; therefore get wisdom" (Proverbs, 4:7)?[1] What purposes did this idea serve? If the concept has changed over time, was this in response to relevant changes in the social and cultural environment? What is likely to be its present value?

It is, of course, impossible to apply this method with anything resembling its ideal intent. There is just too much potentially relevant information to assimilate, and our knowledge of past conditions is necessarily incomplete. Any application will have to be woefully approximate, especially in this first attempt. Yet we believe that the goal to be striven for is worth pursuing even if the means at this point are inadequate. In the present case, we shall explore only three aspects of the concept of wisdom, and we shall limit ourselves to reviewing a narrow selection from mainly the Western classical literature, in the hope of demonstrating the usefulness of evolutionary hermeneutics as well as contributing to the substantive understanding of wisdom as a human trait.

**What is wisdom?**

There is widespread agreement among past thinkers that the concept has three major dimensions of meaning. It can be seen as a *cognitive process*, or a peculiar way of obtaining and processing information; as a *virtue*, or socially valued pattern of behavior; and as a *good*, or personally desirable state or condition. All three dimensions of the concept are relevant for its understanding.

*Wisdom as a cognitive process*

The most obvious meaning of the term *wisdom* refers to a way of knowing. But how does it differ from other cognitive processes, such as intelligence or creativity? The various uses of the term in the past point at several distinguishing characteristics. In contrast to other forms of knowledge, it has been claimed that wisdom:

    a. does not deal with the appearance of fleeting phenomena but with enduring universal truths;
    b. is not specialized but is an attempt to apprehend how the various aspects of reality are related to each other;
    c. is not a value-free way of knowing but implies a hierarchical ordering of truths and actions directed at those truths.

Considering the first of these three characteristics that usually define the cognitive dimension of wisdom, we immediately run into a problem. There is not now, and there has never been, universal agreement about what it is that lies hidden behind the veil of appearances. What is to be counted as "universal truth" varies depending on the particular cosmology of the times. For Plato, the visible world was made up of objects and of their images, to which corresponded an intelligible world of universal ideas *(Republic,* VI, 510, 533–534; *Republic,* VII, 514–24).[2] True knowledge consisted in discovering their nature. Wisdom was the state of the soul when she reflects on eternity and immortality instead of the world of appearances *(Philebus, 30; Phaedo, 79)*. Although Plato and Aristotle's approaches were quite different on many counts, the latter also viewed wisdom as the chief of sciences because its role was to prove the principles on which all the other sciences rested *(Ethics, VI, 7)*.

Christian thinkers like Augustine and Aquinas agreed in several important respects with the viewpoint of the classical philosophers. They also held that wisdom consisted in seeking the invariant and ultimate causes behind the variability of superficial phenomena. They differed, however, in believing that universal truth could only be found with the help of God: "He who considers absolutely the highest cause of the whole universe, namely God, is most of all called wise" (Aquinas, *Summa, 1,* 6). Human reason could reach up to a point, but to behold the real order of things, one needed in addition faith in divine inspiration (Aquinas, *Summa, 2,* 12 passim; *32,* 1). Immanuel Kant also saw wisdom as the discovery of the relation of all cognitions to the ultimate and essential aims of human reason, which were contained in God *(Critique of Pure Reason,* 2nd Div., 2, 3); but he derived the necessary existence of God from the existence of reason rather than the other way around.

What all the ancient thinkers seemed to realize is that without wisdom, ways of knowing are constrained by a tragic paradox: The clearer the view they provide, the more limited the slice of reality they reveal. The integrated thought of "primitive" men and women, who did not distinguish between religion, art, science, habits, and instincts, slowly gave way to more and more specialized "domains" of knowledge. Nowadays knowledge is divided into innumerable branches that appear to be unrelated to each other or to the world as we experience it. Specialization enables us to exert a powerful control on specific, limited aspects of reality. But it does not help us to know what to do with the control thus achieved.

In line with these classical conceptions, much of the impetus for the contemporary study of wisdom is a reaction to the overspecialization of modern culture. For instance, Holliday and Chandler (1986) claim that the present technological zeitgeist has influenced psychology's exclusive concern with behavioral explanations, its concentration on the young, and its devaluation of "essences." They, as well as Meacham (1983), see research on wisdom as attempting to balance scientific/analytic "accumulation" models of truth with integrative hermeneutic inquiries that emphasize critical, historical, and practical dimensions (Habermas, 1972).

Others concerned with higher stages of cognitive development in adulthood (Kramer, 1983; Labouvie-Vief, 1982; Riegel, 1973) echo the same concerns. They try to articulate a stage beyond "formal operations" (abstract, logical, hypothetical, and problem-solving thought; see Inhelder & Piaget, 1958) as the preferred mode of information processing. Kramer (1983) notes the similarity between formal operations and "mechanistic" or "analytic" worldviews (Pepper, 1942; Reese & Overton, 1970), both of which are conducive to an atomistic conception of reality and supposedly less desirable than their mirror opposites, "organismic" and "synthetic" worldviews.

However, in contemporary discussions on wisdom, as in contemporary discussions on almost any human way of knowing, one would seldom come across such integrative notions as "universal truth" or "God." Thus it is legitimate to ask whether or not an essential component of the ancient conception of wisdom has been fundamentally lost or altered. One might take this to be the import of Nietzsche's familiar phrase, "God is dead." But even Nietzsche's epitaph was intended to signal the passing of one conception of teleology so that another integrative aim could be put in its place (Kaufmann, 1966). Thus while it is certainly true that modern variations on the concept of wisdom have taken place (and most likely with an accelerated search for new "Truths" in modern culture), it is unlikely that wisdom – conceived as a relatively holistic cognitive process – has completely disappeared from contemporary thought.

This, in fact, seems to be the case. Consistent with ancient distinctions between a holistic wisdom and other specialized ways of knowing are the results of current empirical studies of the category "wise person" in everyday language. Holliday and Chandler (1986) found a consistent multidimensional picture of the wise person as having:

   a. a general competence (a dimension that overlaps with logical intelligence or technical ability);
   b. an experience-based pragmatic knowledge; and
   c. reflective or evaluative metaanalytic skills.

They fit these three components into a Habermasian framework that recognizes three complementary "types" of knowledge, or knowledge-constitutive interests: technical interests concerned with instrumental action, practical interests concerned with social consensus and understanding, and emancipatory interests concerned with self-critical reflection and autonomy (Habermas, 1972). Clayton and Birren (1980) found a similar multilevel picture of the wise individual as possessing the *integration* of intellectual, affective, and reflective skills for the processing of information. Finally, Sternberg's (1985) analysis of implicit theories of wisdom has uncovered dimensions that overlap with the preceding views. The wise individual is seen as having reasoning ability and superior intellectual functioning but, in addition, good pragmatic judgment and skills of reflection that allow him or her to profit from past mistakes.

A similar portrait of the wise individual is implied by those who postulate a "postformal" operations stage of optimal adult development. Postformal thought supposedly has the following characteristics:

   a. One recognizes the relativity of various formal systems through *life experience* and is able to assume contradictory points of view.

   b. One acknowledges the *interrelatedness* of all experience and the inevitability of change and transformation.

   c. One adopts a more "metasystemic" or *reflective* and integrative approach to thinking (often dialectical).

   d. One makes choices with *commitment* to a certain course of action (Commons, Richards, & Kuhn, 1982; Kramer, 1983; Labouvie-Vief, 1980, 1982; Perry, 1970; Riegel, 1973).

The cognitive picture emerging in contemporary thought concerning wise or optimally functioning adults, although it is incomplete and a long way from being a consensus, is consistent. This consistency is nicely expressed by Kramer's (1983) comment, "Post-formal operational thought is at the same time more practical and concrete, and more detached and abstract" (p. 97). It is more concrete because the individual "transcends reason," which would remain relativistic and detached in formal operations until a commitment is made based on self-examination and life experience (Labouvie-Vief, 1982; Perry, 1970); it is more abstract because of its higher synthetic, process-aware, or metasystemic vantage point (i.e., operations on formal operations, Commons et al., 1982). Compare Emerson's (1929, Vol. 12) remarks on wisdom: "Affection blends, intellect disjoins subject and object" (p. 44); "A blending of these two – the intellectual perception of truth and the moral sentiment of right – is wisdom" (p. 45).

It is easy to stress the differences between the ancient and contemporary ways of conceptualizing the meaning of wisdom. But we shall focus on the commonalities instead, in the belief that those aspects of a meme that remain the same despite great changes in the social and cultural milieu are the ones that will have the more enduring consequences for human survival.

While contemporary discussions of wisdom fail to evoke the traditional categories of universal truth or God to denote the pursuit of wisdom, there is an underlying emphasis in both accounts on the value of holistic cognitive processes that move beyond a fragmented and impassive relativity, toward a more "universal" or metasystemic awareness of interrelated systems. Attributes such as reflectivity or the capacity for self-examination are seen as providing the needed impetus to escape from relativistic intellectualization. What remains the same in these ways of conceiving of wisdom (and the many other similar ones in different cultures), despite many other divergent aspects, is the insight that the specific knowledge of the world we have at any given time is only a pale reflection of reality. Our eyes, our telescopes, the latest scientific theories provide only a narrow glimpse of the structure of the universe. These disjointed views, while clear, can be very deceptive. They make us believe that we know what lies outside, while they only give us selective, and hence misleading information. This message is as relevant today as it was 24 centuries ago, in Plato's time.

In *War and Peace* the Mason, one of Tolstoy's characters, gives this explanation to Pierre: "The highest wisdom is not founded on reason alone, nor on those worldly sciences of physics, chemistry, and the like, into which intellectual knowledge is divided. The highest wisdom is one. The highest wisdom has but one science – the science of all, the science explaining all creation and man's place in it" (Tolstoy, 1968, p. 429).

This view points at what the "universal truth" of our time may turn out to be. Not immutable Platonic ideas, nor the eternal, all-embracing will of God, but a systemic ecological consciousness in which the consequences of events and actions are understood to be causally related and to have long-term effects for the survival of human life and for the environment that sustains it.

The need for understanding the requirements of the total system of nature is foreshadowed by many thinkers of the past. Plato in the *Statesman* writes about the golden age in which men and animals could communicate; Montaigne discourses at length on the human folly of ignoring the natural context of which we are a part *(Essays, 11, 12)*; Kant urges us to develop a morality based on an understanding of the "world as an ordered whole of interconnected goals, as a system of final causes." Wisdom consists in paying attention to the ends of nature and inquiring after the stupendous art that lies hidden behind its forms *(Critique of Teleological Judgement, 86)*. Just as in the earliest times of recorded human thought, but with an even greater urgency, we are becoming increasingly aware of the fact that the separate branches of knowledge are not designed to reveal ultimate truths. For this we need wisdom, or the systematic pursuit of the connection between the branches – a "science of the whole."

## Wisdom as virtue

The sense in which wisdom is a virtue follows from its characteristics as a cognitive process. If it is a mode of knowledge that tries to understand the ultimate consequences of events in a holistic, systemic way, then wisdom becomes the best guide for what is the *summum bonum,* or "supreme good." The knowledge of how causes and effects are connected shows the way for action and is the basis of morality.

This will be true both at the individual and at the social levels. At the individual level, wisdom helps the person decide what is the optimal course of action for his or her own self, by mediating between the local and often conflicting knowledge provided by instincts, habits, and reason (cf. Plato, *Republic,* IV, 442). "All . . . things hang upon the soul," Socrates says in *Meno* (88), "and all things of the soul herself hang upon wisdom." Time after time Plato, as well as many other thinkers of the past, point out that without wisdom other advantages like wealth, health, power, honor, and even good fortune are useless because the person will not know how to get benefit from them (e.g., *Meno,* 87; *Protagoras,* 349, 352, 358). Therefore, "wisdom is the only good, ignorance the only evil" *(Euthydemus,* 281). Inasmuch as he reflects on the "divine order," the lawfulness behind the chaos of appearances, the mind of the philosopher himself will become orderly and divine, as far as the nature of man allows it to be *(Republic,* VI, 500).

Kant saw an even closer connection between the cognitive and the moral aspects of wisdom. To follow the logic of reason is a duty, and to the extent that a person is not distracted by foreign influences in its pursuits, he or she is wise *(Metaphysics of Ethics,* 11). The task of wisdom is to seek the unconditioned totality of the effects of pure practical reason, in other words, what is best for mankind *(Critique of Practical Reason,* I, 1). Thus the goals of radical cognition and of moral action blend into one.

From this it follows that wisdom is also the foremost public virtue, because it is the only approach that takes into account long-term consequences for the entire social system: "First among the virtues found in the state, wisdom comes into view" (Plato, *Republic,* IV, 428). The wise person is the one best equipped to judge (Aristotle, *Metaphysics,* 1, 2) and to keep the commonwealth in order (Aquinas, *Summa,* 1, 8). The ultimate requirement for ruling is knowledge of how to optimize the well-being of the community as a whole *(Republic,* VI, 505). Hence Plato's insistence that only when philosophers become kings, and kings philosophers, will a good society come into being.

The assumption behind the view of wisdom as a virtue is that a person confronted with the knowledge of what *really* goes on – that is, ultimate truth – is unable to resist its logic and will follow the right path. "No man voluntarily pursues evil," writes Plato *(Protagoras,* 358). The divine order is so compelling that those who get a glimpse of it will gladly submit to its pattern.

The findings of modern psychology, and the social sciences in general, may be seen as casting grave doubts on this ancient belief that "truth shall set ye free." We have learned from analytic psychology how dependent on the distorting effects of early experience our interpretations of reality are. We have learned from the behaviorists how much learning is conditioned by fortuitous associations. Social psychologists have shown how strongly other people's opinions affect our judgments. Anthropologists have revealed the deep hold that the cultural patterning of symbols and values have on the mind. Marxists have argued that self-interest built into unequal social position prevents men from ever being impartial. Given these merciless revelations about the limits of our ability to reason objectively, are there any grounds left for hoping that wisdom is possible and that it can lead to a better life?

Here, again, as in the case of searching for universal truth, it seems apparent (at first glance) that modern sensibilities have completely abandoned this hope, as well as Plato's suggestion that a compelling ethics will follow from the contemplation of Truth. It may be, however, that this ethical dimension of wisdom has survived, albeit in new conceptual terminology. Habermas

(1972) has offered an incisive treatment of this very issue, tracing the original connection between ethical formation as "mimesis" in classical thought, through its contemporary rejection, and finally offering his formulation of how philosophy (love of wisdom) can remain "true to its classical tradition" (see pp. 301–317). Since Holliday and Chandler (1986) have suggested how a Habermasian framework helps to make sense of the empirical data on wisdom, a summary of Habermas's conclusions on this point, as well as a few others, may be relevant.

Habermas claims: "Philosophy remains true to its classical tradition by renouncing it" (p. 317). By this he apparently means that the Greek conception of ethical formation through mimesis (contemplation of the Divine Order), which offered the Greeks a sound basis of morality free from contingent and inconstant human interests, was itself based on a *concealment of its actual interest*. This concealed interest in the case of the early philosophers might have involved seeking a new stage of emancipation and individuation beyond the archaic communal powers of the ancient mystery cults. He comments, "The repression of interest appertained to this interest itself" (p. 307). Contemporary scientific and philosophical perspectives have become aware of some, but not all, aspects of this repressed interest. According to Habermas, philosophy can remain true to its classical tradition (i.e., finding a connection between wisdom and virtue) only by first rejecting the ancient ontological formulation, especially its concealed "objectivism." This allows, in turn, a new foundation for the connection of practical efficacy and human knowledge to be built.

Habermas's reformulation is not a radical proposal; ultimately it amounts to the sound methodological advice that informs all epistemology: To free ourselves from narrow interests (in traditional terms, to achieve "disinterest"), we must continually uncover implicit human interests. He focuses on three – technical, practical, and emancipatory – that he claims are part of the "interest structure of the human species" with their basis in the "natural history (both biological and cultural) of the human species." It is the "metalogical necessity of interests . . . with which we must instead *come to terms*" (p. 312, emphasis in original). These statements reflect the extent to which wisdom still *compels* to virtue rather than offers a relative choice.

The essential point of these observations for our purposes here is that as with Nietzsche's rejection of universals, Habermas's rejection of the ancient link between wisdom and virtue (ethical order from divine order) is a preliminary step to the reintroduction of a formulation that *serves a similar function*. Thus, although the concept of wisdom has changed over time, essential attributes of the wisdom-equals-virtue equation have, in this case, been renewed.

The evolutionary perspective suggests that the ancient equation of wisdom and virtue is still viable and, in fact, that it is more relevant now than it ever has been. It can be argued that the various limits on objective perception and reasoning the social sciences have revealed – repressions, defenses, bad faith, false consciousness, ethnocentricism, conditioned responses, suggestibility, and so on – are precisely the concrete "particulars" of experience that Plato argued the philosopher must overcome in order to see the underlying truth, and thus get closer to wisdom. They are also the parochial "interests" with which Habermas claims we must come to terms. So the accumulating knowledge about our imperfections need not paralyze us into helplessness; on the contrary, it should help us make the right decisions with a clearer idea of where the obstacles are.

Wisdom is needed to help make these decisions. As the current empirical studies have shown (Clayton & Birren, 1980; Holliday & Chandler, 1986; Sternberg, 1985), awareness of this important decision-making function of wisdom has not disappeared from everyday language. For instance, the behavioral descriptor with the highest positive loading in the Sternberg study suggests others view the wise individual as possessing "the unique ability to look at a problem or situation and solve it." This emphasis is particularly strong in the work of Baltes, Smith, Staudinger, and Sowarka (in press), who define wisdom as an "expertise (involving good judgement and advice) in the domain, fundamental pragmatics of life" (p. 8). Thus their research agenda focuses on such things as life planning and management, and their methods include asking a subject to "think aloud" when presented with fictitious life problems and dilemmas.

Current research on wisdom may also soon be able to shed light on the actual steps that lead to virtuous decisions. From work thus far one might tentatively suggest the following: The great "width" (empathy), "height" (intelligence), and "depth" (reflectivity) of the wise person allows him or her to form a more complex or *concrete and abstract* perspective on some problem and thus attain the possibility of seeing the wisest course of action. The wise person gains rich life experience through spontaneous and affective involvement with the world and brings clarity and form to this experience by finding an intellectual distance. He or she learns responsibility and self-direction by reflecting on these processes and fitting their unique contributions together in a complete, well-rounded story. In Holliday and Chandler's (1986) framework, the wise individual would have a balance of practical, technical, and emancipatory interests. Since interest would bring sustained attention to all these areas, the wise individual is one who pays attention to interpersonal meanings, instrumental action, and issues of autonomy and responsibility (excluding none of them). A wise decision could not be made until a particular problem has been informed by all three dimensions of analysis. For instance, the wise priest offering advise to a devout young couple caught in the dilemma of an unwanted pregnancy might consider the intricate meaning of the current situation based on his empathy for the couple's perspective and the contemporary milieu, his knowledge of traditional actions based on church doctrine, and his own deep reflections on the situation before offering advice that weaves all these needed sources of information together.

With the important challenges that face modern society, one-dimensional technological thinking will not suffice for finding our location with respect to many critical survival problems. There is no question that now more than ever we need a holistic, long-range understanding of actions and events – let us call it wisdom – so as to avoid the unforeseen consequences of narrowly specialized interests and ways of knowing. It took marvelous ingenuity to invent aerosol sprays based on chlorofluorocarbons – the knowledge that went into this artifact puts all the philosophers of ancient Greece to shame. But how wise will this invention turn out to be if it destroys part of the ozone layer surrounding the planet, causing the harmful ultraviolet components of sunrays to kill much of the life inside the sea and to kill us through skin cancer? Measured against such effects, clean windows and odorless underarms do not seem like such a bargain. If wisdom is a process by which people try to evaluate the ultimate consequences of events in terms of each other, it is more necessary now than Plato could ever have anticipated it to be over two millennia ago.

Unfortunately wisdom is no more a priority now than it was at the time Socrates was invited to drink his hemlock. While specialized knowledge shows immediate effects, the benefits of wisdom are by definition slower to appear and less obvious. Knowledge is expressed in declarative certitudes, whereas wisdom must compare, raise questions, and suggest restraints. Hence wisdom rarely gets much respect and is seldom popular. Yet an evolutionary analysis suggests that unless we cultivate an interdisciplinary knowledge of our systemic needs, we shall not be able to understand what is happening, and we shall not be able to see what is good or bad for us in the long run.

*Wisdom as a personal good*

There is a great unanimity among thinkers of the past about the fact that wisdom not only gets us closer to the truth, and it not only provides a basis for making sound value judgments, but it also is good for us here and now. Two main reasons are advanced for this claim. The first is that without it none of the other "goods" will be rewarding; we need wisdom to get pleasure from health, satisfaction from fame, and good use out of wealth (cf. Plato, *Meno*, 87; *Euthydemus*, 278–279). The second is that the contemplation of universal order wisdom affords is a supreme pleasure in its own right – it is intrinsically rewarding.

In the final chorus of *Antigone*, Sophocles writes: "wisdom is the supreme part of happiness." Plato echoes the thought, " . . . wisdom and intelligence and memory . . . are better and more desirable than pleasure" *(Philebus*, 11), and "All that the soul attempts or endures, when under the guidance of wisdom, ends in happiness" *(Meno, 88)*. So does Aristotle: A large part of the *Nichomachean Ethics* (e.g., Books I and X) is devoted to the question of happiness, concluding that the contemplation of universal truth is the closest human beings can come to perfect happiness. "He who exercises his reason and cultivates it seems to be in the best state of mind and most dear to the gods. . . . And he who is that will presumably be also the happiest: so that in this way too the philosopher will more than any other be happy" *(Ethics, X, 8, 1179a)*.

The scholastics, whose search for universal truth inevitably led to God, also concluded that nothing compared with the happiness one derived from the pursuit of wisdom (e.g., Aquinas, *Summa*, 1, 5; 1, 64). Augustine states: "Contemplation is promised us as being the goal of all our actions, and the everlasting perfection of our joys" *(De Trinitate, 1, 8)*. And according to Spinoza: "It is therefore most profitable to us in this life, to make perfect the intellect or reason as far as possible, and in this one thing consists the highest happiness or blessedness of man; for blessedness is nothing but the peace of mind which springs from the intuitive knowledge of God." And Montaigne echoes the idea: "The most manifest sign of wisdom is continual cheerfulness" *(Essays, 1, 25)*. In the same essay he tells how one day Demetrius the grammarian came across a knot of philosophers merrily chatting in the temple of Delphos. Being obviously a rather obnoxious person, he said to them: "Either I am much deceived, or by your cheerful and pleasant countenances, you are engaged in no very deep discourse." To which one of the group, Heracleon the Megarean, replied that pedantic scholars, discussing trivial little specialized problems, might knit their brows and look serious while discoursing of their science. "But as to philosophical discourses, they always divert and cheer up those that entertain them, and never deject them or make them sad."

In spite of this overwhelming agreement of past thinkers that the pursuit of wisdom brings with it the most intense joy, this aspect of wisdom is clearly the least emphasized and least understood in modern thought. Is the ancient choir of praise an example of the self-delusion to which we are so prone, a whistling in the dark, an effort to seduce prospective students by praising one's craft? Or is there a genuine foundation for the claim that the pursuit of wisdom is so enjoyable?

The current technological zeitgeist has devalued wisdom as the pursuit of universal truth leading to ethical virtue. Our evolutionary perspective has suggested this result – in part – rests on conceptual categories (universal truth, God) that no longer easily mesh with modern scientific sensibilities; yet attempts to translate these categories – to preserve their evolutionary significance – have persisted (see also Burhoe, 1976). The challenge of translation remains the same, and perhaps is even greater, in regards to the ancient conception of wisdom as an enjoyable personal good. In other words, the general devaluation of a universal realm of Truth or Being has closed the door, as it were, to the place of "perfect" joy or happiness. The intuition of a metaphysical realm that wisdom was thought to afford has often been historically associated with ineffable, ecstatic experiences, especially in the Christian tradition. Such experiences would be discounted today as pure fantasy, as would the metaphysical realities that supposedly sparked the experiences.

It is, however, also clear that a belief in such "transcendent" experiences has played an important role in all the world's religions (Eliade, 1959; Jung, 1969) and in the continuity and renewal of preliterate and literate culture (Durkheim, 1954; Turner, 1979). The perpetual historical association of wisdom with perfect joy, self-transcendence, ecstasy, and so on, suggests that this dimension of the concept may have an evolutionary significance that needs to find new expression in terminology that – from our modern perspective – is less grandiose and elusive. There are likely to be many ways for contemporary thinkers to approach this task and attempt to provide new support for the notion that the pursuit of wisdom is a joy in itself; however, judging by the lack of attention to this aspect of wisdom in modern thought, this work has barely begun. One productive approach, we believe, is by appealing to what has been learned about the class of experiences and behaviors referred to as "intrinsically motivating," or enjoyable for their own sake.

If the contemporary frame of mind is primarily interested in technology (and values formal operations cognition), then one may expect the major focus of attention to be on material rewards, for instance, the profit that becomes possible with specialization and control. Contemporary research on intrinsically rewarding behavior has clearly demonstrated the detrimental effects of so-called extrinsic rewards like money on intrinsically rewarding experience (Lepper & Greene, 1978; Lepper, Greene, & Nisbett, 1973). That wisdom gets clouded when it is directed by self-interest has been intuited by the most ancient writers: "The wisdom of a learned man cometh by opportunity of leisure; and he that hath little business shall become wise" (Ecclesiasticus 38:24). "How can he get wisdom . . . whose talk is of bullocks" (Ecclesiasticus 38:34). Similarly Plato argues that philosophy must be intrinsically motivated, detached from politics and business (*Theaetetus*, 172–175), and Aristotle stresses on several occasions that wisdom must be pursued in order to know and not for any utilitarian end (e.g., *Metaphysics*, 1, 2, 982b; *Ethics*, X, 6–9). Wisdom, it seems, presupposes overcoming selfish ends.

Recent characterizations of the wise individual as open to technical, practical, and *emancipatory* (reflective) interests (Holliday & Chandler, 1986) suggests that he or she is open not only to the possibility of experiencing the "extrinsic" rewards of material control but also to the possibility of experiencing intrinsic rewards. For example, Habermas claims that in self-reflection "knowledge and interest are one" (i.e., interest becomes "disinterested"); the emancipatory cognitive interest in autonomy and responsibility pursues "knowledge for the sake of knowledge" or "the pursuit of reflection as such" (see pp. 313–314). Similarly, Plato observes that the wise man knows well the "lower" pleasures of the body but, in addition, has cultivated a higher pleasure in contemplation *(Republic,* IX). Thus one might claim the pursuit of wisdom is intrinsically rewarding based on the fact that the *reflective dimension of wisdom belongs to a class of autonomy or growth-oriented behaviors that do not provide a direct and immediate benefit for the individual in any technical or practical way.* Such autotelic *(auto* = self, *telos* = goal) behaviors produce an optimal state of enjoyment in consciousness and are perceived as rewarding in themselves (Csikszentmihalyi, 1975; Csikszentmihalyi & Csikszentmihalyi, 1988).

Not only does the reflective dimension of wisdom pursue autonomy, but characteristics of the task also make it intrinsically rewarding. For instance, self-reflection requires an inward focusing of attention that effectively blocks any potential distracting stimuli from the environment. This focusing centers on a well-ordered and controllable series of symbolic links in a train of thought, to the exclusion of the more "natural" meandering of the stream of consciousness. Further, inasmuch as reflection on the "big picture" that wisdom pursues poses some of the most challenging obstacles for growth and insight, it is likely that one must utilize one's full attentional capacity to be successful. These aspects of reflection closely resemble some of the *conditions* that facilitate optimal psychological experience (Csikszentmihalyi & Csikszentmihalyi, 1988): a narrowing of attention on a limited stimulus field, high concentration, clear feedback and control, and a strong sense of meaningful challenge requiring the exercise of one's full skills.

When self-reflection leads to emancipation, or the moment when an expanded awareness recognizes the limitations of one's previous perspective, the process of growth is ecstatic in the literal sense of the word – "to place outside." In other words, one is momentarily placed outside ordinary (habitual) awareness, and this experience is exhilarating and intrinsically rewarding. (In studies of optimal psychological experiences, this enjoyable dimension has been described as a loss of ego or self-consciousness.) One need not think of this process as involving a transcendence to a metaphysical realm, but a more limited self-transcendence that arrives at a new *betweenness* with the world, through perceptions (or thoughts) being experienced for the first time. The pursuit of wisdom forces the true lover of knowledge to continually overcome the narrow worldview that selfish interests illuminate in order to climb to the higher perspective that wisdom seeks. Thus it is not at all surprising that such repeated self-overcoming – through reflection or contemplation – would provide numerous opportunities for experiencing the intrinsic rewards of growth and would thus lead to the affirmation that the pursuit of wisdom is a joy in its own right.

The joy of wisdom is arguably one of its most important dimensions in that the cherished past is spun from the axis of momentary joyful experience; so is the anticipated future, as one desires to experience such intense joy again. Maslow (1968) understood this *transformational* power to be the value of so-called peak experiences. Such lasting effects on everyday life seem to be characteristic of what subjects describe as a "flow" experience: egolessness, merged action and awareness, high concentration, clear feedback, control, and enjoyment of the activity for its own sake (Csikszentmihalyi, 1975). Whether or not one overcomes self-limitations through self-reflection, or in the challenge of climbing a new mountain, the intrinsic rewards involved can have an indelible effect. The following quote comes from a rock climber: "Up there you have the greatest chance for finding your potential for any form of learning. . . . Up there you see man's true place in nature, you feel one with nature." Aldous Huxley (1972) – speaking before the XIV International Congress of Applied Psychology in Denmark – made the same point about the value of such experiences: "But if they are properly used, if they are co-operated with, if the memory of them is felt to be important . . . then they can be of immense value to us and of great importance in changing our lives" (p. 56).

The strong impression that a peak or flow experience leaves in the conscious memory of the person may result from the fact that such intense experiences are *felt* to be holistic, ethically compelling, and intrinsically motivating. Thus at their moment of occurrence, they phenomenologically express what has been written for centuries about wisdom as a cognitive process, a virtue, and a personal good. Whether one refers to the "wisdom of the child" when observing the complete involvement (affective and cognitive), respect, and joy of a child who is able to appreciate simple wonders like the graceful flight of a bird or the wisdom of a great philosopher lost in his or her contemplation of the stars, a tight-fitting and intrinsically rewarding connection holds between the person and the world; and the experience is felt to be an absolute end-in-itself. While such experiences can in no way justify any metaphysical claims, one can perhaps interpret the enthusiastic reports concerning the universal truth or virtue revealed by them, not as erroneous but, in this specific sense, as valid. Further insight into the psychology of such experiences may help to salvage the sense of truth expressed in the ancient accounts of wisdom as leading to perfect joy, or the intuition of God, by placing the experience in a new interpretive context, more in line with current psychological perspectives.

The evolutionary perspective suggests that the ancient connection of wisdom as a supreme joy in its own right, and thus as a personal good, is still relevant today in important ways. The joy historically associated with the contemplation of a Divine Order for its own sake manifests the part of our nature interested in growth, freedom from limitations, or as Habermas has suggested, emancipation. Such an interest, like a variation in a phenotype, *risks something* when reaching for a new level of organization and order. The short-term consequences of such a move are not instrumental or practical and, even with much time, may never be. In this sense, the motivation and rewards for growth-oriented behavior are intrinsic; and the use of such terms as "survival" and "adaption" to describe the evolutionary process must be complemented by the notion of "expansion." Nietzsche (1974) has emphatically stressed this point, " . . . the really fundamental instinct of life which aims at *the expansion of power* . . . frequently risks or even sacrifices self-preservation" (pp. 291–292, emphasis in original). Thus the evolutionary importance of wisdom as a personal good (a supreme joy in its own right) lies in its connection to variation, experimentation, curiosity, and other similar *expansive* processes. The process of growth – requiring the use of one's full effort or energy – provides immediate rewards and thus does not have to be justified in any other way.

**Why is wisdom dangerous?**

Despite the enormous credit wisdom had among thinkers of the past, there is, at the same time, a deep streak of ambivalence running through their writings, something akin to suspicion and a note of warning. Early in Genesis (3:5) the devil's first temptation consists in promising Adam and Eve that "Ye shall be as gods, knowing good and evil." There are signs of doom in many parts of the Bible; for instance, in *Ecclesiastes:* "In much wisdom is much grief; and he that increaseth knowledge increaseth sorrow." The classical authors often agreed. In the *Odyssey* (XII, 184–92), as Ulysses and his ship sail by, the Sirens sing a sweet song promising to enrich his mind with knowledge, for everything that happens on the face of the earth is known to them. But all around the green meadow where the Sirens sing lie the rotting corpses of the uncautious sailors who were lured to the rocks by their curiosity. "I know not whether it had not been better for mankind," Cicero wrote, "that . . . reason had not been given to man at all; considering how pestiferous it is to many, and healthful but to few" *(De Natura Deorum, III, 27)*. Trying to understand what dangers the ancients saw in wisdom may turn out to be as useful for understanding the evolutionary meaning of the concept as an examination of its advantages would be.

There seem to be three main reasons for the mistrust of wisdom. Two of these turn out to be trivial; the first because it is based on semantic confusion and hence misunderstanding, and the second because it stems from ignorance, or partial knowledge. The third reason, however, points at what may well be a genuine danger inherent in the project of acquiring wisdom.

### The confusion of wisdom and knowledge

In many texts, including the biblical passage quoted in the preceding section, wisdom fails to be differentiated from knowledge; the two terms appear to be synonymous. In such cases the warning against "too much wisdom" really amounts to warning against excessive specialized knowledge unrelated to common sense and to ultimate goals. When this is the case, warnings against wisdom actually amount to appeals for the necessity of wisdom. When Montaigne asks "Of what is the most subtle folly made, but of the most subtle wisdom?" *(Essays, 11, 12)*, he seems to have in mind primarily the fanatical pedants of his time. The dangers of specialized knowledge in our time are too well known to comment on; a good example would be the physicist Robert Oppenheimer, who, when building the first nuclear bomb, exulted at the "sweet problem" he had on his hands (Wylen, 1984).

As Rabelais wrote, not for the first nor for the last time, *Magis magnos clericos non sunt magis magnos sapientes,* or, "The greatest scholars are not the wisest men" *(Gargantua, I, 39)*. But the whole point of the concept of wisdom is that it is different from domain-related thought and knowledge. Hence this critique turns out to be based on a misunderstanding, and it ends up reaffirming the importance of wisdom rather than undermining it.

### The knowledge-based critique of wisdom

The second and more substantial assault is the one that people who believe to already have achieved perfect knowledge bring to bear on the search for ultimate truth. The prototype is the story of the philosopher Thales, who one evening, as his eyes were wandering among the stars, almost fell into an open well. A milkmaid who saw him stumbling laughed and wondered what wisdom could there be in a man who tries to understand the heavens but knows not where he is going.

In classical Western literature, the best-known explanation of why wise persons appear foolish is given in Plato's allegory of the cave *(Republic, VII, 514–517)*. In this parable of the human condition, a group of men live chained in a dark cave, and the only information they get about the world comes from the confused shadows of outside events projected on the inside walls of the cavern by a flickering fire, which they believe to be the sun. Once in a while a man frees himself from the chains and wanders out to discover to his great amazement the colorful world of real objects and events illuminated by the sun. When such a man returns to tell his companions what he saw, they laugh at him in unbelief. Back in the cave, with his eyes unaccustomed to darkness, the man who beheld the real world is more clumsy and helpless than those who had never seen it. So he loses all credibility, and the cave dwellers go on believing that the shadows they see are all there is to reality.

In other words, the world of appearances in which milkmaids and cave dwellers live is so real to them that any attempt to get at universal truths will seem foolish. In the *Apology,* Socrates repeatedly warns his friends that a philosopher – or lover of wisdom – is bound to be hopelessly outwitted by the lawyers, politicians, and businessmen of the city. Any profession, discipline, or science focuses on a particular subset of reality, and in that artificially delimited domain it is able to provide power and control to those who learn it. Wisdom, which is about understanding underlying causes and the consequences of events in relation to each other, does not provide such power. Therefore in the law courts an attorney is going to be much more knowledgeable than a wise person, and in a chemical laboratory a chemist may laugh at the ignorance of the philosopher.

Yet without attempts to get behind the various symbolic systems that we have invented to represent the world, the ancient writers warn us, we are condemned to see reality as a confusing parade of unrelated shadows. No matter how ridiculous, the attempt to bridge between science and religion, between human greed and nature's need, between what is and what ought to be, has to go on if we are to make sense of what is happening in such a way that humanity is to survive.

## The danger intrinsic to wisdom

The first two problems inherent in wisdom turned out to be illusory: the first because it is based on a confusion with knowledge, the second because it is based on a critique that upholds the superiority of the knowledge of particulars over an understanding of the whole – a position our evolutionary interpretation has attempted to discredit. But there is a third set of warnings implicit in the literature, and this one is more difficult to deal with.

Like so many thinkers of the past, Montaigne often refers back to the danger dramatized in the biblical story of Adam's fall: "the thirst of knowledge, and the desire to become more wise, was the first ruin of humankind, and the way by which it precipitated itself into eternal damnation." And "Presumption is our natural and original disease" *(Essays,* II, 12). These and similar warnings do not refer just to the dangers of runaway specialization but to the entire project of the human effort to achieve rationality.

This effort, especially the evolved "vicarious sense" of science or disciplined thought (Campbell, 1976), presents a risk to self-preservation, as does experimentation with any sense faculty. Nietzsche (1968) observes, "To become wise one must wish to have certain experiences and run, as it were, into their gaping jaws. This, of course, is very dangerous; many a wise guy has been swallowed" (p. 164). It may be that the wise person pursues knowledge much like the rock climber pursues the top of a mountain: The anxious first steps into an uncertain future must be taken with faith in order to diligently pursue a course that may not necessarily lead to the desired destination. The greatest danger may even lie in making it, so to speak, to the top of the mountain where the wise person must live "continually in the thundercloud of the highest problems and responsibilities" (Nietzsche, 1974, p. 293). Of the many burdens this may place on an individual, one particularly dangerous aspect of such *remoteness* lies in the distance it places between the person and the more "natural" state of paradisiacal innocence shared by the majority of the unwise. A disorienting *grandiosity* may be nurtured in such isolation from others.

What this suggests to our contemporary way of thinking is that, even under the best of conditions, knowledge is dangerous. But then so is ignorance. The point is to understand what are the dangers peculiar to wisdom so that we can reap its benefits while avoiding as much as possible its negative effects.

Translating the worries of the ancients into current concepts, we would say that what they intuited was the need to avoid the overwhelming pride that knowledge – even when integrated into wisdom – can produce in the unwary. We can see now clearly how dangerous it is for mankind to assume that because we are so smart, we know what is good for us and for the rest of the universe. The more power we control, the more damage our partial knowledge can do. The potential consequences of this were seen already thousands of years ago, when mankind had only a thousandth of its present capacity to pollute and disfigure the world. Montaigne's answer was to keep a just mean, to observe just limits, to follow nature with humility and submission. Plato thought that wisdom, finally, consisted in not wanting more than what is due to us *(Republic,* I, 350).

## Researching the development and communication of wisdom

There are many important issues related to wisdom that could stimulate fruitful research. Our evolutionary perspective suggests that one of the most important would involve the relationship between wisdom and a systematic ecological awareness that takes into account our place in the environment that sustains us. Regardless, however, of the specific issue that is envisioned as being of crucial importance, and requiring wisdom to meet its challenge, is the need to learn more about the *process* of developing and communicating wisdom. If more is learned about this, perhaps the insights could be applied not only to the threat of ecological disaster but also to the many and diverse challenges that currently face us.

Current research has identified a subtlety or *indirectness* possessed by wise individuals. For instance, they are seen as having the ability to "communicate with non-verbal means" (Clayton & Birren, 1980), as being "metaphorical" (Brent & Watson, 1980), and as having "social unobtrusiveness," or the ability to be discrete, patient, and quiet (Holliday & Chandler, 1986). Yet the sense in which these abilities are important is seldom discussed. Why is a wise individual unobstrusive or indirect? We suggest this skill is important for the *development of wisdom and its communication to others* and is related to the intrinsically rewarding dimension of wisdom.

The process of development and communication could be investigated from multiple perspectives, depending on whether one focused attention on wisdom as a cognitive process, a virtue, or a personal good. Contemporary research has made contributions to the understanding of the former two dimensions; there is, however, little research evidence concerning the intrinsic rewards of wisdom or what makes it a source of joy in its own right. The question why the wise individual possesses indirect social skills, and subtle means of communication, may provide the needed impetus to initiate research in this area. Thus we will explore this question in what follows and offer some research suggestions that will hopefully enrich and complement the advances already being made in this "new" field of study.

Habermas (1972) claims that an autonomy-oriented philosophy (wisdom) should "reflect back on the interest structure that joins subject and object a priori" (p. 314). This comment suggests that wisdom develops with the cultivation of a metaawareness of the intrinsic rewards of experience, or a self-reflection on the biocultural "interests" present at birth. This observation is consistent with other recent perspectives on the connections between wisdom and intrinsically rewarding experience. For instance, some of the Eastern philosophies based on Buddhism place the highest value on the experiential dimension of wisdom through pursuing satori or nirvana (Suzuki, 1971). The attainment of such a state is believed to depend on a disciplined and mature awareness of the childlike ability to get engaged in experience (a childlike attitude without being childish; Clayton & Birren, 1980). The Hindu notion of life course suggests that following stages of life as a student and householder, mature age brings insight into the nature of life's *illusion* (literally "in play") and thus an enhanced ability to enjoy experience for its own sake. Jung (1960) speaks of pursuing this childlike, playful modality consciously in later life for the purpose of exploration and adult growth. Chinen (1984) refers to this later-life potential for wisdom and intrinsically rewarding experience as coming from a "modal awareness" or attention to the forms or process of experiencing, rather than just attending to the content of experience.

That wisdom involves the cultivation of a metaawareness of intrinsic rewards is also evident when considering what has been said about the communication of wisdom. The Eastern emphasis on the experiential dimensions of wisdom has led to a complex understanding of the process of communicating wisdom through the master–pupil tutelage, the master's role being the facilitation of joyful self-discovery in the pupil (Clayton & Birren, 1980; Suzuki, 1971). Jung has discussed the mythic or archetypal figure of the wise man as a storehouse of information, who in times of trouble helps others to find solutions for themselves rather than directly endorsing a course of action (Read, Fordham, Adler, & McGuire, 1979). Before the advent of writing, wisdom was transmitted by oral tradition "through stories that [were] constructed to simultaneously *entertain* and instruct" (Holliday & Chandler, 1986, p. 11, emphasis added). Chinen (1984), in the context of discussing Erikson's idea of generativity, suggests the wise mentor advises the apprentice while allowing him or her to make the decisions and mistakes that facilitate self-discovery.

Wisdom by all these accounts demonstrates a higher awareness of the motivations (interest structures) that lead us to process information in particular enjoyable ways. This metaawareness, we suggest, is what provides the wise individual with the possibility of being a subtle and effective *teacher* (developer/communicator) of wisdom. The wise individual is acutely sensitive to others' enjoyable growth experiences. He or she has gained the ability to subtly communicate through the interest structure already operating in another's consciousness by working with the "natural" focus of attention in a person, rather than against it, and guiding it toward higher states of complexity and order. Indirect communication (nonverbal, metaphorical) aids in this subtle direction of attention in the sense that one does not undermine another's enjoyment of self-discovery by a direct authoritarian assault. In addition, the use of metaphor, suggestion, quiet, wit, paradox, or any other indirect method makes the communication more challenging by introducing some uncertainty or puzzle that must be solved. The effect of this gamelike aspect on the listener is likely to be a heightening of interest or concentration and an increased chance of having a flow experience.

A wise teacher would thus have the necessary qualities – both the broad perspective and subtle communication skills – to direct the attention of others toward long-term goals, so that their energy does not become completely trapped in the immediate gratifications of more basic evolutionary interests (e.g., nutrition, reproduction). This leadership ability (whether conscious or not) – which is embodied in the good parent, teacher, or political leader – helps individuals find in their "little" interests the "big" interests that reveal higher states of order and longer range goals for the individuals, for the culture, and eventually for the entire planetary ecosystem (Csikszentmihalyi and Rochberg-Halton, 1981).

Thus, based on accounts from both Eastern and Western traditions concerning the wise individual's ability to stimulate enjoyable self-discovery in others, one might study wisdom as it operates in interpersonal interaction, especially a context in which there exists a relationship of clearly unequal status (e.g., parent–child, teacher–student, employer–employee). For example, one might first identify "wise teachers" through peer ratings at some institution. Interviews may then be conducted with those teachers to ascertain whether their *methods* are especially sensitive to the pupils' autonomy, growth, self-overcoming, and so on. (The dialogistic method of Socrates was one such indirect approach that displayed an awareness of teaching through self-discovery.) One could further postulate that a metaawareness of intrinsic rewards (presumably necessary for wise teaching) could only have been developed on the basis of a rich personal history with such rewards that provided the "material" on which to reflect. Thus interviews with teachers could focus on both their methods and their retrospective histories in the attempt to establish a connection between them. In other words, methods that display such a metaawareness should more often be used by teachers with a history of rewarding growth experiences.

If it is true that such teachers are themselves the "product" of a life filled with successful growth experiences (this is Erikson's [1959] developmental perspective on the wise), they are likely to display in their demeanor the intensity that comes with the continual pursuit of new challenges to overcome. Such a teacher, like many wise individuals in the past, may have something like *charisma,* or the power to stimulate others through their own intensity, based on their supposed contact with a "vital layer" of reality (Shils, 1975; Weber, 1947). Thus another subtle "skill" that may be used to develop wisdom and communicate it to others – in addition to those already discussed – might simply be modeling the process of acquiring wisdom, thereby inspiring others.

It is likely that an inspirational teacher's thoughts and ideas – their memes – would act as catalysts for the development of wisdom in his or her students. They are likely to view the esteemed teacher with a sense of awe and show great respect for his or her authority. One effect of this disposition in the student would be a great intensification and concentration of attention when in the teacher's presence. If, in addition, the wise teacher used indirect, nonthreatening methods to upgrade the challenge of his or her communications, concentration could reach the intensity necessary to trigger intrinsically rewarding flow experiences. In other words, the intense and authoritative presence of the teacher, combined with his or her use of subtle methods, may lead the student to a greater focusing of attention in the hopes of learning something profoundly important.

This combination of inspiration and subtle skill may be very effective in stimulating the growth of wisdom. The relative lack of such esteemed teachers (as well as esteemed artifacts, ideas, institutions) in contemporary society, and the low value attached to intrinsic versus extrinsic rewards are thus likely to be impediments to the development and communication of wisdom. In the current milieu, fewer opportunities arise in which conditions are conducive for concentration on issues of the utmost importance, in the interest of "disinterested" enlightenment and intrinsic rewards.

Thus another direction for future research may lie in gathering reports from individuals concerning their encounters with others they see as wise. Potential questions:

     a. How did you feel in the presence of this person?
     b. What did you take away from the encounter?
     c. How was wisdom communicated?

If one way that wise individuals effectively transmit their memes is in a manner like that just described, then respondents in such a study may report strong emotional effects surrounding encounters with someone wise.


## Conclusions

The application of evolutionary hermeneutics to the concept of wisdom has shown a number of continuities in the meaning this term has had over a period of over 25 centuries. The assumption underlying our analysis has been that such continuities represent relatively unchanging functional prerequisites of human adaptation, survival, and growth.

In other words, by recognizing a peculiar psychological process called "wisdom," by holding it in high esteem, and by being concerned about its potential dangers, we have forged a powerful conceptual tool for managing information about the world and thus for helping us adapt to it. If we did not differentiate wisdom from other forms of knowledge, if we did not think highly of it, or if we accepted its value without question, presumably we would be less likely to fit in with our environment.

The reasons for this adaptive function are expressed by the characteristics generally attributed to wisdom. We have seen its three main dimensions: as a cognitive process, as a guide to action, and as an intrinsic reward.

As a cognitive process, wisdom refers to attempts at understanding the world in a *disinterested* way, seeking the *ultimate consequences* of events as well as ultimate causes while preserving the *integration* of knowledge. Its survival implication is as an antidote to knowledge that pursues selfish, short-term, and limited goals that often turn out to have disastrous consequences for the very persons they were intended to benefit – not to mention other people or the nonhuman environment. More specifically, wisdom is the approach of choice to such contemporary problems as the escalation of nuclear power, the concentration of energy in any form, the pollution of air and water, the creation and cessation of life, and issues of social inequality.

Wisdom is a virtue because by relating in a disinterested way the broadest spectrum of knowledge, *it provides the most compelling guide to action*. Although we no longer believe in the existence of a perfect divine order beyond appearances on which to base a good life, we still must believe, if we are to survive, that it is possible to improve life by understanding how to order our actions better in ways that will bring us in closer harmony with the laws that constrain the physical universe. As long as we act purely in terms of present needs and desires, it is doubtful the rest of the world will be able to afford keeping us much longer. The egocentric, ethnocentric, anthropocentric impulses of mankind are bringing so much destruction into the planetary environment that the probability of the continuation of life keeps steadily diminishing. Only a truly disinterested, long-range, organic understanding of consequences can pull us back from the brink of disaster.

Finally wisdom is a personal good, an *intrinsically rewarding experience that provides some of the highest enjoyment and happiness* available. When a person *reflects* on the connection between events in a disinterested way, he or she has a chance to enter a *flow experience,* an ecstatic state common to those who concentrate consciousness on a challenging, ordered, goal-directed task. As the goal of wisdom is to understand the ultimate consequences and causes of things, it presents the greatest challenges of any mental activity and hence presumably also the most profound enjoyment. The evolutionary significance of this is twofold: First, it provides the mechanism for cultural evolution by motivating people to ever expanding efforts at understanding; second, it provides an alternative for the extrinsic rewards based on pleasure and materialism, which tend to be zero sum, expensive, and hence conducive to social and ecological conflict.

Our review has suggested that psychologists are currently starting to research the first – or cognitive – dimension of wisdom. The moral aspects have been recognized, but so far little empirical work has focused on them. The third dimension, or wisdom as a personally rewarding and meaningful experience, has barely even been noticed. Given the vital importance of it for human survival and growth and its role in the regeneration of wisdom itself, it is to be hoped that more effort will be directed in the future to understanding how it works and how it can be used.

## Notes

1 Biblical references refer to the King James Version.
2 All volume and page references for classic writers and philosophers refer to the Great Books series published by the Encyclopaedia Britannica, 1987.

## References

Aristotle (384–322 B.C. [1987]). *The Works of Aristotle.* Chicago: Great Books of the Western World, Vols. 8 & 9, Encyclopaedia Britannica.
Baltes, P. B., Smith, J., Staudinger, U. M., & Sowarka, D. (in press). Wisdom: one facet of successful aging? In M. Perlmutter (Ed.), *Late-life potential.* Washington, DC: Gerontological Society of America.

Boyd, R., & Richerson, P. J. (1985). *Culture and the evolutionary process.* Chicago: University of Chicago Press.

Brent, S. B. & Watson, D. (1980). Aging and wisdom: individual and collective aspects. Paper presented at the Meeting of the Gerontological Society of America, San Francisco.

Burhoe, R. W. (1976). The source of civilization in the natural selection of coadapted information in genes and cultures. *Zygon, 11*(3), 263–303.

Campbell, D. T. (1965). Variation and selective attention in socio-cultural evolution. In H. R. Barringer, G. I. Blackstone, & R. W. Monk (Eds.), *Social change in developing areas* (pp. 19–42). Cambridge: Schenkman.

Campbell, D. T. (1975). On the conflict between biological and social evolution and between psychology and moral tradition. *American Psychologist, 30,* 1103–1125.

Campbell, D. T. (1976). Evolutionary epistemology. In P. A. Schipp (Ed.), *The library of living philosophers* (pp. 413–463). LaSalle, IL: Open Court.

Chinen, A. B. (1984). Modal logic: a new paradigm of development and late-life potential. *Human Development, 27,* 42–56.

Clayton, V. P., & Birren, J. E. (1980). The development of wisdom across the life-span: a reexamination of an ancient topic. In P. B. Baltes & O. G. Brim, Jr. (Eds.), *Life-span development and behavior* (Vol. 3, pp. 103–135). New York: Academic Press.

Commons, M. L., Richards, F., & Kuhn, D. (1982). Metasystemic reasoning: a case for a level of systemic reasoning beyond Piaget's stage of formal operations. *Child Development, 53,* 1058–1069.

Csikszentmihalyi, M. (1975). *Beyond boredom and anxiety.* San Francisco: Jossey-Bass.

Csikszentmihalyi, M. (1988). The ways of genes and memes. *Reality Club Review, 1,* pp. 107–28.

Csikszentmihalyi, M., & Csikszentmihalyi, I. (1988). *Optimal experience: psychological studies of flow in consciousness.* New York: Cambridge University Press.

Csikszentmihalyi, M., & Massimini, F. (1985). On the psychological selection of bio-cultural information. *New Ideas in Psychology, 3,* 115–138.

Csikszentmihalyi, M., & Rochberg-Halton, E. (1981). *The meaning of things.* Cambridge: Cambridge University Press.

Durkheim, E. (1954). *The elementary forms of religious life.* Glencoe, IL: Free Press.

Eliade, M. (1959) *The sacred and the profane.* New York: Harcourt, Brace, and World.

Erikson, E. (1959). *Identity and the life-cycle.* New York: International Universities Press.

Emerson, R. W. (1929). *The complete works of R. W. Emerson.* New York: Wise.

Habermas, J. (1972). *Knowledge and human interests.* Boston: Beacon Press.

Holliday, S. G., & Chandler, M. J. (1986). *Wisdom: explorations in adult competence.* Basel, Switzerland: Karger.

Huxley, A. (1972). Visionary experience. In J. White (Ed.), *The highest state of consciousness.* New York: Anchor.

Inhelder, B., & Piaget, J. (1958). *The growth of logical thinking from childhood to adolescence.* New York: Basic Books.

Jung, C. G. (1960). The stages of life. In H. Read, M. Fordham, G. Adler, & W. McGuire (Eds.), *The collected works of C. G. Jung* (Vol. 8). Princeton, NJ: Princeton University Press.

Jung, C. G. (1969). *Psychology and religion: West and East.* Princeton, NJ: Princeton University Press.

Kaufmann, W. (1966). *Nietzsche.* Tucson, AZ: University of Arizona Press.

Kramer, D. A. (1983). Postformal operations? A need for further conceptualization. *Human Development, 26,* 91–105.

Labouvie-Vief, G. (1980). Beyond formal operations: uses and limits of pure logic in life-span development. *Human Development, 23,* 141–161.

Labouvie-Vief, G. (1982). Dynamic development and mature autonomy: a theoretical prologue. *Human Development, 25,* 161–191.

Lepper, M. R., & Greene, D. (Eds.). (1978). *The hidden costs of reward: new perspectives on the psychology of human emotion.* Hillsdale, NJ: Lawrence Erlbaum.

Lepper, M. R., Greene, D., & Nisbett, R. E. (1973). Undermining childrens' intrinsic interest with extrinsic rewards: a test of the overjustification hypothesis. *Journal of Personality and Social Psychology, 28,* 129–137.

Lumsden, C. J., & Wilson, E. O. (1981). *Genes, mind, culture: the coevolutionary process.* Cambridge, MA: Harvard University Press.

Lumsden, C. J., & Wilson, E. O. (1983). *Promethean fire: reflections on the origin of mind.* Cambridge, MA: Harvard University Press.

Maslow, A. H. (1968). *Toward a psychology of being.* New York: Van Nostrand.

Meacham, J. A. (1983). Wisdom and the context of knowledge: knowing that one doesn't know. In D. Kuhn & J. A. Meacham (Eds.), *On the development of developmental psychology* (pp. 111–134). Basel, Switzerland: Karger.

Nietzsche, F. (1968). *The basic writings of Nietzsche.* New York: Modern Library.

Nietzsche, F. (1974). *The gay science.* New York: Vintage.

Pepper, S. C. (1942). *World hypotheses.* Berkeley: University of California Press.

Perry, W. I. (1970). *Forms of intellectual and ethical development in college years.* New York: Holt, Rinehart, & Winston.

Plato (428–348 b.c. [1987]). *The Dialogues* (B. Jowett, Trans.). Chicago: Great Books of the Western World, Vol. 7, Encyclopaedia Britannica.

Read, H., Fordham, M., Adler, G., & McGuire, W. (Eds.) (1979). *The collected works of C. G. Jung* (2nd ed.). Princeton, NJ: Princeton University Press/London: Routledge & Kegan Paul.

Reese, H. W., & Overton, W. F. (1970). Models of development and theories of development. In L. R. Goulet & P. B. Baltes (Eds.), *Life-span developmental psychology.* New York: Academic Press.

Riegel, K. F. (1973). Dialectical operations: the final period of cognitive development. *Human Development, 15,* 1–12.

Shils, E. (1975). *Center and periphery: essays in macrosociology.* Chicago: University of Chicago Press.

Simon, H. A. (1969). *The sciences of the artificial.* Cambridge, MA: MIT Press.

Simonton, D. K. (1988). *Scientific genius: a psychology of science.* New York: Cambridge University Press.

Sternberg, R. J. (1985). Implicit theories of intelligence, creativity, and wisdom. *Journal of Personality and Social Psychology, 49* (3), 607–627.

Suzuki, D. T. (1971). *What is Zen?* New York: Harper & Row.

Tolstoy, L. (1869 [1968]). *War and peace.* (A. Dunnigan, Trans.). New York: New American Library.

Turner, V. (1979). *Process, performance, and pilgrimage.* New Delhi: Concept.

Weber, M. (1947). *The theory of social and economic organization* (A. M. Henderson & T. Parsons, Trans.). New York: Oxford University Press.

Wyden, P. (1984). *Day one: before Hiroshima and after.* New York: Simon & Schuster.

# 4    Wisdom as integrated thought: historical and developmental perspectives

*Gisela Labouvie-Vief*

The notion that wisdom may be the reward of advancing age has become a hoped-for antidote to views that have cast the process of aging in terms of intellectual deficit and regression. The result has been a flurry of recent writings attempting to define the nature of wisdom from philosophical or empirical perspectives (e.g., Clayton & Birren, 1980; Dittmann-Kohli & Baltes, in press; Holliday & Chandler, 1986; Meacham, 1983; Moody, Clayton, & McKee, 1983; Taranto, 1988). There is some emerging consensus that wisdom refers to a set of attributes assumed to be correlated with advanced age and not usually covered under the umbrella of "intelligence." Moral and spiritual integrity, humility and compassion, or insight into the pragmatic, subjective, and psychological dimensions of life all have been associated with the concept of wisdom. It is not clear, however, just what is the underlying theme that holds together these various elements, nor what is their adaptive significance.

In this chapter, I propose that these recent attempts to revive an ancient topic, though important for discussions about the nature of the aging process, have implications of a much more far-reaching nature. They indicate, I suggest, the emergence of a new paradigm within which to discuss intellectual and cognitive functions and their development over the course of life. In Western intellectual tradition, these functions have been described primarily by reference to outer, objective, and logical forms of processing and contrasted with inner, subjective, and organismic ones. Many recent writings suggest, instead, that theories of cognition or intelligence that are based on the assumption of the primacy of objective forms of knowing provide an incomplete and possibly distorted picture of the human mind. Instead, they indicate that a more complete picture of mental functioning ought to emancipate organismic forms of cognition as well. Rather than continuing to identify mental life primarily with objective thought, then, theories of thought need to be based on a duality of two modes of knowing that, although often in competition, ideally function in a dialogic relationship. In that dialogue,

Preparation of this chapter was supported by NIA research grant AG04894.

one mode provides experiential richness and fluidity, the other logical cohesion and stability. It is such smooth and relatively balanced dialogue between two modes that I define as wisdom.

Writings about the nature of wisdom hence have a wide reach, embracing issues relevant for theories of mind and self and their kin domains, whether they refer to such "objective" processes as cognition and intelligence or such "subjective" ones as emotions and interpersonal processes. In the midst of such vastness, it may be useful to pinpoint the particular pathway that has guided my own approach to the topic of wisdom. Starting from the question of why adult development has posed such a vexing theoretical problem to developmental theorists, I began to focus on Piaget's theory of development (see Labouvie-Vief, 1980, 1982). A careful examination of that theory seemed particularly compelling, as I felt it was paradoxical that this rich and sweeping system has failed us as a useful theory of adult cognitive development. Based as it is on the core assumption that intelligence arises from organic and subjective processes and providing, as a result, an integrative view of the cognitive underpinnings of the ontogeny of human adaptive capacities, that theory shows many useful pointers to a theory of wisdom.

Despite its organismic view of the mind, however, Piaget's theory also retained many assumptions from older, more objectivist positions. To examine how those assumptions had infiltrated a theory of such organic breadth and ultimately undermined its usefulness seemed to me an important endeavor. And indeed, continuing on that path I came to realize that Piaget was in no way unique in his objectivist bias, but he was joined by other major theorists of mental development such as Freud, Werner (1948), or G. H. Mead (1934). All of these theorists began affecting an extraordinary redefinition of the nature of the human mind: a redefinition aimed at describing not merely "intelligence" as an objective form of thought but "wisdom" as an integrated one. Yet each in his own way remained profoundly indebted to the objectivist assumptions of past thinkers, thus failing to lead his vision to its logical conclusion.

Indeed, the current concerns with wisdom are the continuation of an age-old project. That project began with the birth of reflective intelligence and the search for a way of life that would be governed by rational reflection rather than the mere living out of tradition. It led, however, to a concept of wisdom that unduly split the rational and the nonrational and that still haunts our major theories of the mind. In order to discern how that project might be continued, I was led, therefore, to examine its historical trajectory and its impact on our conceptions of the growth and decline of intellectual functioning.

Out of this examination gradually evolved my own view of how best to conceptualize processes of intellectual and cognitive development over the life course. In this chapter, I attempt to outline that view and highlight some of its heuristic implications. In so doing, I am following a somewhat inductive course, providing a historical backdrop to a treatment of wisdom as integrated cognition. From that overview I go on to discuss the influence of this background on theory and research on wisdom and the life course.

## Modes of knowing

Our conception of mind, self, and human nature in terms of two modes of thinking and organizing experience is basic to most theories of development. It is well exemplified in Piaget's theory, where assumptions are made about the kind of reality to which the developing individual needs to adapt. That reality, according to Piaget (1976, 1980), is not merely an external given the individual aims to reproduce. Rather it is a psychic reality that is more than a mere copy or internalization of outer reality. Hence it is based on a dialectic between the creative and imaginative externalization of inner reality on one hand and the reproductive and receptive internalization of outer reality on the other.

That view of reality, and the concept of development ensuing from it, is well expressed in Piaget's *Play, Dreams, and Imitation in Childhood* (1962), where Piaget distinguishes between two forms of regulation related in turn to two forms of symbol formation. One of those regulation modes is based on *assimilation* and is best exemplified by play. Here, a ludic orientation prevails in which the individual is not concerned with the demands of outer reality. Rather, those of inner reality prevail, and the outer reality is adjusted to the inner world of desires and private images. The second is based on *accommodation,* where the individual adjusts to the outer constraints of the world of personal and impersonal objects: Imitation is the prototype of that situation.

The notion that two modes of cognitive regulation underlie human cognition and behavior is basic to other theories as well. Freud's (1923) differentiation between primary and secondary process thinking, Werner's (1955; Werner & Kaplan, 1963) distinction between physiognomic and formal-technical modes, or Mead's (1934) description of the duality of self – the spontaneous "I" and the conceptual, social "Me" – all imply such a duality of cognitive functioning. Indeed, most theories of human knowledge and behavior seem to be based on one version or another of such a dual control system. In philosophy, for example, the duality recurs as a debate about which are more authentic sources of knowledge: Our ability to provide inner-directed, imaginative syntheses projected "outward" or our "mirroring" of forms that are objectively given from the outside (e.g., Macmurray, 1978; Rorty, 1979). Religious traditions, too, display a duality between dogmatic and monotheistic positions buttressed by a body of codified law and those that are, in essence, mystical and pantheistic and validated by a subjective sense of union between self and some divine principle (Campbell, 1988; Rubenstein, 1988). Hence, these two modes appear to form two complementary though fundamentally different modes of organizing experience and of experiencing reality. Indeed, some theorists have suggested that these two ways of experiencing reality are founded on different neuroanatomically and neurochemically based processing systems (Goldberg & Costa, 1981; Pribram & McGuiness, 1975; Tucker & Williamson, 1984).

Olson (1977) has offered a somewhat similar historical analysis with his differentiation between two forms of meaning making that are involved in oral, preliterate, and literate societies. In the "oral" mode, Olson argues, meaning is derived from the shared experiences of dialogic participants; it is informal and implicit rather than explicit and based on emotive appeal and subjective interpretation. Truth is psychological rather than logical, and validation is by intuitive criteria of "felt sense." In the "written" mode, on the other hand, meanings are disembedded from this organismic core and the immediate context and are related to more general, standardized systems of interpretation. Meaning is based on explicit premises, stable principles, and precise rules and solution algorithms. Validation is by discursive principles, debate, and analysis, and truth is logical rather than psychological.

Although Olson correlates the two modes with the emergence of a written tradition out of one that was primarily based on oral storage and transmission, subsequent writers have suggested that in actuality, the differentiation between two modes of knowing was part of a much broader and pervasive historical shift that can only in part be explained by the evolution of literacy. Nevertheless, even though the two modes may no longer be primarily related to oral or written settings, the differentiation between two modes remains important. Bruner (1986), more recently, has recast it in terms of a distinction between "narrative" and "paradigmatic" modes of knowing. As in Olson's system, the two modes construe, process, and verify reality in fundamentally different ways. The narrative mode's orientation to reality can best be exemplified by a story, in which a "truthful" (i.e., poignant, gripping, or believable) account is based on figurative language and a psychological causality of human intentionality. In contrast, the paradigmatic mode relies on explicit rules and deductive principles.

In my own work (e.g., Labouvie-Vief, 1989), I have begun to refer to these two modes by the Greek terms *mythos* and *logos*. Although in some sense the connotative sphere of these words is so wide as to be almost embarrassing for scientific discourse, in another sense the etymological roots of these words delineate rather precise meanings. Both of them are terms for "word" but in two different senses (see Klein, 1967; Liddell, 1958). *Mythos* means *speech, narrative, plot,* or *dialogue.* As is true of Olson's oral mode, in the mythos mode experience is holistic and based on a bond of close identification between the self and the object of thought. Thought and thinker,

knower and known, are one single, indivisible unit, and it is from this bond
that derives the meaning of an experience. The object of thought is not
articulated separately from the motivational and organismic states of the
thinker; rather the thinker's whole organism partakes in the articulation of
the object and animates it with its own motives and intentions. Cassirer has
eloquently characterized that feature of *mythos* thought in his essay, *Language
and Myth:*

Mythical thinking...does not dispose freely over the data of intuition, in order to
relate and compare them to each other, but is captivated and enthralled by the intuition
which suddenly confronts it. It comes to rest in the immediate experience; the sensible
present is so great that everything else dwindles before it. For a person whose
apprehension is under the spell of this...attitude, it is as though the whole world
were simply annihilated; the immediate content, whatever it be, commands his...
interest so completely that nothing else can exist beside and apart form it. The ego
is spending all its energy in this single object, lives in it, loses itself in it. (Cassirer,
1946, pp. 32–33)

*Logos* also means "word," but the term refers to the more conceptual aspects
of words and, more generally, of states of the world. *Logos* derives from
*gather, read,* and came to connote *counting, reckoning, explanation, rule,* or
*principle* and, finally, *reason.* In contrast to *mythos,* it refers to that part of
knowledge that is arguable and can be demonstrated and defined with precision and agreement. In *logos* thinking, meaning is disembedded from a
reality of flux and change and related to stable systems of categorization. The
complexity of *mythos* is reduced, canalized into single modalities, contained
in fixed meanings. Ideally, *logos* implies that knowledge can be rendered
purely mechanical, computable, and deductively certain.

   Throughout the course of our intellectual history, there has been considerable controversy over which mode of thinking better represents mature
cognitive functioning. In that debate, there has been a long-standing tendency
to adopt a reductionistic solution by asserting that *logos* provides a better
way of thinking and being, whereas *mythos* only constitutes an immature and
degraded version of *logos.* And even though romantic thinkers critiqued that
rationalist position, they remained embedded in the dualism that had come
to construe the mind in terms of two opposing rather than cooperating forms
of thought. This broad epistemic structure of dualism has shown signs of
breaking down, however, and we are witnessing the rise of a new structure
in which the mind is viewed more integratively as encompassing the two modes
as irreducible and complementary poles.

## Mental models

### The birth of logos

The equation of mature thinking with *logos* processes is a relatively recent
achievement in the history of thought. It presupposes a certain level of self-

reflective awareness that gradually emerged in antiquity and that vigorously developed in classical Greece and found its first culmination with the philosophy of Plato.

Prior to Plato, many philosophers already asked such questions as: What is the nature of reality? or What is our nature, and what is our place in the order of things? To the pre-Platonic philosophers, answers to these questions still were permeated with mythic and highly concrete images. Reality still presented itself as an organismic happening integrated with the world of nature. Like nature, reality was animated with life and subject to growth and decay (see Collingwood, 1945; Frankfort & Frankfort, 1946). Mythic and organic conceptions of the universe were mixed with the beginning of systematic and abstracting thought.

Out of those organic conceptions of reality gradually emerged the view that reality was, in essence, defined by conceptual forms that are no longer tied to material substances. One example is Pythagoras' famous teaching that it is not the material substance of things that define their real essence but rather their mathematical or geometric structure. Thus we can identify the same note though it is played on different musical instruments because the geometric structure of the vibrating waves, not the material structure of the instruments, defines the note (Collingwood, 1945).

Pythagoras' theory of the insubstantial nature of reality was more than an intellectual exercise. It constituted a component of a sweeping reorganization of social fabric and intellectual life in ancient Greece (Jaynes, 1976; Vernant, 1982; Whyte, 1948). That reorganization began several millennia B.C. and reached its culmination around 400 B.C., during Plato's lifetime and work. That span of time brought the worldwide transformation of social life from nomadic, gathering, and hunting communities to ones characterized by complex and stable social hierarchies. It was a reorganization, therefore, that affected not only thinking in the narrower sense of the term, but a total form of life in the fullest sense of that term. Thus it brought with it a redefinition of the nature of reality, of the place of men and women in that reality, and of the kind of characteristics that would permit living in that kind of reality. It is in that very broad and integrative sense that I will discuss issues of wisdom hereafter.

The rise of complex social organizations brought with it, then, the necessity for profoundly different forms of life. In his study of the civilizing process, Elias (1978, 1982) has commented on the way in which the emergence of more complex social networks affect these forms of life and the individual's conduct within them. In simpler societies of the past, Elias claims, life was regulated by a form of control rooted in the predominance of instinctual forms of mediation. Such unmediated control contrasts profoundly with the way the modern individual regulates her or his conduct. Modern life is organized less by a dimension of concrete physicality and the immediacy of more or less automatic and instinctual programs. Rather, it requires that individuals guide

their behavior with reference to a complex web of internalized expectations
and cognitive controls.

The contrast between those different forms of life emerges from comparisons of the way philosophers and poets talked about reality. One important
source of evidence, for example, relies on analyses of the Homeric poems,
written in the eighth century B.C., and the writings of Plato and his contemporaries. Over this relatively short time span a dramatic reorganization occurred in how the actions and capacities of adults are described (see Jaynes,
1976; Onians, 1954; Simon, 1978).

In the Homeric poems, there is little evidence for the self-consciousness
typical of the modern person. The Homeric heroes do not engage in reflection
but are embedded in action. Theirs is a concrete, sensory existence. It shows
little evidence of the mental types of regulation mastered by the modern
adult: impulse delay and monitoring and self-ownership of action and feeling
(Onians, 1954). There is no language of a self different from its concrete
actions and assets – a self as a permanent, persistent agent who authors its
actions but is not identical with them. Indeed, there is no word at all, no
specific designating concept, for the self, since " . . . no one in Homer thinks
by himself, but rather engages in an interaction or dialogue, be it with another
person, with a god, or with a part of himself" (Simon, 1978, p. 72).

Thus the language of the self is one of concrete action and of participation.
Nor is there a specific differentiation between mental and physical bodily
processes. Mental activities such as wishing, thinking, and planning are often
described as the automatic occurrence of bodily processes and physical actions. There is no concept of an individual reflective mind. Rather, mind and
self are inherently interactive, dialogic, and participatory. No clear differentiation is made between inner and outer reality, but the boundaries between
inner processes and states and outer events are fluid, and inner states are
often ascribed to outer events. For example, dreams are seen not as emanating
from within but as originating from without. Thus when Zeus in the *Iliad*
ponders how best to avenge Achilles, he sends an "evil Dream" to go to
Agamemnon to send him a message. "Dream" is not an inner process (as it
will be for Plato) but an outer event, a personified agent; disguised as Nestor,
he stands at Agamemnon's bedside and repeats Zeus' message to him (Simon,
1978, p. 58).

The same tendency to externalize one's inner process is also evident in the
language of emotions, wishes, and desires. In the times of the *Iliad,* there
was no concept of inner motives, but the individual saw him- or herself moved
by divine forces. One's own feelings and intentions were perceived as in-
junctions from the outside. Thus when Achilles is about to slay Agamemnon,
he interrupts himself because "Athena comes down, pulls him by his hair,
and says, 'Cease'" (Simon, 1978, p. 62). The self expressed in such language
is a self, then, undifferentiated from inner organismic states and functions on

the one hand and fused with its physical and psychological environment on the other.

By Plato's lifetime, a dramatic change in the language of the mind had occurred, and Plato's writings represent the culmination of a new way of speaking about the mature adult. For Plato, the adult is no longer embedded in a concrete, organic, and participatory reality. Rather, the new reality is one defined by a new function, *psyche,* variously translated as *soul, mind,* or *spirit.* Most of Plato's writing is concerned with delineating the new faculty that allows us to live in that new reality and with differentiating it from a reality of concrete sensory textures.

For Plato, mental functioning is no longer identified with the organic and the mythic – with the senses, with actions, with poeticized accounts of reality. Rather, it resides in our ability to step back from the purely sensory. Plato addresses this issue in the dialogue *Thaetetus,* where Socrates challenges Thaetetus' belief that knowledge is a form of perception. Neither knowledge, suggests Socrates, nor the faculty from which it springs – the mind – is to be identified with sensory functions. The senses, he argues, are merely the *instruments* of knowledge and the mind, but they are not *identical* with them. The senses merely point to the workings of a more abstract agency, the *psyche* or mind. Mind draws on the activity of the senses, yet it is something that goes beyond them, an inner abstract agency that does not merely act but that coordinates activity and operates on it.

With that inward movement the mind has become an autonomous agency. This autonomy is evident in its changing social nature as well. As it turns inward, as it claims ownership and conscious control of bodily impulse and sensory activity, it also becomes less dependent on constant, concrete social monitoring. The new mind thus is more individuated and self-authored. It becomes distanced from a concrete reality of interpersonal exchanges and instead is located inside the individual. It is no longer communal but becomes the purely internal discourse of a solitary agent, the self, with itself. Thus in his dialogue with Thaetetus, Socrates maintains that thinking is

... a discourse that the mind carries on with itself about any subject it is considering. ... So I should describe thinking as discourse, and judgment as a statement pronounced, not aloud to somebody else, but silently to oneself. *(Thaetetus,* 189e–190a, 895–896)

## The dissociated mind

The writings of Plato and his contemporaries are witness to the emergence of the concept of mind that is earmarked with a sense of individuality and responsibility, of a self as a cognitive and moral author and decision maker. Plato's theory of the mind is aimed at delineating those functions of the mind that would accomplish a new way of life. The person who would think and behave according to the new theory, Plato asserts throughout his work, is a person of virtue and wisdom. However, Plato's theory of wisdom remains extremely limited, since it is based on a very limited concept of the mind and its functions.

These new functions are based on a series of differentiations not previously explicit: mind and body, inner and outer, flux and change, being and becoming, knowledge and opinion, universal and particular, all are dualities around which the new concepts of mind and self are structured. Such differentiation between two modalities of mental life is an accomplishment of abstraction essential in the progress of cultural evolution. The Greek model of reality, however, provided no synthesis of these dual terms. According to the new philosophy, all valid knowledge was of the *logos* kind, whereas *mythos* was considered a less desirable form of knowledge, a more primitive one, a mere degradation of *logos*. That dissociation affected both more collective and outer dimensions of life and ones that were more private and inner.

*Thought without thinkers.* One consequence of reducing *mythos* to *logos* was the rationalist claim that the mature mind could be described without reference to an intersubjective, collective reality. Instead, thinking was to be described exclusively by propositional forms, universal ideas, and stable principles that transcended the dynamics of social order and interpersonal exchanges. These new laws of thinking were to replace forms of decision making of the past, forms that had relied primarily on the authority of myth, tradition, and social power (DeLong, 1970; Vernant, 1982). Instead, the Greeks envisioned a new form of decision making that was located purely in the realm of the abstract and the universal. In that realm, everybody could examine statements and be led to the same conclusion. The individuality of the thinker, then, no longer entered into the process of thinking except in the sense that one might make an error of logic (see Macmurray, 1978). The qualitative individuality of participants in dialogue was completely transcended, however, by universal laws. There were no unique selves, therefore, to be accounted for in a theory of thinking. Rather, each self was a mere replica of other, similarly universal selves, and the self entered into thought merely quantitatively.

The attempt to come up with universal decision forms resulted in the formulation of laws of logic, which were assumed to transcend subjective personal and interpersonal forms of decision making (DeLong, 1970; Vernant, 1982). Truth claims and the laws of thinking on which they were based were taken out of the communal and interpersonal and referenced only with respect to universal, thinker-independent forms.

The belief that thinking could be described as a thinker-independent process was contrary to the Sophists' doctrine that the expert logician should be able to manipulate abstract argument structures so as to serve his or her self-interest. DeLong (1970) notes that in that awareness, the Sophists' logical theory was extraordinarily modern in its recognition that abstract argument structures alone do not yield judgments about truth. Rather, since those argument structures must assign truth values to empirical statements, another, subjective ingredient enters logical procedures. To be truthful, the thinker must be able not only to follow the logical structure of arguments, but also to evaluate how reasonably truth values have been assigned to premises. Hence, truth cannot be dissociated from, or even displace, a general discussion of wisdom.

Plato (1961), however, would have no theory of truth or thought that opened the door for the discussion of such subjective processes. In the *Protagoras,* he opposes truth, which is based on logic alone, to rhetoric, which aims at argumentation and persuasion. Protagoras, the Sophist, is compared to a mere peddler who by using the tools of narrative seduces people, "charming them with his voice like Orpheus, and they follow spellbound" *(Protagoras,* 315b, 314). Thus he tries to lead the soul away from its necessary aliment, truth:

[W]e must see that the Sophist in commending his wares does not deceive us, like the whole saler and the retailer who deal in food for the body. These people do not know themselves which of the wares they offer is good or bad for the body, but in selling them praise all alike, and those who buy from them don't know either. *(Protagoras,* 313c–d, 313)

Plato thus thinks Sophism a shameful practice, based as it is on the folly of the body. Following his lead, for centuries to come, theories of truth and logic focused on rational structures only (see Blumenberg, 1987). With the assumption that thinking can be mechanized in terms of thinker-independent processes, theories of thought thus may have committed what Gregory (1981, p. 223) calls "the most profound mistake in human history."

*Mind without body.* One correlate of the devaluation of the communal and narrative aspects of knowing was a similar degradation of the individual's inner world, of the material and organic aspects of knowledge. Plato's theory, accordingly, defined the new way of life in direct opposition to the sensual, bodily, and organic. The ideal man's thinking – and thinking was very much a masculine activity – was no longer supported by the concrete texture of sensory impressions and interpersonal exchanges; rather these were defined as mere perils, and it was necessary that the philosopher aim at "despising the body and avoiding it, and endeavoring to become independent" *(Thaetetus,* 65d, 48). In Plato's writings, there is a constant disparagement, even contempt, of everything associated with the body and the senses:

[A]s long as we possess the body, and our soul is contaminated by such an evil, we'll surely never adequately gain what we desire – and that, we say, is truth. Because the body affords us countless distractions . . . it fills us up with lusts and desires, with fears and fantasies of every kind, and with any amount of trash, so that really and truly we are . . . never able to think of anything at all because of it . . . for all these reasons it leaves us no leisure for philosophy. And the worst of it all is that if we do get any leisure from it, and turn to some inquiry, once again it intrudes everywhere in our researches, setting up a clamour and disturbance, and striking terror, so that the truth can't be discerned because of it. *(Thaetetus,* 66b-d, 49)

Just as the mind must maintain the most rigid discipline over the body and its impulses, Plato claimed in the *Republic,* so it must cultivate a deep suspicion over everything concerned with the imagination. For Plato, the inner life of feelings and the imagination lurks with dangers. As a consequence, his project of denaturalizing and demythifying mind and self is carried to such imaginative products as dreams, myth, and art. For example, in the *Republic,* Plato says of dreaming that desires

. . . are awakened in sleep when the rest of the soul, the rational, gentle and dominant part, slumbers, but the beastly and savage part, replete with food and wine, gambols and, repelling sleep, endeavors to sally forth and satisfy its own instincts. You are aware that in such case there is nothing it will not venture to undertake as being released from all sense of shame and all reason. It does not shrink from attempting to lie with a mother in fancy or with anyone else, man, god, or brute. It is ready for any foul deed of blood; it abstains from no food, and, in a word, falls short of no extreme of folly and shamelessness. *(Republic,* 571c-d, 798)

In a similar vein, Plato wants to ban other imaginative activities from the *Republic.* The artistic, the poetic, and the mythic, he claims, deal not with the truthful eternal nature of things, but rather with their phenomenal appearance. Pictorial representations, for example, are lies and apparitions only, superficial and illusory. "That kind of art," says Plato, " . . . seems to be a corruption of the mind of all listeners who do not possess as an antidote a knowledge of its real nature" *(Republic,* 595b, 820). The activities of poets are no less dangerous since, by aiming at mere appearances, they distract us from seeing truth.

The mind hence is completely stripped of its mythos roots. What, however, happens to these split-off parts of self and mind? They are projected outward toward those who do not conform to the *logos* model. Thus individual differences are accommodated by positing a principle by which some individuals were degraded versions of those *logos* forms. Children, for example, were seen to represent the animal, inferior part of our nature, while adulthood brought the ability to be rational. Similarly, the new mental and spiritual faculties were identified with the masculine, whereas the feminine indicated the organic and material aspects of reality. Although less pronounced in Plato, this devaluation of the feminine was explicit in Aristotle, who argued that it was evident in processes of sexual reproduction. He theorized that the woman contributed the more primitive and material principle to the embryo but denied that the man's contribution also was of a material sort. Instead, he held that the masculine contribution was more spiritual and "divine" (Aristotle, 1921, 729a, 28–34; see also Lerner, 1986).

## The reconnected mind

The rationalist theory of classical Greece persisted, in essence, until the beginning of this century. However, with the geographic and intellectual expansion of the world in the 17th and 18th centuries, the problem of subjectivity emerged in more modern form that itself had various variants. For Kant, for example, it initiated what he called a "Copernican revolution" in epistemology, in which the problem of subjectivity was put squarely at the base of a theory of knowledge and thought. However, that revolution did not result in an upgrading of the *mythos* mode. Thus, when Kant claimed that "we can know a priori of things only what we put ourselves into them" (Cassirer, 1981, p. 158), he realized that this inversion involved the threat of completely surrendering any notion of the "objective." This threat could be averted, in turn, by maintaining a model of the mind that was, in essence, logical rather than psychological.

Nevertheless, a path had been opened for the discussion of subjectivity, and competing with Kant's rationalism grew positions that maintained that knowledge results, not from a receptive discipline, but rather from a productive spontaneity of mind. These philosophical positions – ranging from Rousseau through later romantic positions to Nietzsche – were framed as a mere antithesis to rationalism, however, and did not provide a synthesis. They merely inverted the rationalist hierarchy, insisting on an emotive rather than cognitive reductionism. Just as Descartes had split these two domains into two incommensurables, so epistemology remained divided into the realms of disembodied mind and of mindless matter.

In this century, the problem of how to reconnect the two domains has reemerged in a new form, however, in which the separability of the two domains, *logos* and *mythos,* is completely denied. Beginning with the demise of the doctrine that empirical systems could be based on logical forms whose existence was beyond intuition and doubt (see Hofstadter, 1979; Labouvie-Vief, 1980), philosophy soon was swept with critiques that logic alone could lead to incontrovertible truth. Instead, truth was relocated into and relativized by specific systems within which it could be said to be meaningful: the communal and conventional (Geertz, 1983; Habermas, 1984; Wittgenstein, 1968), the rhetorical and practical (Blumenberg, 1987), the mythic and symbolic (Popper, 1963; Ricoeur, 1970), and the organic and emotional (Lakoff, 1987). This deconstruction of the dogma of the primacy of *logos* has led to a thorough relativism in which any unitary concept of reason based on transcendent truth is completely denied. Instead, reason is purely immanent and absorbed in specific cultural or linguistic practices and biological processes.

From that position of relativism, however, some recent philosophers have gone on to search for more transcendent views of reason. Putnam (1987) argues that positions that would reduce the rational merely to what language we are using or what context we are in retain an element of profound irrationalism. They do not permit a critique of cultural practice, as if such practice constituted an algorithm to be slavishly followed. By confusing the contingent with the desirable, they foster a degree of solipsism and closure, locking each self in an egocentric void. Thus, it would be a mistake to eliminate the normative notion of justifiable truth from philosophical discourse. This implies that reason can't be reduced "to our favorite science, be it biology, anthropology, neurology, physics, or whatever." Instead we need to accept that reason is both immanent and transcendent and that "philosophy, as culture-bound reflection and argument about eternal questions, is both in time and in eternity" (p. 242).

What, then, constitutes a concept of reason that, though grounded in the immanent, reaches beyond it toward a more normative meaning? One example is offered by Habermas (e.g., 1984), who has proposed to ground the concept of reason in the communicative process. Habermas's critique of traditional objectivist notions of reason proposes that even though these notions are framed in opposition to "knowledge constitutive interests" such as communication, practice, and ideology, they nevertheless interact with them. Still, he does not wish to reduce them to such interests because to do so would constitute mere pluralism. One characteristic of reason is that it is reflexive and thus can problematicize and criticize validity claims, and a transformation of the concept of reason needs to retain that self-critical attitude. For Habermas, such a transformation is possible by relocating rational processes from a monologic framework to a communicative one in which validity claims are subject to critique in interpersonal settings and in which each participant is willing to surrender his or her ties to ideology, power, and other interests that can distort the communication process. Respect for qualitative differences and individuality thus is an essential ingredient from which a higher-order concept of rationality can emerge (see also Kohlberg, 1984; Rawls, 1971).

While Habermas is primarily concerned with the constraints emanating from the outer world, Lakoff (1987) has discussed those emanating from the inner world. Critiquing the objectivist view of the transcendent and disembodied nature of reason, Lakoff argues that rational processes reflect the bodily nature of thinking human beings: their activities, movements, physiological patterns. Conceptual processes are grounded in such basic level processes; those that are not directly grounded in biological experience employ metaphor, metonymy, and mental imagery to extend basic categories of bodily experience. Yet such grounding does not commit the thinker to a subjectivist prison. Rather, a more overarching perspective can be gained if each thinker knows his or her role in the process of thinking so that he or she can overcome it and take on the perspective of others. Though grounded in the immanent, then, the new concept of reason nevertheless reaches toward more transcendent meanings as well.

## The loss and gain of wisdom

### Growth and the loss of wisdom

The rationalist model of the mind has had a profound influence on Western conceptualizations of mental functioning, and the paradigmatic view of mind has formed the epistemological background for many studies of cognitive functioning throughout the life course. In those theoretical frameworks, intellectual processes are described primarily as *logos* processes, oriented toward outer, verifiable thinking (see Sternberg & Powell, 1982). In doing so, however, they do not specify mature thought as a balance but rather deal with "nonrational" modes of adaptive functioning only in pejorative terms. As Susanne Langer (1942) put it, "everything that falls outside the domain of analytical, propositional, and formal thought is merely classified as emotive, irrational, and animalian. . . . All other things our minds do are dismissed as irrelevant to intellectual progress; they are residues, emotional disturbances, or throwbacks to animal estate" and indicate "regression to a pre-logical state" (pp. 292–293).

That *logos* bias is evident in most major theories of intellectual development. This is true despite the fact that many of these theories have started from the assumption that thought is grounded in the organic nature of our being. A good example is Piaget's theory, which is based on the assertion that intelligence arises out of a series of core organic schemata that provide adaptations for such basic biological needs as nourishment, contact, and exploration. Nevertheless, his account of development places emphasis on this organicity of thought only early in the life span, whereas later intelligence is said to free itself from that organic ground.

That bias toward disembodied, transcendent structures of thinking is evident in Piaget's discussion of symbolism. With regard to the ludic symbol, for example, Piaget (1962) very much maintains that progress in development brings a decrease in private symbolism, as play is transformed into an "objective imitation of reality" (p. 139). Thus rather than being a mere "affective modification of reality" (p. 285), its function becomes to reproduce the external world. Thus Piaget's reality is very much an external, collective, and impersonal one.

The same bias toward disembodied intellectual structures is also evident in Piaget's discussion of linguistic symbolism, more generally. Piaget's theory, as Turner (1973) has noted, is based on a contrast between symbols, which are private and individual, and signs, which are public and collective and independent of the subject's identity, feelings, and purposes. As children mature, they are more and more able to give up private meanings and relate to collective signs. Indeed, as Watkins (1986) has noted, inner aspects of speech for Piaget are considered inferior and childish: Inner speech "creates a dream world of imagination . . . it tends not to establish truths, but to satisfy desires, and remains strictly individual and incommunicable" (Piaget, 1955, p. 63). As the individual progresses in development, that speech form is driven out, remaining only in such cases of pathology as autism. Thus, even though for Piaget intellectual development emerges from an organic core, the mature adult is idealized almost purely in terms of *logos* processes, whereas *mythos* is devaluated as childish and immature. It does not, therefore, have its own line of development.

This tendency toward an objectivist account of development is even more pronounced in Piaget's discussion of the role of interpersonal processes in development. Such processes do not constitute part of the individual's organicity but instead are reduced to advances in cognitive development. Thus, for example, Piaget's description of the infant is one of an individual interacting with an impersonal world of objects rather than a reality that is primarily social. Piaget asserts that with the acquisition of the object concept, the infant is able to develop an attachment to the caretaker. Social bonding is not assumed to be a major variable in development from the outset, only to be transformed with advances in cognitive development (see Piaget, 1965, 1981). Rather, it is caused by the emergence of new cognitive structures. Thus here we have a basic conception of the human being as an egocentric and isolated entity who can only break out of that isolation and construct a social network through the means of *logos*.

The tendency to devalue *mythos* is not unique to Piaget, however. Freud's theory, too, assumes that primary process constitutes a primitive mode of functioning that in development must give way to the control of an outward-oriented ego. More generally, development during the first part of the life span has been primarily described in terms of the rise of knowledge systems that are aimed at abstraction and control over ones that are characterized by more receptive and imaginative processes.

The resulting process of dissociation and hierarchization does, of course, have importance in the process of early development. Here, the individual needs to idealize the self in terms of outer, conventional definitions of reality and acquire family- and culture-defined domains of competencies. These systems permit the novice adult to categorize experience in a stable and reliable manner. Hence it is not surprising that many domains of research suggest that in this process of adjusting to the outer world, the child does indeed acquire a cognitive and epistemological structure that downgrades aspects of the inner world. As summarized elsewhere (Labouvie-Vief, 1989), this process is demonstrated in several areas of research. First, research on children's imaginative activities suggests that in realizing that the imagery of dreams and play has no objective existence, the inner world is downgraded epistemologically, and the symbolisms emanating from it become divested of the attribute "real" (Foulkes, 1979; Kohlberg, 1969). This results in an increasing negation of the subjective world with the result that much inner symbolism is given up in favor of that imposed by the outer world (Bettelheim, 1977; Fromm, 1951). Similarly, in play and artistic activities, development also appears to bring a degree of conventionalization. More generally, with increasing language development also appears to come a loss of certain figurative, analogical, and paralinguistic features of language (Gardner, 1983; Werner & Kaplan, 1963). Indeed, self and reality come to be defined by conventional labels, social consensus, mental control, or disembodied ideals (see Damon & Hart, 1982; Flavell, 1985; Stern, 1985; Wellman, 1985).

## Adulthood and reintegrated thought

The acquisition of cultural knowledge systems and the resulting idealization of the self in terms of collective processes appears to constitute an important and perhaps necessary part of the early process of development (e.g., Neumann, 1973; Stern, 1985). This initial solution provides, however, only a partial one, and one that brings many problems for adult development. The opposition between ego and principle on the one hand and desire and impulse on the other, which is so basic to a youthful concept of rationality, in adulthood easily can bring with it such consequences as conventionality, rationalization, and rigidity. Unless transformed, the youthful concept of rationality hence can lead to adult irrationality. The goal of adulthood, therefore, is somewhat opposite to that of early development: It consists of a balancing of *logos* as *mythos* is upgraded.

A number of recent theoretical developments indicate that adulthood may be a major site of such balancing operations. These theoretical developments have come not only from a cognitive tradition but also from psychodynamic discussions of the process of development. They suggest that the traditional separation of formal and informal thought is based on an invalid dualism, which is especially limiting when discussing the thought of mature adults.

On the cognitive side, a number of recent studies suggest that such a reintegration is organized by continued developments in the complexity of thought beyond those described by Piaget. Although Piaget stressed the adolescent's ability to operate within abstract systems, these studies suggest that the formal-operational abilities of the youth are still quite limited in their abstractive powers. Following Perry's (1968) lead, research on "postformal" aspects of cognitive development (see Commons, Richards, & Armon, 1984) has located this limitation in a specific cognitive feature – the restriction to single abstract system thinking. Although the individual is able to unify parts of single abstract systems and function systematically and coherently within them, he or she cannot as yet construct a metalanguage to compare systems and coordinate them. As a result, thinking remains dominated by static categories and dualistic constructions of reality. Eventually, many adults transcend these constructions and move on to more transformational, dynamic, and dialectical thought (e.g., Basseches, 1984; Kramer, 1983, Chapter X; Labouvie-Vief, 1982; Riegel, 1973; Sinnott, 1984).

Such movements now have been reliably demonstrated (see also Arlin, 1984; Commons, Richards, & Kuhn, 1982; Kitchener & Brenner, chapter 10 in this volume; Kitchener & King, 1981; Kramer & Woodruff, 1986), although many specifics still remain to be studied. Still, it appears rather firm to state that they continue well into middle adulthood and possibly into later life. However, I suggest that taken by themselves, these movements do not necessarily constitute wisdom per se. Rather they probably form a necessary though not sufficient cognitive base from which the individual may begin a broad epistemic restructuring of interpersonal and intrapersonal dimensions of the world.

*Self and other in thinking.* Interest in the epistemological consequences of continued cognitive complexity has been stimulated by Perry's (1968) landmark study of intellectual development in the college years. Perry showed that in their belief that only one single, "objective" perspective exists on such abstract notions as *truth* or *reality,* many youth externalize processes of judgment and determine them by outer criteria for objective and absolute truths. The objective is understood as firm and unambiguous and opposed to subjective and inner dynamics. College life, Perry showed, slowly erodes that dichotomy and exposes the fact that thought is relative to its author, the thinker. This realization ushers in a period of radical subjectivism and contextual relativism in which any possibility of determinate judgment is denied. Eventually, Perry argues, this relativism is resolved as the individual gives up claims to the objective nature of reason and fully affirms subjectivity, both in self and other.

Perry's research demonstrates that there is a thorough interpenetration of epistemological understanding and aspects of self-development. The cognitive structure of the objectivist leads him to search for truth criteria outside of the self, in authorities who are deemed invulnerable, and to provide a firm perspective on truth. At the core of this epistemic structure is a self, therefore, that construes the social world along lines of vastly differing competence or power. Extending Perry's work to a sample of women, Clinchy and Zimmerman (1981) also comment on that asymmetry, noting that advances in cognitive development bring to the fore a new sense of self empowered with an awareness of her own efficacy and responsibility as a thinker (see also Belenky, Clinchy, Goldberger, & Tarule, 1986).

For Perry, relativism is resolved by a subjectivism enhanced by critical thought and reduced egocentrism and, hence, characterized by a degree of objectivity. Subsequent work has, however, suggested that from this position of personal "commitment in relativism," many individuals begin to reach for resolutions that reject the solipsism inherent in relativism and provide a more objective answer. Kitchener and King (1981), for example, show that the search for more overarching objective principles becomes a moving and integrating force as the individual moves beyond relativism. (See also Kitchener and Brenner, chapter 10 in this volume.) The new concept of objectivity that emerges is, however, no longer opposed to the subjective. Rather, it provides an integration of both concepts since objectivity is seen to result from subjecting one's truth claims to a critical forum. Thus truth claims are relocated from the self to a collective of thinkers and from the search for a single valid solution as product to the identification of such objectivity-enhancing procedures as critical thinking and discussion.

In my own work, I have proposed a similar sequence moving through three levels of adult logical development (Labouvie-Vief, 1982). At the *intrasystemic* level, the individual is able to coordinate the elements that comprise a single abstract system. This system is grounded in conventional language, symbols, and norms that emphasize certainty and stability. The individual can coherently function within those systems but does not yet have a reflective language for them. Such a metalanguage is gradually differentiated at the *intersystemic* level, where multiple systems are acknowledged. Constraints and conflicts between systems (e.g., mind and body, self and other, inner and outer, reason and emotion) are now discussed and elaborated upon, but these systems cannot yet be integrated and transformed reciprocally. Though conflict and tension are increasingly tolerated, they still limit full openness of functioning. At the *integrated* level, historical change and contextual diversity are valued, resulting in an open flexibility tempered by responsibility and self-reflection. Self-chosen principles result in the potential for mature action and self-regulation.

This general epistemic progression has consequences for several domains of research. One of those relates to qualitative differences in how younger and older adults interpret text (Adams, Labouvie-Vief, Hobart, & Dorosz, in press). Adolescents and college students are highly text dependent and do not differentiate account from interpretation. Thus they believe that the reading of a text involves the application of objective procedures or algorithms and that this procedure produces solutions automatically and with certainty. In contrast, the mature individual realizes that account and interpretation are thoroughly interpenetrated and that the duality of objective versus subjective processes is false. As a result, qualitative differences in text processing between younger and more mature adults emerge: The more mature individual construes text not only logically but also psychologically and symbolically.

A somewhat similar qualitative progression emerges in problem solving between younger and older adults. Adams, Labouvie-Vief, Hakim-Larson, DeVoe, and Hayden (1988) provide data to suggest that adolescents and some youth operate within a simple deductive structure within which problems are seen as unambiguous and not requiring interpretation of the self. These individuals are highly text dependent, believing that conclusions are immanent in the text rather than emerging from the active thinking process of the thinker. Ambiguity hence is attributed to faulty thinking and monitoring rather than to rationally justified qualitative differences between different readers of a text. The more mature problem solver, in turn, is aware that problems are necessarily interpreted by the reader: thus a greater awareness of complexity and tolerance of ambiguity emerges, along with more careful checks on the possible limitations of one's own particular viewpoint (Adams, Labouvie-Vief, Hakim-Larson, DeVoe, & Hayden, 1988; see also Blanchard-Fields, 1986; Kitchener, 1983; Kuhn, Pennington, & Leadbeater, 1983; Sinnott, 1984; Wood, 1983). Such a progression suggests, then, that the mature adult evolves a problem-solving style that is uniquely suited to solving "ill-structured" problems (Arlin, 1984; Kitchener, 1983; Wood, 1983) rather than the explicit and well-structured problems at which young research subjects excel.

A second major consequence also becomes apparent when examining problem-solving styles. Since our assumption in the text-processing study was that these styles are mediated by cognitive assumptions about the nature of logical certainty versus individual diversity, we (Adams et al., in press; see also Labouvie-Vief & Lawrence, 1985) also examined how the individual makes epistemological sense out of individual diversity. Our results show that the adolescents' epistemological model – based on the notion of a single valid, certain answer – cannot reconcile individual differences in the solution process with the notion of valid and rationally motivated disagreement. Since only one answer is deemed valid, logical competency is concretely identified with the ability to produce the single correct solution, and individual differences are thought to derive from simple unilinear, hierarchically ordered differences in that competence (smartness or intelligence). For the more mature individual, perspective enters and valid qualitative differences are acknowledged to result from differences in interpretation.

The discussion in the previous paragraphs is not to state that the younger individual has no concept of the validity of individual differences because our subjects *do* on occasion assert that "everybody thinks differently." However, they are not able to reconcile the domain of valid qualitative individual differences with that of rationally motivated solutions. As a result, they come to construe individual differences in an asymmetrical fashion. Such asymmetrical constructions are apparent in our study of individuals' conceptions of their emotional processes (Labouvie-Vief, Hakim-Larson, DeVoe, &

Schoeberlein, 1989). When subjects discussed their experience of anger, those at less mature levels polarized self and other. Blame and responsibility for conflict were attributed to the other, whose behavior was held to high standards of rationality and explained in terms of intentional processes. In contrast, the self was free of blame. More mature adults, however, were able to create more symmetrical representations of self and other. They were able to accept responsibility for the conflict and to understand that the other is not necessarily motivated by malevolent intentions. Thus for anger, lack of maturity involved an overpolarization of self and other, whereas maturity brought a compensating ability to experience empathy and to maintain connectedness. Elsewhere, Blanchard-Fields (1986) has suggested that this overcoming of the "fundamental attribution error" constitutes a major developmental task for adult development, and our data support that contention.

The upgrading of individual differences hence not only is important for relatively formal problem-solving processes, but also enters into more informal domains. Many theories of adult development affirm that a major characteristic of higher levels of development is the emergence of a deep respect for individual differences and diversity. Kohlberg (1984), for example, discusses postconventional morality in terms of the emergence of ideal perspective taking, in which the individual attempts to transcend the self's perspective and to understand and even embrace that of the other. Similarly, Loevinger's (1976) levels of ego development are predicated on the assumption that the mature individual evolves an appreciation for the uniqueness of self and other. Kegan's (1982) theory also proposes a movement from interpersonal dependence to a firmer sense of identity in which the individual tolerates diversity and individuality. Finally, in our own research on emotional regulation (Labouvie-Vief, Hakim-Larson, DeVoe, & Schoeberlein, 1989), we observed that the role of reference groups in helping mediate emotional conflict changes from youth to mature adulthood. The adolescents primarily sought to validate their own emotion by relating to a reference group that would affirm their feeling. In contrast, the more mature adults appeared to be keenly aware of the problematic nature of claims to objectivity in the emotional realm and thus sought out others primarily as aides to evaluate and critique their own perceptions of the situation.

Examining such rational processes in the emotional realm highlights the profound relationship between the individual's progression on a dimension of cognitive complexity and one of social power. It was inherent in the philosophical project of philosophers since Plato to define intellectual "power" as a source of decision making that would transcend the power of traditional structures of authority. Piaget, similarly, has emphasized that the two progressions are intimately intertwined and that with increases in cognitive development comes a shift from a "heteronomous" to an "autonomous" interpersonal orientation. In a similar vein, I suggest that cognitive maturity is earmarked by the understanding that rational choice is possible only in a community of potential equals.

How important that understanding is for issues of adult adaptation was examined in a recent study in which we analyzed how individuals conceptualized sources of stressful events (Labouvie-Vief, Hakim-Larson, & Hobart, 1987). Our data showed that there is a systematic progression from early adolescence to mature adulthood. The younger individual's stress results from a sense of self as relatively powerless and dependent on the mediating efforts of more powerful others; thus coping efforts depend to a high degree on projecting blame and responsibility on more powerful others. The more mature adult, in contrast, comes to construe social power more symmetrically. In that process, he or she comes to accept responsibility for stressful experience and is less dependent on external mediating efforts. Indeed, a similar progression from asymmetrically to more symmetrically conceived power structures appears to be deeply rooted in *mythos* processes, emerging in domains as diverse as faith (e.g., Fowler, 1981), mythic constructions (e.g., Chinen, 1985), and dream images (Young-Eisendrath & Wiedemann, 1987).

These developmental movements found in contemporary adults, then, dovetail rather well with the more systematic efforts of many recent thinkers. All of these individuals suggest that in both cultural and individual development, we are moving toward a conception of reason in which traditional concepts of mind and self are thoroughly transformed. The young individual looks for transcendence in outer, objectified structures that are opposed to principles of subjectivity and communality. Yet that very schism reveals a profound conceptual dependence on others who would help resolve the resulting conceptual paradoxes. The mature individual, in turn, realizes that the subjective and communal are a necessary part of one's endeavors to be objective. Still, they do not remain a goal in themselves. Rather, they become a vantage from which the individual searches for a new concept of objectivity – however, no longer one that is rooted in a "God's-eye view" of certainty but one that is more open, tentative, and human sized.

*Embodied thinking.* Whereas one correlate of the understanding of objectivity and subjectivity as complementary poles of the mind is that it leads to a reestablishment of the communal and transpersonal nature of mind, another is that it leads to an inward exploration of more private dimensions of mental functioning and of the self. The notion that aging brings an inward turn has long been an important concept in the literature on later life processes (Neugarten, 1968). However, we are only beginning to realize the adaptive significance and heuristic importance of that notion of an inward turn. Here, I propose that this dual significance derives from the fact that the individual gradually gives up a definition of self in terms of abstract idealizations and elaborates one that reaffirms the significance of an organic ground: of the bodily, the figurative, and the mythic.

Early socialization is aided by the evolution of a notion of the mind as an organ of individual volition, decision making, and rational thinking and that is opposed by bodily processes that are not subject to volitional control. Young children do not master this conceptual differentiation, however, but display an undifferentiated understanding of bodily processes as ones that are psychologically motivated. For example, for children 4 to 5 years old, such functions as eating, elimination, or growth are understood to have relevance for pleasing important reference figures. By age 10, children begin to differentiate subsystems of the body in a mechanical way and to abstract biological principles that govern the existence of living things. This marks the emergence of biological processes as a domain of explanation that is differentiated from volition and mental function (Carey, 1985; Nagy, 1953; Wellman, 1985). According to Broughton (1980), these functions are arranged in a hierarchy of mind–body processes in which the body is associated with involuntary and unconscious processes, whereas the brain–mind is characterized by higher order rational, logical, and abstract thinking.

The hierarchy of mind–body processes offers a basis of youthful thinking and self-regulation. It also offers the basis of youthful self-definitions. Damon and Hart (1982) showed, for example, that the adolescent's self-definition is based on the ability to see the self as a mental and idealized entity. More generally, most theories of self and self-development have primarily emphasized the "egoic" and conscious functions of the self (see Harter, 1983).

In our own work, we have begun to examine this issue in a study of individuals' conceptions of their emotional processes (Labouvie-Vief, DeVoe, & Bulka, in press). Emotions are a good example of the complementarity of psychological processes since their dual nature as organismic and involuntary processes, on the one hand, and as mental and willed ones, on the other, are as problematic for the developing individual as they are for the philosopher. In order to regulate her or his impulse life, the individual needs to acquire abstract idealized standards of normative behavior; yet in this reliance on others, impulse regulation necessitates the devaluation of inner experiences that cannot be expressed in terms of such collective ideals. This results in a characteristic language of emotional regulation. From the midteens to early twenties, emotional control is based on the notion of an ideal abstract state. Emotion language now is preoccupied with the mental control of emotions or the failure of such control. Emotions and actions are justified by social norms binding for all, whereas their characterization as private, organismic processes is almost entirely absent. Overall, the language of emotions is one of containment and repression rather than vividly felt emotional experience.

In mature adulthood, however, the individual begins to elaborate a more complementary concept of feelings and impulses as biological processes that are not necessarily dependent on one's cognitive efforts. Aware that organismic processes have their own lawfulness that is only obscured and even distorted with excessive efforts at censoring, the individual now explores and acknowledges inner tendencies. The aim here is to examine such tendencies so one can understand their workings and use them as a check on behavior. On the surface, such increased subjectivity sometimes appears to mimic the impulsivity of the younger individual. In the mature adult, however, it emerges in a structurally more complex form, in which a degree of spontaneity is wedded to conscious choice and flexible modulation. Thus the mature adult is able to combine free emotional expression with conscious regulation. At the same time, greater tolerance of feeling in the self leads the individual to better accept others' feelings, intentions, and thoughts as separate in oneself.

That one core task of adulthood is a broadening and reorganization of emotional life and of the self-concept is a major ingredient of theories of the self in adulthood. Jung (1933) anticipated those in his view of adulthood, according to which a major task is to give up identification with the conscious ego and to open oneself to the more organismic self-processes in which the ego is embedded. Indeed, for Jung, the self is this more inclusive embedding and regulating process, and the major task of midlife is to give up the egoic, idealized definition of self and open oneself up to this broader organismic structure.

This general notion of a reuniting of *logos* and *mythos* aspects of self and thinking is in line with several emerging research domains. In one set of studies, for example, we (Adams, Labouvie-Vief, Hobart, & Dorosz, in press) propose that later life may bring the reemergence of a more figurative, symbolic processing style. In our research, we have found that the younger individual often reads text analytically, examining aspects of internal structure and keeping inferences to such intratextual processes. For the older adult, however, the interest of text often lies not in the delineation of a particular action–event sequence but rather in the fact that it signifies truths about the human condition. Hence inferencing is based on a symbolic processing style in which inner and psychological processes rather than purely logical ones are important.

Contrary to Piaget, who states that symbolic thought is an immature form, then, we are suggesting that the symbolic emerges in adulthood in a uniquely mature form. Accordingly, a new approach to the development of imaginative processes may be called for. Early in life, the approach is reductionistic, and this may well correspond to the individual's emerging defense structure. Later in life, however, the individual may come to accept the symbolic as an independent source of knowing in its own right. Indeed, it may no longer be viewed as a childish form but as a uniquely mature adult form of meaning making.

Thus far, we have scant data on what these mature forms may be, but suggestions from writing grounded in myth are rich indeed. For example, writers of a Jungian persuasion (e.g., Jung, 1956; von Franz, 1956) claim that themes of the organic grounding of abstract mental ideals are expressed in dream symbols unique to later life development. Chinen (1985) has argued that this theme is reflected, as well, in myth and fairy tales depicting later-life issues. Tales featuring young protagonists, according to Chinen, feature the ego in formation and emphasize mastery of the unconscious and heroically exploring the outer world. In contrast, tales featuring adults depict the search for wisdom rather than adventure, mastery of self rather than others, and rather than seeking personal victory and salvation, the self becomes oriented toward the "emancipation of the world." From a somewhat similar perspective, Campbell (1988) maintains that the theme of the inward journey after midlife is an almost universal theme in mythic writings of the world. Although the myths from different cultures may vary in their specific content, they all reduce basic aspects of the experience of living in a human body to a limited and repeatable set of symbols. Thus, says Campbell, "the themes are timeless, and the inflection is to the culture" (p. 10).

On a more solid empirical footing, a lessened concern with control and an increased openness to unconscious processes emerges as one of the most stable findings on the literature on personality changes during adulthood. In Loevinger's (1976) model of ego development, for example, the impulsiveness of the child gives way to a conventional mode in which one's own subjective inner life is suppressed and subordinated to social norms. The mature individual, however, evolves a greater degree of flexibility in which the conflicts between impulse and norm, self and society, or inner and outer are acknowledged and integrated within a more autonomously chosen structure. This evolution appears to be related to a profound restructuring of processes of coping and defense, with a lessening of denial, projection, and hostility and an increase in sublimation, suppression, and humor (Haan, 1977, 1981; Ihelevich, & Glaser, 1986; Labouvie-Vief et al., 1987; McCrae, 1982; Vaillant, 1977).

One consequence of that restructuring is a reorganization of concepts of the masculine and the feminine. Just as the youthful model of rationality is based on a devaluation of organic processes, so it often adopts a "devaluating and defensively belittling attitude towards the female" (Blos, 1962, p. 25; see also Gilligan, 1982). Thus the reemergence of the organic for a traditional psychoanalytic perspective has signaled the beginning of age-associated losses. In contrast, Gutmann (e.g., 1987) has argued that it earmarks a period of new growth. As aggressive sexual impulses are phased out in men whose parenting cycle is completed, it frees them to integrate "feminine" qualities into their own structure. Thus they cathect otherness rather than self-interest, inner process rather than outer result. Women, similarly, are able to integrate the more agentic and aggressive aspects usually associated with masculinity.

Thus older individuals are able to attain an androgynous sexuality, knowledge of the inner world, and even moral and spiritual leadership. Their position as caretakers of the social system thus exemplifies Erikson's (e.g., 1978) claim that the adult moves toward a generative investment in others.

A somewhat similar proposal is that of McAdams (1985), who, in contrast to Gutmann's energic interpretation, proposes a cognitive one. Examining individuals' biographical constructions from the perspective of how the themes of power and relatedness are balanced, McAdams notes that individuals younger or of lower developmental levels (as assessed by Loevinger's ego level) represent their biographies in terms of a single predominant theme. At later levels, that polarization is given up, and individuals are better able to integrate these two themes. Indeed, McAdams (1985) has suggested that the balancing of these two themes is at the core of the development of generativity.

Another consequence of moving beyond cultural form may be a change in one's mode of creation. Jacques (1965), for example, has proposed that breaking out of conventional form constitutes a major crisis in the lives of artists as well as normal adults. Although not all adults are able to resolve this crisis in a positive manner, those who do may experience a surge of creative vitality and the evolution of a unique style which transcends personal and cultural experience and distills core patterns of the human experience (see also Munsterberg, 1983). A prime example is the painter Henri Matisse, who gave up painting during the last years of his life to create the works of his final maturity in a medium (paper cutouts) he had only taken up at around 60 years of age. "I have attained," he said toward the end of his life, "a form filtered to its essentials" (Elderfield, 1978, p. 7).

### Retrospect and prospect

In this chapter, I have proposed to define wisdom as the grounding of intellectual operations – those usually associated with *logos* – in *mythos*, an organismic core of interpersonal and intrapersonal processes. Providing a broad outline of the separation of these two modes in history and individual development, I suggest that recent concerns with wisdom reflect a move toward a reintegration of these two modes both in historical and in individual development. Such a reintegration brings with it a broadened definition of intellectual processes as including emotional, ethical, expressive, and mythic ones.

By suggesting that a theory of mental processes be broadened in its organismic significance, I am not suggesting, however, that it can be reduced to organismic processes. As Piaget has argued so vigorously, intellectual operations arise out of a process of negating the organismic, of straining beyond it to search for integrative frameworks that transcend local applicability. Wisdom, similarly, cannot imply a mere return of *mythos* but requires that the individual hold the paradoxical tension of thought being both immanent and transcendent. It is out of that tension, after all, that novelty and progression can emerge. Thus, although suggesting that the notion of reflective intelligence needs to be more thoroughly grounded in a theory of organic life, a theory of wisdom must retain an undiminished emphasis of processes of reflection and critical evaluation. Indeed, such an emphasis is mandatory if we are to distinguish true wisdom as integrated thought from a more regressive relinquishment of rationality.

The view of wisdom I am proposing, therefore, retains many of the elements significant in Plato's theory. It squarely rejects the position that the abstract and theoretical and the concrete and practical constitute incommensurable domains of mental functioning. Instead, it accepts the position that a theory of mind, self, and reason for better or worse also implies a prescription for how to conduct and evaluate one's life. The limits of the Platonic vision of wisdom as it has persisted through the ages derive, however, from the attempt to dissociate the two poles that are necessary to the evolution of wisdom. Hence, the objectivist Platonic vision proposes a concept of reason that rejects rational evaluation of elements deriving from one of these poles, *mythos*. Thereby it opens itself to profound irrationality.

I have argued that both in contemporary intellectual history and in the lives of many adults, the realization of that irrationality and the search for a broader, more grounded vision of rationality constitute a driving force. The notion of wisdom hence becomes an essential ingredient for concepts of adult adaptation. Indeed, I have suggested that the emergence of wisdom in mature adulthood has many important real-life adaptive implications relating to coping, defending, understanding of self and other, and creative productivity. If in that somewhat sweeping view I have bracketed many complex questions, I have done so in the belief that it is most useful first to elaborate a core structure within which to discuss the development of wisdom and then to proceed to the discussion of more differentiated issues.

One of these issues is just how, in a practical sense, the current position differs from views that discuss wisdom from a more formal perspective, say, by specifying the level of complexity of thinking about a particular domain. On the present view, whereas wise thinking, with its ability to embrace paradox and transformation, certainly requires a specific level of cognitive complexity, it is not identical with formally complex thought. Complex thinking can be in the service of organismic integration, as in wisdom, or of fragmentation, as in dissociation. Similarly, I suggest that wisdom cannot be reduced to a cognitive theory of expertise. Although aspects of expert cognition may well mimic certain aspects of wisdom, the concept of wisdom necessarily is directed away from specialization and toward more integrative, organismic knowledge. Thus, what makes the artist, the poet, or the scientist wise is not expert technical knowledge in their respective domains but rather knowledge of issues that are part of the human condition, more generally. Wisdom consists, so to say, in one's ability to see through and beyond individual uniqueness and specialization into those structures that relate us in our common humanity.

Nevertheless, I am not claiming that wisdom is independent of a particular domain studied. I would suggest, however, that these domains need to be derived from a theory of *mythos* – those adaptations that constitute part of our age-old heritage and that we cannot compromise without compromising our humanity. While *logos* has insisted on the separation of such realms as reason versus faith, thinking versus feeling, outer versus inner, or mind versus body, wisdom maintains that these two realms constitute but complementary and interacting poles of thought. Since at the core of wisdom is an understanding of the necessary relatedness of these two poles, the domains of wisdom would encompass such issues as moral and ethical understanding, understanding one's own emotions and inner life and differentiating them from those of others, and using such understanding reflectively in the striving for a rational attitude that unites the search for objective validation with that for subjective significance.

One important task for research may be to describe such domains of wisdom and examine the degree to which they form separate or interrelated domains. Another strategy might be aimed, however, at examining more intraindividual variation. In developing my own research approach and examining that of my colleagues, I have been astounded by the degree to which seemingly diverse domains are intercorrelated, and I have come to assume – if only as a well-meaning and falsifiable speculation – that indeed something akin to a single competence of wisdom may underlie the diverse domains I have attempted to tie together in this chapter. This is not to state that variability is not an important factor; however, it often appears to enter as a result of intrapsychic dynamic factors. For example, episodic catastrophic stresses or childhood trauma may create special areas of vulnerability that create variability in functioning. Or rigidified belief systems at the level of culture or family may prevent the individual from moving to optimal integration.

A second general set of questions relates to whether the integration I am proposing is a necessary sequence or whether it is dependent on certain facilitating conditions. Certainly, the movements I have discussed in this chapter can be documented throughout history. However, the breadth and urgency with which they are occurring now is probably a contemporary phenomenon and linked, as I have argued, to the emergence of a certain worldview or broad epistemic structure. Thus I would suggest that although wisdom is certainly a potentiality within the reach of human nature, its development needs a set of nurturing conditions: the availability of a cultural and familial *ethos,* of mythological themes, of an open attitude toward the life of imagination, of respect for individuality, all are among the factors that may make useful candidates for research on wisdom.

Finally, we need to return to the beginning of this chapter and ask if wisdom is a characteristic uniquely associated with old age. In my own research project, we have not found this to be so. Usually, wisdom – as measured by the procedures my collaborators and I have devised – appears to reach its apex in middle adulthood (approximately the fourth or fifth decade). As a group, adults in their sixties and older may actually score somewhat lower. However, this may be a result of a historical shift in epistemic orientation rather than reflect regression. Indeed, in my research I have consistently found that age, per se, is not the most meaningful criterion to study wisdom-related processes in adulthood. When charted along age, the criteria we have studied usually have shown a curvilinear relationship, abating in adulthood. More striking patterns were obtained, in turn, if we rely on age-independent measures of developmental complexity: In that case, our measures tend to show a strong and linear relationship.

Not all adults, however, are wise, and wisdom appears to constitute an ideal reached by a relatively few adults. The notion that wisdom is the prerogative of old age, then, may be an adage that requires some correction. In past societies the old may well have constituted a more strongly selected subgroup in which wisdom proved related to longevity. In contemporary society, however, the concept is best defined conceptually and decoupled from age per se.

Even while being a somewhat idealistic construct, however, wisdom is one of enormous heuristic significance. As I have argued in this chapter, wisdom is a construct of considerable analytic power and pertaining to many significant real-life adaptive criteria. Like a concept of optimal health, which is realized by few if any individuals, it may not only describe an ideal end state to the process of development, but also offer a vehicle to study those factors that cause individuals to deviate from an optimal developmental trajectory. Thus our current concerns with wisdom may bring to fruition an ancient hope – that of constructing a theory of human potentialities oriented by a normative view of transcendent ideals yet firmly grounded in the organic texture of life.

# References

Adams, C., Labouvie-Vief, G., Hakim-Larson, J., DeVoe, M., & Hayden, M. (1988). *Modes of thinking and problem solving: developmental transitions from preadolescence to middle adulthood.* Unpublished manuscript.

Adams, C., Labouvie-Vief, G., Hobart, C. J., & Dorosz, M. (in press). Adult age group differences in story recall style. *Journal of Gerontology.*

Aristotle (1921). *De generatione animalium.* In W. D. Ross (Ed.), *The works of Aristotle.* Oxford: Clarendon Press.

Arlin, P. (1984). Adolescent and adult thought: a structural interpretation. In M. L. Commons, F. A. Richards, & C. Armon (Eds.), *Beyond formal operations: late adolescent and adult cognitive development* (pp. 258–271). New York: Praeger.

Basseches, M. A. (1984). Dialectical thinking as a metasystematic form of cognitive organization. In M. L. Commons, F. A. Richards, & C. Armon (Eds.), *Beyond formal operations*. New York: Praeger.

Belenky, M. F., Clinchy, B. M., Goldberger, N. R., & Tarule, J. M. (1986). *Women's ways of knowing*. New York: Basic Books.

Bettelheim, B. (1977). *The uses of enchantment: the meaning and importance of fairy tales*. New York: Knopf.

Blanchard-Fields, F. (1986). Reasoning on social dilemmas varying in emotional saliency: an adult developmental perspective. *Psychology and Aging, 1,* 325–333.

Blos, P. (1962). *On adolescence: a psychoanalytic interpretation*. New York: Free Press.

Blumenberg, H. (1987). An anthropological approach to the contemporary significance of rhetoric. In K. Baynes, J. Bohman, & T. McCarthy (Eds.), *After philosophy: end or transformation?* Cambridge, MA: MIT Press.

Broughton, J. (1980). Genetic metaphysics: the developmental psychology of mind–body concepts. In R. Rieber (Ed.), *Body and mind* (pp. 177–207). New York: Academic Press.

Bruner, J. (1986). *Actual minds, possible worlds*. Cambridge, MA: Harvard University Press.

Campbell, J. (1988). *The power of myth*. New York: Doubleday.

Carey, S. (1985). *Conceptual change in childhood*. Cambridge, MA: MIT Press.

Cassirer, E. (1946). *Language and myth*. New York: Harper and Brothers. Reprinted 1953, Dover Publications, New York.

Cassirer, E. (1981). *Kant's life and thought*. New Haven: Yale University Press.

Chinen, A. B. (1985). Fairy tales and transpersonal development in later life. *Journal of Transpersonal Psychology, 17,* 99–122.

Clayton, V., & Birren, J. E. (1980). The development of wisdom across the life span: a reexamination of an ancient topic. In P. B. Baltes and O. R. Brim (Eds.), *Life span development and behavior*. New York: Academic Press.

Clinchy, B., & Zimmerman, C. (1981). Epistemology and agency in the development of undergraduate women. In P. Perun (Ed.), *The undergraduate woman: issues in educational equity*. Boston: D. C. Heath.

Collingwood, R. G. (1945). *The idea of nature*. Oxford: Clarendon Press.

Commons, M. L., Richards, F. A., & Armon, C. (1984). *Beyond formal operations*. New York: Praeger.

Commons, M. L., Richards, F. A., & Kuhn, D. (1982). Systematic, metasystematic, and cross-paradigmatic reasoning: a case for stages of reasoning beyond Piaget's stage of formal operations. *Child Development, 53,* 1058–1068.

Damon, W., & Hart, D. (1982). The development of self-understanding from infancy through adolescence. *Child Development, 53,* 841–864.

DeLong, H. (1970). *A profile of mathematical logic*. Reading, MA: Addison-Wesley.

Dittmann-Kohli, F., & Baltes, P. B. (in press). Toward a neofunctionalist conception of adult intellectual development: wisdom as a prototypical case of intellectual growth. In C. Alexander & E. Langer (Eds.), *Beyond formal operations: alternative endpoints to human development*. New York: Cambridge University Press.

Elderfield, J. (1978). *The cut-outs of Henri Matisse*. New York: G. Braziller.

Elias, N. (1978). *The civilizing process*, Vol. 1, *The History of Manners*. New York: Pantheon Books.

Elias, N. (1982). *The civilizing process*, Vol. 2, *Power and civility*. New York: Pantheon Books.

Erikson, E. (1978). Reflections on Dr. Borg's life cycle. In E. Erikson (Ed.), *Adulthood* (pp. 1–31). New York: W. W. Norton.

Flavell, J. H. (1985, August). *The development of children's knowledge about the appearance-*

*reality distinction.* Invited address presented at the American Psychological Association, Los Angeles.

Foulkes, D. (1979). Children's dreams. In B. Wolman (Ed.), *Handbook of dreams: research, theories, and applications.* New York: Van Nostrand Reinhold.

Fowler, J. W. (1981). *Stages of faith: the psychology of human development and the quest for meaning.* San Francisco: Harper & Row.

Frankfort, H., & Frankfort, H. A. (1946). *Before philosophy: the intellectual adventure of ancient man.* Baltimore, MD: Penguin Books.

Freud, S. (1923). The ego and the id. In J. Rickman (Ed.) (1957), *A general selection from the works of Sigmund Freud.* Garden City, NJ: Doubleday.

Fromm, E. (1951). *The forgotten language.* New York: Grove Press.

Gardner, H. (1983). *Frames of mind: the theory of multiple intelligences.* New York: Basic Books.

Geertz, C. (1983). *Local knowledge.* New York: Basic Books.

Gilligan, C. (1982). *In a different voice.* Cambridge, MA: Harvard University Press.

Goldberg, E., & Costa, L. (1981). Hemisphere differences in the acquisition and use of descriptive systems. *Brain and Language, 14,* 144–173.

Gregory, R. L. (1981). *Mind in science.* New York: Cambridge University Press.

Gutmann, D. (1987). *Reclaimed powers: toward a new psychology of men and women in later life.* New York: Basic Books.

Haan, N. (1977). *Coping and defending: processes of self-environment organization.* New York: Academic Press.

Haan, N. (1981). Common dimensions of personality development: early adolescence to middle life. In D. Eichorn (Ed.), *Present and past in middle life.* New York: Academic Press.

Habermas, J. (1984). *The theory of communicative action,* Vol. 1, *Reason and the rationalization of society.* Boston: Beacon Press.

Harter, S. (1983). Developmental perspectives on the self system. In E. M. Hetherington (Ed.), *Handbook of child psychology* (Vol. IV, pp. 275–385). New York: Wiley & Sons.

Hofstadter, D. R. (1979). *Goedel, Escher, Bach: an eternal golden braid.* New York: Vintage Books.

Holliday, S. G., & Chandler, M. J. (1986). Wisdom: explorations in adult competence. In J. A. Meacham (Ed.), *Contributions to human development* (Vol. 17). Basel, Switzerland: Karger.

Ihelevich, D., & Glaser, G. (1986). *Defense mechanisms.* Oswego, MI: DMI Associates.

Jacques, E. (1965). Death and the mid-life crisis. *International Journal of Psychoanalysis, 46,* 502–514.

Jaynes, J. (1976). *The origin and history of consciousness in the breakdown of the bicameral mind.* Boston: Houghton Mifflin.

Jung, C. G. (1933). *Modern man in search of a soul.* New York: Harcourt, Brace & World.

Jung, C. G. (1964). *Man and his symbols.* New York: Dell.

Kegan, J. (1982). *The evolving self.* Cambridge, MA: Harvard University Press.

Kitchener, K. S. (1983). Cognition, metacognition, and epistemic cognition. *Human Development, 26,* 222–232.

Kitchener, K. S., & King, P. M. (1981). Reflective judgement: concepts of justification and their relationship to age and education. *Journal of Applied Developmental Psychology, 2,* 89–116.

Klein, E. (1967). *A comprehensive etymological dictionary of the English language.* Amsterdam: Elsevier.

Kohlberg, L. (1969). Stage and sequence: the cognitive–developmental approach to socialization. In G. A. Goslin (Ed.), *Handbook of socialization theory and research* (pp. 347–380). Chicago: Rand McNally.

Kohlberg, L. (1984). *Essays on moral development,* Vol. II, *The psychology of moral development.* San Francisco: Harper & Row.

Kramer, D. A. (1983). Post-formal operations? A need for further conceptualization. *Human Development, 26,* 91–105.

Kramer, D. A., & Woodruff, D. (1986). Relativistic and dialectical thought in three adult age-groups. *Human Development, 29,* 280–290.

Kuhn, D., Pennington, N., & Leadbeater, B. (1983). Adult thinking in developmental perspective. In P. B. Baltes & O. G. Brim, Jr. (Eds.), *Life-span development and behavior* (Vol. 5, pp. 158–195). New York: Academic Press.

Labouvie-Vief, G. (1980). Beyond formal operations: uses and limits of pure logic in life span development. *Human Development, 23,* 141–161.

Labouvie-Vief, G. (1982). Dynamic development and mature autonomy. *Human Development, 25,* 161–191.

Labouvie-Vief, G. (1989). Modes of knowledge and the organization of development. In M. L. Commons, J. D. Sinnott, F. A. Richards, & C. Armon (Eds.), *Beyond formal operations II: comparisons and applications of adolescent and adult development models.* New York: Praeger.

Labouvie-Vief, G., DeVoe, M., & Bulka, D. (in press). Speaking about feelings: conceptions of emotion across the life span. *Psychology and Aging.*

Labouvie-Vief, G., Hakim-Larson, J., DeVoe, M., & Schoeberlein, S. (1989). Emotions and self-regulation: a life span view. *Human Development, 32,* 279–299.

Labouvie-Vief, G., Hakim-Larson, J., & Hobart, C. J. (1987). Age, ego level, and the life-span development of coping and defense processes. *Psychology and Aging, 2,* 286–293.

Labouvie-Vief, G., & Lawrence, R. (1985). Object knowledge, personal knowledge, and processes of equilibration in adult cognition. *Human Development, 28,* 25–39.

Lakoff, G. (1987). *Women, fire, and dangerous things.* Chicago: The University of Chicago Press.

Langer, S. (1942). *Philosophy in a new key: a study in the symbolism of reason, rite, and art.* Cambridge, MA: Harvard University Press.

Lerner, G. (1986). *The creation of patriarchy.* New York: Oxford University Press.

Liddell, S. (1958). *Greek lexicon.* Oxford: Clarendon.

Loevinger, J. (1976). *Ego development.* San Francisco: Jossey-Bass.

McAdams, D. (1985). *Power, intimacy, and the life story.* Homewood, IL: Dorsey Press.

McCrae, R. R. (1982). Age differences in the use of coping mechanisms. *Journal of Gerontology, 37,* 454–460.

Macmurray, J. (1978). *The self as agent.* Atlantic Highlands, NJ: Humanities Press.

Meacham, J. A. (1983). Wisdom and the context of knowledge: knowing what one doesn't know. In D. Kuhn & J. A. Meacham (Eds.), *On the development of developmental psychology,* Vol. 8 in *Contributions to human development.* Basel: Karger.

Mead, G. H. (1934). *Mind, self, and society.* Chicago: University of Chicago Press.

Moody, H., Clayton, V., & McKee, P. (1983). Wisdom in old age: the highest stage of cognitive development? *The Gerontologist, 23,* 263.

Munsterberg, H. (1983). *The crown of life: artistic creativity in old age.* New York: Harcourt, Brace Jovanovich.

Nagy, M. H. (1953). Children's conceptions of some bodily functions. *Journal of Genetic Psychology, 83,* 199–216.

Neugarten, B. L. (1968). The awareness of middle age. In B. L. Neugarten (Ed.), *Middle age and aging* (pp. 93–98). Chicago: University of Chicago Press.

Neumann, E. (1973). *The origins and history of consciousness.* Princeton, NJ: Princeton University Press.

Olson, D. R. (1977). From utterance to text: the bias of language in speech and writing. *Harvard Educational Review, 47,* 257–281.

Onians, R. B. (1954). *The origins of European thought: about the body, the mind, the soul, world, time, and fate.* Cambridge: Cambridge University Press.

Perry, W. G. (1968). *Forms of intellectual and ethical development in the college years.* New York: Holt, Rinehart, & Winston.

Piaget, J. (1955). *The language and thought of the child.* New York: New American Library.

Piaget, J. (1962). *Play, dreams, and imitation in childhood.* New York: Norton.

Piaget, J. (1965). *The moral judgment of the child.* New York: Free Press.

Piaget, J. (1976). *The grasp of consciousness: action and concept in the young child.* Cambridge, MA: Harvard University Press.

Piaget, J. (1980). *Experiments in contradiction.* Chicago: University of Chicago Press.

Piaget, J. (1981). *Intelligence and affectivity: their relationship during child development.* Palo Alto, CA: Annual Reviews.

Plato (1961). Collected Dialogues. In E. Hamilton & H. Cairns (Eds.), *The collected dialogues of Plato, including the letters.* Princeton, NJ: Princeton University Press.

Popper, K. R. (1963). *Conjecture and refutations: the growth of scientific knowledge.* New York: Harper & Row.

Pribram, K. H., & McGuiness, D. (1975). Arousal, activation, and effort in the control of attention. *Psychological Review, 82,* 116–149.

Putnam, H. (1987). Why reason can't be naturalized. In K. Baynes, J. Bohman, & T. McCarthy (Eds.), *After philosophy: end or transformation?* Cambridge, MA: MIT Press.

Rawls, J. (1971). *A theory of justice.* Cambridge, MA: Harvard University Press.

Ricoeur, P. (1970). *Freud and philosophy: an essay on interpretation.* New Haven, CT: Yale University Press.

Riegel, K. F. (1973). Dialectical operations: the final period of cognitive development. *Human Development, 16,* 346–370.

Rorty, R. (1979). *Philosophy and the mirror of nature.* Princeton, NJ: Princeton University Press.

Rubenstein, R. L. (1988). Religion and cultural synthesis. *International Journal of the Unity of the Sciences, 1,* 99–118.

Simon, B. (1978). *Mind and madness in ancient Greece.* Ithaca, NY: Cornell University Press.

Sinnott, J. (1984). Postformal reasoning: the relativistic stage. In M. L. Commons, F. A. Richards, & C. Armon (Eds.), *Beyond formal operations* (pp. 298–325). New York: Praeger.

Stern, D. L. (1985). *The interpersonal world of the infant.* New York: Basic Books.

Sternberg, R. J., & Powell, J. S. (1982). Theories of intelligence. In R. J. Sternberg (Ed.), *Handbook of human intelligence.* Cambridge: Cambridge University Press.

Taranto, M. A. (1988). *Facets of wisdom: a theoretical synthesis.* Unpublished manuscript, Nassau Community College.

Tucker, D. M., & Williamson, P. A. (1984). Asymmetric neural control systems in human self-regulation. *Psychological Review, 91,* 185–215.

Turner, T. (1973). Piaget's structuralism. *American Anthropologist. 75,* 351–373.

Vaillant, G. E. (1977). *Adaptation to life.* Boston: Little, Brown.

Vernant, J. P. (1982). *The origins of Greek thought.* Ithaca, NY: Cornell University Press.

von Franz, M. (1964). The process of individuation. In C. G. Jung (Ed.), *Man and his symbols* (pp. 157–254). New York: Dell.

Watkins, M. (1986). *Invisible guests: the development of imaginal dialogues.* Hillsdale, NJ: Analytic Press.

Wellman, H. M. (1985). The child's theory of mind: The development of concepts of cognition. In S. Yussen (Ed.), *The growth of reflection in children.* (pp. 169–206). New York: Academic Press.

Werner, H. (1948). *Comparative psychology of mental development.* New York: International University Press.

Werner, H. (1955). *On expressive language.* Worcester, MA: Clark University Press.

Werner, H., & Kaplan, B. (1963). *Symbol formation.* New York: Wiley.

Whyte, L. L. (1948). *The next development in man.* New York: Holt.

Wittgenstein, L. (1968). *Philosophical investigations.* Oxford: Blackwell.

Wood, P. K. (1983). Inquiring systems and problem structure: implications for cognitive development. *Human Development, 26,* 249–265.

Young-Eisendrath, P., & Wiedemann, F. (1987). *Female authority.* New York: Guilford Press.

*Part III*

**Approaches informed by folk conceptions of wisdom**

# 5    Toward a psychology of wisdom and its ontogenesis

*Paul B. Baltes and Jacqui Smith*

The conceptual focus of our approach is to conceive of wisdom as an expert knowledge system (expertise). Specifically, we view wisdom as a highly developed body of factual and procedural knowledge and judgment dealing with what we call the "fundamental pragmatics of life." The fundamental pragmatics of life concern important but uncertain matters of life. Specifically, they involve knowledge and judgment about the course, variations, conditions, conduct, and meaning of life. Before we describe this approach in more detail, we present some of the historical background and theoretical rationales that have stimulated us to pursue research and theory on the topic of wisdom.

## Conceptual background

Our interest in the psychological study of wisdom is motivated by three *general* lines of psychological inquiry. A first is our interest in the study of high levels of human performance, the kind of performance that can be labeled as exceptional and expertlike (Baltes & Kliegl, 1986; Ericsson, in press; Kliegl & Baltes, 1987; Smith & Baltes, in press; Smith, Dixon, & Baltes, 1989). The second line of inquiry is our search for positive aspects of the aging mind (Baltes & Baltes, in press; Baltes & Labouvie, 1973; Baltes & Schaie, 1976). The third line of interest is work on conceptions of intelligence that reflect a concern with the contextual and pragmatic features of everyday functioning (Cornelius & Caspi, 1987; Denney, 1984; Dixon & Baltes, 1986; Rogoff & Lave, 1984; Sternberg & Wagner, 1986). These three general lines of inquiry are described in more detail in later sections of this chapter.

Aside from this general backdrop associated with the search for high levels of human performance, successful aging, and contextual conceptions of intelligence, our work on wisdom has been motivated by two more *specific* lines

The present chapter describes the theoretical and methodological framework of a research program on wisdom codirected by the two authors. We thank our current and past colleagues in the research group (Freya Dittmann-Kohli, Claudia von Grote-Janz, Silvia Sörensen, Doris Sowarka, and Ursula Staudinger) for their many valuable contributions to the work presented here. We are also grateful to Steven Cornelius and Laura Thompson for their helpful comments on an earlier draft.

87

of investigation stemming from research and theory in life span developmental psychology. These are associated with theoretical propositions of life span cognitive psychology (P. B. Baltes, 1987) and the developmental study of cognition in the context of personality and the pragmatics of life (Baltes, Dittmann-Kohli, & Dixon, 1984; Cantor & Kihlstrom, 1987; Dixon & Baltes, 1986; Labouvie-Vief, 1986).

For example, life span cognitive psychologists have begun to explore the nature of knowledge and thinking that may uniquely reflect the ecologies and experiences of the second half of life and features of high-level functioning peculiar to adults. A concern with dialectical and relativistic thinking (Commons, Richards, & Armon, 1984; Kramer, 1983; Kuhn, Pennington, & Leadbeater, 1983; Mines & Kitchener, 1986), reasoning involving uncertainty (Meacham, 1983), and the integration of affect and cognition into a new postformal level of reasoning (Labouvie-Vief, 1982, 1986) is illustrative of this effort. In this context, wisdom has been singled out as a prime example of an adulthood-based form of advanced knowledge (Clayton, 1975; Clayton & Birren, 1980; Dittmann-Kohli & Baltes, in press; Holliday & Chandler, 1986; Meacham, 1983; Smith et al., 1989; Sternberg, 1985a). Similarly, life span personality psychologists have made an effort to identify prototypical developmental themes and goals (Ryff, 1982, 1984) that may serve as organizers for developmental progression during the second half of life. In this framework as well, and following G. Stanley Hall's (1922) and Erik Erikson's (1959) ground-breaking work, wisdom has been identified as one of the concepts intended to encapsulate the general direction of progressive personality change during adulthood.

The work on wisdom conducted at the Max Planck Institute for Human Development and Education in Berlin represents an effort to interconnect these several research avenues into a single framework generative of programmatic theory-driven empirical inquiry. The goal is to formulate an integrative psychological theory of wisdom and to examine its validity and usefulness on several levels of analysis. The framework used is informed by concepts and methods associated with cognitive psychology and with the study of knowledge systems (Anderson, 1981, 1987; Glaser, 1984; Simon, 1983). The substantive domains chosen for the definition of wisdom and the predictions made about its development are based on life span theory (P. B. Baltes, 1987).

The present chapter is a progress report. To date, our work on wisdom, especially its empirical part, truly is in its infancy. Thus, there is much unfinished business involving the scope, precision, and deployability of the psychological theory of wisdom we are able to offer in this chapter. At best, what we submit here can be labeled as a prolegomenon to a theory of wisdom, something akin to a prototheory.

## Science and wisdom

Empirical efforts by behavioral scientists to study wisdom have been rare. In our view, this dearth of empirical research is related, in some degree, to the hesitation on the part of many behavioral science researchers to approach wisdom with principles of the scientific method. Indeed, research into the psychology of wisdom is likely to stretch the limits of what empirical analysis can accomplish.

For some, researchers and laypersons alike, it may even be unwise to try to study wisdom. In their view, wisdom is the prototype of the class of psychological phenomena that by definition are unapproachable and unexplainable through scientific analysis. Wisdom is seen as part of the societally hidden and private reality. Efforts to make wisdom transparent and to transform it into a subject matter of public knowledge and scientific debate is bound to change its basic foundation.

Such skeptical perspectives are weighty and deserve attention. Wittgenstein (1953) can be called upon as a witness. He proffered several warnings against naïveté on the part of the scientifically minded empirical psychologists who want to study complex human experiences. The following quotation from Wittgenstein exemplifies this concern: "The existence of the experimental method makes us think we have the means of solving the problems which trouble us; though problem and method pass one another by" (1953, p. 232).

We are sympathetic to this call for moderation and reflectiveness about the value of scientific, empirical analysis of complex phenomena, such as wisdom, and we acknowledge that a scientific analysis of wisdom will never result in an isomorphic representation of the human and cultural reality of wisdom. The scientifically constructed phenomena should, of course, be expected to bear a certain measure of similarity to the cultural phenomena singled out for scientific investigation. At the same time, it is likely that application of the scientific, empirical method will transform the phenomenon at hand. Occasionally, this transformation occurs in ways that some consider too distant from the point of departure.

We offer this note of caution because we continue to be awed by what wisdom may be as an individual and cultural product. Thus, we believe that research on wisdom is likely to lead to some immediate resistance and disappointment unless one is willing to acknowledge the boundaries of scientific analysis. The scientific analysis of wisdom is not only an effort to capture wisdom as we experience it in our daily lives and as we recognize it as a pinnacle of human knowledge. Application of the scientific approach also results in a new kind of reality: As we study wisdom scientifically, the phenomenon is constructed according to a new set of rules and principles, namely, those of science.

## Wisdom as a high-level and peak performance

Wisdom is often considered as a peak performance, perhaps even as a possible end state of human knowledge and its development. This point of departure is relevant because the study of the nature and process of high levels of performance is of central interest to any theory of development, whether ontogenetic or cultural (Berlin, 1988; Lerner, 1984; Nisbett, 1980; Schmidt, 1970; Werner, 1948). The essence of the concept of development is a focus on the idea of progress toward a higher level outcome and on conditions that are facilitative of the acquisition of such higher levels of competence and performance.

We do not wish to argue, of course, that singular definitions of the end state of development and progress are appropriate. Nor do we want to characterize wisdom as an end state in any absolute sense of the word. This would be inappropriate in view of the dominance of contextualistic and pluralistic viewpoints about the nature of development (P. B. Baltes, 1987; Dixon & Lerner, 1988; Lerner, 1984; Montada, 1987). A certain degree of pluralism and openness is a key ingredient in theories of development that are sensitive to a process of cultural evolution (Edelstein, 1983) and to the role of the individual as a producer of his or her own development (Brandstädter, 1984; Ford, 1987). However, we do proffer that the study of high-level and peak performances was a central topic from the time when developmental psychology emerged as a field (Lehman, 1953; Pressey, Janney, & Kuhlen, 1939; Tetens, 1777) and that the study of wisdom exemplifies this continued search for end state–like developmental outcomes.

For several thousands of years (Assmann & Assmann, 1987; Cicero, 1979; Clayton & Birren, 1980; Holliday & Chandler, 1986), wisdom has been mentioned as the capstone of human knowledge. The wisdom tree, a prominent piece of art during the Middle Ages, was a concrete expression of this view in the Western world (Sears, 1986). In the wisdom tree, the seven "liberal arts" (astronomy, geometry, music, arithmetic, grammar, rhetoric, and dialectics) were identified and arranged like branches of a tree with wisdom being at the top. The joining of the liberal arts into a coherent new whole of knowledge constituted "wisdom." No wonder, therefore, that the acquisition of wisdom was judged to take a lifetime and to be reserved for only a few (Clayton & Birren, 1980; Holliday & Chandler, 1986).

In our view, the enduring search for a better understanding of peak performances and end state–like outcomes, of which wisdom is an exemplar, has been central to developmental scholarship for several reasons. First, peak performances can be seen as general instantiations of the human potential. Knowledge about the processes and factors involved in peak performances provides a scenario for the "optimization" of ontogenesis and for what is possible in principle. Further, the analysis of high levels of performance offers evidence about the nature of societal and personal goals, that is, about the question of directionality(ies) of human development as a cultural phenomenon. It is likely, for example, that high levels of achievement are possible only if individuals and cultures invest a considerable amount of effort into the production of such outcomes (Ericsson, in press; Simonton, 1984; Zuckerman, 1977). In this sense, studies of peak performances during ontogenesis reveal the power of individuals and societies as actors in the process of individual and cultural development.

### Wisdom and the search for positive aspects of aging

In addition to our general interest in understanding the directional nature of human development and the antecedents and forms of peak performance, of which wisdom is a prototype, there is another intellectual commitment that has prompted us to study wisdom. This second motivator is the search for positive features of human aging. Much of our work is set within the context of gerontological questions. Since its origin as a science, the field of gerontology has included the quest for positive aspects of human aging and the search for indicators of "successful" aging (Baltes & Baltes, in press; Birren & Renner, 1980; Labouvie-Vief, 1981; Rowe & Kahn, 1987; Ryff, 1982).

This quest was evident, for example, in Stanley Hall's (1922) first major effort at a psychological treatment of old age, where wisdom (*sapientia*) was singled out as a promising domain. The same applies to perhaps the first major essay on old age in the Western world, written some 50 years B.C. by the Roman philosopher Cicero, *De Senectute* (1979). During the second half of the 20th century, there have been several other theorists who have proposed higher level stages or states for the last phases of life. The work of Erik Erikson on late-life changes in adult personality is a good example (Erikson, 1959; Erikson, Erikson, & Kivnick, 1986). Furthermore, there has been much theoretical discussion concerning the tasks and settings of adult life (M. Baltes, 1987; Dixon & Baltes, 1986; Featherman, 1983, 1987; Havighurst, 1972; Neugarten, 1968; Ryff, 1984) and the structures and functions of the mind that could possibly elicit advances in select domains of subjective experience and overt behavior (Commons et al., 1984; Labouvie-Vief, 1981, 1982; Perlmutter, 1988; Piaget, 1972; Riegel, 1973).

To date, however, and despite much theoretical fervor, the empirical harvest is relatively small. We do know, for example, that certain facets of crystallized intelligence remain stable into old age (Horn, 1970; McArdle & Horn, 1988). Such evidence, however, does not speak explicitly to the question whether there are new, more advanced forms of intelligence that emerge during the process of human aging. Perhaps more relevant is evidence from cognitive training research (Baltes & Lindenberger, 1988; Denney, 1984; Willis, 1987) demonstrating that many older adults, in principle and if they are spared from brain-related diseases, possess the capacity to engage in further efforts toward their own development by acquiring new cognitive skills or by nurturing their past strengths. The careers of older top artists and experts in various professional fields also illustrate the assertion that skills can be maintained and extended in late adulthood (Arnheim, 1986; Baltes & Kliegl, 1986; Charness, 1985; Ericsson, in press; Lehman, 1953; Simonton, 1984). Further, there is growing evidence that older adults may be superior in some tasks of cognitive reasoning associated with questions of social and practical intelligence and the integration of affect into cognitive systems (Blanchard-Fields, 1986; Cornelius & Caspi, 1987; Labouvie-Vief, 1981, 1986).

Skeptics argue, however, that such evidence is not enough to persist in the view that human aging includes a major reservoir for further development and true "peak" performances (e.g., Salthouse, 1985). The argument made, for example, is that solid replications are rare and that there is no empirical evidence that older adults *on the average* are better than younger adults on any task that has been brought under tight control in the laboratory. In addition, it is argued that there is no evidence that older persons hold the "world record" in any domain of life. Thus, skeptics can continue to advocate the position that the case for truly superior performances of older adults, especially in the domain of the mind, has not been made.

Our approach to this state of affairs is twofold (Baltes, 1987; Baltes, Smith, Staudinger, & Sowarka, in press; Dixon & Baltes, 1986; Staudinger, Cornelius, & Baltes, 1989). First, and here we join others with similar positions (Labouvie-Vief, 1981, 1982, 1985; Perlmutter, 1988; Ryff, 1984), we interpret the existing body of empirical research on cognitive functioning in old age as insufficient, especially because extant measures and criteria of performance quality are youth oriented. We suggest that any cognitive task on which older adults perform as well as (or occasionally better than) younger adults should be seen as carrying novel and important information that warrants further amplification. At present, the pool of tasks used in cognitive aging research has not been developed with adequate attention to the possible uniqueness and strengths of old age.

Second, we also argue for the *fundamental significance of rare exceptions* to the generally obtained pattern of late-life decline. Even if one older adult were to perform at or near peak levels of functioning, this would imply that positive functioning in old age is possible *in principle*. That such high levels of functioning have not been attained for most older adults in the present times may simply reflect the state of an "underdeveloped culture" with its lack of medical and cultural success in achieving an "optimized" state of old age. A high level of cultural evolution, in other words, has not yet reached the period of old age. Therefore, cultural evolution awaits another critical test: the construction of a world in which reaching old age entails the possibility of continued, albeit possibly only select, growth.

Research directed toward understanding the nature and manifestation of wisdom and wise judgment is a testing ground for the search for what may be possible in principle. This choice of research focus is not unreasonable because wisdom reflects extensive knowledge and expertise and, therefore, could be expected to have "long life" as one necessary precursor. In reviews on the nature of exceptional performances (Ericsson, 1985; Ericsson & Crutcher, in press), it has persuasively been shown that a long-term investment involving decades and thousands of hours of practice is necessary to acquire an expertise. Thus, wisdom may be the prototype of an area of cognitive functioning in which older adults, because of their age, have the opportunity to hold something akin to a world record.

## Wisdom and conceptions of intelligence

The third theoretical perspective underlying our research program on wisdom relates to the concept of intelligence. Although we do not want to designate wisdom as fully defined by the conceptual territory of intelligence, we believe that research into wisdom is helpful in advancing more comprehensive models of intelligence. For many years, the study of intelligence has been dominated by the study of performance on intelligence tests in the context of school-related curricula. During the recent decade, there has been an increasing dissatisfaction with this focus, and there have been significant efforts to re-examine the structure and function of intelligence (Gardner, 1983; Goodnow, 1986; Neisser, 1979; Resnick, 1976; Snow, 1980; Sternberg & Detterman, 1986; Sternberg & Wagner, 1986).

These new efforts at defining intelligence, on the one hand, have benefited from advances in componential theories of the mind and investigations of cognitive processes (e.g., Anderson, 1983; Jäger, 1982; Klix, 1984; Sternberg, 1985b). On the other hand, and much influenced by earlier discussion of the question of ecological validity and everyday relevance of intelligence tests, there has been a major push toward broadening the substantive scope of intellectual behavior (Rogoff & Lave, 1984; Sternberg & Wagner, 1986). The primary focus on school-related knowledge and skills has been questioned, and new sectors of life (i.e., social, work, art, leisure, and family contexts) have been singled out as domains within which factual and procedural forms of intelligence can be properly studied.

Our research on wisdom is an instantiation of these developments. The goal is to examine one substantive area that exemplifies a body of factual and procedural knowledge not covered in traditional definitions of intelligence. By selecting such a possibly vague and complex subject matter as wisdom, we are forced either to test the scope of existing theories or to move beyond the charted territories in the search for novel conceptions of intelligence.

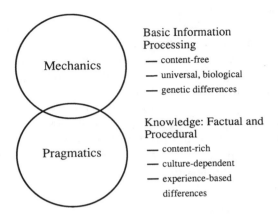

Basic Information
Processing
— content-free
— universal, biological
— genetic differences

Knowledge: Factual and
Procedural
— content-rich
— culture-dependent
— experience-based
  differences

Figure 5.1. A dual process model of intelligence (after Baltes, Dittmann-Kohli, & Dixon, 1984). The model is much influenced by Cattell's (1971) and Horn's (1970) theory of fluid-crystallized intelligence.

## Conceptualization of wisdom

In the following, we first describe in more detail our general approach to the study of life span intelligence. We do this to characterize how research on wisdom is embedded in a larger framework of the developmental study of the human mind. Subsequently, we describe our prototheory of wisdom as an expert knowledge system about the fundamental pragmatics of life.

### A dual process framework of intelligence

In our general theoretical framework of life span intelligence, the knowledge-based "pragmatics" of intelligence are juxtaposed with the basic "mechanics" of intelligence (P. B. Baltes, 1987; Baltes et al., 1984; Baltes & Kliegl, 1986). This heuristic distinction between the knowledge-free mechanics (Hunt, 1978) and the knowledge-rich pragmatics (Dixon & Baltes, 1986) of intelligence is similar to and extends the original conceptual framework of the Cattell–Horn theory of fluid-crystallized intelligence (Cattell, 1971; Horn, 1970). The defining characteristics of the mechanics and the pragmatics of intelligence are summarized in Figure 5.1.

What about the life span developmental course of the mechanics and the pragmatics of intelligence? Although we expect aging loss in the "hardware-like" mechanics of intelligence, especially if measured near limits of functioning (Kliegl & Baltes, 1987), we assume that some late-life advances are possible in the "softwarelike" pragmatics of intelligence. Thus, we suggest that the hallmark of positive cultural evolution and positive lifelong development lies in the possibility of growth (advances) in the knowledge-based

Table 5.1. *Wisdom: a working framework*

---

*Everyday definition*
Good judgment and advice about important but uncertain matters of life.

*Theoretical definition*
An *expert knowledge system* in the domain, fundamental life pragmatics (e.g., life planning, life management, life review).
*Functional consequence:* exceptional insight into human development and life matters, exceptionally good judgment, advice, and commentary about difficult life problems.

*Family of five criteria*
1. *Rich factual knowledge:* general and specific knowledge about the conditions of life and its variations
2. *Rich procedural knowledge:* general and specific knowledge about strategies of judgment and advice concerning matters of life
3. *Life span contextualism:* knowledge about the contexts of life and their temporal (developmental) relationships
4. *Relativism:* knowledge about differences in values, goals, and priorities
5. *Uncertainty:* knowledge about the relative indeterminacy and unpredictability of life and ways to manage

---

pragmatics. Recently, Perlmutter and her colleagues (e.g., Perlmutter, 1988) have proposed a three-tier model of intellectual development that is consistent with our general approach. Perlmutter's second and third tier are subsumed in our model under the heading of pragmatics.

Within this dual process distinction between the mechanics and pragmatics of life span intelligence, wisdom is considered one of the adulthood prototypes of growth in the pragmatics of intelligence (another prototype may be associated with various forms of professional specialization; see Featherman, 1986, 1987). We propose that the specific substantive domain related to wisdom encompasses knowledge about the conduct of life and the human condition, that is, knowledge about the course, variations, dynamics, and conflicts of life. We assume that the concept, wisdom, is reserved for high levels of knowledge in this domain. Therefore, we characterize wisdom as an expert knowledge system (Smith & Baltes, in press; Smith et al., in press).

## Theoretical definition of wisdom and its operationalization

Table 5.1 summarizes our approach toward defining wisdom. Our analysis starts from an everyday conception, namely, that wisdom involves "good judgment and advice about important but uncertain matters of life" (Baltes et al., 1984; Dittmann-Kohli & Baltes, in press; Smith et al., 1989). Theoretically, we characterize wisdom as *"expert knowledge involving good judgment and advice in the domain, fundamental pragmatics of life."* We also have defined a family of five criteria that index this expertise: rich factual knowledge, rich procedural knowledge, life span contextualism, relativism, and the ability to understand and manage uncertainty (Smith & Baltes, in press). These five criteria of wisdom (described in what follows in more detail) are presented as "ideals" (Barsalou, 1985; Chaplin, John, & Goldberg, 1988), as a set of characteristics that should be evident in a given body of knowledge about the fundamental pragmatics of life in order to approximate wisdom as we have defined it.

The implications of this analogue of wisdom as an expert knowledge system are considered in the next section. However, three observations are made here. First, our general assumption is that aspects of knowledge in the domain, fundamental life pragmatics, are within reach of every individual. Second, as with other domains (Ericsson, in press), we expect that very few people become experts. Third, we distinguish between the characteristics of a "wise person" and the definition of "wisdom" as an expert knowledge system. Our current emphasis is on wisdom as a body or system of knowledge rather than on the description of individuals who might be called the carriers of wisdom. At a later stage, and following on from our empirical work, we may be interested in developing proposals about the personal and life characteristics of wise persons.

We consider this conceptual emphasis on a body of knowledge and not on "wise" individuals important (which, incidentally, is similar to Piaget's approach to the definition of intelligence) because individuals such as wise persons represent but one carrier of wisdom-related knowledge. Other possible carriers are, for example, texts of social institutions (e.g., a constitution or the law of a country), religious documents, or collections of proverbs and prescriptions about values and human conduct. Our chosen emphasis on wisdom as a body of knowledge distinguishes our approach from other researchers on the same topic and also explains why our initial focus is less on personality characteristics than on a specification of the nature of the knowledge system.

In the following sections, we will describe each of the concepts used as defining elements in our theoretical framework in more detail.

*The domain: fundamental pragmatics of life.* The domain fundamental pragmatics of life encompasses knowledge about *important matters of life, their interpretation and management.* Included is knowledge about the variations, conditions, and historicity of life span development, human nature and conduct, life tasks and goals, social and intergenerational relationships, and life's uncertainties. Knowledge about one's self and one's own life biography and goals is also part of the domain.

A historical note may be helpful to understand the choice of the phrase *fundamental pragmatics of life.* In line with a functionalist orientation (Dixon & Baltes, 1986), the term *pragmatics* as used here is much influenced by one of the philosophical counterparts of functionalism, that is, pragmatism. In pragmatism (e.g., Bridgewater & Kurtz, 1963), thought is considered instrumental to the aims of an individual. Occasionally, when using the term pragmatic, it is also assumed that the aims or matters involved are "important" (i.e., fundamental) ones. An example is the term *pragmatic sanction* in political history. Pragmatic sanction involves a decision of state that deals with matters of great importance to a community or state. It is in this sense that we consider matters of fundamental pragmatics of life to be at the core of knowledge about human conduct and the human condition. We do this, although our initial research efforts may have involved more issues and topics of what was labeled in another paper "practical" rather than "philosophical" wisdom (Dittmann-Kohli & Baltes, in press).

Although we restrict wisdom to knowledge about fundamental, that is, important, matters of life, it is likely that wisdom is related to bodies of knowledge that are less fundamental but are parts of what others have called social intelligence (Cantor & Kihlstrom, 1987; Ford & Tisak, 1983; Keating, 1978) and everyday or practical intelligence (Cornelius & Caspi, 1987; Sternberg & Wagner, 1986). Thus, it is likely that knowledge about fundamental life pragmatics is built upon, and in some sense assumes, the presence of a knowledge of everyday routines (e.g., knowledge of common activities and events, social norms, available human services, and social institutions).

To enable the empirical investigation of wisdom-related knowledge in individuals, we have nominated three central task contexts: *life planning, life review,* and *life management.* It is clear from the everyday understanding of these contexts that there are no "recipes," for example, with which to plan for the future, interpret the past, or organize one's decisions about dilemmas of life. To engage in everyday discourse or conversation about such topics requires, of course, a general level of knowledge of life matters. In comparison, the ability to consistently produce insightful commentary, to show good judgment, or to offer good advice in contexts of life planning, life review, or life management is indicative, we suggest, of exceptional or expert knowledge in the domain fundamental life pragmatics.

There are, of course, other vehicles by which wisdom-related knowledge could be located or elicited. One example is proverbs that entail core summaries of factual and procedural knowledge about the process of life development and its management (Smith et al., 1989). Consider the following examples: "appearances are deceptive," "look before you leap," "variety is the spice of life," "when things are at their worst, they begin to mend," or the Chinese saying "it takes a long journey to find out which horse is the strongest." Proverbs such as these represent a distillation of personal (Polyani, 1962) and cultural knowledge about life (Berger & Luckmann, 1967). Their production is usually only possible and their message can usually only be effectively decoded and translated into practice by someone with sufficient background knowledge on a relevant topic. Moreover, access to opportunities to learn the accepted phrases associated with a society's maxims may be restricted to particular social and educational levels.

*The analogue to expert knowledge.* The definition of wisdom as an expert knowledge system permits further specification of the nature of the knowledge system from a cognitive psychological perspective (Chi, Glaser, & Rees, 1983; Glaser, 1984; Hoyer, 1986; Weinert, Schneider, & Knopf, 1988). Three features of the expertise analogue are particularly important to our conceptualization of wisdom. The expertise analogue contributes (1) a general model of the form and organization of expert knowledge, (2) a methodology to access this knowledge, and (3) theories of acquisition of a high level of performance.

To illustrate, studies of expertise by cognitive psychologists (Chi et al., 1983; Glaser, 1984; Weinert et al., 1988) indicate that experts in a particular domain can be differentiated from novices in that domain on both quantitative (i.e., sheer amount of knowledge) and qualitative (i.e., flexible use and organization) levels. Qualitative aspects, in particular metaknowledge and strategies (e.g., use of intuition), appear to best distinguish the top experts in domains where many people are able to specialize or acquire knowledge through formal education (e.g., medicine, physics).

The set of five wisdom-defining criteria shown in Table 5.1 is consistent with such models of expert knowledge. Together, these criteria describe the nature of wisdom-related knowledge and its "summative" manifestation in terms of exceptional insight into life matters and good judgment and advice about difficult life problems. In addition to two generic criteria of expert knowledge, rich factual knowledge about life and rich procedural knowledge about life, we have specified three metalevel dimensions along which this knowledge (both factual and procedural) could be organized. These metalevel dimensions are life span contextualism, relativism (associated with an awareness of variations in values, goals, and life priorities), and the recognition and management of life's uncertainty. These criteria define some of the critical dimensions around which life problems are interpreted, life goals and priorities are evaluated and established, and advice is offered.

How can wisdom-related knowledge be measured? Here, the second feature of our use of the analogue to expert knowledge is relevant. Central to the study of expert knowledge by cognitive psychologists is the assumption that the analysis of protocols (written or verbal) allows access to the content and structure of knowledge in a domain (Anderson, 1987; Ericsson & Simon, 1984). We have adopted this assumption and the relevant methodology to study wisdom. The collection and analysis of "thinking aloud" protocols to wisdom-related tasks and written texts concerning life matters and life decisions provides a body of data that allows examination of our theoretical model. In-depth protocol analysis also enables us to describe the strategies and heuristics of knowledge application in this domain. Later in this chapter we describe two wisdom-related tasks (dealing with life planning and life review) and a method of analysis that we have developed to operationalize this approach.

An additional feature of the expert knowledge analogue that we have adopted concerns the acquisition of knowledge and the idea that experts are exceptions rather than the rule. In most domains, experts have devoted considerable time and effort to their area of expertise (Ericsson, in press). Estimates indicate 10 years as a minimum and a well-designed program of practice, training, and mentorship. In many domains, opportunities to acquire knowledge and to achieve recognition as an expert (or potential expert) are constrained by societal structures. Experts can therefore rightly be considered as exceptions. The same is likely to be true for experts in the domain of fundamental life pragmatics.

The usefulness of the expert knowledge analogue, however, like any model (Reese & Overton, 1970), may also suffer from possible disadvantages. In our deliberations, we have focused on one such possible disadvantage. It involves the fact that most work in the field of expertise has been restricted to relatively well-structured systems of knowledge such as chess or physics. Wisdom, on the other hand, is considered as an instantiation of an ill-structured and open system of expert knowledge. It is knowledge at the frontiers rather than textbooklike standardized knowledge. Our current response to this possible criticism is twofold. First, we argue that the expertise analogue is not necessarily restricted to well-structured domains. Thus far, expertise has only been studied more easily in such domains. Second, even in well-structured domains of knowledge, we believe that experts have knowledge not covered by highly routinized schemata of factual and procedural knowledge. When it comes to top performances, it is likely that experts demonstrate knowledge beyond that which is already part of the standardized body of knowledge. To counteract possible misunderstandings associated with a narrow view of the term *expertise,* we have come to use the term *expert knowledge system.*

*Five wisdom-related criteria*

What is the specific meaning of the five criteria listed in Table 5.1? As mentioned before, the first two criteria, rich factual knowledge and rich procedural knowledge, are essential components of general models of expert knowledge. Any expertise entails rich factual and procedural knowledge. The remaining three criteria (life span contextualism, relativism, and uncertainty) specify characteristics of the metalevel organization of expert knowledge in the wisdom-related domain, fundamental pragmatics of life. These metalevel criteria encompass facets of previous descriptions of wisdom and optimal adult thought (Arlin, 1984; Holliday & Chandler, 1986; Kramer, 1983; Kuhn et al., 1983; Labouvie-Vief, 1985; Meacham, 1983; Mines & Kitchener, 1986). In addition, they reflect what has become known as the family of perspectives characteristic of life span theory (P. B. Baltes, 1987).

*Rich factual knowledge.* Having rich factual knowledge implies having, in long-term memory, an extensive data base about life matters analogous to a multiply cross-referenced encyclopedia. There have been many attempts to specify the organization of such a data base. A valuable example is that of Schank and Abelson (1977) and their colleagues. According to their conception, knowledge is organized around a meaningful representation of life content and events. They propose two classes of knowledge, general and specific:

General knowledge enables a person to understand and interpret another person's actions simply because the other person is a human being with certain standard needs who lives in a world which has certain standard methods of getting those needs fulfilled. ... Specific detailed knowledge about a situation allows us to do less processing and wondering about frequently experienced events. (1977, p. 37)

Schank and Abelson refer to specific knowledge as "scripts," a representation of the expected sequential flow of events in a particular situation (e.g., going to a restaurant, applying for a job). To understand new situations, individuals construct "plans" based on their general knowledge about the connectivity of events. General knowledge includes information about and interpretations of "human intentions, dispositions, and relationships" (p. 4) organized in terms of "goals" (e.g., satisfaction, enjoyment, achievement, preservation, crisis, instrumental) and "themes" (e.g., role themes, interpersonal themes, and life themes).

Schank and Abelson developed their model of knowledge organization to describe "the world of psychological and physical events occupying the mental life of ordinary individuals" (1977, p. 4). Their interest was in modeling text and conversational understanding. We consider that such a model could be developed further to describe an expert data base and to focus more directly on knowledge about the fundamental pragmatics of life rather than everyday life. For example, it is likely that an expert data base exhibiting rich factual knowledge would contain a wide scope of detailed scripts (specific knowledge) and an elaborate set of interpretative frameworks (generalized knowledge about the conditions of life). An expert in the domain fundamental life pragmatics would have general knowledge about the nature of typical events and decisions, the vulnerability, emotions, and needs of individuals (e.g., attachment, sense of self, health), and the controllability of developmental goals across the life span (Heckhausen & Baltes, 1988; Heckhausen, Dixon, & Baltes, 1989).

*Rich procedural knowledge.* Procedural knowledge about fundamental life pragmatics is a repertoire of mental procedures (or heuristics) used to select, order, and manipulate the information in the data base and to use it for purposes of decision making and action planning (e.g., Brown, 1982; Dörner, 1981; Kahneman, Slovic, & Tversky, 1984). These mental procedures are adapted to specific task demands and are somewhat independent of the cognitive mechanisms that implement them (Anderson, 1987). According to Anderson, learning can occur only at the level of facts and procedures; at the implementation level, the basic cognitive mechanisms are fixed and cannot be modified by learning.

What types of procedures might be included in the repertoire of an expert in the fundamental pragmatics of life? Some suggestions can be drawn from cognitive science research, although work focusing on procedural knowledge is at an early stage. In the context of social domains of knowledge, Kahneman et al. (1984) and Nisbett and Ross (1980), for example, have distinguished several heuristics (e.g., availability, representativeness, satisfying) commonly observed when individuals construct scenarios or make judgments and decisions given incomplete or uncertain information. In addition, recent descriptions of pragmatic reasoning schemes (Cheng & Holyoak, 1985; Holland, Holyoak, Nisbett, & Thagard, 1986) appear to delineate procedures relevant to the domain of life knowledge. Cheng and Holyoak argue that reasoning rules are primarily based on pragmatic interpretations of situations developed as a function of recurring experience with these situations. Pragmatic reasoning schemas consist of "generalized context-sensitive" rules "defined in terms of classes of goals (e.g., taking desirable actions or making predictions about possible future events) and relationships to these goals (e.g., cause and effect or precondition and allowable action)" (Cheng & Holyoak, 1985, p. 395). In addition to efficiently using such pragmatic schemas, it might well turn out that an expert in the domain fundamental life pragmatics is less likely to exhibit some of the typical biases (e.g., failure to consider base rate information or confirmation bias) that occur in social judgment (Nisbett & Ross, 1980).

To what degree the domain of wisdom is characterized by a specific type of procedural knowledge is not yet known due to a lack of relevant research. Birren's (1969) suggestions on strategies that characterize older adults' goals and life decisions and Meacham's (1983) proposition that wisdom entails the heuristic that "the more one knows the more one knows that one doesn't know" are examples of possible procedural heuristics associated with wisdom. Other examples are access to a rich set of proverbs mentioned earlier that, in their core meaning, offer interpretive orientations to a problem (e.g., "you can't win them all") and strategies associated with extracting information most relevant in a given life problem.

*Life span contextualism.* The criterion life span contextualism connotes an understanding that life development and life events are embedded in multiple life span contexts (age-related, sociohistorical, idiosyncratic) involving thematic (family, education, work, leisure, etc.) and temporal relationships. Included also in this criterion is the understanding that life span contexts are not always coordinated but can involve tension and conflict.

Taken as a whole, an understanding of life span contextualism involves knowledge about ontogenetic and historical changes in the coordination, relative salience, and priority of life themes and their implications for the specification of the ends and means of life. For example, how does one balance career priorities with family and leisure priorities? Are there some life phases or situations where one theme has a priority over the other? How are life span contexts coordinated to optimize both short- and long-term goals? What are the contextual conditions under which a good person–environment fit is achieved (Lerner & Lerner, 1983)?

*Relativism.* Our definition of relativism is not identical with other efforts available in the literature on adult cognition (e.g., Kramer, 1983; Kuhn et al., 1983). We have defined the criterion relativism in terms of knowledge about differences in individual and cultural goals, values, and priorities. Individual differences in personal style, motives, values, interests, and ability imply that individuals will choose different life paths and interpret events in their lives from different perspectives. Recent work in social cognition, for example, has documented the role of personal goals in organizing and mediating behavior (e.g., Brandtstädter & Baltes-Götz, in press; Dweck & Leggett, 1988; Elliott & Dweck, 1988). In a similar vein, individuals developing their lives in different cultures or cultural subgroups are likely to acquire a different set of expectations and schemes of evaluation.

Thus, we expect an expert in the domain fundamental life pragmatics to show sufficient value flexibility when interpreting life histories and life decisions of others. In particular, their knowledge system will involve an awareness that all judgments are a function of, and are relative to, a given cultural and personal value system. In this respect, experts are likely to have particular strategies that allow them to separate their personal values, goals, and life experiences from consideration of the lives and goals of others. Wisdom-type experts are able to acknowledge that there are a number of different interpretations and solutions. Despite this recognition of individual and cultural relativism, however, we do not maintain that such knowledge would result in rampant relativism and the inability to evaluate. On the contrary, we assume that wise knowledge implies the potential to judge which interpretation or solution is most appropriate relative to a particular value perspective. In contexts where experts are asked for critique or advice, they are likely to adopt strategies that involve the generation of alternative problem definitions and solutions despite a core set of possibly "invariant" human values.

*Uncertainty.* We introduce the criterion uncertainty to denote knowledge about the relative indeterminacy and unpredictability of life. This acknowledges the fact that one can *never* know everything about a problem or an individual's life. The future is not fully predictable and not all aspects of the past or present can be known. In this respect, Meacham (1983) suggests that wise people ought to excel at asking questions since they have a greater insight into the uncertainties and doubts surrounding life matters and into those areas of knowledge that they do not know about. Moreover, he notes that one measure of wisdom may be the ability to admit not knowing.

The recognition of uncertainty, however, is not sufficient to define expert knowledge in the domain, fundamental life pragmatics. What is needed as well is knowledge of strategies for managing and dealing with uncertainty (Dörner, 1976, 1981; Tversky & Kahneman, 1981). An expert, we suggest, would focus both on the recognition of uncertainty and on its management. Expert knowledge would, for example, most likely include an elaborate set of subjective probability estimates about the likely occurrence of events at different life phases and their relationships. On the basis of these estimations, advice could be given about the risk of success or failure of a decision taken in the face of uncertainty.

*Application of the five wisdom criteria.* The five criteria outlined in the preceding section provide a framework for conceptualizing the content and organization of expert knowledge in the domain, fundamental life pragmatics. In our own work, the manifestation of this knowledge is observed in discourse and commentary about life matters. Table 5.2 indicates how ideas offered in response to a problem of life management can be related to the family of wisdom criteria.

The dilemma given in Table 5.2, actually not one used in our work, is based on a "life management" question: "A fourteen-year-old girl is pregnant. What should she, what should one, consider and do?" Another example may be the question: "A sixteen-year-old boy wants to marry soon. What should he, what should one, consider and do?" In Table 5.2, statement categories are offered to illustrate instantiations of the five criteria of wisdom. An expertlike answer indicative of wisdom would reflect solid evidence for the entire family of criteria. In general, we argue that in a given protocol ideas and statements related to each of the criteria need to be identifiable for the response to qualify as truly wise.

### Predictions about ontogenesis of wisdom

Several kinds of predictions guide our research. Some of the predictions are basic to our general conceptualization of wisdom as a body of expert knowl-

Table 5.2. *Use of the wisdom criteria to evaluate discourse about life matters (Example: A 14-year-old is pregnant. What should she consider and do?)*

| Criterion | Instantiation in verbal discourse |
|---|---|
| Factual knowledge | Who, when, where?<br>Specific knowledge, examples, variations<br>General knowledge of emotions, vulnerability, and multiple options (parenting, adoption, abortion) |
| Procedural knowledge | Strategies of information search, decision making, and advice giving<br>Timing of advice<br>Monitoring of emotional reactions<br>Heuristics of cost–benefit analysis |
| Life span contextualism | Likely age sequence<br>Sociohistorical and idiosyncratic context<br>Coordination of life themes (family, education, work) and temporal changes<br>Contextual conflicts and tensions |
| Relativism | Religious and personal preferences<br>Current/future values, goals, motives<br>Cultural relativism |
| Uncertainty | No perfect solution<br>Optimization of gain/loss<br>Future not fully predictable<br>Back-up solutions |

edge about the fundamental pragmatics of life. Others involve expectations about the ontogenesis of wisdom.

A first class of predictions concerns the existence of social consensus about wisdom and its manifestations and the location of wisdom in people's belief systems about life span development. For example, if wisdom is indeed a prototype of a high level of cultural evolution and personal functioning, concepts such as wisdom and wise should be easily identifiable in everyday language and carry a specific meaning that distinguishes them from other related concepts such as social or academic intelligence. Furthermore, if wisdom is a prototypical end state or outcome of extensive ontogenetic development (Erikson et al., 1986), wisdom should be identifiable as a subjective marker of late-life positive change.

A second class of predictions involves the nature of ontogenesis. Figure 5.2 summarizes the elements of the research framework that guides our thinking about the antecedents of wisdom. As already mentioned, two indicators are advanced as markers of wisdom products: exceptional knowledge about the human condition and advice giving.

The general prediction is that the development of wisdom in individuals is dependent on general, specific, and modifying factors. General factors include

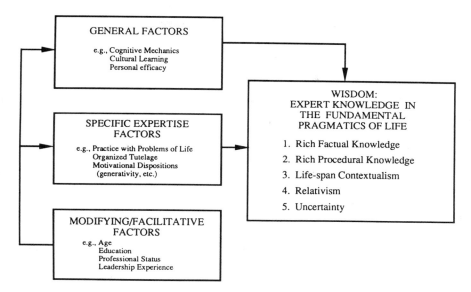

Figure 5.2. A research framework describing antecedent factors for the knowledge system, wisdom. Not shown are the correlates and consequences of wisdom: expert insightful judgment and advice giving.

a certain level of cognitive, personal, and social efficacy. Specific factors denote those conditions that are intrinsic to the expertise involved, that is, wisdom. In our view, specific factors necessary for acquiring wisdom include (1) extensive experiences with a wide range of human conditions as is often associated with work in the human services, (2) organized practice including mentorship, and (3) motivational dispositions such as generativity.

The third set of antecedent conditions involves factors that possibly regulate the likelihood of having the life experiences necessary for the acquisition of wisdom. In Figure 5.2, we label these as modifying or facilitative factors. Because of the amount of practice and the range of experiences involved, living longer (reaching an older age) is likely to be a facilitative (but not sufficient) condition for the acquisition of wisdom. The degree to which age is necessary will depend, in part, on the time span and the body of experiences required to acquire the wisdom-relevant knowledge. A major limiting condition would be if the experiences would need to occur directly rather than vicariously. Education, professional status, and leadership experience are listed as additional factors likely to facilitate the acquisition of wisdom.

There are additional developmental conditions worthy of consideration. For example, learning theory would suggest that some mixture of success as well as failure experiences is most likely important together with periods of structured study. Bloom's (1985) work on the development of talent would imply that access to mentors may also be a critical ingredient. In this sense, an individual who has reached an expert level of wisdom-related knowledge need not be seen as having led a wise life him- or herself.

The framework presented in Figure 5.2 also makes explicit that expert knowledge in the fundamental life pragmatics is not necessarily restricted to old age. Chronological age is but a facilitative condition. A strong life span developmental prediction would be that all persons with wisdom are older adults. A weak life span developmental hypothesis is that among wise persons there is a disproportionately large number of older persons. This weak life span developmental hypothesis guides our work on wisdom. *We expect "world records" in wisdom to be held by older adults, although on the average older adults may not be wiser than younger adults.*

In the following, two lines of empirical research are presented that address some of the predictions made about the nature of wisdom and its ontogenesis. The first type of work describes evidence about the subjective meaning of wisdom in everyday language. The second line summarizes initial work aimed at the age-comparative study of wisdom as an expertise dealing with judgment and advice about important but uncertain matters of life.

*Research on everyday conceptions of wisdom*

How is wisdom understood in everyday language and what is its relevance in subjective, "naïve," or implicit conceptions of life span development? Earlier research by Clayton and Birren (1980), Sternberg (1985a), and Holliday and Chandler (1986) has shown that the concepts wisdom and wise persons are firmly embedded in everyday language. In our own laboratory, the work by Sowarka (1987, 1989) offers additional evidence. Moreover, research by Heckhausen et al. (1989) supports the expectation that individuals, when asked about the nature of life span development, identify wisdom as a late-life goal.

The key data from Holliday and Chandler (1986) are summarized in Table 5.3. These authors conducted a series of studies that included an analysis of the words people use to describe wisdom and wise persons and the attributes judged to be most "typical" indicators of these concepts. They also examined to what degree wisdom is perceived to be different from other related competencies such as intelligence. A factor analysis of the attributes judged to be high in prototypicality revealed the two factors described in Table 5.3. These factors identify two aspects of wisdom-related characteristics as evident in wise persons and wise behavior: exceptional understanding and the ability to communicate relevant knowledge and judgment to others.[1] The meaning system reported by Holliday and Chandler (1986) correlates well with our own conceptualization of wisdom as expert knowledge involving good judgment and advice about important but uncertain matters of life (Dittmann-Kohli & Baltes, in press; Smith & Baltes, in press; Smith et al., 1989).

Table 5.3. *Everyday (naïve) theory of wisdom and wise persons: factor analysis of high prototypicality ratings*

| Factor I:<br>Exceptional understanding | Factor II:<br>Judgment and communication skills |
|---|---|
| Uses common sense | Aware |
| Has learned from experience | Is a source of good advice |
| Sees things within larger context | Comprehending |
| Observant/perceptive | Understands life |
| Understands him- or herself | Worth listening to |
| Sees the essence of the situation | Considers all options in a situation |
| Open-minded | Thinks carefully before deciding |
| Thinks for him- or herself | Sees and considers all points of view |

Based on Holliday and Chandler (1986).

That wisdom is a concept easily accessible to adults was also shown in dissertation work conducted in our laboratory by Sowarka (1987, 1989). She analyzed interviews with older adults about wise persons and wisdom collected by Johnson (1982). The analysis dealt with the descriptors of wisdom, the settings and tasks mentioned as requiring wisdom, and the traits perceived to be characteristic of wise persons. Sowarka's work points to one aspect of wisdom or wise persons that needs consideration. In her analysis, elderly subjects emphasized the notion that wise persons also have an "excellent character." At present, our focus is to study wisdom as a body of knowledge. We are currently exploring whether we should explicitly add this aspect to our theoretical definition. This may be necessary if the knowledge system of wisdom is defined to include characteristics of effective advice giving.

Is wisdom perceived to be a late-life goal or a desired state? This question was the topic of a study by Heckhausen et al. (1989). These authors sought the views of young, middle-aged, and older adults about the nature of development and aging. More than 300 psychological attributes (e.g., aggressive, curious, excitable, intelligent, materialistic, proud, wise) covering a wide range of personality and intelligence characteristics were used as an item pool. Subjects were asked which of these attributes they expected to change with age ("become more apparent, stronger and/or more frequent") during the decades from 20 to 90 of adult life. In addition, subjects indicated the timing (onset and offset) and the degree of desirability of the expected change.

The entire pattern revealed that subjects believed that the attributes likely to change in early adulthood were more desirable than what is expected to begin to change in later adulthood. Of the entire set of development-sensitive attributes, there were only two "desirable" attributes that were expected to become more frequent and stronger during late adulthood. As shown in Figure 5.3, "wise" was one of these two attributes. On average, subjects believed

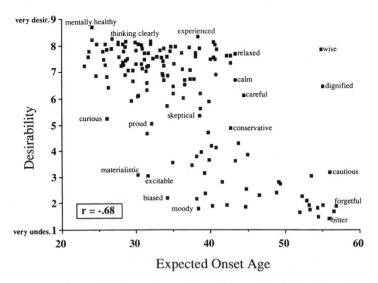

Figure 5.3. Expected ages of onset for psychological attributes judged to change during adulthood and their desirability. (Based on Heckhausen, Dixon, & Baltes, 1989.)

that wisdom begins to evolve (become stronger) after 55 years of age. In addition, the growth of wisdom was expected, on average, to continue into the ninth decade (average expected closing age: 85 years). The other late-life onset and desirable attribute was "dignified." Its developmental span was practically identical with that of wise.

Such research on subjective or implicit theories of wisdom supports an often stated conjecture in the literature, namely, that wisdom represents a positive phenomenon associated with late life (Clayton & Birren, 1980; Holliday & Chandler, 1986; Meacham, 1983). Wisdom is manifest in everyday language and in beliefs about positive change during late adulthood. Further, as shown in our research, the onset of wisdom is expected to occur fairly late in life. Thus, it seems justifiable to posit that wisdom represents something akin to a developmental goal that gives directionality to cognitive and personality functioning during adulthood.

*Research on wisdom as expert knowledge*

As mentioned before, we have operationalized the measurement of wisdom by developing a method to simulate discourse about life matters and by using rating scales based on the family of five wisdom criteria (described in the preceding sections) to evaluate the quality of this discourse. Subjects respond verbally to short vignettes covering various types of life problems and tasks (Smith & Baltes, in press; Smith et al., 1989; Staudinger, 1988).

Table 5.4. *Examples of life planning and life review tasks*

| | |
|---|---|
| Subjects are asked to "think aloud" about the following: | |
| Life planning | Joyce, a widow aged 60 years, recently completed a degree in business management and opened her own business. She has been looking forward to this new challenge. She has just heard that her son has been left with two small children for whom to care. Joyce is considering the following options: She could plan to give up her business and move to live with her son, or she could plan to arrange for financial assistance for her son to cover child care costs. What should Joyce do and consider in planning for her future? What extra information would you like to have available? |
| Life review | Martha, an elderly woman, had once decided to have a family and not to have a career. Her children left home some years ago. One day Martha meets a woman friend whom she has not seen for a long time. The friend had decided to have a career and no family. She has retired some years ago. This meeting causes Martha to think back over her life. What might her life review look like? Which aspects of her life might she remember? How might she explain her life? How might she evaluate her life retrospectively? |

*Note:* Tasks vary in type of problem (e.g., normative vs. nonnormative), age, and gender of target character. Furthermore, prompting questions are given at the completion of the spontaneous protocol (see Smith & Baltes, in press; Staudinger, 1988).

The vignettes are presented to subjects with the instruction that they discuss the problem faced by the fictitious person and offer advice. Subjects are instructed in the method of thinking aloud (Ericsson & Simon, 1984) to facilitate the reporting of their knowledge and thoughts. In addition, after spontaneously offered protocols are collected, a set of prompt questions are used to probe further into the knowledge systems available to subjects. The protocols are scored by trained raters for evidence of the five wisdom criteria.[2] In addition, the texts are content analyzed.

At present, our research has involved the analysis of discourse about difficult life matters in two contexts: life planning and life review. Cross-sectional studies have been carried out in which we sought the responses of young, middle-aged, and older adults to various life problems. To increase the probability of wise responses and to minimize cohort effects, the subjects represented a positive selection of adults in terms of educational and intellectual levels. They were, however, not selected on a criterion of wisdom.

A first study elicited wisdom-related knowledge in the context of problems involving life planning (Smith & Baltes, in press; Smith et al., 1989); a second focused on a life review task (Staudinger, 1988; Staudinger, Smith, & Baltes, 1989). Table 5.4 gives examples of a life-planning and life review problem. We consider that responses to the life-planning task involve the generation of future scenarios, evaluation of the implications and consequences of these scenarios, selection of one or more goals, planning to attain these goals, and suggestions about ways to monitor progress. The life review task requires subjects to construct a life story and to interpret and evaluate this constructed life course.

Subjects' responses to the life-planning and life review tasks were transcribed and then evaluated by panels of trained raters in terms of the five-criterion set (rich factual knowledge, rich procedural knowledge, life span contextualism, relativism, uncertainty) chosen to define wisdom-related knowledge. The raters were selected on the basis of their demonstrated extensive knowledge about life matters. They included lawyers, social scientists, experienced journalists, social workers, and specialist teachers. The interrater agreements are satisfactory and range usually from .60 to .80.

Analyses of the data await completion. However, among the preliminary findings are the following. First, and in line with our "weak" life span prediction, older adults are among the top performers. Second, and again in line with our definition of wisdom as an expert knowledge system, there are few responses judged to be wise. Third, average age/cohort differences are small, indicating much age-related stability. In addition, it seems that the entire period of adulthood is involved in the acquisition and transformation of wisdom-related knowledge. This conclusion is suggested by the fact that there is evidence for age-specific domains of wisdom-related expertise.

*Life planning.* Responses to four life-planning problems were obtained from 60 men and women (Smith & Baltes, in press). The problems differed on two dimensions: (a) target age of the principal character (a young adult of about 30 years of age vs. an older adult of about 60 years) and (b) type of life decision (normative vs. nonnormative). Problems were grouped as more or less normative according to our assessment of their age-graded statistical frequency, commonness, and "on-time/off-time" nature (Brim & Ryff, 1980; Hagestad & Neugarten, 1985). These distinctions represented a first effort at varying the age specificity of the problems and their degree of familiarity. A major theme present to some degree in all problems was the relationship between work and family.

Only 5% of the protocols from this sample were considered by our raters to be close to (but not identical with) the ideal defined by the five wisdom-related criteria. Agreement between 13 raters was high in this respect. Top performances were spread equally across the three age groups. For the nonnormative–old age problem (see Table 5.4), however, all of the top-rated responses came from older subjects.

Both young and older adults performed best when dealing with nonnormative life problems specific to their own age period (see Figure 5.4). Compared to their own performance on other problems, young adults were rated significantly lower on the old–nonnormative problem. In contrast, older adults were rated higher on this problem than on the other three problems. Older adults' ratings on the criteria of rich factual and procedural knowledge and

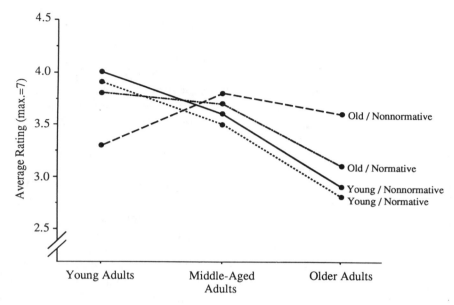

Figure 5.4. Age cohort differences on the life-planning task as a function of the target age and normativeness of the problem. Young and old subjects performed best when the age of the character in the problem matched their own age. (Based on Smith & Baltes, in press.)

relativism were significantly higher for the old compared to the young target problems.

A content analysis of the themes discussed by subjects (Sörensen, 1988) enabled a further portrayal of the background knowledge about life that individuals brought to the life-planning task. For example, when speaking about both the young and old nonnormative problems, subjects focused on the attributes and characteristics of the people involved, in particular, the main character. This was especially true for the young adults. Other themes that predominated concerned the desires of significant others and family relationships in general. Surprisingly, few subjects talked about health issues, goals, or motives.

These findings from the life-planning task point to age-specific peaks in select areas of knowledge about life pragmatics. At less-than-expert levels, this may well be the case. We expect that subjects specifically selected or nominated for their expertise will display a pattern of performance that is less tied to the target age of the problem. We are currently collecting data to address these questions.

*Life review.* In the doctoral study of Staudinger (1988), 63 women constructed a life review for Martha, a fictitious character described as being young, middle-aged, or old, who was prompted to look back over her life by a chance meeting with a school friend. The study design allowed comparison of the knowledge of young adults about the review of an older woman with that of older adults about reviews by young women.

Old and young subjects showed comparable levels of knowledge. Indeed, across all wisdom-related criteria and all review problems, older adults were never rated significantly lower than young adults. For the criterion awareness of uncertainty older adults in this sample were rated higher than the young adults. Again, however, it should be pointed out that the sample of responses was not considered to be within the range of the ideal described by the five wisdom criteria.

The results of these two initial studies demonstrate primarily that the method chosen to study wisdom-related knowledge seems to be practicable. Moreover, the data collected indicate that not unlike other areas of crystallized as well as social and practical intelligence (Blanchard-Fields, 1986; Cornelius & Caspi, 1987; Denney, 1984; Kuhn et al., 1983), older adults do not exhibit an aging loss. In fact, there is some evidence in the present data that older adults continue to evolve their knowledge and, further, that they are among the top performers. Thus, the initial empirical results are promising. It is now possible to carry the research paradigm to its next step, that is, the study of persons nominated to be wisdom experts. Such research is in progress.

### Summary and outlook

Since ancient Greek philosophy and throughout modern times, wisdom has been considered as the peak, the capstone of knowledge about the human condition. Recently, this longstanding cultural heritage has attracted psychological researchers interested in exploring facets of successful aging and the potential for growth in late adulthood. Such an approach seems important because it pushes the boundaries of the nature of aging beyond current realities. Thus, even in the absence of sufficient and current empirical evidence demonstrating wisdom as an area of late-life potential, the basic tenet is important. Like scholarship on world utopias, the search for wisdom in old age is likely to open new vistas on what might be possible in principle if societal conditions were different.

In our own research strategy, we have defined wisdom as a body of expert knowledge in the domain fundamental pragmatics of life. The conceptual focus, then, is on knowledge rather than carriers of knowledge. Because of our interest in positive aspects of human aging, we have also speculated about the performance of individuals of different ages. In this instance, we proceed from the assumption of a "weak" life span hypothesis. On the one hand, we argue that not all older persons will be wise. On the other hand, we suggest that among wise persons there may be a disproportionately large number of older individuals. We do not expect many older adults, to outperform young adults, in part because of limitations in the degree of cultural evolution. In our view, cultural evolution has not yet reached anything approaching a state of optimality for old age, and so the opportunities for older persons to display characteristics of wisdom are limited.

However, because we define wisdom as expert knowledge about the nature of human development and the human condition, we expect that the acquisition and maintenance of wisdom is facilitated by living longer. Such an expectation is in agreement with theories of exceptional performance (Ericsson & Crutcher, in press) that state that it takes many years and thousands of hours of structured and guided practice to reach truly high levels of expertise. Of course, although living longer together with extensive experience and organized practice are necessary conditions for the acquisition of an expert level of knowledge, they are not sufficient. Various life history, personal, and motivational factors may also be involved in the acquisition and maintenance of wisdom.

Our initial empirical findings and those of others (e.g., Clayton & Birren, 1980; Holliday & Chandler, 1986; Sternberg, 1985a) are encouraging and suggest that wisdom is a viable topic for scientific psychological research. Wisdom seems to be a well-marked concept in language and in people's beliefs and knowledge about human behavior and its development. People can easily speak about wisdom and wise persons and can identify some of the salient characteristics of the phenomenon. In terms of people's beliefs about changes during adulthood and old age (Heckhausen et al., 1989), wisdom appears to be one of the very few attributes in our mental scenarios about aging that typifies positive late-life goals and accomplishments. Furthermore, the attributes mentioned by subjects when describing their everyday views of wisdom and wise persons are similar to what we have specified as the essence of a theoretical definition of wisdom.

We also consider as promising our emerging work on behavioral indicators of wisdom as expert knowledge in the fundamental pragmatics of life. Researchers interested in immediate demonstration of the superiority of older persons in tasks of wisdom may be disappointed because so far we have found few older persons who display a level of knowledge that can be categorized as wise. We are less affected by this finding because our research strategy has not yet focused on the question of top performance (however, see the next paragraph). Rather, we are committed to developing a conceptual and methodological tool that shows promise for future investigation of the nature of wisdom. In this vein, the research approach that involves collecting thinking-aloud protocols about life dilemmas and evaluating these protocols against a family of wisdom-related criteria seems to work from a methodological point of view. It results in reliable and seemingly meaningful findings. There are few age/cohort differences, and older adults are among the top performers. These findings are preliminary, but they are consistent with our theoretical expectations and the notion that wisdom may be a positive late-life goal that, under supportive conditions, could be attained by older adults.

Ongoing and future research about wisdom at the Max Planck Institute in Berlin is aimed primarily at three objectives each of which is expected to add an important facet to our general conceptualization:

   a. the construction of additional tasks or tests associated with wisdom-related knowledge;
   b. the identification of top wisdom performances through a process of nomination of wisdom experts and by evaluation of criterion groups selected on the basis of their relevant life and professional experiences (e.g., medical doctors and clinical psychologists as respondents); and
   c. microanalytic content analysis of wisdom protocols.

We hope that this research will allow further specification of the scope, precision, and applicability of the theory of wisdom advanced.

One concluding observation. Throughout, we have emphasized that our conceptual approach to the study of wisdom is to define it as a body of expert knowledge and not to restrict wisdom to characteristics of individuals, that is, wise persons. At the risk of redundancy, we would like to highlight again the point that the research framework presented and the method used to identify wisdom-related knowledge in terms of a family of criteria is not restricted to the use of life dilemmas and the discourse products of individuals. As long as verbal protocols about the domain of wisdom or related topics associated with the pragmatics of life are available, they can be evaluated using the proposed set of five criteria (rich factual knowledge, rich procedural knowledge, life span contextualism, relativism, uncertainty) as a yardstick. Thus, we believe that the research analogue can be applied to a whole gamut of language-based documents ranging from interviews, diaries, and essays about life to historical documents such as religious documents or other texts on human conduct. This feature seems important as it makes the theoretical and methodological approach chosen applicable to a broad range of products that are possibly of interest to researchers in search of new facets of intelligence, positive aspects of human aging, or other high levels of performance in the domain of social knowledge.

## Notes

1 Holliday and Chandler (1986) report three other factors – general competencies, interpersonal skills, and social unobtrusiveness – but the items loading on these factors had been judged to be less typical of a "truly wise person."
2 A manual describing the problems and method is available from the authors.

## References

Anderson, J. R. (Ed.) (1981). *Cognitive skills and their acquisition.* Hillsdale, NJ: Erlbaum.
Anderson, J. R. (1983). *The architecture of cognition.* Cambridge, MA: Harvard University Press.

Anderson, J. R. (1987). Methodologies of studying human knowledge. *Behavioral and Brain Sciences, 10,* 467–505.

Arlin, P. K. (1984). Adolescent and adult thought: a structural interpretation. In M. L. Commons, F. A. Richards, & C. Armon (Eds.), *Beyond formal operations: late adolescent and adult cognitive development* (pp. 258–271). New York: Praeger.

Arnheim, R. (1986). On the late style. In R. Arnheim (Ed.), *New essays on the psychology of art* (pp. 285–293). Berkeley: University of California Press.

Assmann, A., & Assmann, J. (1987, September). *Weisheit II.* Paper presented at the meeting of the Werner-Reimers-Stiftung, Heidelberg, Federal Republic of Germany.

Baltes, M. (1987). Erfolgreiches Altern als Ausdruck von Verhaltenskompetenz und Umweltqualität. In C. Niemitz (Ed.), *Erbe und Umwelt* (pp. 353–374). Frankfurt: Suhrkamp.

Baltes, P. B. (1987). Theoretical propositions of life-span developmental psychology: on the dynamics between growth and decline. *Developmental Psychology, 23,* 611–626.

Baltes, P. B., & Baltes, M. M. (in press). Psychological perspectives on successful aging: the model of selective optimization with compensation. In P. B. Baltes & M. M. Baltes (Eds.), *Successful aging: perspectives from the behavioral sciences.* New York: Cambridge University Press.

Baltes, P. B., Dittmann-Kohli, F., & Dixon, R. A. (1984). New perspectives on the development of intelligence in adulthood: toward a dual-process conception and a model of selective optimization with compensation. In P. B. Baltes & O. G. Brim, Jr. (Eds.), *Life-span development and behavior* (Vol. 6, pp. 33–76). New York: Academic Press.

Baltes, P. B., & Kliegl, R. (1986). On the dynamics between growth and decline in the aging of intelligence and memory. In K. Poeck, H. J. Freund, & H. Gänshirt (Eds.), *Neurology* (pp. 1–17). Heidelberg: Springer.

Baltes, P. B., & Labouvie, G. V. (1973). Adult development of intellectual performance: description, explanation, modification. In C. Eisdorfer & P. Lawton (Eds.), *The psychology of adult development and aging* (pp. 157–219). Washington, DC: American Psychological Association.

Baltes, P. B., & Lindenberger, U. (1988). On the range of cognitive plasticity in old age as a function of experience: 15 years of intervention research. *Behavior Therapy, 19,* 283–300.

Baltes, P. B., & Schaie, K. W. (1976). On the plasticity of intelligence in adulthood and old age: where Horn and Donaldson fail. *American Psychologist, 31,* 720–725.

Baltes, P. B., Smith, J., Staudinger, U. M., & Sowarka, D. (in press). Wisdom: one facet of successful aging? In M. Perlmutter (Ed.), *Late-life potential.* Washington, DC: Gerontological Society of America.

Barsalou, L. W. (1985). Ideals, central tendency, and frequency of instantiation as determinants of graded structure in categories. *Journal of Experimental Psychology: Learning, Memory, and Cognition, 11,* 629–654.

Berger, P. L., & Luckmann, T. (1967). *The social construction of reality.* Garden City, NY: Doubleday.

Berlin, I. (1988). On the pursuit of the ideal. *New York Review of Books, 35,* 16.

Birren, J. E. (1969). Age and decision strategies. *Interdisciplinary topics in gerontology.* Basel, Switzerland: Karger.

Birren, J. E., & Renner, V. J. (1980). Concepts of mental health and aging. In J. E. Birren & R. B. Sloane (Eds.), *Handbook of mental health and aging* (pp. 3–33). Englewood Cliffs, NJ: Prentice-Hall.

Blanchard-Fields, F. (1986). Reasoning in adolescents and adults on social dilemmas varying in emotional saliency: an adult developmental perspective. *Psychology and Aging, 1,* 325–333.

Bloom, B. (1985). *Developing talent in young people.* New York: Ballantine.

Brandtstädter, J. (1984). Personal and social control over development: some implications of an action perspective in life-span developmental psychology. In P. B. Baltes & O. G. Brim, Jr. (Eds.), *Life-span development and behavior* (Vol. 6, pp. 1–32). New York: Academic Press.

Brandtstädter, J., & Baltes-Götz, B. (in press). Personal control over development and quality of life perspectives in adulthood. In P. B. Baltes & M. M. Baltes (Eds.), *Suc-*

*cessful aging: perspectives from the behavioral sciences.* New York: Cambridge University Press.

Bridgewater, W., & Kurtz, S. (Eds.) (1963). *The Columbia encyclopedia.* New York: Columbia University Press.

Brim, O. G., Jr., & Ryff, C. D. (1980). On the properties of life events. In P. B. Baltes & O. G. Brim, Jr. (Eds.), *Life-span development and behavior* (Vol. 3, pp. 368–388). New York: Academic Press.

Brown, A. L. (1982). Learning and development: the problem of compatibility, access, and induction. *Human Development, 25,* 89–115.

Cantor, N., & Kihlstrom, J. F. (1987). *Personality and social intelligence.* Englewood Cliffs, NJ: Prentice-Hall.

Cattell, R. B. (1971). *Abilities: their structure, growth and action.* Boston: Houghton Mifflin.

Chaplin, W. F., John, O. P., & Goldberg, L. R. (1988). Conceptions of states and traits: dimensional attributes with ideals as prototypes. *Journal of Personality and Social Psychology, 54,* 541–557.

Charness, N. (Ed.) (1985). *Aging and human performance.* Chichester, England: John Wiley.

Cheng, P. W., & Holyoak, K. J. (1985). Pragmatic reasoning schemas. *Cognitive Psychology, 17,* 391–416.

Chi, M. T. H., Glaser, R., & Rees, E. (1983). Expertise in problem-solving. In R. Sternberg (Ed.), *Advances in the psychology of human intelligence* (Vol. 7, pp. 7–76). Hillsdale, NJ: Erlbaum.

Cicero, M. T. (1979). *Cato major* [His discourse of old age] (Original work *De Senectute*, J. Logan, Trans.). New York: Arno Press.

Clayton, V. (1975). Erikson's theory of human development as it applies to the aged: wisdom as contradictory cognition. *Human Development, 18,* 119–128.

Clayton, V., & Birren, J. W. (1980). The development of wisdom across the life span: a re-examination of an ancient topic. In P. B. Baltes & O. G. Brim, Jr. (Eds.), *Life-span development and behavior* (Vol. 3, pp. 103–135). New York: Academic Press.

Commons, M. L., Richards, F. A., & Armon, C. (Eds.) (1984). *Beyond formal operations: late adolescent and adult cognitive development.* New York: Praeger.

Cornelius, S. W., & Caspi, A. (1987). Everyday problem solving in adulthood and old age. *Psychology and Aging, 2,* 144–153.

Denney, N. W. (1984). A model of cognitive development across the life span. *Developmental Review, 4,* 171–191.

Dittmann-Kohli, F., & Baltes, P. B. (in press). Toward a neofunctionalist conception of adult intellectual development: wisdom as a prototypical case of intellectual growth. In C. Alexander & E. Langer (Eds.), *Beyond formal operations: alternative endpoints to human development.* New York: Oxford University Press.

Dixon, R. A., & Baltes, P. B. (1986). Toward life-span research on the functions and pragmatics of intelligence. In R. J. Sternberg & R. K. Wagner (Eds.), *Practical intelligence: nature and origins of competence in the everyday world* (pp. 203–234). New York: Cambridge University Press.

Dixon, R. A., & Lerner, R. M. (1988). History and systems of developmental psychology. In M. H. Bornstein & M. E. Lamb (Eds.), *Developmental psychology: an advanced textbook* (2nd ed., pp. 3–50). Hillsdale, NJ: Erlbaum.

Dörner, D. (1976). *Problemlösen als Informationsverarbeitung.* Stuttgart: Kohlhammer.

Dörner, D. (1981). Über die Schwierigkeiten menschlichen Umgangs mit Komplexität. *Psychologische Rundschau, 3,* 163–179.

Dweck, C. S., & Leggett, E. L. (1988). A social-cognitive approach to motivation and personality. *Psychological Review, 95,* 256–273.

Edelstein, W. (1983). Cultural constraints on development and the vicissitudes of progress. In F. S. Kessel & A. W. Siegel (Eds.), *The child and other cultural inventions* (pp. 48–81). New York: Praeger.

Elliott, E. S., & Dweck, C. S. (1988). Goals: an approach to motivation and achievement. *Journal of Personality and Social Psychology, 54,* 5–12.

Ericsson, K. A. (1985). Memory skill. *Canadian Journal of Psychology, 39*(2), 188–231.

Ericsson, K. A. (in press). Peak performance and age: an examination of peak performance in sports. In P. B. Baltes & M. M. Baltes (Eds.), *Successful aging: perspectives from the behavioral sciences*. New York: Cambridge University Press.

Ericsson, K. A., & Crutcher, R. J. (in press). The nature of exceptional performance. In P. B. Baltes, D. L. Featherman, & R. M. Lerner (Eds.), *Life-span development and behavior* (Vol. 10). Hillsdale, NJ: Erlbaum.

Ericsson, K. A., & Simon, H. A. (1984). *Protocol analysis: verbal reports as data*. Cambridge, MA: MIT Press.

Erikson, E. H. (1959). Identity and the life cycle. *Psychological Issues Monograph I*. New York: International Universities Press.

Erikson, E. H., Erikson, J. M., & Kivnick, H. Q. (1986). *Vital involvement in old age: the experience of old age in our time*. New York: Norton.

Featherman, D. L. (1983). The life-span perspective in social science research. In P. B. Baltes & O. G. Brim, Jr. (Eds.), *Life-span development and behavior* (Vol. 5, pp. 1–59). New York: Academic Press.

Featherman, D. L. (1986). Biography, society, and history: individual development as a population process. In A. B. Sorensen, F. E. Weinert, & L. R. Sherrod (Eds.), *Human development and the life course: multidisciplinary perspectives* (pp. 99–149). Hillsdale, NJ: Erlbaum.

Featherman, D. L. (1987, July). *Work, adaptive competence, and successful aging: a theory of adult cognitive development*. Paper presented at the Ninth Biennial Meeting of the International Society for the Study of Behavioural Development, Tokyo, Japan.

Ford, D. H. (1987). *Humans as self-constructing living systems: a developmental perspective on behavior and personality*. Hillsdale, NJ: Erlbaum.

Ford, M. E., & Tisak, M. S. (1983). A further search for social intelligence. *Journal of Educational Psychology, 75*, 196–206.

Gardner, H. (1983). *Frames of mind: the theory of multiple intelligences*. New York: Basic Books.

Glaser, R. (1984). Education and thinking. *American Psychologist, 39*, 93–104.

Goodnow, J. J. (1986). Some lifelong everyday forms of intelligent behavior: organizing and reorganizing. In R. J. Sternberg & R. K. Wagner (Eds.), *Practical intelligence: nature and origins of competence in the everyday world* (pp. 143–162). New York: Cambridge University Press.

Hagestad, G., & Neugarten, B. L. (1985). Age and the life course. In R. H. Binstock & E. Shanas (Eds.), *Handbook of aging and the social sciences* (pp. 35–81). New York: Van Nostrand Reinhold.

Hall, G. S. (1922). *Senescence: the last half of life*. New York: Appleton.

Havighurst, R. J. (1972). *Developmental tasks and education* (3rd ed.). New York: McKay.

Heckhausen, J., & Baltes, P. B. (1988). *Perceived controllability of expected psychological change*. In preparation.

Heckhausen, J., Dixon, R. A., & Baltes, P. B. (1989). Gains and losses in development through-out adulthood as perceived by different adult age groups. *Developmental Psychology, 25*, 109–121.

Holland, J. H., Holyoak, K. J., Nisbett, R. E., Thagard, P. R. (1986). *Induction: processes of inference, learning, and discovery*. Cambridge, MA: MIT Press.

Holliday, S. G., & Chandler, M. J. (1986). *Wisdom: explorations in adult competence*. Basel, Switzerland: Karger.

Horn, J. L. (1970). Organization of data on life-span development of human abilities. In L. R. Goulet & P. B. Baltes (Eds.), *Life-span developmental psychology: Research and theory* (pp. 423–466). New York: Academic Press.

Hoyer, S. (1986). Clinical aspects of the dementias. In K. Poeck, H.-J. Freund, & H. Gänshirt (Eds.), *Neurology* (pp. 21–25). Heidelberg: Springer.

Hunt, E. (1978). Mechanics of verbal ability. *Psychological Review, 85*, 109–130.

Jäger, A. O. (1982). Mehrmodale Klassifikation von Intelligenzleistungen: Experimentell kontrollierte Weiterentwicklung eines deskriptiven Intelligenzstrukturmodells. *Diagnostica, 28,* 195–225.

Johnson, R. E. (1982). *A study of wisdom as reported by older adults in America.* Ann Arbor, MI: University Microfilms International.

Kahneman, D., Slovic, P., & Tversky, A. (Eds.) (1984). *Judgment under uncertainty: heuristics and biases.* Cambridge, MA: Cambridge University Press.

Keating, D. P. (1978). A search for social intelligence. *Journal of Educational Psychology, 70,* 218–233.

Kliegl, R., & Baltes, P. B. (1987). Theory-guided analysis of mechanisms of development and aging through testing-the-limits and research on expertise. In C. Schooler & K. W. Schaie (Eds.), *Cognitive functioning and social structure over the life course* (pp. 95–119). Norwood, NJ: Ablex.

Klix, F. (Ed.) (1984). *Gedächtnis, Wissen, Wissensnutzung.* Berlin: Deutscher Verlag der Wissenschaften.

Kramer, D. A. (1983). Postformal operations? A need for further conceptualization. *Human Development, 26,* 91–105.

Kuhn, D., Pennington, N., & Leadbeater, B. (1983). Adult thinking in developmental perspective. In P. B. Baltes & O. G. Brim, Jr. (Eds.), *Life-span development and behavior* (Vol. 5, pp. 157–195). New York: Academic Press.

Labouvie-Vief, G. (1981). Proactive and reactive aspects of constructivism: growth and aging in life-span perspective. In R. M. Lerner & N. A. Busch-Rossnagel (Eds.), *Individuals as producers of their development* (pp. 197–230). New York: Academic Press.

Labouvie-Vief, G. (1982). Dynamic development and mature autonomy: a theoretical prologue. *Human Development, 25,* 161–191.

Labouvie-Vief, G. (1985). Intelligence and cognition. In J. E. Birren & K. W. Schaie (Eds.), *Handbook of the psychology of aging* (2nd ed., pp. 500–530). New York: Van Nostrand Reinhold.

Labouvie-Vief, G. (Ed.) (1986). *Developmental dimensions of adult adaptation: perspectives on mind, self, and emotion.* Unpublished manuscript, Department of Psychology, Wayne State University, Detroit.

Lehman, H. C. (1953). *Age and achievement.* Princeton, NJ: Princeton University Press.

Lerner, R. M. (1984). *On the nature of human plasticity.* New York: Cambridge University Press.

Lerner, J. V., & Lerner, R. M. (1983). Temperament and adaptation across life: theoretical and empirical issues. In P. B. Baltes & O. G. Brim, Jr. (Eds.), *Life-span development and behavior* (Vol. 5, pp. 197–231). New York: Academic Press.

McArdle, J. J., & Horn, J. L. (1988). *A mega-analysis of the WAIS: structure and function of abilities in adulthood.* Unpublished manuscript, University of Virginia, Department of Psychology.

Meacham, J. A. (1983). Wisdom and the context of knowledge: knowing that one doesn't know. In D. Kuhn & J. A. Meacham (Eds.), *On the development of developmental psychology* (pp. 111–134). Basel, Switzerland: Karger.

Mines, R. A., & Kitchener, K. S. (1986). *Adult cognitive development: methods and models.* New York: Praeger.

Montada, L. (1987). Themen, Traditionen, Trends. In R. Oerter & L. Montada (Eds.), *Entwicklungspsychologie* (2nd ed., pp. 1–86). München–Weinheim: Psychologie Verlags Union.

Neisser, U. (1979). The concept of intelligence. *Intelligence, 3,* 217–227.

Neugarten, B. L. (1968). Adult personality: toward a psychology of the life cycle. In B. L. Neugarten (Ed.), *Middle age and aging: a reader in social psychology* (pp. 137–147). Chicago: University of Chicago Press.

Nisbett, R. (1980). *History of the idea of progress.* New York: Basic Books.

Nisbett, R., & Ross, L. (1980). *Human inference: strategies and shortcomings of social judgment.* Englewood Cliffs, NJ: Prentice-Hall.

Perlmutter, M. (1988). Cognitive development in life-span perspective: from description of differences to examination of changes. In M. Hetherington, R. Lerner, & M. Perlmutter (Eds.), *Child development in a life span perspective* (pp. 191–217). Hillsdale, NJ: Erlbaum.

Piaget, J. (1972). Intellectual evolution from adolescence to adulthood. *Human Development, 15,* 1–12.

Polyani, M. (1962). *Personal knowledge: towards a post-critical philosophy.* Chicago: University of Chicago Press.

Pressey, S. L., Janney, J. E., & Kuhlen, R. G. (1939). *Life: a psychological survey.* New York: Harper.

Reese, H. W., & Overton, W. F. (1970). Models of development and theories of development. In L. R. Goulet & P. B. Baltes (Eds.), *Life-span developmental psychology: research and theory* (pp. 115–145). New York: Academic Press.

Resnick, L. (Ed.) (1976). *The nature of intelligence.* Hillsdale, NJ: Erlbaum.

Riegel, K. F. (1973). Dialectical operations: the final period of cognitive development. *Human Development, 16,* 346–370.

Rogoff, B., & Lave, J. (1984). *Everyday cognition.* Cambridge, MA: Harvard University Press.

Rowe, J. W., & Kahn, R. L. (1987). Human aging: usual and successful. *Science, 237,* 143–149.

Ryff, C. D. (1982). Successful aging: a developmental approach. *The Gerontologist, 22,* 209–214.

Ryff, C. D. (1984). Personality development from the inside: the subjective experience of change in adulthood and aging. In P. B. Baltes & O. G. Brim, Jr. (Eds.), *Life-span development and behavior* (Vol. 6, pp. 243–279). New York: Academic Press.

Salthouse, T. A. (1985). *A theory of cognitive aging.* Amsterdam: North-Holland.

Schank, R., & Abelson, R. (1977). *Scripts, plans, goals, and understanding: an inquiry into human knowledge structures.* Hillsdale, NJ: Erlbaum.

Schmidt, H. D. (1970). *Allgemeine Entwicklungspsychologie.* Berlin: Deutscher Verlag der Wissenschaften.

Sears, E. (1986). *Ages of man: medieval interpretations of the life cycle.* Princeton, NJ: Princeton University Press.

Simon, H. A. (1983). *Reason in human affairs.* Stanford, CA: Stanford University Press.

Simonton, D. K. (1984). *Genius, creativity, and leadership.* Cambridge, MA: Harvard University Press.

Smith, J., & Baltes, P. B. (in press). A study of wisdom-related knowledge: age/cohort differences in responses to life planning problems. *Developmental Psychology.*

Smith, J., Dixon, R. A., & Baltes, P. B. (1989). Expertise in life planning: a new research approach to investigating aspects of wisdom. In M. L. Commons, J. D. Sinnott, F. A. Richards, & C. Armon (Eds.), *Beyond formal operations II: comparisons and applications of adolescent and adult developmental models.* New York: Praeger.

Snow, R. E. (1980). Intelligence for the year 2001. *Intelligence, 4,* 185–199.

Sörensen, S. (1988). *Age differences in wisdom-related expertise: content analysis of verbal protocols about life pragmatics.* Master's thesis, Free University Berlin, Federal Republic of Germany.

Sowarka, D. (1987). *Wisdom in the context of persons, situations, and actions: common-sense views of elderly women and men.* Unpublished manuscript, Max Planck Institute for Human Development and Education, Federal Republic of Germany.

Sowarka, D. (1989). Weisheit und weise Personen: Common-Sense-Konzepte älterer Menschen. *Zeitschrift für Entwicklungspsychologie und Pädagogische Psychologie, 21,* 87–109.

Staudinger, U. (1988). *The study of life review: an approach to the investigation of intellectual development across the life span.* Ph.D. Dissertation, Free University of Berlin & Max Planck Institute for Human Development and Education, Berlin, Federal Republic of Germany.

Staudinger, U., Smith, J., & Baltes, P. B. (1988). *Wisdom-related knowledge: the sample case of life review.* In preparation.

Staudinger, U. M., Cornelius, S. W., & Baltes, P. B. (1989). The aging of intelligence: potential and limits. *Annals of the Academy of Political and Social Sciences, 503,* 43–59.

Sternberg, R. J. (1985a). Human intelligence: the model is the message. *Science, 230,* 1111–1118.

Sternberg, R. J. (1985b). Implicit theories of intelligence, creativity, and wisdom. *Journal of Personality and Social Psychology, 49,* 607–627.

Sternberg, R. J., & Detterman, D. K. (Eds.) (1986). *What is intelligence?* Norwood, NJ: Ablex.

Sternberg, R. J., & Wagner, R. K. (Eds.) (1986). *Practical intelligence: nature and origins of competence in the everyday world.* Cambridge: Cambridge University Press.

Tetens, J. N. (1777). *Philosophische Versuche über die menschliche Natur und ihre Entwicklung.* Leipzig, GDR: Weidmanns Erben und Reich.

Tversky, A., & Kahneman, D. (1981). The framing of decisions and the psychology of choice. *Science, 211,* 453–458.

Weinert, F. E., Schneider, W., & Knopf, M. (1988). Individual differences in memory development across the life span. In P. B. Baltes, D. L. Featherman, & R. M. Lerner (Eds.), *Life-span development and behavior* (Vol. 9, pp. 39–85). Hillsdale, NJ: Erlbaum.

Werner, H. (1948). *Comparative psychology of mental development.* New York: International Universities Press.

Willis, S. L. (1987). Cognitive training and everyday competence. In K. W. Schaie (Ed.), *Annual Review of Gerontology and Geriatrics* (Vol. 7, pp. 159–188). New York: Springer.

Wittgenstein, L. (1953). *Philosophical investigations.* New York: Macmillan.

Zuckerman, H. (1977). *Scientific elite: Nobel laureates in the United States.* New York: Free Press.

# 6    Wisdom in a postapocalyptic age

*Michael J. Chandler with Stephen Holliday*

## A disquieting suggestion

Alasdar Macintyre begins his provocative book *After Virtue* (1981) with what he refers to as "a disquieting suggestion." He asks us to imagine that in some previous time, now lost to memory, the natural sciences suffered a monumental catastrophe, perhaps at the hands of some know-nothing political movement, in which laboratories were burned down, books and instruments destroyed, and scientific teaching abolished. Much later, according to this fictional account, other more enlightened people undertake the task of rebuilding science, although they have largely forgotten what it was. In doing so, they salvage the charred remains of half-chapters from books, single pages from articles, and instruments whose use they no longer understand. Out of this patchwork of unrelated fragments they struggle to reembody what was once physics and chemistry and biology. Like a cargo cult filled with persons with names like "handle with care" or "this side up," the would-be scientists of this scavenger society learn various incantations about "neutrinos" and "atomic weights," but nobody, or almost nobody, has any grounds for even suspecting that such sloganeering does not sum to the actual doing of natural science in any proper sense at all. That is, the fragmented thinking of the persons living in such a disordered culture would need to be numbered among the symptoms of the disaster whose consequences they were trying to overcome, and as a result, the magnitude and perhaps even the very occurrence of the catastrophe they had suffered would inevitably prove invisible to them.

The point that Macintyre wishes to advance through his account of this imaginary world inhabited by fictitious pseudoscientists blind to their own fate is that in the actual contemporary world we inhabit our own conception of morality is in the same state of grave disorder as the conception of natural science in the imaginary world he describes. Although he does not propose that the earlier fabric of some more coherent moral order actually underwent precisely the same salutary collapse described in his fictional account, he does seriously wish to suggest that something amounting to such a catastrophe did unfold over a much longer period of time, leaving us

121

with a contemporary conception of morality that has been fragmented to the point that we no longer have the moral means to recognize the disaster that has befallen us.

My own reasons for repeating this cautionary tale are much the same in form if not in content and are intended to prepare the way for a similar line of argument regarding our contemporary conceptions of knowledge and what it could possibly mean to be wise. In a way that is intended to parallel Macintyre's account of the collapse of a once more inclusive and more integral moral order, I will argue, following Habermas (1970), that our modern conception of the knowing process is a much fragmented and highly restricted version of a once much more elaborated conceptual scheme that held a meaningful place for a whole panoply of possible knowledge forms and provided real room for both the notion of wisdom and the existence of wise persons (Marcel, 1951).

Both Marcel (1951) and, in a more general form, Habermas (1970) have argued that the intellectual conditions of modern life have fostered a dismissive attitude toward alternative modes of knowing and sponsored a tendency to equate all legitimate knowledge with the products of scientific activity. Although not easily summarized, the essence of Habermas's position on this topic is that the knowing enterprise requires being understood as a pluralistic undertaking mediated by what he characterizes as technical, practical, and emancipatory knowledge-constitutive interests. Technical interests, which he describes as mediating our understanding of natural events, are described as having their prescientific roots in attempts at mastery over nature through labor and as extending in modern times into a science that is concerned with predicting and controlling natural events. Practical interests, by contrast, are portrayed as those cognitive concerns primarily at work in the intersubjective domain focally concerned with the maintenance of social and communicative practices and commonly manifested in the study of history and in the arts. Finally, emancipatory interests are seen by Habermas as being concerned with freedom that is achieved by transcending both the preoccupations with biological preservation that mark technical interests and the dependency on social-historical configurations that mark practical interests. Emancipation, then, is portrayed as a movement to free oneself from both the arbitrary forces of nature and the social structures that limit self-understanding.

Like Macintyre, I will undertake to trace responsibility for the collapse of this once more inclusive view to a dramatic turn of historical events that largely abolished much of what the concept of knowledge was formerly understood to include. Similar claims will also be made that because this revolutionary change occurred before, or largely before, the founding of an academic psychology, most of the ensuing accounts of the knowing process generated by the discipline have derived from what were already highly restricted forms of conceivable knowledge, rendering our own sustaining hand in this affair largely invisible.

Finally, it needs to be pointed out that a prerequisite for understanding the disordered state of Macintyre's imaginary world, and by implication our own, was a history that had to be written in three distinct stages. In the imaginary case of the natural sciences the first stage was that in which such sciences flourished, the second that in which they suffered catastrophe, and the third that in which they were restored but in a damaged and distorted form. The argument to be pursued here necessarily follows a similar itinerary. In brief, Stage I in this train of real events is held out as largely identical with the history of philosophy, at least until the threshold of the 19th century. During this protracted period elaborating the many possible forms of conceivable knowledge was philosophy's primary task and the study of wisdom its characteristic endeavor. Stage II, as philosophers of history such as Marcel (1951) and Habermas (1970) have made us aware, was made up of a string of intellectual disasters, perhaps due in part to "capitalism" or the industrial revolution, and brought to a fine point by a variety of "positivistic" philosophers of science whose legislative brand of "scientism" (Habermas, 1970) succeeded in largely ruling out of court all possible forms of knowledge save a neutered brand of technical expertise that renders the concept of wisdom essentially meaningless. By this account we are currently living through the dark ages of Stage III, and our difficult task is to somehow bootstrap ourselves out of our present truncated conception of knowledge and into a position that allows for the possibility of understanding the proper place of wisdom in the process of successful aging. The pages that follow are meant to contribute to this bootstrapping operation.

## An orientation to the present chapter

The existence of this volume and numerous other recent articles on the same subject stands as testimony to a felt need on the part of many life span developmental psychologists. What is generally experienced as missing by all of these authors is some serviceable way of considering the optimistic prospect that there might still be room for intellectual development beyond adolescence. One contingent of this new work force is busy with the task of trying to identify possible cognitive changes in the postadolescent period immediately following the consolidation of the familiar structures of formal operational reasoning (e.g., Commons, Richards, & Armon, 1984).

A second group, whose efforts are the principal subject of this chapter, has been more concerned with trying to pin down some optimal end state to successful intellectual development by salvaging from the ashes of an older but now derelict intellectual tradition remnants of what might still be known about becoming wise. These rehabilitative efforts have commonly pursued one or another or both of two approaches. The first amounts to a kind of intellectual archaeology concerned with gleaning through the vestiges of an older wisdom tradition that rose and fell largely before psychology's emergence as a separate discipline. Unlike Macintyre's hypothetical case, the products of various earlier efforts to explicate the meaning of wisdom were not in fact literally destroyed but only removed from lists of recommended readings. Consequently, those concerned with rehabilitating such vestigial ideas are free to rummage through stacks of largely noncirculating volumes and dust off what earlier generations once had to say on the subject of wisdom. The second of these search strategies is more empirical and arises as an option as a consequence of the fact that there tends to be more inertia in the corpus of common languages than is true of the lexicons of scientific discourse, which are often subjected to a seasonal house cleaning. One consequence of this lack of parallelism is that although early psychologists worked hard to root out of their technical vocabularies what had come to be perceived as a thicket of unconscionably vague central state notions, persons on the street did not and so went right on talking about wise actions and wise people in general ignorance of the fact that doing so was no longer fashionable among those moving in presumably more sophisticated scientific circles. As a result, there are good reasons to assume that still sedimented within the common language are ideas about what it might mean to be wise that can be profitably mined by those newly interested in recovering some systematic understanding of the concept.

Some part of my own research efforts, and those of my colleague Stephen Holliday, have included attempts to pursue these two lines of possible inquiry by both rummaging through older writings on the subject of wisdom and developing systematic strategies for querying ordinary people about what they understand wisdom to mean. A progress report on these efforts will make up a large part of the details of this chapter. Because there is nothing especially unique about deciding to look things up or ask when you do not know, however, it should come as no surprise that other investigators (e.g., Brent & Watson, 1980; Clayton & Birren, 1980; Dittmann-Kohli & Baltes, 1985; Meacham, 1983; Thorngate, 1981) have adopted much the same research strategy by also attempting to get at what earlier experts and contemporary laypersons have judged to be prototypically wise. Some comparison of our own findings with those of others involved in this same enterprise consequently is required. In carrying out this comparative analysis, special attention will be focused on the recent work of Baltes and his Berlin colleagues (e.g., Baltes, Smith, Staudinger, & Sowarka, in press; Dixon & Baltes, 1986), both because their research program has been particularly ambitious and because it has been used to promote an account of wisdom importantly different from the one to be advocated here.

## Stage I: a backward glance at wisdom's golden age

While modernity, at least Western modernity, has taken a rather jaundiced view of wisdom, seeing the classic quest after its meaning as a kind of fool's errand, best left to those in the business of compiling almanacs and penning messages for fortune cookies, quite the opposite was true during the centuries immediately preceding the emergence of psychology as an independent discipline, an extended period during which the study of wisdom was widely understood as the primary task of philosophers and an intellectual obligation upon all thoughtful persons. In an earlier backward glance into this previous intellectual tradition Holliday and I (Holliday & Chandler, 1986) distinguished and attempted to summarize three closely interwoven strands of thought concerned with the fundamental questions of: What can I know; what ought I do; and what may I hope? By this earlier account, the first and most widely discussed of these questions, which focuses primarily upon matters of learning and erudition, gradually became a primary concern of professional philosophers, who came to equate wisdom with various heady, theoretically oriented enterprises aimed at achieving abstract insights into what were imagined to be the formal structures of the world. Although also initially committed to addressing questions pertaining to the ability to judge rightly in matters related to prudent conduct and to the setting of virtuous goals, philosophic interests in these pragmatic and emancipatory matters progressively came to take a back seat and were eventually subordinated to the goal of developing formal investigatory systems. There still survive, of course, fragments of even older religious and secular wisdom traditions that attempt to convey, through various parables, proverbs, and wise sayings, distilled answers to more pragmatic and value-laden questions concerning matters of hope and correct living. As Marcel (1951) has pointed out, however, these old saws gradually fell into disrepute in a modern technical world that has as its primary aim the rapid development of circumscribed skills and techniques capable of increasing our dominance over the natural world.

Taken together, these historical trends all but guaranteed the modern eclipse of the notion of wisdom. Abstract philosophic concerns about wisdom, defined as a search for underlying essences, came to have little place in a world where all such essences had been happily traded in for more manageable and measurable surface manifestations. By the same token, once highly prized advice about likely routes to human happiness or appropriate means to good ends came to sound cliché, worn, and platitudinous in a contemporary world relentlessly committed to a form of technical progress viewed as independent of all value considerations. Wisdom, then, by this account, was already "on the ropes" by the middle of the past century. A further account of the final killing blows that eventually floored the classic wisdom tradition is the subject of the section to follow.

## Stage II: a description and postmortem of wisdom's sudden demise

Despite, then, what amounts to more than 2,000 years of written history in which the concept of wisdom has played a central part, the notion appears to have essentially vanished from the modern scientific scene. In psychology, at least, this disappearance has been all but complete. One measure of this total turnabout can be had by checking the indexes of psychological texts written in the past 50 years, most of which skip blithely from "WISC" to "wish fulfillment" without so much as a fare-thee-well to "wise" or "wisdom." Similarly, neither the *Psychological Abstracts* nor any of the several popular dictionaries of psychological terms contain any mention of "wisdom" as a category of possible interest. What seems required in the face of this sudden disappearance is a kind of coroner's inquest aimed at unearthing whatever Macintyreian disaster is responsible for having erased all traces of the notion of wisdom from the modern register of legitimate scientific concerns.

Without presuming this analysis to be exhaustive, at least three deeply interrelated factors can be identified that together may help to account for this modern eclipse of the study of wisdom. Central among these factors has been the late 19th and early 20th century tendency to equate the whole of human knowledge with the sum of those empirical facts obtained through applications of the methods of natural science inquiry. From the monopolistic vantage of this positivistic view of science only direct perception can lead to legitimate knowledge, and any pretense that things might be otherwise tends to be dismissed as misguided. The general effect of this insistence that all clear and distinct knowledge must coincide with those products of objective inquiry generated according to the logic of science has been to immunize modern thought against the possibility that wisdom might still somehow count as a legitimate knowledge form.

A second factor, largely derived from the first, which has served to all but guarantee that the concept of wisdom would play only the most marginal of roles in modern thought, has been 20th century psychology's romance with behaviorism. As Brunswik (1952) and many others have made clear, vague central state notions such as wisdom were just the sort of excess baggage held responsible for philosophy's announced failure to accompany the natural sciences into the apparent progress of the 20th century (Holliday & Chandler, 1986). Wisdom and other similarly "metaphysical" central state notions, once thought to occupy procedurally inaccessible regions of the body, consequently were accorded the status of so many indwelling spirits (Skinner, 1953) and permanently struck from the list of authorized research topics.

Finally, the technological era ushered in by the industrial revolution also promoted a penchant for machine metaphors that has seriously undermined the credibility of wisdom or any other positive construct historically associated with persons of advanced age (Marcel, 1951). Planned obsolescence is an

accepted standard of our modern industrial age, and any concept that threat-
ens to promote the idea that an otherwise derelict population of elderly
persons might somehow exhibit progressive forms of psychological functioning
is seen automatically as a kind of fairy story.

While the set of forces outlined in the preceding have summed to something
amounting to disaster for the classic wisdom tradition, it also is important to
temper these fatalistic claims by pointing out that the rumors describing wisdom's premature demises may have been exaggerated. Throughout psychology's history there have always been a few (e.g., Erikson, 1968) for whom
the concept of wisdom functioned as a kind of theoretical anchor point. More
recently, however, psychologists and others in growing numbers also have
come to doubt the correctness of any view that automatically equates knowledge with the empirical-analytic truths of science. Such critics are perhaps to
be forgiven if they question the conclusion that all of the seemingly untrack-
able problems of contemporary life will be solved by still another technological
breakthrough and continue to hold out some hope that there are still deeper
and wiser ways of understanding these problems.

While the contributor list of this volume is largely made up of persons
optimistic enough to spend energy attempting to breathe life back into the
body of the failing concept of wisdom, the potential danger that awaits all
such resuscitative efforts, if we are to continue to take instruction from Macintyre's cautionary tale, is that precisely the same forces that promoted the
original eclipse of this notion will continue to operate to spoil any such re-
constitutive measures. That is, there is a real and present danger that without
some fundamental overhaul in what we are prepared to regard as possible
knowledge forms, the new work in this area will get off on the wrong foot
by falling victim to a kind of assimilation bias that reduces wisdom to some
already familiar and properly sanitized psychological construct such as crystallized intelligence (Cattell, 1971; Horn, 1970) or technical expertise (Baltes
et al., in press). As with members of other such cargo cults, our task in coming
to understand what wisdom might entail is unlikely to be best accomplished
by simply deciding that it is a synonym for some charred psychometric fragment left over from the scorched earth practices of an earlier positivistic
science. Attempting to decide whether this is so is the primary focus of the
following section, which takes up the task of exploring existing Stage III efforts
to salvage and rebuild upon an earlier wisdom tradition.

## Stage III: the new wisdom revival

Whatever the prior status of an earlier wisdom tradition, the future shock
that has accompanied the technical progress of the last century has served,
according to critical theorists such as Habermas (1970), to stun us into the
false expectation that all hopes for solutions to society's problems lie along

a path paved with empirical facts. Because such facts would appear best assembled by a youthful breed of psychometric athletes especially skilled at inventing such technical solutions, little hope is held out for the prospect that elderly persons, best known for their preoccupation with a discarded past, are likely to contribute to this endeavor. Wisdom, if it has retained any meaning at all, is generally thought best understood as a kind of vestigial organ of the mind, still relevant only within those few remaining folk cultures that have not as yet joined the modern technological revolution. This, then, is how things have been and would likely have remained had it not been for certain unanticipated perturbations in the population growth curve that have made aging a growth industry and added new legitimacy and new incentives to the search for some up side to the otherwise downward spiral of getting old. As a consequence of this and perhaps other less pecuniary climatic changes, the intellectual atmosphere surrounding gerontologic studies has taken a recent turn for the best. Spurred along by this newly recovered interest in "successful aging" (Baltes, 1987), the once moribund topic of wisdom recently has streaked ahead to become one of the most promising dark horses in adult development's stable of new constructs. In the place of the previously sanctioned view that older persons are somehow intellectually derelict, such changes have prompted a variety of contemporary authors to reconsider the prospect that getting older need not necessarily mean getting worse and to begin to search out ways in which the intellectual functions of the elderly might be different from and yet not automatically inferior to those practiced by younger persons.

One of the first steps taken in this new enterprise has involved various efforts to hold up to more careful methodologic scrutiny all of those older data that had contributed to the conviction that psychometric intelligence was on some automatic slow slide into senility. Armed with their newly found optimism on the behalf of the elderly and prompted by their suspicion that the typically substandard test performance of older persons might prove to be an artifact of poorly conceived measurement and sampling practices, this new breed of life span developmental psychologists began to amass evidence that eventually demonstrated that seniors typically retain at least a subset of their intellectual faculties and often only appeared to become enfeebled because of biased testing practices and invidious cohort comparisons (Labouvie-Vief & Chandler, 1978). While clearly this was progress, it was recognized to fall importantly short of constituting any positive endorsement of the prospects of getting old. What seemed required instead of, or in addition to, these still apologetic findings was some new line of evidence capable of making the case that there might be intellectual advantages to as well as compensations for getting older. Enter wisdom, stage left.

The general prospect that getting wise might prove to be that good intellectual thing available to persons of a "certain age" but not to their junior counterparts was a natural, even for those of us living through a historical period in which wisdom, along with God and other such arcane things, had been declared officially dead. Wisdom, or what we remember of it, was known to occasionally come out of the mouths of babes, but more generally, if it was to appear at all, it was meant to especially characterize those who already had lived for a very long time, and so the prospects for this line of reasoning have seemed especially good. The problem, of course, is that if Macintyre is right, we have not only forgotten what it might mean to be wise, and largely forgotten the intellectual disaster that brought us to this know-nothing state, but are also cognitively poorly prepared to recognize an act of wisdom even if confronted with it directly. Consider the following hard cases:

1. Washed up upon an otherwise pristine shore an isolated cult of postmodern psychologists stumbles upon a crate of bumper stickers saying things like "you're not getting older, you're getting better" and "wisdom is never having to say your senile." Much later representatives of the religion founded upon these castaway items make a bid to infiltrate some learned society concerned with successful aging, and we are cast in the role of sergeant at arms, charged with the task of blocking these interlopers at the door; change of scene.

2. This time it is Polonius undertaking to advise us about how we should live. "To thine own self be true" he suggests, followed by "Neither a borrower nor a lender be" (Hamlet: Act I, Scene III) and still other worn clichés and tired platitudes that may simultaneously express enduring truths about the human situation (Kekes, 1983).

3. Finally, Tolstoy's (1974) Ivan Ilyich, on his deathbed, is filled with terminal self-doubt but skillful in the performance of his official duties until the end: cheerful, worldly, sociable, clever, expert Ivan, tragically uncertain that his life was really a life worth living.

Clearly, the problem is in knowing how to decide. Are Ivan and Polonius actually wise, or is it that Ivan is to be pitied and Polonius simply tolerated as a fool because he has only learned to say all the things a wise person might say on a more auspicious occasion? Ivan certainly knows, as John Meacham's (1983) definition of wisdom requires, that he has failed to understand and so might qualify as wise by that negative standard. Similarly, Polonius, although obviously ignorant about certain matters, is still a specialized expert, full of technically detailed and hard-won knowledge about the pragmatics of living, and so might make it under the definitional wire of wisdom currently being promoted by Baltes and his colleagues (i.e., Baltes et al., in press; Dixon & Baltes, 1986). Shakespeare and Tolstoy, both of whom coincidently lived through historical periods less blind to the possibility of wisdom than our own, would of course be disappointed in us for missing the point of their stories, but still by some current criteria Ivan and Polonius do legitimately qualify.

The cargo cult of would-be life span psychologists is a harder case still. The problem is that these devotees do not claim to be personally wise but only to have empirically stumbled upon evidence regarding wisdom's true meaning.

What needs to be decided here is whether or not they got it right. While we may not be especially impressed by the flotsam and jetsam evidence upon which they stake their claims, there is nothing especially unusual about this since theorists of different persuasion rarely have much respect for evidence said to support conclusions different from their own. What we are left with, then, as is almost always true, is the responsibility for bringing forward a more persuasive set of data than what is otherwise casually carried in by the tide.

## Contemporary wisdom research

Almost without exception the handful of investigators who have undertaken to get some fix upon the possible meaning of wisdom have followed a common course by undertaking to resurrect whatever residual knowledge may lie sedimented within the common language conceptions of ordinary persons by carrying out some form of survey of their opinions. Clayton and Birren (1980), for example, used a multidimensional scaling procedure in an effort to identify factors underlying common perceptions of wisdom. Brent and Watson (1980) asked their subjects to describe wise people and then undertook to group the attributes named into related clusters. Holliday (1981) employed common language Q-sort items that subjects were asked to distribute over a set of target persons labeled as simply "old," "intelligent," or "wise." Finally, both the Berlin group (i.e., Baltes et al., in press) and Holliday and Chandler (1986) capitalized on categorization theory models (Rosch, 1975) and prototype analyses as techniques for soliciting information about the ordinary ways in which persons distinguish wise individuals from members of other closely adjoining categories.

Although, as one would naturally expect, the various samples of individuals studied and the various survey techniques employed by these several groups of investigators did not generate perfectly identical lists of descriptors, the more impressive fact is the degree of actual overlap that was obtained. Considered on an item-by-item basis there is little reason to suspect that the subjects of these various studies would have found very much to disagree with one another about, which, of course, is as it should be if there really exists some discriminating and prototypically well-organized conception of what it means to be wise.

Where these several studies do importantly differ is with regard to the ways in which these first-order data are imagined to somehow "organize themselves." A simple head count of the number of importantly different dimensions or clusters or factors these various groups have turned up is somewhat instructive in this regard. Baltes and his colleagues (i.e., Baltes, Dittmann-Kohli, & Dixon, 1984; Baltes et al., in press; Dixon & Baltes, 1986; Smith, Dixon, & Baltes, 1989; Sowarka, 1987) manage to fit their data to a *two*-factor or "dual process" model concerned with the "mechanics" as opposed to the "pragmatics" of intelligence. Clayton and Birren's (1980) data indicated *three* distinct clusters of attributes that defined for them what are cognitive, affective, and reflective dimensions of wisdom. Brent and Watson's (1980) data identified *four* clusters of attributes they labeled person-cognitive, practical experiential, interpersonal, and moral-ethical. Finally, Holliday and Chandler (1986) report a total of *five* distinct factors (i.e., exceptional understanding, judgment and communication skills, general competence, interpersonal skills, and social unobtrusiveness) but go on to locate these item clusters along three dimensions they relate to Habermas's (1970) model of technical, practical, and emancipatory knowledge-constitutive interests.

The empirical generalization easily afforded by these several contrastive claims is that it will likely prove always to be the case that there are exactly as many factorally distinct solutions to the structure of wisdom as there are investigative teams at work on the problem. Immediately troublesome as all of this may seem, no one who is at all familiar with the soft and interpretive side of various formal and informal data-clustering techniques is likely to come away too surprised that Baltes and his colleagues, who take their lead from Cattell and Horn's notions of "fluid" and "crystallized" intelligence, should be drawn to a two-factor solution, whereas Holliday and Chandler, whose work betrays a certain snake fascination with Habermas's tripartite model, should eventually settle upon a three-dimensional solution.

Much more meaningful than any such numbers game is a harder question concerning the extent to which the interpretive efforts of these various investigative groups need to be understood as somehow symptomatic of a damaged and distorted form of understanding brought on by the earlier eclipse of our lost wisdom tradition. That is, if there is any inherent rightness to the picture of wisdom's rise and fall from grace painted in earlier sections and if Macintyre's "disquieting suggestion" has relevance to our own circumstances, then it would likely follow that even the best of our current efforts to rehabilitate the concept of wisdom all run the serious risk of mistaking what it means to be wise for some limited and technologic brand of knowing that is more a part of the disease that the concept of wisdom has already suffered than a part of its cure. In an effort to evaluate this dark possibility, the section that follows undertakes a conceptual analysis of the impressive body of work on wisdom now generating from Berlin's Max Planck Institute, not because there is reason to suspect that these investigators are more at risk to mistake diseases for the cures than is anyone else, but because the sheer size of their ongoing effort makes them the best available test case.

### The "dual processing" model

The wisdom project of Baltes and his co-workers has involved two lines of empirical research. The first of these, already discussed briefly in the preceding section, concerns people's understanding of the concept of and their beliefs about the salient characteristics of wisdom and wise persons. The second involves initial attempts to specify behavioral indicators of wisdom and to investigate wise judgment in the context of discourse about difficult life problems (Baltes et al., in press). Both of these aspects of their project are taken up briefly in this section using, when appropriate, the Holliday and Chandler (1986) study as a foil.

In both of these lines of research the work of the Berlin group is informed by what they refer to as a "dual-process framework of intelligence," in which what they call the knowledge-based "pragmatics" of intelligence are juxtaposed with what they take to be its basic "mechanics" (Baltes, 1987; Dixon & Baltes, 1986). In striking this primary dichotomy these authors explicitly draw upon the earlier Cattell–Horn theory of crystalized and fluid intelligence (Cattell, 1971; Horn, 1970) while still making often subtle distinctions between these two models. Based upon their own and others' earlier research, they concede from the outset that younger persons typically display more talent than do older individuals on standard measures of the "mechanics" of intelligence and so are obliged to stake all of their claims about what wisdom might mean on the residual category of pragmatics. Off on this foot, they alternatively define wisdom as either the ability "to exercise *good* [emphasis added] judgment about important matters of life" (Smith, Dixon, & Baltes, 1989) or as a specialized form of old age intelligence (Baltes, 1984) involving *expertise* in a domain having to do with the "fundamental pragmatics of life" (Baltes et al., in press). For good reasons, no formal attempt is made to chart the limits of this domain, but as a way of beginning, it is said to encompass knowledge about the variations and conditions of life span development, human nature and conduct, life tasks and goals, social and intergenerational relationships, and life's uncertainties. Persons who traffic in this domain in ways that reflect wisdom are said to do so because they satisfy the "summative" criteria of showing rich factual and procedural knowledge and of approaching uncertain matters in ways that are both contextualized and relativized.

As these authors point out, "There are many ways of carving up the conceptual space of intelligence, and all are more or less useful" (Dixon & Baltes, 1986, p. 221). On the basis of similar generous sentiments, there is no special quarrel to be had here with the usefulness of this dual process model, particularly if it is judged, as it has a right to be, on its success at stimulating research. The real concern that does remain has more to do with the question of whether there is any room within such an interpretive framework for any kind of followable or familiar conception of wisdom as it is popularly understood.

So long as they are reasonably clear and consistent, people are, of course, in some sense free to use words such as *wisdom* in any way they like; in just the same way as they can, if they choose, name their children things like "handle with care" and "this side up." On these grounds Baltes and his colleagues are at least as clear and consistent as anyone else working on this thorny problem and so perhaps should be left to go about their business as they see fit. If, however, Macintyre's cautionary tale has relevance here, it is important to ask whether a model whose key concepts are "expertise" and "specialization" (Dixon & Baltes, 1986) also leaves a meaningful place for concepts such as wise and wisdom as ordinarily understood. In the postapocalyptic world left over after wisdom's mid–19th century demise, numerous things still remain possible. Those living through this neopositivistic period:

1. are still free to amass "rich stores of factual and procedural knowledge" (Baltes et al., in press);
2. are licenced to accumulate "elaborate repertoires" of "action plans, scripts and heuristics" useful for "speeding up" their "production systems" (Smith et al., 1989);
3. are allowed to become "expert" in "specialized" solutions to well-structured problems (e.g., typing) (Baltes, 1987); and
4. may even learn to cast appraising (but not truly evaluative) judgments such as "this is a *good* (i.e., sound, effective, practical, action-guiding) instance of that" (Baltes et al., in press).

Best of all, they are still in the running to:

5. become "world record" holders in areas where they are not otherwise pressed by more youthful contenders (Baltes et al., in press).

Were it not for the puzzling fact that the doing of all of these technical, expert, and specialized things was being promoted as the new definition of wisdom, the open question would remain – can such persons still become wise? Ivan Ilyich and Polonius would no doubt qualify by such standards. Both have their own specialties, both their hard-won areas of expertise, and Polonius, at least, is if anything overfilled with wise council and good advice. In point of fact, however, the real problem, as Kekes (1983) reminds us, is in learning how to avoid confusing truly wise persons with just such local experts, narrow specialists, and purveyors of esoteric information. The contemporary woods, as everyone knows, are full of technical experts of narrowly specialized skill whom we would never suspect of being wise. Academics and other bookish types, who are forever being reminded of how little else they know, need hardly also be reminded of this distinction. But imagine your surprise when, upon reaching that Himalayan mountain or that damp cave where truly wise persons are purported to live, you are told that the particular expert on your particular problem in living happens to reside on the next mountain or in the next cave. The obvious reason that you would be taken aback is that wisdom, to the best of our memories, has nothing to do with narrow forms of specialized and restricted expertise and everything to do with a broader form of human understanding capable of cutting across unique particulars in order to arrive at some view that has the widest scope of possible application. Again, as Kekes (1983) reminds us, becoming wise is not a matter of learning new esoteric truths but one of rediscovering the significance of old truths that, at some level, everybody already knows.

The point being driven home here has not escaped the attention of the Berlin group. Dixon and Baltes (1986), for example, point with some concern to the fact that the notion of cognitive expertise has its roots in studies of performance in comparatively well-structured formal domains such as chess, physics, and mathematics and wonder aloud by what criteria we should judge expertise in things like music composition or painting. Actually the answer to this question is straightforward: The "expert" painter is a talented copyist whose specialized skills are relatively easily judged. The hard question is by what criteria we should judge the great or creative painter. If philosophers such as Churchland (1984) are correct, the approach required in considering such ill-structured questions relies upon cognitive processes far removed from those needed to solve more straightforward "puzzles" of the sort having to do with "expert" painters and composers.

A similar premonition that their enterprise might somehow have gotten off on the wrong foot is reflected in the concern expressed by Baltes et al. (in press) that the finding of their colleague Sowarka (1987), indicating that wise people also have "excellent character," does not fit comfortably into their model. Much the same concern is also in order regarding a large number of highly prototypically rated descriptors of wise people (i.e., tolerant, humble, moral, etc.) identified by Holliday and Chandler (1986) and others, that would also be difficult to account for in any system that defines wisdom only as a state of cognitive expertise.

Much the same point could be made with reference to the Berlin group's handling of the notion that wise persons are a source of "good" judgment regarding the conduct of life. Within the interpretive content of their value-neutral dual processing model the only available meaning of the word *good* is as a synonym for appraising terms such as "sound, effective, practical, and action-guiding" (Dixon & Baltes, 1986, p. 225). This is precisely the sort of good (read prudent and practical) life that finally drove Ivan Ilyich to despair (Kekes, 1983) and not at all an answer to our own and Habermas's (1970) question about the good things for which we might hope.

Finally, before going on to soften what is perhaps too pointed a critique of the Berlin group's position, it is worth briefly considering the second phase of their ongoing wisdom project concerned with their attempts to specify behavioral indicators of wisdom by sampling people's judgments about difficult life problems. In their initial empirical efforts these authors (Smith, Dixon, & Baltes, 1989) have involved subjects of different ages in a "thinking-aloud" procedure that requires them to work through several hypothetical life-planning problems. The protocols resulting from these interviews are then analyzed in terms of five criteria (rich factual knowledge, rich procedural knowledge, relativism, contextualism, and uncertainty) chosen to define wisdom-related knowledge. Although, to date, the results generated by this procedure have produced little in the way of significant age cohort differences, at least it has proved to be the case that some of the older subjects in these studies were among the top performers (Baltes, 1987).

The problem here is in knowing what to make of such data. Two general sorts of problems present themselves. The first centers upon what Kekes (1983) labels the "Polonius-Syndrome" and concerns again the now overworked point that "a fool can learn to say all the things a wise man says and to say them on the same occasions" (Kekes, 1983, p. 286). The second centers on the fact that decisions about what is wise and what is foolish can rarely be accomplished in advance. As Freeman (1985) points out, we often find ourselves celebrating after the fact someone's good or wise judgment in having elected to pursue a course that, at the time it was taken, we were absolutely convinced was foolish. That is, the question of whether a particular choice of actions is or is not wise simply may not belong to that category of things that lend themselves to being decided or recognized in advance. As Freeman (1985) has shown, there exist whole constellations of contextualized and time-bound events whose cohesive pattern is not manifestly or nakedly "there" for us to observe or verify at the time but rather whose intelligibility is only detectable in retrospect after everything is said and done. Matters requiring such historical forms of explanation do not adhere, then, to normal criteria of predictability or verifiability but need to conform instead to standards of intelligibility and public acceptability that are not simply equivalent to prediction turned upside down. The existence of such pattern explanations are relevant to the present discussion in two ways. First, the possibility is worth considering that being especially competent in rendering such cohesive patterns through an active process of after-the-fact translation may itself prove to be an important part of what it means to be wise. Others (e.g., Neugarten, 1969) have frequently commented upon the fact that whereas the outlook of youth is commonly forward in time, the orientation of older individuals tends to be fundamentally retrospective in character. If pattern or historic explanation depends upon such a looking back over the flow of past events, then there is in this fact a potentially new way of understanding why wisdom is the all-but-exclusive province of persons of "a certain age." Second, if it should prove to be the case that not only wisdom in general but also individual wise acts take on their proper meaning only retrospectively, then any plan to develop testing procedures of the sort promoted by Smith, Dixon, and Baltes (1989), which depend upon deciding in advance which problem solutions are wise and which are not, will ultimately flounder for lack of available scoring criteria.

In brief summary, then, the efforts of Baltes and his colleagues to both define wisdom as a feature of crystallized intelligence and develop procedures for its measurement, although clearly straining the envelope of older monopolistic one-note conceptions of possible knowledge forms, still suffer an eventual contortion back into the shape of limited technical expertise. The focus of this group upon matters of practical knowledge and its emphasis upon the pragmatic resolution of life issues does go some important distance toward breaking faith with traditional psychometric conceptions of intelligence, consequently clearing some room for the possible reemergence of a viable conception of wisdom. In the end, however, this insight seems to devolve back into another only slightly modified species of other predominantly technical accounts of possible knowledge according to which wisdom amounts to no more than the simple accumulation of esoteric information or expertise, where the good life is confounded with the prudent life and where standard psychometric ploys permit wise persons to be picked out of the crowd.

The open question, in light of all of the concerns raised in this section, is in what sense the Holliday and Chandler (1986) study imagines itself to escape the same difficulties. Both sets of authors inhabit the same postapocalyptic dark age, belong to the same cargo cult, and are equally handicapped by their inherited inability to either fully recall the disaster that was visited upon their intellectual forebears or effectively recover an older and less confining conception of knowledge or wisdom. Both proceeded in roughly the same fashion, collected highly similar data sets, and analyzed their findings with nearly identical statistical procedures. Given all of these near identities, the likely answer should be and is that in most of their details these two studies are much more similar than different. Where they do tend to part company is with regard to the particular procrustian bed into which they attempted to tuck their findings. In the place of the Berlin group's "dual processing" framework, the Holliday and Chandler findings were seen to better conform to Habermas's (1970) triumvirate of technical, practical, and emancipatory forms of knowledge-constitutive interests. Before undertaking to justify this interpretive choice, however, it is better to begin with what was done and what was found.

## The Holliday–Chandler study

In this research (Holliday & Chandler, 1986), only a part of which will be described here, a series of separate studies involving approximately 500 subjects was carried out in an effort to collect and analyze people's common language descriptions of wise people and to evaluate how such conceptions influence their problem-solving efforts. The primary goal of this series of studies was to test the hypothesis that the terms wise and wisdom, as commonly used, reference a constellation of coherently organized and psychologically meaningful attributes and behaviors that include but are not coextensive with what it means to be simultaneously old and intelligent. Employing a Roschian framework of interpretation (Rosch, 1975) and trading upon the methods and procedures of others who had already attempted similar prototype approaches to the study of other psychological descriptors (i.e., Broughton, 1984; Buss & Craik, 1981; Cantor & Mischel, 1979; Neisser, 1979; Sternberg, Conway, Ketron, & Bernstein, 1981), an attempt was made to determine:

1. whether wisdom can be construed as a prototype-organized concept;
2. whether such a prototype is consistent across age groups;
3. whether the concept of wisdom is held importantly distinct from other partially overlapping constructs; and
4. what particular shape the underlying dimensions of the structure of this prototype take.

In the first study of this series 150 individuals representing three age cohorts (young adults, middle-aged adults, and senior citizens) were asked to generate multiple lists of attributes or characteristics judged by them to be especially descriptive of persons who are wise, intelligent, perceptive, shrewd, and spiritual. Subjects of different ages were included in an effort to provide for a test of the cross-generational consistency of the wise prototype. The lists of these descriptors were then distilled through a series of data reduction steps to eventually yield a nonredundant set of the most frequently nominated characteristics. In general, there were no important age cohort differences in these or any subsequent analyses and, as would be expected if some coherent and prototypically organized conception of wisdom actually is sedimented in the natural language, these subjects were remarkably repetitive in what they had to say about wise persons.

In Study 2, which involved another sample, similarly selected by age, the most consistently chosen of the descriptors to emerge from Study 1 (supplemented by a subset of other terms intended to reflect some dominant themes appearing in the psychological and philosophical wisdom literatures) were presented as stimuli to be rated as to how characteristic they were of wise people. In general, subjects of all ages had definite and closely related opinions about these matters, clearly differentiating between what they took to be good, bad, and indifferent descriptions of wise persons. Interestingly, with the single exception of terms drawn from Eriksonian theory, the descriptors characteristic of various formal psychological and philosophical accounts of wisdom but absent from common language descriptions received generally low prototypicality ratings.

The analyses of these prototype ratings yielded a number of converging lines of evidence that, taken together, lend strong support to the hypothesis that wisdom needs to be thought of as a well-defined, multidimensional, prototypically organized competency descriptor. More specifically, a series of five factors emerged from the principal components analysis undertaken on these data. Factor 1, labeled Exceptional Understanding as based on ordinary experience, rested upon items such as "has learned from experience," "sees things in a larger context," and so on. Factor 2, defined by items such as "is a good source of advice" and "understands life" and referred to as Judgment and Communication Skills, focuses on the ability to understand and judge correctly in matters of daily living. Factors 3, 4, and 5, referred to as General Competence, Interpersonal Skills, and Social Unobtrusiveness, rested upon items such as "intelligent" and "educated" (Factor 3), "sensitive" and "sociable" (Factor 4), and "discrete" and "non-judgmental" (Factor 5) and appear in each case to refer to enabling factors people think of as necessary but not especially prototypic aspects of wisdom.

What would appear to be the most important result of these analyses is the general demonstration that people construe this prototype descriptor list in a multidimensional manner and that the specific dimensions of this factor structure are straightforwardly interpretable in terms of recognizable types of psychological abilities. That is, across three generations, respondents to this procedure revealed a complex, multifaceted, but consistent prototypically organized conception of what it means to be wise.

Finally, several analyses were conducted to examine the similarity between wisdom and other conceptually related competency indicators including intelligent, perceptive, spiritual, and shrewd. Here the data made it apparent that these subjects maintained a sufficiently well-differentiated notion of wisdom to allow them to keep clear about the differences assumed to divide wise persons from those who are more simply only intelligent or perceptive or shrewd or spiritual.

These are the data, and now the matter that needs to be settled is how such findings might open some new crack of light into our dark and monopolistic view of knowledge and our consequently stunted conception of wisdom. This task is taken up in the next and final section.

## Moving toward a multidimensional account of wisdom

In contrast to the more straightforwardly univariate account of wisdom offered by the Berlin group that discounts the "mechanics" of intelligence as a young person's game and lays primary responsibility for what it might mean to be wise upon the "pragmatics" of intelligence, the responses of the subjects of Holliday and Chandler's studies were not so easily contained within the horizon of possible meanings afforded by conventional unitary conceptions of empirical-analytic knowledge. Instead, if we are to take seriously the reports of these subjects, their accounts promote a much more elaborated picture. The General Competency factor that emerged, and that shows clear overlap with the common language conception of intelligence, makes it apparent that, for these subjects, a certain continuing facility with a purely *technical* kind of ability, closely akin to the Berlin group's notion of intellectual "mechanics," continues to be a working aspect of their prototype of wise persons. The Judgment and Communication Skills factor would appear to be a close approximation of what Baltes and his colleagues have in mind by their notion of "expertise in the fundamental pragmatics of life" and makes clear contact with more classic conceptions of what Habermas (1970) describes as a second form of pragmatic or practical knowledge. Finally, the Exceptional Understanding factor, which focuses attention upon those interpretive and meta-analytic abilities that allow wise persons to identify essences and to establish life goals and values rather than merely identify simple prudential choices and mundane means–ends relations, points to a third dimension that is especially foreign to modern views that equate all true knowledge with the products of empirical science.

On balance, then, it would appear that the claims about wise persons promoted by our subjects fit awkwardly or not at all within the conventional one-note interpretive framework left over to us after the eclipse of all more classic accounts of possible knowledge forms. Whether this is to be seen as a good or bad thing is likely to prove a function of whether one is largely content with or alarmed by the prospect of living in a world that sees all the solutions to its problems as lying along a course of increased technical expertise. For our own part, Holliday and I fall in the camp of those who are deeply alarmed and look with some hopefulness on the prospect that there may be wise persons who see things within some more expanded framework. Whereas deciding exactly what such a framework might look like is, by definition, a task that necessarily must be left to those who are wise rather than to those who simply study wisdom, some general instruction was taken and a real intellectual debt is owed by us to the work of Marcel (1951) and Habermas (1970), who perhaps more than any others have struggled to recover a broader sense of what it might mean to know.

In particular, Habermas has argued that the modern tendency to see knowledge in terms of technical expertise has obscured the possibility that there actually may be several related forms of what he characterizes as technical, practical, and emancipatory knowledge-constitutive interests. The underlying interest in technical knowledge, he argues, is the need to control the natural environment, and our modern tendency to equate all knowledge with it has blinded us to the need to serve our interests through practical and emancipated modes of knowledge. Of the remaining but often discounted possibilities, he characterizes practical knowledge as involved with our interests in maintaining social and communicative practices. His account of emancipatory knowledge is more elusive but crystallizes around the themes of promoting rather than restricting human possibilities and of finding answers to the question of what we might hope. The point to be made in reciting these aspects of Habermas's theory is that his notions of technical, practical, and emancipatory knowledge-constitutive interest bears a remarkable similarity to the dimensions that appear to make up our common language conception of wisdom. If this is so, wise persons may prove to be those who successfully peer through the gloom of our present dark age and recover some preapocalyptic vision of types of knowledge we have long since forgotten. Such prospects should lend new motivation to those of us interested to learn more about what it might mean to be wise.

## References

Baltes, P. B. (1984). Intelligenz im Alter. *Spektrum der Wissenschaft, 5*, 46–60.

Baltes, P. B. (1987). Theoretical propositions of life-span developmental psychology: on the dynamics between growth and decline. *Developmental Psychology, 23*, 611–626.

Baltes, P. B., Dittmann-Kohli, F., & Dixon, R. A. (1984). New perspectives on the development of intelligence in adulthood: toward a dual-process conception and a model of selective optimization with compensation. In P. B. Baltes & O. G. Brim, Jr. (Eds.), *Life-span development and behavior* (Vol. 6, pp. 33–76). New York: Academic.

Baltes, P. B., Smith, J., Staudinger, U. M., & Sowarka, D. (in press). Wisdom: one facet of successful aging? In M. Perlmutter (Ed.), *Late-life potential*. Washington, DC: Gerontological Society of America.

Brent, S. B., & Watson, D. (1980). Aging and wisdom: individual and collective aspects. Paper presented at the Meetings of the Gerontological Society of America, San Francisco.

Broughton, R. (1984). A prototype strategy for construction of personality scales. *Journal of Personality and Social Psychology, 47*, 1334–1346.

Brunswik, E. (1952). *The conceptual framework of psychology*. Chicago: The University of Chicago Press.

Buss, D., & Craik, K. (1981). The frequency concept of disposition. Dominance and prototypically dominant acts. *Journal of Personality, 48*, 379–392.

Cantor, N., & Mischel, W. (1979). Prototypes in person perception. In L. Berkowitz (Ed.), *Advances in experimental social psychology*. New York: Academic Press.

Cattell, R. B. (1971). *Abilities: their structure, growth, and action*. Boston: Houghton Mifflin.

Churchland, P. M. (1984). *Matter and consciousness*. Cambridge, MA: MIT Press.

Clayton, V. P., & Birren, J. E. (1980). The development of wisdom across the life span: a reexamination of an ancient topic. In P. B. Baltes & O. G. Brim, Jr. (Eds.), *Life-span development and behavior* (Vol. 3, pp. 103–135). New York: Academic Press.

Commons, M. L., Richards, F. A., & Armon, C. (Eds.) (1984). *Beyond formal operations: late adolescent and adult cognitive development*. New York: Praeger.

Dittmann-Kohli, F., & Baltes, P. B. (1985). Toward a neofunctionalist conception of adult intellectual development: wisdom as a prototypical case of intellectual growth. In C. Alexander & E. Langer (Eds.), *Beyond formal operations: alternative endpoints to human development*. New York: Oxford University Press.

Dixon, R. A., & Baltes, P. B. (1986). Toward life-span research on the functions and pragmatics of intelligence. In R. J. Sternberg & R. K. Wagner (Eds.), *Practical intelligence: nature and origins of competence in the everyday world* (pp. 203–234). New York: Cambridge University Press.

Erikson, E. H. (1968). *Identity: youth and crisis*. New York: W. W. Norton.

Freeman, M. (1985). Paul Ricoeur on interpretation: the model of the text and the idea of development. *Human Development, 28*, 295–312.

Habermas, J. (1970). *Knowledge and human interests*. Boston: Beacon Press.

Holliday, S. G. (1981). *A comparison of wise, intelligent and old individuals.* Unpublished manuscript.

Holliday, S. G., & Chandler, M. J. (1986). *Wisdom: explorations in adult competence.* Basel, Switzerland: Karger.

Horn, J. L. (1970). Organization of data on life-span development of human abilities. In L. R. Goulet & P. B. Baltes (Eds.), *Life-span developmental psychology: research and theory* (pp. 423–466). New York: Academic Press.

Kekes, J. (1983). Wisdom. *American Philosophical Quarterly, 20,* 277–286.

Labouvie-Vief, G., & Chandler, M. (1978). Cognitive development and life-span developmental theory: idealistic vs. contextual perspectives. In P. B. Baltes (Ed.), *Life-span development and behavior* (Vol. 1). New York: Academic Press.

Macintyre, A. (1981). *After virtue. A study in moral theory.* London: Duckworth.

Marcel, G. (1951). *The decline of wisdom.* London: Harvill Press.

Meacham, J. A. (1983). Wisdom and the context of knowledge: knowing that one doesn't know. In D. Kuhn & J. A. Meacham (Eds.), *On the development of developmental psychology* (pp. 111–134). Basel, Switzerland: Karger.

Neisser, U. (1979). The concept of intelligence. *Intelligence, 3,* 217–227.

Neugarten, B. L. (1969). Continuities and discontinuities of psychological issues into adult life. *Human Development, 13,* 121–130.

Rosch, E. (1975). Cognitive representations of semantic categories. *Journal of Experimental Psychology: General, 104,* 192–233.

Skinner, B. F. (1953). *Science and human behavior.* New York: Macmillan.

Smith, J., Dixon, R. A., & Baltes, P. B. (1989). Expertise in life planning: a new research approach to investigating aspects of wisdom. In M. L. Commons, J. D. Sinnott, F. A. Richards, & C. Armon (Eds.), *Beyond formal operations II: comparisons and applications of adolescent and adult development models.* New York: Praeger.

Sowarka, D. (1987). *Wisdom in the context of persons, situations, and actions: common-sense views of elderly women and men.* Unpublished doctoral dissertation, Free University of Berlin and Max Planck Institute for Human Development and Education, Berlin, Federal Republic of Germany.

Sternberg, R. J., Conway, B. E., Ketron, J. L., & Bernstein, M. (1981). People's conceptions of intelligence. *Journal of Personality and Social Psychology, 41,* 37–55.

Thorngate, W. (1981). *The experience of wisdom.* Report submitted to the Social Sciences and Humanities Research Council of Canada, Ottawa, Canada.

Tolstoy, L. (1974). The death of Ivan Ilyich. In *The Cossacks and Other Stories* (R. Edwards, Trans.). Harmondsworth, England: Penguin.

# 7    Wisdom and its relations to intelligence and creativity

*Robert J. Sternberg*

When we think of Solomon, we think of him as having been wise. Einstein we remember as intelligent, and Milton as creative. What makes one man wise, another intelligent, and a third creative? Clearly, any one of these men might be remembered for any of these three attributes. Certainly Solomon's solution to the problem of how to determine the true mother of a child was intelligent and creative as well as wise. Einstein's formulation of the theory of relativity bore extraordinary elements of creativity and elements of wisdom as well as of intelligence. And Milton's *Paradise Lost* shows prodigious intelligence and wisdom as well as creativity. Yet, we remember each of these great men for a different attribute. Much as the attributes may overlap, they also seem to have distinctive characteristics that set them apart.

The goal of this chapter is to formulate a theory of wisdom that specifies its common as well as its distinctive attributes with respect to intelligence and creativity. To accomplish this goal, I will draw on two approaches to the study of wisdom: use of implicit theories and use of explicit theories. What, exactly, constitutes an implicit or an explicit theory?

Implicit theories are constructions by people that reside in the minds of these people. They thus constitute people's *folk psychology*. Such theories need to be discovered rather than invented because they already exist, in some form, in people's heads. Discovering such theories can be useful in helping to formulate the common-cultural views that dominate thinking about a given psychological construct, for example, whatever it is that renders descriptions of Solomon as wise, Einstein as intelligent, and Milton as creative. Understanding implicit theories can also help us understand or provide bases for explicit theories. The latter generally provide a deeper understanding of psychological phenomena, although sometimes a less broad one.

Explicit theories are constructions of psychologists or other scientists that are based or at least tested on data collected from people performing tasks

Preparation of this chapter was supported by Contract MDA90385K0305 from the Army Research Institute.

142

presumed to measure psychological functioning. These are the theories that form the basis for countless articles in the various journals of psychology. Explicit theories derive, in large part, from implicit theories of the scientists formulating the explicit theories. To understand current explicit theories fully, one would want to understand the implicit theories from which they derive.

Wisdom has been the subject of both implicit and explicit theorizing, as shown in this volume. Consider some examples of each kind of work.

Clayton and Birren (1980; see also Clayton, 1982) used an implicit-theories approach. They multidimensionally scaled ratings of pairs of words potentially related to wisdom for three samples of adults differing in age (younger, middle-aged, older). In her earliest study (Clayton, 1975), the terms that were scaled were ones such as *experienced, pragmatic, understanding,* and *knowledgeable.* In each study, subjects were asked to rate similarities between all possible pairs of words. The main similarity in the results for the age cohorts for whom the scalings were done was the elicitation of two consistent dimensions of wisdom, which Clayton referred to as an affective dimension and a reflective dimension. There was also a suggestion of a dimension relating to age. The greatest difference among the age cohorts was that mental representations of wisdom seemed to become more differentiated with increases in the age of the subjects.

Holliday and Chandler (1986) also used an implicit-theories approach to understanding wisdom. Approximately 500 subjects were studied across a series of experiments. They were interested in determining whether the concept of wisdom can be understood as a "Roschian prototype" (Rosch, 1975) or a central concept. Principal-components analysis of one of their studies revealed five underlying factors: exceptional understanding, judgment and communication skills, general competence, interpersonal skills, and social unobtrusiveness.

There is very little explicit-theoretical research on wisdom. The most well-known program of such research is that of Baltes and Smith. For example, Baltes and Smith (1987) gave adult subjects life management problems, such as "A fourteen-year-old girl is pregnant. What should she, what should one, consider and do?" and "A fifteen-year-old girl wants to marry soon. What should she, what should one, consider and do?" Baltes and Smith tested a five-component model on subjects' protocols in answering these and other questions. The five components in the model are factual knowledge, procedural knowledge, life span contextualism, relativism, and uncertainty. An expert answer should reflect more of these components, whereas a novice answer should reflect fewer of them. The data were generally supportive of their model.

In this chapter, I will describe my own explorations of wisdom. In the next part of the chapter, I will describe research based on an implicit-theoretical approach. In the subsequent part, I will describe an explicit-theoretical account of wisdom that incorporates the results of the implicit-theoretical account. In the final part, I will summarize the main points of the chapter.

### An implicit-theoretical approach to wisdom

In a series of four experiments plus a prestudy, I sought to understand people's implicit theories of wisdom and its relations to intelligence and creativity (Sternberg, 1986). The project differed from other implicit-theoretical projects in its emphasis on understanding how wisdom relates to intelligence and creativity and in its use of not just lay subjects but also professors of art, business, philosophy, and physics as a basis for comparing implicit theories across domains of inquiry.

*Behavioral listings*

In the prestudy, roughly two dozen each of professors of art, business, philosophy, and physics as well as laypersons were asked to spend a few minutes listing whatever behaviors they could think of that were characteristic of an ideally wise, intelligent, or creative person in their respective fields of endeavor (or, in the case of laypersons, in general). Well over 100 behaviors were obtained from each population.

*Behavioral ratings*

In a first main experiment, 200 professors each of art, business, philosophy, and physics were asked to rate the characteristicness of each of the behaviors obtained in the prestudy from the corresponding population with respect to their ideal conception of each of an ideally wise, intelligent, or creative individual in their occupation. Laypersons (nonstudents) were also asked to provide these ratings but for a hypothetical ideal individual without regard to occupation. Ratings were on a 1 (low) to 9 (high) scale, with a rating of 1 meaning *behavior extremely uncharacteristic* and a rating of 9 meaning *behavior extremely characteristic*. The numbers of respondents per field ranged from 65 to 85. There were 30 laypersons as well. Each participant provided all three ratings in counterbalanced order across subjects.

Mean ratings for wisdom on the 9-point scale ranged from 6.3 to 7.1 with a median of 6.4 across groups, indicating that the listed items did tap wisdom-related behaviors. Subject reliabilities (internal consistency across subjects) by group ranged from .86 to .96 with a median of .94. Item reliabilities, also of the internal-consistency variety, ranged from .89 to .97 with a median of .92. These high reliabilities indicate considerable consistency within occupational group and within the item set, suggesting that the results are interpretable without undue concern about individual differences (within group) or incoherence of the item set.

Correlations were computed across items for the three ratings. These correlations enabled me to determine the extent to which people show similar patterns of item ratings for wisdom, intelligence, and creativity. The patterns of correlation were clear: In each group except philosophy, the highest correlation was between wisdom and intelligence; in philosophy, the highest correlation was between intelligence and creativity. The correlations between wisdom and intelligence ratings ranged from .42 to .78 with a median of .68. For all groups, the lowest correlation was between wisdom and creativity. Correlations between wisdom and creativity ratings ranged from − .24 to .48 with a median of .27. In the middle was the correlation between intelligence and creativity, ranging from .29 to .64 with a median of .55. Perhaps of greatest interest in these correlations is the single negative correlation – that between wisdom and creativity for the business professors. Whereas in other groups these two constructs were seen as weakly positively related, in the business group, they were seen as negatively related. In other words, in the business group, wisdom and creativity were seen as actually somewhat antithetical to each other. For those of us who have spent some time studying managerial intelligence (see Wagner & Sternberg, 1985, 1986), this finding is not surprising, although it is nevertheless disturbing. Managers often tend to see the creative people within an organization as not quite fitting in and certainly not as the people who should be running the organization.

## The structure of wisdom and its relation to intelligence and creativity

In a second experiment, 40 college students were asked to sort three sets of 40 behaviors each into as many or as few piles as they wished. These 40 behaviors in each set were the top-rated wisdom, intelligence, and creativity behaviors from the previous experiment. The sortings were then each subjected to nonmetric multidimensional scaling.

For wisdom, six components emerged. These components, in order of strength, together with behaviors showing the highest loadings, were as follows:

1. *Reasoning ability:* has the unique ability to look at a problem or situation and solve it; has good problem-solving ability; has a logical mind; is good at distinguishing between correct and incorrect answers; is able to apply knowledge to particular problems; is able to put old information, theories, and so forth together in a new way; has a huge store of information; has the ability to recognize similarities and differences; has rationality (ability to reason clearly); makes connections and distinctions between ideas and things.

2. *Sagacity:* displays concern for others; considers advice; understands peo-

ple through dealing with a variety of people; feels he or she can always learn from other people; knows self best; is thoughtful; is fair; is a good listener; is not afraid to admit making a mistake, will correct the mistake, learn, and go on; listens to all sides of an issue.

3. *Learning from ideas and environment:* attaches importance to ideas; is perceptive; learns from other people's mistakes.

4. *Judgment:* acts within own physical and intellectual limitations; is sensible; has good judgment at all times; thinks before acting or making decisions; is able to take the long view (as opposed to considering only short-term outcomes); thinks before speaking; is a clear thinker.

5. *Expeditious use of information:* is experienced; seeks out information, especially details; has age, maturity, or long experience; learns and remembers and gains information from past mistakes or successes; changes mind on basis of experience.

6. *Perspicacity:* has intuition; can offer solutions that are on the side of right and truth; is able to see through things – read between the lines; has the ability to understand and interpret his or her environment.

Comparable components for intelligence were

1. practical problem-solving ability,
2. verbal ability,
3. intellectual balance and integration,
4. goal orientation and attainment,
5. contextual intelligence, and
6. fluid thought.

For creativity, the components were

1. nonentrenchment,
2. integration and intellectuality,
3. aesthetic taste and imagination,
4. decisional skill and flexibility,
5. perspicacity,
6. drive for accomplishment and recognition,
7. inquisitiveness, and
8. intuition.

All three scalings well fit the data, accounting respectively for 87% (wisdom), 82% (intelligence), and 93% (creativity) of the variance in the data.

The obtained dimensions are consistent with the results of the first study, suggesting that in dimensions as in correlations between ratings of behaviors, wisdom and intelligence are closest in character and wisdom and creativity furthest. For example, the first components for each of wisdom and intelligence – reasoning and practical problem-solving ability – are quite similar to each other. Indeed, 5 of the 9 behaviors with the highest positive loadings on the first dimension for intelligence are also among the 10 behaviors with the highest positive loadings on the first dimension for wisdom. In contrast, the first component for creativity – nonentrenchment – is wholly different in its behavioral composition from the comparable components for wisdom and intelligence.

## Correlations with psychometric tests

Multidimensional scaling provides a means of internal validation; that is, it fits a model (multidimensional scaling) to data without respect to how these data relate to any outside measures. But it would be possible to obtain an excellent fit of the model to the data without the data showing any relation to anything outside the study. Hence, it is important to validate data externally as well as internally, showing relations to measures not generated by the theory or method being used within the given paradigm.

In a third experiment, 30 nonstudent adults were asked to fill out the wisdom, intelligence, and creativity questionnaires, but for themselves rather than for some ideal individual. Thus, they indicated the extent to which each behavior characterized themselves. Each subject's pattern of responses was then correlated with the ideal prototype for the given attribute – wisdom, intelligence, or creativity – as obtained in the first experiment. This correlation reveals the similarity between each subject's rating of him or herself and other subjects' ratings of the ideal. The higher the correlation, the closer the subject is to the ideal prototype. The correlation, then, is in a sense a score, indicating the match of the subject in each of wisdom, intelligence, and creativity to a hypothetical ideal for each of these attributes.

Subjects were also given four psychometric tests: the Cattell and Cattell Test of $g$ and the Embedded Figures Test, both commonly used tests of intellectual ability; and the George Washington Social Intelligence Test and the Chapin Social Insight Test, both measures of social judgment, which was believed to be close, although not identical, to wisdom. No creativity tests were used because of my judgment that none of the ones available at the time provided anything approaching an adequate assessment of creativity.

Convergent validity would be indicated by the wisdom prototype-resemblance score showing high correlations with the social judgment tests but low correlations with the intellectual ability tests and the intelligence prototype-resemblance score showing the reverse pattern. In fact, for the wisdom prototype-resemblance score, its correlations were .38 with the George Washington and .46 with the Chapin, both statistically significant. In contrast, the correlations were − .01 with the Cattell and − .14 with the Embedded Figures, neither significant. Thus, the wisdom prototype-resemblance score showed the predicted pattern of correlations. The intelligence prototype-resemblance score correlated .48 with the Cattell and .54 with Embedded Figures, both statistically significant. It also correlated − .06 with the George Washington, which was not significant, but .43 with the Chapin, which was significant. Thus, three of four correlations were as predicted for the intelligence prototype-resemblance score. The creativity prototype-resemblance score was not expected to correlate significantly with any of the psychometric tests, and it did not.

These data indicate a high degree of external (convergent and discriminant) validity for the wisdom prototype-resemblance score. It truly does seem to measure social judgment skills separate from cognitive intelligence, as indicated by its pattern of correlations with the cognitive and social tests.

*Use of prototypes*

The first three experiments suggest that people have prototypes somehow stored in their heads for intelligence and creativity as well as for wisdom. These prototypes are not only internally consistent and sensible but also related externally to psychometric measures targeted to the relevant constructs. But do people actually use these prototypes? It is possible that people have prototypes stored in their heads that are essentially inert. They may be there but unused in ordinary social relations. For the prototypes to have maximum psychological interest, it should be the case that not only do they exist, but they are used as well.

In a fourth experiment, 40 nonstudent adults were presented with 54 simulated letters of recommendation. Consider examples of two such letters:

> *Gerald:* He possesses the ability for high achievement; he has the ability to grasp complex situations; he has good problem-solving ability; he attaches importance to well-presented ideas.
> *Doris:* She is motivated by goals; she questions societal norms, truisms, and assumptions; she thinks quickly; she is not materialistic; she is totally absorbed in study.

Descriptions were generated so as to vary predicted levels of wisdom, intelligence, and creativity. Each description was four, five, or six sentences in length and was paired equally often with names of males and with names of females. A given subject saw a given description only once – either with a male name or with a female name. The subject's task was to rate the wisdom, intelligence, and creativity of each of the described individuals. Ratings were made on a 9-point scale, where 1 indicated that the individual to be rated was not at all wise, intelligent, or creative and 9 indicated that the individual was extremely wise, intelligent, or creative. All subjects rated all descriptions on each of the three attributes.

It was possible to obtain predicted ratings for wisdom, intelligence, and creativity by summing up the ratings of laypersons from the first experiment on each attribute for each described person and then dividing by the number of attributes given for the hypothetical individual. Averages rather than sums of ratings were used because the number of behaviors was not the same for each of the descriptions.

Suppose, for example, that five behaviors were given for Susan. The predicted wisdom ratings would be the mean of the characteristicness ratings for wisdom in the first experiment (plus a constant). The more closely the description of the hypothetical individual resembles the ideal of the first experiment on each of the three attributes, the higher should be the rating that hypothetical individual receives in the present experiment.

First, one can look at the correlations between each possible pair of ratings in order to determine how close each construct is perceived to be to each other construct in the context of recommendation ratings. The correlations between ratings were .94 for wisdom and intelligence, .62 for wisdom and creativity, and .69 for intelligence and creativity. Thus, once again, the highest correlation was that between wisdom and intelligence and the lowest that between wisdom and creativity. In this experiment, the correlation between wisdom and intelligence was particularly high.

We can also compute the correlation between the actual ratings for each attribute and the expected ratings, not only for the corresponding attribute but for the noncorresponding attributes as well. The correlation should be highest for the corresponding attribute. The correlation between wisdom ratings and expected wisdom ratings was .96. The correlation between wisdom ratings and expected intelligence ratings was .88, and that between wisdom and expected creativity ratings was .54. Thus, the expected pattern of convergent-discriminant validity was again shown. Comparable results were obtained for intelligence and creativity. For intelligence, the correlations were .89 with the intelligence prototype, .87 with the wisdom prototype, and .48 with the creativity prototype. For creativity, the correlations were .89 with the creativity prototype, .40 with the wisdom prototype, and .46 with the intelligence prototype. Again, wisdom and intelligence are quite a bit closer than is creativity to either of them.

## Comparisons across domains

It was possible to compare implicit theories of wisdom (as well as of intelligence and creativity) across the domains studied in this research. Implicit theories of wisdom show considerable overlap across fields of specialization. Nevertheless, there are some differences in implicit theories. Art professors emphasize insight, knowing how to balance logic and instinct, knowing how to transform creativity into concepts, and sensitivity. These aspects of wisdom would seem quite relevant in the mature appreciation and evaluation of art. Business professors emphasize maturity of judgment, understanding of the limitations of one's actions and recommendations, knowing what one does and does not know, possession of a long-term perspective on things, knowing when not to act as well as when one should act, acceptance of reality, good decision making, the ability to distinguish substance from style, and appreciation of the ideologies of others. These aspects of wisdom would seem particularly relevant in making and evaluating business decisions. Philosophy professors emphasize balanced judgment, nonautomatic acceptance of the "accepted" wisdom, concentration on fundamental questions, resistance to fads, looking for fundamental principles or intuitions behind a viewpoint, concern with larger purposes, openness to ideas, ability to use facts correctly, avoidance of jargon, possession of a sense of where future progress is possible, unwillingness to become obsessed with a single theory, attention to both detail and scope, and a sense of justice. All of these talents would seem relevant to the construction and evaluation of philosophical arguments. Finally, physicists emphasize appreciation of the various factors that contribute to a situation, familiarization with previous work and techniques in the field, knowing if solving a problem is likely to produce important results, awareness of the important problems in the field, knowledge of the human and political elements of scientific work, contemplation, and recognition of the aspects of physical phenomena that underlie the concepts of physics. These skills would seem to be helpful in attaining a deep understanding of the nature of physics and its place both in science and in the world.

## Implications

The study described in the preceding section suggests that implicit theories can provide a useful way to obtain a "lay of the land" in the search for understanding of wisdom and its relations to intelligence and creativity. The results were construct valid in terms of convergent and discriminant validity and also were consistent with results from other studies of implicit theories. For example, the scaling results for wisdom confirmed and elaborated on those of Clayton and Birren (1980) using the same technique (multidimensional scaling) but a very different method for generating behaviors. My reasoning component closely resembles Clayton and Birren's reflective dimension, and my sagacity component closely resembles their affective one. If wisdom differs from intelligence and creativity, it appears most to differ in the sagacity component, which was clearly unique to the scaling of wisdom.

Studies of implicit theories, by their nature, have limitations. They apply to a given subject population at a given time in a given place. As we have seen, implicit theories differ somewhat even across groups in a given time and place. If studies of implicit theories of intelligence are any indication (see Berry, 1984; Sternberg, 1987), implicit theories of psychological constructs can differ radically cross-culturally and can differ as well across age levels. Moreover, studies of implicit theories tell us people's conceptions of a construct. They may serve as a useful basis for explicit theories of the construct, but they are not themselves explicit theories. My own explicit theory, which draws in part upon the implicit-theoretical results described in the preceding section, is presented in the next part of the chapter.

## An explicit-theoretical approach to wisdom

My goal in this part of the chapter is to present an explicit-theoretical account of wisdom and its relations to intelligence and creativity. I believe it is necessary at the outset to distinguish between two uses of these three terms. One use is what might be referred to as a "narrow" one. The other use is a "broad" one. I believe it necessary to distinguish these two uses because they actually refer to somewhat different senses of the terms, and people can easily talk past each other when they use the same terms to mean different things.

The narrow use of the terms is as descriptors for a set of strictly cognitive abilities that enable behavior that is labeled "wise," "intelligent," or "creative." Such narrow use is the prevalent one in the study of intelligence, going back to psychometric theories of the construct and continuing today even among many information-processing theorists of intelligence (see Sternberg [1977, 1985], for a discussion of these issues). Creativity has also been studied in the narrow sense by those who choose to view it in wholly cognitive terms (e.g., Guilford, 1950). Wisdom does not have a long tradition of empirical research, and a purely cognitive view has never taken off. To the contrary, most of the views expressed in this volume go beyond the strictly cognitive. Rather, they view wisdom in a broad sense.

The broad sense of the terms *wisdom, intelligence,* and *creativity* allows for generation of behavior by psychological elements that need not be strictly cognitive, although cognitive elements may be included. My own theory of intelligence (Sternberg, 1985) would be an example of a broader theory, as would most of the theories of creativity expressed in a book I edited on the topic (Sternberg, 1988c). In my discussion here, I will be using the terms wisdom, intelligence, and creativity in the broad sense. My concern will be with the attributes, external as well as internal, that would lead a person to be labeled as wise, intelligent, or creative. The study of implicit theories showed the terms – particularly wisdom and intelligence – to be overlapping in meaning. I will concentrate on how the terms are distinctive, although I will pay some attention as well to how they are similar.

It is useful to distinguish the concepts of wisdom, intelligence, and creativity in terms of six background variables that lead to the use of one particular term rather than one of the others to label a person. The six background variables are knowledge, cognitive processing, intellectual style, personality, motivation, and environmental context (see also Sternberg [1988b] and Sternberg & Lubart [in press] for how these variables can be applied particularly to the understanding of creativity). The account given in the next section is summarized in Table 7.1.

Table 7.1. *Summary, simplified comparison among wisdom, intelligence, and creativity*

| Aspect | Construct | | |
| --- | --- | --- | --- |
| | Wisdom | Intelligence | Creativity |
| Knowledge | Understanding of its presuppositions and meaning as well as its limitations | Recall, analysis, and use | Going beyond what is available |
| Processes | Understanding of what is automatic and why | Automatization of procedures | Applied to novel tasks |
| Primary intellectual style | Judicial | Executive | Legislative |
| Personality | Understanding of ambiguity and obstacles | Eliminating ambiguity and overcoming obstacles within conventional framework | Tolerance of ambiguity and redefinition of obstacles |
| Motivation | To understand what is known and what it means | To know and to use what is known | To go beyond what is known |
| Environmental context | Appreciation in environment of depth of understanding | Appreciation in environment of extent and breadth of understanding | Appreciation in environment of going beyond what is currently understood |

## Knowledge

Knowledge is important to wisdom, intelligence, and creativity but in different ways.

The wise person is someone who *probes inside knowledge* – who understands the meaning of what is known. This person excels in what is often called metacognition, that is, knowledge about knowledge. Wise people

1. know what they know,
2. know what they do not know,
3. know what they can know given the limitations of present understandings and of knowledge itself, and
4. know what they cannot know, again given the limitations imposed on them (see also Meacham, 1983).

They understand the significance of the knowledge they do and do not and can and cannot have as well as its potential meaning for life endeavors.

The intelligent person is someone who is able to *recall, analyze, and use* knowledge. The person may be characterized by a good memory for knowledge, or by the ability to analyze implications of knowledge, or by the ability to use knowledge effectively. In terms of my triarchic theory (Sternberg, 1985), memory and analysis fall within the "componential domain" and (practical) use within the "contextual domain." Intelligent people may also be able to go beyond existing knowledge (experiential subtheory), but this part of intelligence is the part that overlaps with creativity. Similarly, the analysis of knowledge can overlap with wisdom if that analysis concerns the meaning and presuppositions of what is known.

The creative individual is someone who *goes beyond existing knowledge.* This is the person who creates new knowledge and whose interest in existing knowledge is often primarily in figuring out how to go beyond its limits. The wise person seeks to understand the meaning and limitations of this knowledge. The intelligent person seeks to make optimal use of this knowledge. The creative person, though, wishes to be freed from this knowledge. If we view existing knowledge as setting constraints, much like a prison, we might view the wise person as seeking to understand the prison and just what its boundaries are, the intelligent person as seeking to make the best of life in the prison, and the creative person as seeking to escape from the prison.

## Intellectual processes

The processes of wisdom, intelligence, and creativity are the same. What differs is their use. The componential subtheory specifies a set of mental processes that are common to higher cognitive functioning (Sternberg, 1985). But what sets apart wisdom, intelligence, and creativity is how these processes are applied to experience.

The wise person *resists automatization of thought but seeks to understand it in others.* In what scripted ways do people behave, and why? What are their automatic assumptions and use of assumptions, and why? How will a true mother react to the dismemberment of a baby as opposed to someone who is not a true mother (in the case of Solomon)?

The intelligent person *welcomes automatization.* He or she is intelligent largely by virtue of the number of automatized routines available for information processing. Indeed, it is such routines that are explicitly measured by tests of crystallized intelligence and often implicitly measured by fluid ability tests as well (see Cattell, 1971). Intelligent people can do automatically tasks that for others are controlled and nonroutine. It is for this reason that more intelligent people so often seem to be faster than less intelligent ones.

The creative person eschews automatization but, unlike the wise person, has no great interest in understanding it. Rather, he or she wishes *to go beyond automatization – to deal with the novel,* the nonentrenched. In terms of my experiential subtheory, the wise person seeks to understand automatization, the intelligent person seeks to automatize, and the creative person seeks to resist automatization so as to deal with novelty.

*Intellectual style*

Intellectual style refers to the way a person uses, or directs, his or her intellectual functioning. My own theory of styles is based on a notion of mental self-government, whereby people are viewed as using styles in order actively to govern their thinking and their behavior (Sternberg, 1988a). One aspect of style is particularly relevant in my comparison of wisdom, intelligence, and creativity, namely, the functions of mental self-government.

Governments serve three primary functions: legislative, which is concerned with the formulation of laws and procedures; executive, which is concerned with the execution of laws and procedures; and judicial, which is concerned with the evaluation of laws and procedures and with the evaluation of the extent to which the laws and procedures are being followed. People have predilections for these various styles of functioning. They do not employ one or another style exclusively but rather have a preference toward which they will gravitate when the task or situation renders it possible for them to act upon their preference.

The wise person is someone who is likely to lean toward a *judicial style*. But the person is not simply someone who enjoys evaluation for the sake of passing on what is good and what is bad. Indeed, the evaluations of wise persons are likely to be less explicitly judgmental than those of others. They seek to understand why and what it means that people think what they think, say what they say, and do what they do. They are likely to be much more concerned with understanding a framework for thought, speech, and action than with simply judging it as good or bad.

An intelligent person may have any of the three styles (hence, the overlap between intelligence, on the one hand, and wisdom and creativity, on the other), but traditionally, intelligence is most associated with the *executive style*. In order to see the truth of this statement, one need only look at conventional intelligence tests: All of the tasks are executive, requiring the test taker to accept the terms of the given problem and to solve it. But the wise person is likely to question why the problems even appear on a test of intelligence, whereas the creative person may accept the problems but provide answers that go beyond those of the test constructor in their cleverness or even correctness. Schools, too, for the most part, label people intelligent who prefer the executive style. The good student is the one who does what he or she is told and does it well. Students who question the values or assumptions of assignments or who make assignments into something other than the teacher intended are not likely to be appreciated by their teachers.

The creative person, as implied in the preceding paragraph, is likely to show a predilection for the *legislative style*. This person does not like to be told what to do or how to do it: He or she wants to decide what to do and how to do it. Creative people do not want to be locked into conventional ways of doing things, whereas wise people want to understand these ways of doing things and why people have chosen these ways. The creative person will not always be legislative, but at least in the domain of his or her creativity, the person will want to go beyond where things are, to stretch what is known and even how people think about what is known.

*Personality*

Wise, intelligent, and creative people – to the extent that they are non-overlapping – exhibit somewhat different personality attributes that tend to generate behavior that is labeled in one way or another. I shall be concerned in particular with two related attributes.

Consider first how the individual deals with ambiguity. The wise person *is comfortable with ambiguity* and, indeed, sees it as inherent in virtually all interactions people have with the world. The wise person views him- or herself and others as engaged in an unending dialectic with each other and with the world, with the result that truly nonambiguous situations never exist. Ambiguity is something to be understood, appreciated, and treated as fundamental to the nature of things. Hence, the wise person can be serene in the face of challenges that would distress the less wise.

The conventionally intelligent person is someone who *sees ambiguity as something to be resolved, preferably sooner rather than later.* Ambiguity interferes with optimal problem solving, and hence ambiguities need to be resolved in order to ensure that the solution that is reached for a given problem is indeed an optimal one. If an ambiguity presents itself, it is to be resolved so that it will no longer be a stumbling block to problem solving. Of course, a more broadly intelligent person may understand and appreciate ambiguity (the person who is wise as well as intelligent) or tolerate it (the person who is creative as well as intelligent). But again, how a person reacts will depend upon his or her partaking of just one, or two, or all three of the attributes here under examination.

The creative person learns to tolerate ambiguity, although he or she is uncomfortable with it. Such a person realizes that in creative endeavors, there will be periods of time, sometimes long ones, when things do not quite make sense or do not hang together. The creative person learns that premature closure results in a solution that is less than optimally creative. Hence, ambiguity must be tolerated with discomfort in the hope that it will eventually lead to a creative formulation of the kind being sought.

Consider a second personality attribute, namely, how a person handles obstacles. The wise person seeks to understand obstacles – why they are there, what they mean, how general or specific they are, and what their implications are for others as well as oneself. The intelligent person seeks to get around obstacles within the definition of the problem that presents the obstacles. Thus, he or she will seek ways around the obstacles while acknowledging that there are obstacles to be overcome. The creative person is likely to seek an alternative definition of the problem where the obstacles no longer exist. He or she, in essence, attempts to define away the obstacles by redefining the task at hand.

*Motivation*

I suggest that wise, intelligent, and creative people are motivated by different goals. The wise person is motivated toward deeper understanding and particularly toward understanding the structure, assumptions, and meaning underlying phenomena and events. This person seeks the deepest possible understanding of a phenomenon, even one that may seem mundane to others. The intelligent person is motivated toward understanding of more phenomena. The creative person is motivated toward understanding of new kinds of phenomena, particularly toward new understandings of phenomena. The creative person wants to see things in a way different from the way others see them.

Consider the meaning of personal growth in light of these differences. For the wise person, growth means deeper understanding of phenomena and their meaning. For the intelligent person, growth means understanding of more existing phenomena. For the creative person, growth means understanding of new kinds of phenomena or new understandings of existing phenomena. The creative person is not happy just to understand what others understand: He or she wants to understand what they do not understand, or to understand what they understand but in a different way.

*Environmental context*

Whether or not someone is perceived as wise, intelligent, or creative will depend a great deal on environmental context. If what has been described as wise is valued in an environment, then a person exhibiting these attributes will be labeled as wise. But if these attributes are ignored or even devalued, the person may not be appreciated or may be labeled as a fool or as someone who makes mountains out of molehills or as someone who gets lost in thought. A person who is labeled as intelligent in one environment may be labeled as pretentious, naïve, or useless in another environment. And a person labeled as creative in an environment that rewards the attributes of creativity may be labeled as a behavior problem, a nonconformist, or even an outcast in another. The critical point, of course, is that no matter what internal attributes a person may have, these attributes can be perceived in a variety of ways depending on what is rewarded and punished within a given environment.

## Conclusion

My goal in this chapter has been to convey an implicit-theoretical and an explicit-theoretical account of wisdom. The implicit-theoretical account is based on people's conceptions of the nature of wisdom. The explicit-theoretical account, which draws on the implicit-theoretical one, is my own view of wisdom. In each account, I have analyzed wisdom and how it relates to intelligence and creativity. Wisdom overlaps with intelligence and, to a lesser extent, with creativity. Thus, in discussing the three constructs, one can concentrate either on their areas of overlap or on their areas of uniqueness. I have attempted to discuss both. What appears to be unique about wisdom is what was labeled "sagacity" in the implicit-theoretical account. Sagacity involves more than just cognitive skills. It involves as much an attitude toward knowledge as knowledge itself. In particular, in the explicit-theoretical account of what leads people to be labeled as wise, I have dwelled upon six kinds of antecedents – those of knowledge, intellectual processes, intellectual style, personality, motivation, and context.

The wise person is characterized by a metacognitive stance. Wise people know what they know and what they do not know as well as the limits of what can be known and what cannot be. They apply the processes of intellect in a way that eschews automatization. They recognize that stances and procedures people follow automatically are subject to inherent as well as environmentally imposed limitations. What is automatically considered correct in one time or place can be automatically considered wrong in another time or place because there is an ongoing dialectic that places limitations upon any kind of absolute "correctness." Nevertheless, the wise person seeks truth to the extent it is knowable and evaluates information so as to understand how it relates to truth. Wise people welcome ambiguity, knowing it is an ongoing part of life, and try to understand the obstacles that confront themselves and others in life. They are motivated toward in-depth understanding of phenomena, at the same time that they recognize the limitations of their own understanding. They seek understanding of what will "work" not only for them but for society as well.

The implicit and explicit theories described in this chapter show considerable, although not complete overlap. The group implicit theory is far more detailed with respect to the intellectual side of wisdom, describing in some detail the components of reasoning, sagacity, learning, judgment, expeditious use of information, and perspicacity. The explicit theory is more detailed in specifying noncognitive aspects of wisdom, which tend to be mixed with cognitive ones in the implicit theory. A complete explicit theory of wisdom would have to provide more fine-grained detail than the present explicit theory has.

The account of wisdom given in this chapter is a preliminary one: Indeed, any modestly wise person knows that no account of wisdom is likely ever to be final. But I hope it contributes to the dialogue of wisdom by researchers in their attempts to understand one of the most elusive constructs they can attempt to study.

## References

Baltes, P. B., & Smith, J. (1987, August). *Toward a psychology of wisdom and its ontogenesis.* Paper presented at the Ninety-Fifth Annual Convention of the American Psychological Association, New York City.

Berry, J. W. (1984). Towards a universal psychology of cognitive competence. In P. S. Fry (Ed.), *Changing conceptions of intelligence and intellectual functioning: current theory and research* (pp. 35–61). Amsterdam: North-Holland.

Cattell, R. B. (1971). *Abilities: their structure, growth, and action.* Boston: Houghton Mifflin.

Clayton, V. (1975). Erikson's theory of human development as it applies to the aged: wisdom as contradictory cognition. *Human Development, 18,* 119–128.

Clayton, V. (1982). Wisdom and intelligence: the nature and function of knowledge in the later years. *International Journal of Aging and Development, 15,* 315–321.

Clayton, V., & Birren, J. E. (1980). The development of wisdom across the life-span: a re-examination of an ancient topic. In P. B. Baltes & O. G. Brim (Eds.), *Life-span development and behavior* (Vol. 3, pp. 103–135). New York: Academic Press.

Guilford, J. P. (1950). Creativity. *American Psychologist, 5,* 444–454.

Holliday, S. G., & Chandler, M. J. (1986). *Wisdom: explorations in adult competence.* Basel, Switzerland: Karger.

Meacham, J. A. (1983). Wisdom and the context of knowledge: knowing that one doesn't know. In D. Kuhn & J. A. Meacham (Eds.), *On the development of developmental psychology* (pp. 111–134). Basel, Switzerland: Karger.

Rosch, E. (1975). Cognitive representations of semantic categories. *Journal of Experimental Psychology: General, 104,* 192–233.

Sternberg, R. J. (1977). *Intelligence, information processing, and analogical reasoning: the componential analysis of human abilities.* Hillsdale, NJ: Erlbaum.

Sternberg, R. J. (1985). *Beyond IQ: a triarchic theory of human intelligence.* New York: Cambridge University Press.

Sternberg, R. J. (1986). Implicit theories of intelligence, creativity, and wisdom. *Journal of Personality and Social Psychology, 49,* 607–627.

Sternberg, R. J. (1987). Implicit theories: an alternative to modeling cognition and its development. In J. Bisanz, C. J. Brainerd, & R. Kail (Eds.), *Formal methods in developmental psychology: progress in cognitive development research* (pp. 155–192). New York: Springer-Verlag.

Sternberg, R. J. (1988a). Mental self-government: a theory of intellectual styles and their development. *Human Development, 31,* 197–224.

Sternberg, R. J. (Ed.) (1988b). *The nature of creativity: contemporary psychological perspectives.* New York: Cambridge University Press.

Sternberg, R. J. (1988c). A three-facet model of creativity. In R. J. Sternberg (Ed.), *The nature of creativity: contemporary psychological perspectives* (pp. 125–147). New York: Cambridge University Press.

Sternberg, R. J., & Lubart, T. (in press). An investment model of creativity and its development. *Human Development.*

Wagner, R. K., & Sternberg, R. J. (1985). Practical intelligence in real-world pursuits: the role of tacit knowledge. *Journal of Personality and Social Psychology, 48,* 436–458.

Wagner, R. K., & Sternberg, R. J. (1986). Tacit knowledge and intelligence in the everyday world. In R. J. Sternberg & R. K. Wagner (Eds.), *Practical intelligence: nature and origins of competence in the everyday world* (pp. 51–83). New York: Cambridge University Press.

# 8 The study of wise persons: integrating a personality perspective

*Lucinda Orwoll and Marion Perlmutter*

The primacy of cognitive explanations of wisdom in recent research has failed to incorporate personality prerequisites. Fundamental links between wisdom and adult personality development, elucidated by several personality theorists, are summarized in the first part of this chapter. We identify two key indicators of personality-based wisdom: advanced self-development and self-transcendence. Wisdom depends on an unusually integrated personality structure that enables people to transcend personalistic perspectives and embrace collective and universal concerns. We assume, however, that these personality attributes presuppose complementary cognitive development and that wisdom is rare precisely because it entails both exceptional personality and cognitive growth.

In the second part of this chapter, we propose an empirical approach to the study of wisdom that capitalizes on the integration of personality and cognition by intensively studying adults who are considered wise. In this approach, subject selection is guided by nominations of wise people and measure selection is guided by both cognitive and personality theories. We elaborate how this approach can be applied to the study of wisdom by discussing useful ingredients from several other research traditions. Finally, we provide an empirical foundation for the study of wise people by summarizing current research.

## Personality conceptualization of wisdom

Hypotheses about a personality dimension of wisdom can be drawn from three personality theorists who have dealt explicitly with wisdom: Erikson, Jung, and Kohut. Although these theorists have different orientations to personality (i.e., Erikson's psychosocial, Jung's analytical, and Kohut's object relations), each discussed self-development and self-transcendence as key attributes of the wise personality. These attributes denote an unusually integrated and mature personality structure that transcends preoccupation with self-referent thoughts and feelings and structures interactions with self, others, and the world.

160

## Self-development

Self-development helps define the personality component of wisdom. For Erikson (1968, 1978, 1982; Erikson, Erikson, & Kivnick, 1986), a phenomenological self, "I," or ego comes to full fruition as a result of the negotiation of the conflicts inherent in the final life stage, Integrity versus Despair. Wisdom is its associated virtue. These stage-related concerns include responsible acceptance of life as it was lived; positive adaptation to physical deterioration and impending death; and relinquishment of leadership to the future while maintaining continuity with the past. Wisdom develops not only in old age but incrementally throughout life by actuation of growth rather than foreclosure in response to numerous age-associated challenges. In balancing syntonic and dystonic tendencies throughout the life course, wise persons accomplish a daunting and rare feat of self-development.

For Jung (1953a,b, 1959a,b, 1971), individuation of the self is the road to wisdom. His theory places the source of wisdom intrapsychically, in confronting progressively deeper aspects of the self. This process begins with access to the personal unconscious, integration of the shadow or dark side of the self, and balance among opposing forces, such as inner and outer reality, good and evil, and male and female tendencies. Such self-awareness, which builds the basis for wisdom, requires considerable effort, to which few people are committed. Even fewer explore rich reservoirs of knowledge and wisdom in deeper layers of the self.

Kohut (1977, 1978a,b) similarly postulated that an experiential self is the source of wisdom. Extending his usual focus on early child–parent relationships, Kohut speculated about how the self develops in adulthood, particularly in relation to "narcissism." Kohut's concept of narcissism as a natural, essential part of a healthy developmental course differs from Freud's notion of regressive and immature self-love. For Kohut, healthy narcissism begins in early childhood with age-appropriate fantasies of omnipotence and grandiosity and later with internalization of an idealized parent who represents omniscience and perfection. These two phases of the narcissistic self mature into a cohesive adult, who effectively copes with life's vicissitudes and relies on firm values and ideals to guide behavior. Maturation of early narcissistic needs into adaptive adult forms constitutes a forerunner to wisdom, whose full development hinges on other transformations resulting in empathy, mature humor, and acceptance of transience. The final transformation of narcissism into wisdom represents the farthest point in the development of an integrated personality.

In summary, these theories build on a constructivist view of personality development in which an active, organizing self participates in a dynamic process involving both conscious and unconscious influences. Wisdom, whether conceived as cumulative and age-related ego development, individuation, or transformed narcissism, entails uncommon levels of self-awareness and psychological growth. Wise persons should evince such characteristics indicative of exceptionally mature and integrated personalities.

Personality psychology suggests that the mature personality has a productive orientation and capacity for mature love (Fromm, 1955, 1956), based on openness to present experience and trust in one's organismic response to situations (Rogers, 1961). Others describe self-extension, achieved by involvement in meaningful pursuits and interests; self-objectivity, including insight and a sense of humor; and a unifying philosophy of life as benchmarks of psychological maturity (Allport, 1937). These qualities, although descriptive of wise persons, are not adequate in themselves to define a personality component of wisdom. We argue that another aspect of personality, self-transcendence, makes wisdom unique.

### Self-transcendence

One consequence of advanced personality development is the ability to transcend the self, that is, to move beyond individualistic concerns to more collective or universal issues. We believe that self-transcendence is an essential component of wisdom and accounts, in part, for wise people's long-range perspectives and deep understanding of philosophical and epistemological issues. The developmental course of wisdom is linked with the maturation of the self, which moves from an egocentric focus to a universalistic apprehension of reality.

In defining the last stage of life, Erikson pinpointed "ultimate concerns" and described a person's transcendence of "the limitations of his identity and his often tragic or bitterly tragicomic engagement in his one and only life cycle within the sequence of generations" (Erikson, 1968, p. 140). He discussed a transpersonal sense of "I" that might develop in old age and that transcends "timebound identities" and senses an "all-human and existential identity like that which the world religions and ideologies have attempted to create" (Erikson et al., 1986, p. 53).

This transcendency appears also in Erikson's notion of ego growth within an "ever widening social radius" that makes demands appropriate to each stage of life. The social radius of infancy, confined to the primary caretakers, gradually expands from family to peers and intimate partners to offspring and occupational groups; at the end of life, the social radius eventually encompasses humankind in general. Thus, Erikson suggested (1982) that wisdom involves an expansion of the context in which the subjective sense of "I" is placed to a broader, more global, and philosophical perspective.

In an elaboration of Erikson's later stages, Peck (1968) advanced "ego-transcendence vs. ego-preoccupation" as developmental markers of old age. Ego transcendence is an adaptive orientation in late life to the prospect of personal death. Reconciliation with one's finitude is propelled by investment in the well-being of friends, family, and culture rather than one's individual identity.

Jung considered self-transcendent themes as precipitated by an inner shift toward collectivistic consciousness, attainable through self-knowledge:

This widened consciousness is no longer that touchy, egotistical bundle of personal wishes, fears, hopes, and ambitions which always has to be compensated or corrected by unconscious countertendencies; instead, it is a function of relationship to the world of objects, bringing the individual into absolute, binding, and indissoluble communion with the world at large. The complications arising at this stage are no longer egotistic wish-conflicts, but difficulties that concern others as much as oneself. (Jung, 1953a, p. 176, ¶275)

At this level, information not usually accessible to awareness is made conscious through dreams and symbols. This arcane realm, called the "collective unconscious," contains universal or archetypal information and is the source of wisdom. In self-transcendence, unabsorbed by individualistic passions, the self learns from these archetypal sources and is psychically open to the insight and understanding they hold. Whether or not one takes this unconscious realm literally, Jung's formulation prescribes openness to collective images of wisdom to find fundamental and timeless truths about universal human experiences.

Self-transcendence is paramount in Kohut's theory of wisdom. Transformation of narcissism into its most complete form is possible only when the psychic energy of the self is transferred "to the supraindividual ideals and to the world with which one identifies" (Kohut, 1978a, p. 458.) With this orientation, the self suspends its own importance, experiences others' empathically, and responds to its own impermanence with humor and an expanded sense of self. Essentially, wisdom involves acknowledgment of the limitations of the self's powers as a concrete and finite person through a sense of "cosmic narcissism." Wisdom is hewed in the process of expanding the self to a timeless, universal identity rather than with an individualistic and mortal one.

### Implications of personality development for wisdom

In summary, three personality theories suggest that wisdom entails extraordinary personality development and transcendence of conventional levels of self-absorption. This freedom from self-absorption permits attention to more universal, collective, or global concerns. We suggested earlier that these personality attributes in combination with cognitive attributes structure how wise people view themselves, others, and the world. People with advanced personality development may experience their affects in largely undefended and open ways, fostering self-awareness; people with advanced cognitive development may use cognitively complex appraisals of themselves in self-

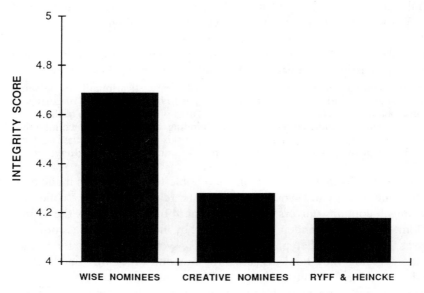

Figure 8.1. Mean integrity score of wise and creative nominees in Orwoll study and average subjects in Ryff and Heincke (1983) study.

reflection. A synthesis of affective clarity and cognitive complexity probably is a precursor to high levels of self-insight, a quality associated with wisdom (Holliday & Chandler, 1986). In interaction with others, exceptionally integrated people predictably show empathy, understanding, and caring. When these dispositions are catalyzed with complex and dialectical cognition, they reappear as penetrating interpersonal insight and discernment. Similarly, self-transcendence facilitates perception of the world with humanitarian and global feelings of concern. When these attributes combine with deep reflection about universal themes, they may manifest a far-seeing, global perspective.

While we know of no direct empirical support for the conception of wisdom that we have described, the findings of a study by Orwoll (1988) are consistent with it. In her study, older adults nominated as wise were compared to older adults nominated as creative. Wise nominees were found to be no different from creative nominees on general measures of psychological well-being but were significantly higher on a measure thought to reflect wisdom (i.e., Eriksonian-based measure of ego integrity, constructed by Ryff and Heincke, 1983). As indicated in Figure 8.1, wise nominees also scored higher on integrity than older adults from the general population who participated in Ryff and Heincke's study.[1] As indicated in Figure 8.2, wise respondents were also more likely to express a global perspective (i.e., concern for the world state or humanity as a whole) compared with creative nominees. These results

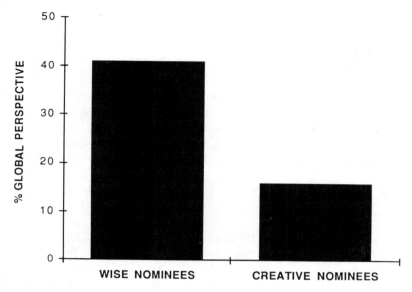

Figure 8.2. Percentage of wise and creative nominees showing global perspective (Orwoll, 1988).

begin to sift out personality variables that seem to be distinctively applicable to wisdom.

Better understanding of the personality development of wise people will not only illuminate the personality component of wisdom but also explain how cognitive aspects of wisdom become expressed in the whole person. It is from the perspective of the whole person that we believe wisdom should be studied. In the following section, we articulate a methodology for the study of the wise person.

## Methodology for the study of wisdom

Thus far studies of wisdom have considered personality and cognitive components separately. We propose a methodology for studying them together. The main premise of this approach is that wisdom can be better understood by the intensive study of people believed to be wise. This approach should not only isolate component aspects of wisdom for intra- and inter-individual comparisons but also reveal their organization and patterning within and across individuals. It directs attention more holistically on the study of people who cluster at the upper end of the continuum of wisdom instead of componentially on isolated variables as expressed in a wide range of individuals. Study of exceptionally wise people should provide insight into

1. the nature of wisdom, including the interrelationships among various affective, cognitive, and social correlates of wisdom;
2. the development of wisdom, including life course processes and events that contribute to wisdom; and
3. the consequences of wisdom, that is, what it means to live a wise and meaningful life.

To illustrate this methodology, we discuss three research approaches that outline useful ways to study wise persons: an "exemplar approach," which suggests a research strategy for subject selection; a personological approach, which suggests some of the types of data that would be useful to collect; and a developmental approach, which helps chart wisdom across changes in adulthood.

## Exemplar approach

In studies of exemplars, subjects who exemplify a salient characteristic are investigated to illuminate its personality, cognitive, and life history correlates. This typological approach has been deployed effectively in the study of creativity (e.g., Baron, 1969; Bloom, 1985; Gruber, 1981), another uncommon, multidimensional attribute. Other excellent examples of the use of this approach include Helson's studies of creative mathematicians (Helson, 1971; Helson & Crutchfield, 1970a,b), in which subjects were identified as creative by others in their field through both nominations and ratings. In-depth assessments yielded extensive information about family background, personality, and intellectual styles of creative persons, delineating the distinctive psychology of creativity. Further precedent for this research strategy can be found in studies of people with exceptional adjustment (Vaillant, 1977), intelligence (Goertzel & Goertzel, 1962; Simonton, 1984), and ego development (Helson, 1985a).

This approach also launched Maslow's (1970) study of self-actualizing people, from which he proposed a typology of optimal human functioning. Although unsystematic, his work has been theoretically and descriptively useful. Moreover, his focus on growth potential rather than deficiency provides a useful precedent for the study of wisdom.

The exemplar approach, although providing integrative data, raises several legitimate methodological questions. First, how capable are nominators in identifying wise persons? Considerable evidence from research on laypersons' implicit theories of wisdom, detailed later in this chapter, indicates that a widely shared conception of wisdom exists and that it differs from other related traits (Clayton & Birren, 1980; Holliday & Chandler, 1986; Perlmutter, Adams, Nyquist, & Kaplan, 1988; Sternberg, 1985). High social consensus in natural language meanings of wisdom have been found across a range of samples and cohorts. These findings suggest shared cognizance of the major attributes of wisdom in the general population. Confidence in the nomination procedure can be enhanced further with multiple nominators and particularly qualified nominators. This latter strategy has been relied upon extensively by anthropologists who use "focused key informants" (Tremblay, 1957).

Second, how accurate are the nominators in identifying wise people? Meager empirical data on wise people make evaluation of this question difficult. However, Orwoll's (1988) preliminary work on the personality characteristics of wise persons, discussed earlier, offers initial confirmation of the utility of peer nominations in the study of wisdom. Two types of data support the use of nominees as exemplars of wisdom. Wise and creative samples differed in self-descriptive Adjective Check List profiles in ways predicted by prototypical descriptors of wisdom and creativity. In addition, the nominated samples differed on an objective measure of integrity, which is allied closely with wisdom. Furthermore, although validational support for peer nominations is still sparse in the study of wisdom, it is ample in the creativity literature (see Helson, 1985b, 1987).

Third, against what comparison groups shall a wise criterion group be measured? Evaluation of sages qua sages presupposes a comparable group of persons inherently lower in sageness with whom to compare them. Choice of comparison samples should be theoretically driven and evaluated for validity. Nominators might rate nominees on a number of attributes thought to be compatible and incompatible with wisdom and with the targeted comparison. This strategy helps decipher overlap between criterion and comparison groups and supplies observer-based indices of nominees' characteristics. Similar descriptive information can be obtained from self-reports. Random samples of the general population, or theoretically targeted samples, offer opportunities to test hypotheses about the distribution and nature of wisdom.

## Personological approach

The personological approach in personality research offers the study of wisdom a vital research tradition. The works of Murray (1938), White (1975), and Allport (1962) are examples of this approach in which individual lives form the basic unit of investigation. Some researchers within this tradition focus idiographically; many use a hybrid approach, applying idiographic data to illuminate nomothetic principles. The methodologies include clinical assessment (Murray, 1938; White, 1969), psychobiography (Runyan, 1984), personal narrative (McAdams, 1985), and personal documents (Allport, 1942; Franz, 1988; Stewart, Franz, & Layton, 1988). Particularly when combined with the exemplar approach, such research provides a contextual and integrated body of information about the influence of transformative experiences and events across the life span.

*Developmental approach*

Life span developmental methodologies might also strengthen the study of wise people. Applying the techniques of longitudinal (Eichorn, Clausen, Haan, Honzik, & Mussen, 1981; Vaillant, 1977) and cross-sectional (Levinson, Darrow, Klein, Levinson, & McKee, 1978; Neugarten 1964) designs with the use of multimeasure assessments would facilitate a more holistic conception of the development of wisdom than provided by previous life span investigations of discrete wisdom-related variables. Such studies would clarify whether wisdom is best considered an individual difference variable or one associated with particular stages of life. This question has become of increasing empirical interest as findings have failed to identify a solid age trajectory (Smith, Dixon, & Baltes, 1987; see also Labouvie-Vief, chapter 4 in this volume).

*Summary*

Each of the research approaches discussed so far offers some useful methodological ingredients for the study of wise people. Although often overlapping, these paradigms grew, in some cases, out of very different intellectual traditions that have unique elements to offer. When drawn together, they convey bodies of knowledge and procedural expertise usefully appropriated for an integrated study of wisdom.

**Empirical information about wise people**

Research on implicit theories of wisdom has outlined laypersons' beliefs about wisdom, providing a grounding for further empirical work. Table 8.1 summarizes the major overlaps in characteristics of wisdom generated in three studies. Clayton and Birren (1980) sought to explore the underlying structure of contemporary views of wisdom by asking subjects to rate the similarity of a number of descriptors of a wise individual. The ratings pointed to a multidimensional conception of wisdom similar to that found in historical writings. That is, they found a clustering of attributes into three major dimensions that they labeled affective ("peaceful," "empathetic," "understanding," and "gentle"); reflective ("introspective" and "intuitive"); and cognitive ("pragmatic," "observant," and "intelligent").

More recently, Sternberg (1985) used implicit theory to study the relationship between intelligence, creativity, and wisdom. In a preliminary study, he gathered laypersons' descriptions of ideally intelligent, creative, and wise individuals. Based on this list of behaviors, subjects rated how characteristic the behavior was with respect to their conceptions of ideally intelligent, creative, and wise persons. A subsequent group of subjects sorted the most

Table 8.1. *Overlapping descriptors generated by three studies of implicit theories of wisdom*

| Clayton and Birren | Sternberg | Holliday & Chandler |
|---|---|---|
| understanding; introspective | understands people through dealing with a variety of people; knows self best; is thoughtful; is fair; is a good listener; is not afraid to admit mistakes; listens to all sides of an issue | understands people; understands self; is thoughtful/thinks a great deal; is fair; is a good listener; has learned from experience; sees and considers all points of view |
| knowledgeable; observant | has huge store of knowledge; is perceptive; is sensible; thinks before acting or making decisions; is able to take the long view; thinks before speaking; seeks out information, especially details | is knowledgeable; observant/perceptive; uses common sense; thinks carefully before deciding; weighs consequences of actions; foresightful/farseeing; sees things in larger context; discreet; curious |
| experienced | is experienced; age, maturity, or long experience | experienced; mature, older |
| intuitive | has intuition; can offer solutions on the side of right and truth; is able to see through things, read between lines; has the ability to understand and interpret environment | intuitive; moral; sees essence of situation; understands/evaluates information |
| empathetic; intelligent | — | empathic; intelligent |

characteristic behaviors for each trait based on the likelihood that the set of behaviors would appear together in the same person. Multidimensional scaling specified dimensions that accounted for the most variance of these traits. Wisdom was perceived as more like intelligence than creativity but also as comprised of a distinguishing set of qualities. Based on the multidimensional space describing wisdom, Sternberg defined the wise individual as one who:

... listens to others, knows how to weigh advice, and can deal with a variety of different kinds of people. In seeking as much information as possible for decision making, the wise individual reads between the lines as well as makes use of the obviously available information. The wise individual is especially able to make clear, sensible, and fair judgments, and in doing so, takes a long-term as well as a short-term view of the consequences of the judgment made ... is perceived to profit from the experiences of others, and to learn from others' mistakes, as well as from his or her own ... is not afraid to change his or her mind as experience dictates, and the solutions that are offered to complex problems tend to be the right ones. (Sternberg, 1985, p. 623)

In another study of implicit theories of wisdom, Holliday and Chandler (1986) asked people to generate lists of prototype descriptors of wise people. Other subjects rated the prototypicality of these generated descriptors as well as attributes from wisdom literature and attributes that described other types of people (intelligent, perceptive, spiritual, shrewd, and foolish). A factor analysis of prototypicality ratings resulted in five factors. The first factor, Exceptional Understanding, contained such attributes as "has learned from experience," "sees things within a larger context," "understands him/herself," and "empathic." The second factor, Judgement and Communication Skills, contained such attributes as "is good source of advice," "reflective," and "thinks carefully before deciding." The third factor, General Competencies, had attributes with moderate prototypicality ratings, including "curious," "intelligent," "self-actualized," and "experienced." The fourth factor, Interpersonal Skills, contained such attributes as "fair," "reliable," "mature," and "kind." The fifth factor, Social Unobtrusiveness, included "discreet," "non-judgmental," "non-impulsive," "quiet," and "plans carefully."

Like Sternberg, Holliday and Chandler (1986) sought to compare the descriptors of wisdom with those of other traits varying in possible similarity to wisdom. In general, they found that wisdom is a distinct, nonredundant concept that overlaps with related concepts in ways that are reasonable and nonarbitrary. Holliday and Chandler concluded that "the dimensions referencing understanding and pragmatic skills serve as a distinctive core of meaning for the concept of wise, and serve to differentiate wise people from other people and to highlight their unique abilities" (p. 81).

In those studies, subjects generated descriptors of ideal or hypothetical wise people, revealing socially shared definitions of wisdom. Some of our own work has taken a different approach, asking subjects to describe the characteristics of actual people they nominate as wise. In one such study, Perlmutter et al. (1988) compared nominators' general beliefs about the characteristics of wisdom with the characteristics of wise people that they nominated. In one part of the study, adults ranging in age from 20 to 90 were asked whether they thought wisdom is related to age, gender, and education. As may be seen in Figure 8.3, 78% of the subjects thought that wisdom is related to age, 16% to gender, and 68% to education. These findings indicate that people in our culture generally believe wisdom is more prevalent in older and more educated people but that it is not limited to individuals of one particular gender.

To determine whether people's general beliefs about wisdom are reflected in the kinds of people they think of as wise, subjects also were asked to nominate the three wisest people they could think of and to specify the age, gender, and educational backgrounds of the wise nominees. As can be seen in Figure 8.4, the findings pertaining to age of nominees corresponded closely to the findings concerning general beliefs about wisdom and age. The nominees tended to be middle-aged to old, with an average age of approximately 50 years for young nominators and 65 years for older nominators. This positive correlation between age of nominator and age of nominee is probably due to differences in the average age of the nominator's circle of acquaintances.

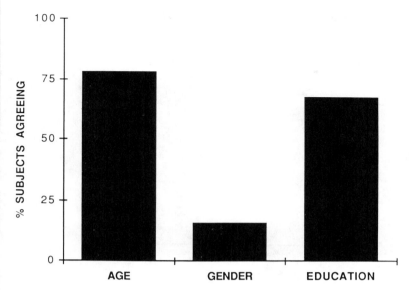

Figure 8.3. Percentage of subjects agreeing that age, gender, and education are related to wisdom (Perlmutter, Adams, Nyquist, & Kaplan, 1988).

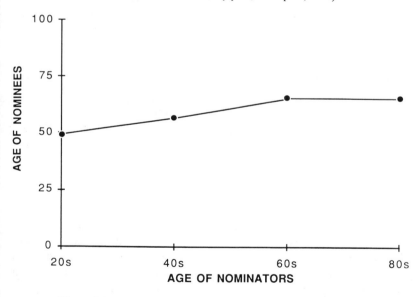

Figure 8.4. Age of wise nominees (Perlmutter, Adams, Nyquist, & Kaplan, 1988).

Although people's nominations with respect to age tended to be consistent with their general beliefs, as assessed by direct questioning, a rather different picture emerged when people were asked to rate their own wisdom. As may be seen in Figure 8.5, when adults aged 20 to 90 were asked to rate how wise

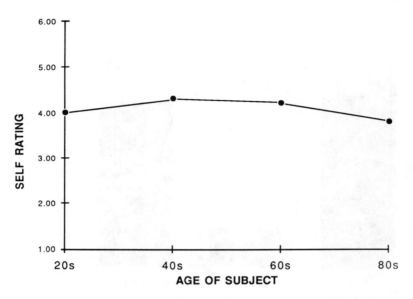

Figure 8.5. Self-rating of wisdom (Perlmutter, Adams, Nyquist, & Kaplan, 1988).

they believed they were, there was little overall age difference, and indeed, there was a slight tendency for self-ratings of wisdom to increase until about age 40 and then to level off or decrease. It appears, then, that whereas people hold a general belief that wisdom increases with age, and older people are more likely to be nominated as wise than young people, subjects do not rate their own wisdom in a manner that is consistent with this age-related conception of wisdom. The relationship between age and wisdom should, therefore, be examined more carefully. One possible explanation of the discrepancy is that recognition of the limitations of one's own wisdom is, in fact, characteristic of being wise (e.g., Meacham, 1983).

Figure 8.6 shows that findings relevant to nominees' gender did not correspond to general beliefs about the relationship between wisdom and gender. Although few subjects explicitly stated that wisdom is related to gender, there was a clear tendency for males to be nominated as wise more frequently than females. Interestingly, males were more likely to nominate males than were women. This finding of overrepresentation of males may reflect that wisdom is a socially valued characteristic (Heckhausen, Dixon, & Baltes, 1989) and thereby often more associated with males than with females in our culture (Broverman, Vogel, Broverman, Clarkson, & Rosenkrantz, 1972).

Finally, as is shown in Figure 8.7, it appears that highly educated people are more likely than less educated people to be nominated as wise. This finding corresponds to people's general statements about the relationship between education and wisdom. It should be noted, however, that the sample

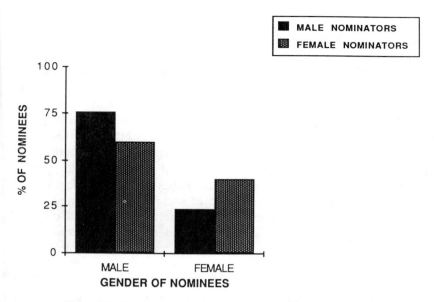

Figure 8.6. Gender of wise nominees (Perlmutter, Adams, Nyquist, & Kaplan, 1988).

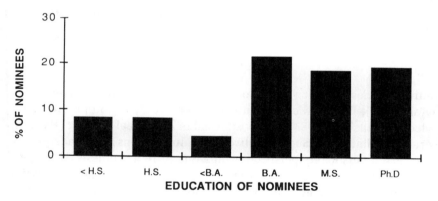

Figure 8.7. Educational level of wise nominees (Perlmutter, Adams, Nyquist, & Kaplan, 1988).

of nominators used in this study was fairly well educated (>12 years) and thus probably nominated people they knew of comparable education level. Moreover, at least a few of the wise nominees had very little education, suggesting that education is not necessary for wisdom. In open-ended questions, none of the subjects indicated they thought that education is in any way sufficient for achieving wisdom.

*Summary*

Taken together, the findings of Clayton and Birren (1980), Sternberg (1985), and Holliday and Chandler (1986) indicate that the category of "wise person" has a widely shared meaning in our culture. These studies show that wisdom, although comprised of multidimensional characteristics, is a concept that is distinct from other concepts that may be similar to it, such as intelligence, creativity, and perceptiveness. Such consensus about meaning provides some assurance that wise people can be identified for study and that they are likely to possess many of the characteristics believed to covary with wisdom.

Studies by Perlmutter et al. (1988) suggest that people show fairly high agreement about some demographic characteristics of wise people and less about other characteristics. The influence of social stereotypes and social biases in the evaluations of wisdom must therefore be considered. To better understand the influence of such variables, a broader sampling of nominators reflecting a range of socioeconomic, educational, ethnic, and cultural backgrounds should be undertaken.

Moreover, to really know what wise people are like, it is important to actually study them. Studying wise people should help determine the veridicality of implicit ideas about wisdom, the universality of characteristics of wisdom, and the influence of the social environment in shaping wisdom. Life history information about wise people will chart developmental antecedents of wisdom, and information about current abilities, concerns, and perspectives will detail its expression.

## Conclusion

Cognitive theories have viewed wisdom as social and interpersonal knowledge (Clayton, 1982), life knowledge (Dittmann-Kohli & Baltes, in press), meta-knowledge (Meacham, 1983), and postformal or dialectical thought (Rybash, Hoyer, & Roodin, 1986). Such cognitive conceptualizations have inadequately incorporated a personality perspective on wisdom. In a synthesis of the personality literature, we located two markers of wisdom that may be useful stakes on which to tie empirical investigations. Wisdom, we found, requires remarkable negotiation of the personality domain, evident in unusual self-development and self-transcendence. Both of these attainments are inherently contingent on concomitant cognitive maturation.

If wisdom is an integration of cognition and personality (Labouvie-Vief, chapter 4 in this volume; Kramer, chapter 13 in this volume), studying wise persons affords an opportunity to learn about the fluid interactions among its components. We have argued that people identified as wise be studied using measures derived from both cognitive and personality theories of wisdom. Without empirical grounding, however, we can only speculate about how personality indicators reciprocally relate to cognitive indicators of wisdom. We conjecture that with personality development mature detachment from egocentric psychic demands promotes mental processing of new information and clearer perception of existing information. Reciprocally, incremental growth in wisdom-related cognition restructures and raises affective insight to more mature levels. A cognitive stance, such as Meacham's (1983) link between wisdom and awareness of limits in personal knowledge, can be thought of as having both antecedents in and consequences for affective development. That is, if wisdom is to be understood as a holistic disposition, it is necessary to begin to link definitive cognitive processes with definitive personality processes.

Taking this perspective, one might consider such questions as: Does cognitive realization of self-limitation initiate an affective search for self-transcendent truths or foster compassion for the limitations of others? Conversely, do certain affective experiences or life transitions predispose a cognitive shift in the subjective ratio of acquired to perceived knowledge? Empirical investigations of the dynamic interplay between personality and cognition in the development of wisdom will illuminate how feelings impel new cognitive frameworks and cognitive advances promote personality integration. These interrelationships may emerge through the patterns observed in studies of wise people, whose lives are likely to illuminate the nature and development of wisdom.

## Note

1 We gratefully acknowledge Carol Ryff for providing us with her data.

## References

Allport, G. W. (1937). *Personality: a psychological interpretation.* New York: Henry Holt.
Allport, G. W. (1942). *The use of personal documents in psychological science.* New York: Social Science Research Council.
Allport, G. W. (1962). The general and the unique in psychological science. *Journal of Personality, 30,* 405–422.
Baron, F. (1969). *Creative person and creative process.* New York: Holt, Rinehart, & Winston.
Bloom, B. S. (1985). *Developing talent in young people.* New York: Ballantine Books.
Broverman, I., Vogel, S., Broverman, D., Clarkson, F., & Rosenkrantz, P. (1972). Sex-role stereotypes: a current appraisal. *Journal of Social Issues, 28,* 59–78.
Clayton, V. (1982). Wisdom and intelligence: the nature and function of knowledge in the later years. *International Journal of Aging and Human Development, 15*(4), 315–321.
Clayton, V., & Birren, J. E. (1980). The development of wisdom across the life span: a reexamination of an ancient topic. In P. B. Baltes & O. G. Brim (Eds.), *Life span development and behavior* (Vol. 3). New York: Academic Press.
Dittmann-Kohli, F., & Baltes, P. B. (in press). Toward a neofunctionalist conception of adult intellectual development. In C. Alexander & E. Langer (Eds.), *Beyond formal operations: alternative endpoints to human development.* New York: Oxford University Press.

Eichorn, D. H., Clausen, J. A., Haan, N., Honzik, M. P., & Mussen, P. H. (1981). *Present and past in middle life.* New York: Academic Press.

Erikson, E. H. (1968). *Identity: youth and crisis.* New York: W. W. Norton.

Erikson, E. H. (1978). Reflections on Dr. Borg's life cycle. In E. H. Erikson (Ed.), *Adulthood.* New York: W. W. Norton.

Erikson, E. H. (1982). *The life cycle completed.* New York: W. W. Norton.

Erikson, E. H., Erikson, J. M., & Kivnick, H. Q. (1986). *Vital involvement in old age.* New York: W. W. Norton.

Franz, C. E. (1988). *A case study of adult psychosocial development: identity, intimacy, and generativity in personal documents.* Unpublished doctoral dissertation, Boston University.

Fromm, E. (1955). *The art of loving.* New York: Harper & Row.

Fromm, E. (1956). *The sane society.* New York: Ballantine Books.

Goertzel, V., & Goertzel, M. (1962). *Cradles of eminence.* Boston: Little, Brown.

Gould, R. L. (1978). *Transformations.* New York: Simon & Schuster.

Gruber, H. E. (1981). *Darwin on man.* Chicago: University of Chicago Press.

Heckhausen, J., Dixon, R. A., & Baltes, P. B. (1989). Gains and losses in development throughout adulthood as perceived by different adult age groups. *Developmental Psychology, 25*(1), 109–21.

Helson, R. (1971). Women mathematicians and the creative personality. *Journal of Consulting and Clinical Psychology, 36*(2), 210–220.

Helson, R. (1985a). Lives of women who became autonomous. *Journal of Personality, 53*(2), 257–285.

Helson, R. (1985b). Which of those young women with creative potential became productive? Personality in college and characteristics of parents. In R. Hogan & W. H. Jones (Eds.), *Perspectives in personality* (Vol. 1). Greenwich, CT: JAI Press.

Helson, R. (1987). Which of those young women with creative potential became productive? II. From college to midlife. In R. Hogan & W. H. Jones (Eds.), *Perspectives in personality* (Vol. 2). Greenwich, CT: JAI Press.

Helson, R., & Crutchfield, R. S. (1970a). Creative types in mathematics. *Journal of Personality, 38,* 177–197.

Helson, R., & Crutchfield, R. S. (1970b). Mathematicians: the creative researcher and the average Ph.D. *Journal of Consulting and Clinical Psychology, 34*(2), 250–257.

Holliday, S. G., & Chandler, M. J. (1986). *Wisdom: explorations in human competence.* New York: Karger.

Jung, C. G. (1953a). *Two essays on analytical psychology.* New York: Pantheon Books.

Jung, C. G. (1953b). *Psychology and alchemy.* New York: Princeton University Press.

Jung, C. G. (1959a). *The archetypes of the collective unconscious.* New York: Princeton University Press.

Jung, C. G. (1959b). *Aion: researches in the phenomenology of the self.* New York: Princeton University Press.

Jung, C. G. (1971). The stages of life. In J. Campbell (Ed.), *The portable Jung.* New York: Penguin Books.

Kohut, H. (1977). *Restoration of the self.* New York: International Universities Press.

Kohut, H. (1978a). Forms and transformations of narcissism. In P. Ornstein (Ed.), *The search for the self.* New York: International Universities Press.

Kohut, H. (1978b). Thoughts on narcissism and narcissistic rage. In P. Ornstein (Ed.), *The search for the self.* New York: International Universities Press.

Levinson, D. J., Darrow, C., Klein, E., Levinson, M., & McKee, B. (1978). *The seasons of a man's life.* New York: Knopf.

McAdams, D. P. (1985). *Power, intimacy, and the life story: personological inquiries into identity.* New York: Guilford Press.

Maslow, A. H. (1970). *Motivation and personality.* New York: Harper & Row.

Meacham, J. A. (1983). Wisdom and the context of knowledge: knowing that one doesn't know. In D. Kuhn & J. A. Meacham (Eds.), *On the development of developmental psychology.* Basel, Switzerland: Karger.

Murray, H. A. (1938). *Explorations in personality.* New York: Oxford University Press.

Neugarten, B. L. (1964). *Personality in middle and late life.* New York: Atherton Press.

Orwoll, L. (1988). *Wisdom in later adulthood: personality and life history correlates.* Unpublished doctoral dissertation, Boston University.

Peck, R. C. (1968). Psychological developments in the second half of life. In B. L. Neugarten (Ed.), *Middle age and aging.* Chicago: University of Chicago Press.

Perlmutter, M., Adams, C., Nyquist, L., & Kaplan, C. (1988). *Beliefs about wisdom.* Unpublished data.

Rogers, C. R. (1961). *On becoming a person.* Boston: Houghton Mifflin.

Runyan, W. M. (1984). *Life histories and psychobiography.* New York: Oxford University Press.

Rybash, J. M., Hoyer, W. J., & Roodin, P. A. (1986). *Adult cognition and aging.* New York: Pergamon Press.

Ryff, C. D., & Heincke, S. G. (1983). The subjective organization of personality in adulthood and aging. *Journal of Personality and Social Psychology, 44,* 807–816.

Simonton, D. K. (1984). *Genius, creativity and leadership.* Cambridge, MA: Harvard University Press.

Smith, J., Dixon, R. A., & Baltes, P. B. (1987). *Age differences in response to life planning problems: A research analog for the study of wisdom. Related knowledge.* Unpublished manuscript.

Sternberg, R. J. (1985). Implicit theories of intelligence, creativity, and wisdom. *Journal of Personality and Social Psychology, 49*(3), 607–627.

Stewart, A. J., Franz, C. E., & Layton, L. (1988). The changing self: using personal documents to study lives. *Journal of Personality, 56,* 41–74.

Tremblay, M. A. (1957). The key informant technique: a nonethnographic application. *American Anthropologist, 59*(4), 688–701.

Vaillant, G. E. (1977). *Adaptation to life.* Boston: Little, Brown.

White, R. W. (1969). *The study of lives.* New York: Atherton Press.

White, R. W. (1975). *Lives in progress.* New York: Holt, Rinehart, & Winston.

*Part IV*

**Approaches informed by
psychodevelopmental conceptions
of wisdom**

*John A. Meacham*

> Our wisdom, we prefer to think, is all of our own gathering, while, if the truth be told, it is, most of it, the last coin of a legacy that dwindles with time.
> – Evelyn Waugh (1945)

A contemporary image of wisdom typically associated with presumed Eastern philosophies is of the experienced, enlightened, and respected elder. Yet Erikson (1982, p. 79) has reminded us that the name of Lao-tze, the founder of Taoist philosophy, means old child and refers to a newborn with a tiny white beard. Is it possible that in associating wisdom with old age we risk losing sight of what is the true essence of wisdom, an essence that in its simplicity is within the reach even of a child? With this possibility in mind, I have first endeavored to consider what might be the nature of wisdom apart from its association with age. In doing so, I have concluded that the essence of wisdom is to hold the attitude that knowledge is fallible and to strive for a balance between knowing and doubting. Second, I draw support for this conception of wisdom from the research literature on wisdom. Third, I consider the question of whether wisdom increases with age and conclude that support for this hypothesis is lacking. Fourth, I suggest that although the potential for wisdom is present throughout the life course, unfortunately most people lose their wisdom as they grow older. Finally, I argue that the developmental origin of wisdom is in interpersonal relations, and I suggest some ways in which wisdom can be maintained across the life course.

## To be wise is to know and to doubt

*Shorter is not easier, nor wiser*

The Coast Range of California is a younger mountain range than, for example, the Appalachian Mountains of the Atlantic states. On the youthful land surface of the Coast Range, the stream gradients are steep, erosion has been rapid, the valleys make sharp cuts in the land, and the hillsides are steep. In

181

contrast, on the mature surface of the Appalachians, the streams are gentle, erosion has slowed, and the slopes are shallow. The hillsides of the Coast Range are wooded primarily in the valleys facing the Pacific Ocean, where moisture is retained from the winter rains and the summer fog to sustain groves of redwood trees. But unlike the heavily wooded hills of the Appalachians, many of the slopes of the Coast Range are bare, except for grasses, green in spring, brown in summer and fall.

I have memories of hiking over the hills of the Coast Range, starting from about the age of 10, for I grew up in a town nestled among the foothills, close enough for hikes of an hour or two with classmates after school, longer hikes in the summer. Many of the open, grassy fields had been used for the grazing of cattle, but I cannot recall having seen many, if any, cattle. I do remember, however, that we were cautious whenever we crossed barbed wire into an open field, for we knew that bulls would spare no effort to gore us before we could reach the safety of the woods.

Many of the grassy hillsides were enveloped in a tracery of narrow paths, the result of grazing cattle having trampled the muddy ground year after year. I remember hiking along one of these paths with a childhood friend, Richard, and talking about why it was that the path we were following went around the hillside rather than up the hillside, which was where *we* wanted to go. All of the paths maintained a more or less constant elevation around the hillside, varying only a foot or so up or down so as to intersect with roughly parallel paths. I do not know whether it occurred to me then or later that the paths were evidence of an adaptive intelligence, if not a wisdom, on the part of the cows. It requires less effort to graze a steep hillside with successive passes from side to side than with repeated ascents and descents of the hillside.

This bovine wisdom (if I might be permitted such an oxymoron) apparently is not possessed by 10-year-old boys, for Richard and I more often than not attempted to hike directly up the steep slopes toward the crest of the hill rather than meander back and forth in a longer but gentler ascent. We were seduced by the apparent closeness of the crest of the hill to take what seemed to be the easier route, but the more we climbed, the more the apparent crest of the hill receded, so that our climb took much longer and left us more exhausted than we had anticipated it would.

Richard's and my knowledge that the crest of the hill was within easy reach was fallible. Our surprise at having the crest of the hill recede from us as we climbed higher and higher illustrates the lack of an attitude that is essential to wisdom. Our error in believing that in the course of our ascent we could see our destination, the crest of the hill, was encouraged by the shape of the young hills, steep and convex upward, and by the open grassy fields, which appeared to provide an unobstructed view toward the crest. As we looked along the tangent up the hillside toward the top, we were unable to see the actual crest until, after considerable effort, we had at last climbed quite close to the top. Of course, when we reached the crest of the first hill, we realized that this was merely the first in a series of more distant and higher hills to be climbed on later occasions.

## Knowledge is fallible

Similarly, a lack of wisdom is illustrated by the error of believing that one can see all that can be seen, that one knows all that can be known. This error is an implicit assumption within many traditional models of the growth of information, learning, and knowledge. The assumption is that there is a fixed upper boundary or crest on the knowledge that might be acquired and that the growth of knowledge can be understood in terms of progress toward this upper boundary. This boundary can be conceived differently according to various psychological theories or measurement procedures, for example, the set of items on an intelligence test, the content of a textbook or a professor's lectures for a semester, or all the books in a large library. In psychology, the growth of knowledge has been conceived in terms of accumulation of skills, habits, vocabulary, information, concepts, and so forth, as each person strives to come closer to the fixed boundary of what can be known. Brown (1982, p. 107), for example, reviewing the extent to which traditional learning theories, computer metaphors, and schema theories successfully address questions of growth and learning, comments that "many current theories offer little more than an accretion mechanism."

Yet there is no final crest, there is no fixed boundary on what it is possible to know (Meacham, 1983b). The higher my friend and I climbed, the more the apparent crest of the hill receded. Similarly, and more generally, the more one knows, the more one realizes the extent of what one does not know, and so learning and development necessarily continue. The boundary on all possible knowledge is not fixed but rather can only be understood and continues to expand in relation to what is already known. Each new domain of knowledge appears uncomplicated from the vantage point of ignorance; yet the more we learn about a particular domain, the greater the number of uncertainties, doubts, questions, and complexities that arise.

The essence of wisdom, therefore, is to hold this attitude toward knowledge, that knowledge is fallible. For individuals the easiest course of learning and development is that described by traditional models in psychology, to acquire more and more knowledge. The danger in such a course is to engage in action overly confident that one knows all or most of what can be known when in fact this cannot be so. The challenge of wisdom is to avoid this easy course of merely acquiring more and more knowledge and instead to strive simultaneously to construct new uncertainties, doubts, and questions about what might be known. In this way, one's actions can be guided by a more appropriate consideration of what one does know within the context of what one does not know. If my friend and I had been wise as 10-year-olds, we would have understood that the closeness of the crest of the hill was an illusion, and we would therefore not have been surprised to see it recede into the distance as we struggled toward it.

## The knowledge context matrix

This particular conception of wisdom – knowing that one does not know, appreciating the fallibility of knowledge – was presented along with supporting arguments and evidence in an earlier work (Meacham, 1983b). In that work, traditional accumulation models of the growth of information, learning, and knowledge were criticized and a new model, termed the *knowledge context matrix,* was presented. The term *knowledge context* was employed in order to emphasize that the meaning and value of any knowledge depends upon the context within which that knowledge is known. The knowledge context matrix is determined jointly by one's perception of the extent of all knowledge that can be known and by one's perception of the proportion of what one does know to all that can be known. Clearly two persons can hold the same objective amount of knowledge, yet the first might feel that he or she knows a substantial proportion of all that can be known whereas the second might feel that he or she knows relatively little. In the extreme, (a) the first may feel knowledgeable and confident in taking action and perhaps be closed-minded, rigid, and lacking in curiosity, whereas (b) the second may feel cautious and uncertain in acting, due to lack of confidence in what is known for certain, yet perhaps be more open-minded and even eager to acquire new knowledge. To be wise in one's actions is to avoid both of these extremes.

Six distinct types of movement (*a* through *f*) within the knowledge context matrix were defined and illustrated in my earlier work as well as a particular case of movement for which the knowledge context matrix degenerates into the traditional accumulation model of knowledge (e.g., memorization of a list of letters, numbers, or words). Although all six types of movement in the knowledge context matrix have implications for our understanding of wisdom, only two of these need to be briefly described in order to continue with the present chapter (for derivation and examples, see Meacham, 1983b):[1]

> *a.* The most common course of movement is to accumulate knowledge as rapidly as possible. Within the knowledge context matrix, this course of movement is associated with modest increases in the perception of what remains to be known and with substantial increases in one's confidence in already knowing a great proportion of what can be known. Uncorrected movement of type *a* leads to the first extreme described in the preceding paragraph, overconfidence.
>
> *b.* In movement of type *b,* uncertainties, doubts, and questions arise faster than they can be resolved. This occurs when there are only modest increases in the accumulation of knowledge but more substantial increases in the perception of what remains to be known. Uncorrected movement of type *b* leads to the second extreme, excessive cautiousness.

The course of wisdom is to engage in both types of movement, maintaining a balance between these two extremes, adding to the knowledge that one does hold while simultaneously recognizing that there is much that one does not know.[2]

It would be convenient to have shorthand labels for these two types of movement, labels such as *knowing* and *doubting*. These are not quite appropriate labels, for in the knowledge context matrix movement of type *a* includes not only increased knowing but also modest increases in not knowing, that is, in the perception of what remains to be known; and movement of type *b* includes modest increases in knowing, substantial increases in not knowing, and substantial increases in doubting, that is, decreased confidence in what is known (see figure 1 in Meacham [1983b] for details). In short, knowing and doubting are not polar opposites: One can know that one does not know, one can know what one does not know (I do not know many foreign languages), one can know that one has doubts as well as what one has doubts about, one can not know what one knows (but the information might be recalled on a later occasion), one can doubt that one knows (but be surprised at one's success upon giving it a try), one can doubt that one does not know (but be embarrassed at not knowing the answer), and so forth.

Despite the fact that knowing and doubting are not polar opposites, in order to save time and space, I will avoid further recapitulation of the knowledge context matrix and adopt the terms *knowing* and *doubting* to stand for movement of types *a* and *b,* respectively. To struggle directly toward the crest of a hill, to merely accumulate knowledge, is to know; to yield ground, to become overwhelmed by what one does not know, is to doubt; to follow a more gentle upward path, suspecting that the crest is higher than it appears and so harboring one's strength, to both accumulate knowledge while remaining suspicious of it and recognizing that much remains unknown, is to be wise.

## Knowing, doubting, and the wisdom literature

### Supporting argument and evidence

Support for the conception of wisdom derived from the knowledge context matrix, that to be wise is to know and to doubt, can be garnered from a variety of sources, including the philosophy of science, the ontogeny of knowing, and the philosophy of wisdom. What distinguishes science from nonscience? Although many possible distinctions might be offered, certainly the process of science entails precisely that attitude that is the essence of wisdom: knowing that one does not know, appreciating that knowledge is fallible. The anthropologist Ashley Montague has employed this distinction between science and nonscience in commenting on the controversy surrounding laws enacted in the states of Arkansas and Louisiana requiring the story of creation to be taught as a "scientific" theory in the public schools. Advocates of the laws had pointed out that there is controversy and doubt within the scientific community regarding the details of the theory of evolution. Montague took advantage of their observation and neatly captured the distinction between science and nonscience: "Science has proofs without certainty. Creationists have certainty without any proofs" (cited in Hilts, 1981). Science is more than the accumulation of evidence or "facts"; it also entails the doubting and the continual evaluation of that evidence as well as a willingness to discard ideas that are no longer supported. Thus, continued controversy over the precise mechanisms of evolution is consistent with the process of science; an unwavering commitment to the story of creation is not. All the facts and interpretations of science must remain open to falsification. As Bronowski (1973, p. 353) has noted, "There is no absolute knowledge. And those who claim it, whether they are scientists or dogmatists, open the door to tragedy. All information is imperfect. We have to treat it with humility."

The struggle to avoid the extremes of too confident knowing and too cautious doubting is captured within Chandler's (1987) essay setting forth parallels between traditional philosophic concerns, on the one hand, and the epistemological problems that arise in the intellectual development of adolescents and young adults, on the other. Chandler characterizes the first extreme as dogmatism, a reaction against the personal, subjective, and relativistic nature of human knowledge. One strives to ground one's knowledge in such presumably more objective bases as omniscient authority, religion, scientism, and so forth. Chandler's second extreme is skepticism. Because nothing can be known with absolute certainty, one is forced to adopt inadequate means of deciding how to act, such as impulsivism, intuitionism, conformism, and indifferentism (p. 151). Neither extreme resembles wisdom, although the middle course between the two, which Chandler has termed postskeptical rationalism, certainly does. The postskeptical rationalist requires merely that actions be guided by knowledge that is as certain as possible and/or as certain as it is necessary to be. That is, one abandons both the hope for absolute truth and the prospect that nothing can be known; in wisdom, one is able to act with knowledge while simultaneously doubting.

A philosophy of wisdom based on an avoidance of extremes and a search for the moderate course between extremes has been outlined by Hartshorne (1987). Hartshorne illustrates this philosophy by drawing numerous examples from ethics, aesthetics, metaphysics, religion, and daily life. The extremes expressed in such oppositions as ugliness versus orderliness, monism versus pluralism, determinism versus indeterminism, materialism versus idealism, rationalism versus empiricism, atheism versus theism, and pessimism versus optimism are plainly false. The sense of beauty, for example, arises in the middle ground between ugliness and orderliness, between confusing chaos and boring mechanism, between discord and harmony. The problem, according to Hartshorne, is to find the judicious mean between these extremes. Finding the moderate course is made difficult, in some cases, by "the fact that one of the two extremes is so obviously untenable that by comparison the opposite extreme appears imperative" (p. 8) and, in others, by the fact that "sometimes there seems almost a conspiracy among extremists to see to it that moderate positions should be ignored" (p. 22).

Hartshorne's philosophy of wisdom appears consistent with the notion, derived from the knowledge context matrix, that wisdom entails both knowing and doubting. For Hartshorne, "Caution can go too far; so can boldness" (p. 1). Nevertheless, because Hartshorne illustrates his philosophy primarily through examples involving opposite extremes, it can be seen as a special case of what is described by the knowledge context matrix. If we were to understand doubting to imply knowledge of some entity that is opposite to the doubted entity, then the differences between Hartshorne's philosophy of wisdom and the knowledge context matrix would be reduced considerably. Yet, aside from the sorts of oppositions described by Hartshorne, it seems that in the more general case the nature of doubting does not necessarily entail knowledge of or belief in something other than that which is doubted. One can merely doubt what one knows, or doubt that one knows. (Dorothy remarks, in *The Wizard of Oz,* "Toto, I have a feeling we're not in Kansas anymore.") Indeed, Hartshorne appears to undercut his own oppositional model by noting that "to assert 'both–and' is not always the right way to do justice to two contrasting conceptions" (p. 12). Thus Hartshorne's philosophy of wisdom as the moderate course between two known extremes is a special case of the more general knowledge context matrix in which wisdom is the moderate course between knowing and doubting.

## What wisdom is not

The essence of wisdom, as argued in the preceding and elsewhere (see, e.g., Meacham, 1983b, p. 127), lies not in what is known but rather in the manner in which that knowledge is held and in how that knowledge is put to use. To be wise is not to know particular facts but to know without excessive confidence or excessive cautiousness. Wisdom is thus not a belief, a value, a set of facts, a corpus of knowledge or information in some specialized area, or a set of special abilities or skills. Wisdom is an attitude taken by persons toward the beliefs, values, knowledge, information, abilities, and skills that are held, a tendency to doubt that these are necessarily true or valid and to doubt that they are an exhaustive set of those things that could be known.

Consider, for example, an early scene from the film *The Graduate,* a scene that elicits a good laugh from audiences. Ben (Dustin Hoffman) is accosted by his father's friend, Mr. Maguire:

MAGUIRE: Come with me for a minute. I want to talk to you. I just want to say one word to you. Just one word.

BEN: Yes, sir.

MAGUIRE: Are you listening?

BEN: Yes, sir, I am.

MAGUIRE: Plastics.

*(long pause)*

BEN: Exactly how do you mean it?

The humor in this scene is carried not by any consideration of whether the advice regarding plastics, clearly intended by Maguire to be his wise gift to the new graduate, is valid or not. Instead, the humor turns on the excessive confidence with which the advice is held by Maguire and with which it is offered to Ben. Maguire's incautious attitude with regard to what he knows violates the definition of wisdom, so that the advice regarding plastics cannot possibly be perceived as wise.

In contrast, an early scene in the movie *Wall Street* illustrates the holding of a wise attitude toward what one knows. Indeed, the scene presages the eventual tragedy of the other major characters, a tragedy arising from their excessive confidence. The novice stockbroker Bud Fox (Charlie Sheen) makes an announcement to the senior stockbroker Lou Mannheim (Hal Holbrook):

FOX: Lou, I got a sure thing. Anacott Steel.

MANNHEIM: No such thing, except death and taxes. . . . What's going on, Bud? You know something? Remember, there are no shortcuts, son. Quick-buck artists come and go with every bear market.

Later in the film, Mannheim comments: "You're on a roll, kid. Enjoy it while it lasts. 'Cause it never does." Both scenes are sobering, not titillating, for audiences because Mannheim's expressions of doubt toward the knowledge Fox proffers are recognized as a hallmark of wisdom. The validity of the particular knowledge about Anacott Steel – whether the stock will rise or fall in price – is not relevant to the scene, just as the question of whether the time is right for plastics was not relevant. Good advice is not necessarily the same as wise advice. The essence of wisdom is not in what is known but in how that knowledge is held and put to use.

## Additional supporting analyses

This conception of wisdom as both knowing and doubting receives additional support from several analyses of the concept of wisdom appearing recently in the psychological literature. Wisdom has been conceived by Baltes, Dittmann-Kohli, and Dixon (1984) and Dixon, Kramer, and Baltes (1985) as good judgment about practical matters in life, especially those matters that are complex and uncertain regarding problem definition and solution. They propose five aspects of or criteria for wisdom: "an expertise in selected domains of knowledge, the pragmatics of life as the content domain of expertise, contextual richness in problem definition, uncertainty of problem definition, and relativism in judgment" (Baltes et al., 1984, p. 66). There is an approximate correspondence between these five criteria and my own conception of wisdom as both knowing and doubting. Expertise, good judgment, and insight, the first criterion of wisdom, can be seen as based upon both the second criterion of factual knowledge, or *knowing,* and the third, fourth, and fifth criteria, which involve complexity, relativism, and uncertainty, that is, the *doubting* of what is known.

Sternberg (1985) has provided data to support a multidimensional scaling model of wisdom-related behaviors, contrasting this model with those for intelligence and creativity. In the case of wisdom, separate interpretations are provided for the positive and negative polarities of each of three dimensions: The first dimension is interpreted as including reasoning ability and sagacity, the second as including learning from ideas and environment and judgment, and the third as including perspicacity and expeditious use of information. Sternberg (1985, p. 617) notes that the behaviors associated with the first dimension for wisdom (reasoning ability) are quite similar to those that represent the first dimension of intelligence (practical problem-solving ability).

The dimension with the least overlap with either intelligence or creativity, so that it might be taken as revealing what is most distinctive about wisdom, is sagacity (Sternberg, 1985, p. 623). Sagacity includes behaviors such as considers advice, feels he or she can always learn from other people, is thoughtful, is a good listener, is not afraid to admit making a mistake, and listens to all sides of an issue. These behaviors can also be interpreted as reflecting an understanding of the fallibility or limitations of one's own knowledge, a lack of dogmatism, a tolerance of uncertainty, and a willingness to doubt. If so, then Sternberg's (1985) data are not inconsistent with the conception of wisdom derived from the knowledge context matrix.

According to the historical review of Holliday and Chandler (1986), the notion that doubting, as well as knowing, is central to the concept of wisdom was held even by classical Greek philosophers. For Aristotle, who focused on speculative, abstract, or theoretically oriented wisdom rather than wisdom in practical matters, wisdom involved not only knowing all things to the extent possible but also being acutely aware of the limitations of knowledge. For the skeptics, on the other hand, who focused on practical wisdom, wisdom was also seen as "the ability to recognize the limits of one's knowledge" (Holliday & Chandler, 1986, p. 15). Thus both speculative and pragmatic wisdom were thought to include doubting as an important dimension, as in the present conception.

Holliday and Chandler (1986) also carried out a prototype analysis of the concept of wisdom, collecting descriptions of wise people and ratings of how typical each attribute is of wise people, and subsequently conducting a principal-components analysis on these ratings. A five-factor solution was obtained: exceptional understanding, judgment and communication skills, general competencies, interpersonal skills, and social unobtrusiveness. These five factors subsume factors obtained in earlier studies, such as that of Clayton and Birren (1980). The last three of the five factors are less significant, for the general competencies, interpersonal skills, and social unobtrusiveness factors were also associated with distractor categories such as intelligence, perceptiveness, spirituality, and shrewdness. The remaining two factors, Holliday and Chandler suggest, serve as the "distinctive core of meaning for the concept of 'wise'" (1986, p. 81). The first of these, exceptional understanding, can also be understood in a general sense as *knowing;* it includes descriptors such as has learned from experience, sees things within a larger context, uses common sense, observant/perceptive, thinks for him- or herself, understands him- or herself, sees the essence of situations, and so forth (Holliday & Chandler, 1986, p. 61).

Holliday and Chandler's (1986) remaining factor, judgment and communication skills, can be interpreted as doubting. This factor includes four descriptors related to communication skills (is a source of good advice, worth listening to, knows when to give/not give advice, and uncondescending) but also includes six descriptors that can be taken to reflect awareness of the limitations of knowledge, cautiousness in decision making, or *doubting:* thinks carefully before deciding, sees and considers all points of view, considers all options in a situation, reflective, weighs the consequences of action, and foresightful/farseeing. In my view, this factor might have readily been named caution in judgment, a label more consistent with my own conception of wisdom.

Holliday and Chandler (1986, p. 83) suggest that Clayton and Birren's (1980) reflective dimension corresponds with their exceptional understanding category, apparently because of the similarity between intuitive, myself, and introspective, on the one hand, and intuitive and understands him- or herself, on the other. But Clayton and Birren's terms might also be taken to correspond with reflective, understands life, and aware, descriptors associated with Holliday and Chandler's judgment and communication skills, the factor that I have reinterpreted as doubting. If so, then Clayton and Birren's (1980) results can also be interpreted in terms of a *knowing* dimension, including intelligent, pragmatic, observant, experienced, and knowledgeable, and a reflective or *doubting* dimension, including intuitive and introspective.

Sternberg (1985, p. 625), similarly commenting on the results of Clayton and Birren (1980), aligns their reflective dimension with his reasoning polarity and their affective dimension, which includes understanding, empathetic, peaceful, and gentle, with his sagacity polarity. Nevertheless, it would seem as reasonable to align Clayton and Birren's (1980) reflective dimension, which includes introspective and myself, with Sternberg's (1985) sagacity polarity, which includes thoughtful and knows self best. To do so would bring all three of these empirical analyses of wisdom into alignment with the present conception that wisdom must include doubting.

Naming factors is a risky business, renaming them even riskier. Still, it appears that the analyses provided by Baltes et al. (1984), Sternberg (1985), Holliday and Chandler (1986), and Clayton and Birren (1980) can be taken as not inconsistent with the present conception of wisdom as involving both knowing and doubting. It is not my intent to argue against multidimensional conceptions of wisdom. I do believe, however, that it is important to distinguish

1. those dimensions that characterize not only wisdom but also other categories of cognitive and interpersonal functioning (Sternberg [1985, p. 617] and Holliday and Chandler [1986, p. 81] are especially good on this point)

from

2. those dimensions that although strongly associated with wisdom are nevertheless secondary to or derived from wisdom (certain interpersonal skills such as being uncondescending, empathic, a good listener, kind, and so forth, might follow from first being wise)

and from

3. those dimensions or aspects that are essential to our definition of wisdom.

My thesis is that the indispensable core is the combination of both knowing and doubting.

## Does wisdom increase or decrease with age?

### *The argument against ad hoc observations*

Wisdom is commonly linked in the life span development literature with development in late adulthood and old age (e.g., Baltes, Smith, Staudinger, & Soworka, in press; Clayton & Birren, 1980; Erikson, 1982; Perlmutter & Hall, 1985, p. 262), yet good empirical evidence for this association of wisdom and aging is notably lacking. In the absence of empirical evidence that wisdom increases with age, at least two other possible developmental functions (Wohlwill, 1973) should be considered: that wisdom decreases with age and that wisdom is not age related. In the remainder of this chapter, I will argue against the notion that wisdom increases with age and for the reasonableness of these other developmental functions.

Why has wisdom been linked with late adulthood and old age? There are two major reasons, the first having to do with our inadequate, ad hoc observations on the incidence of wisdom, the second having to do with our own needs as (for the most part) younger adults to attribute wisdom to older persons. When we reflect upon those few occasions in which the behavior or speech of someone has been so remarkable – that is, it stands out from what seems to be typical behavior or speech – that we make the attribution of wisdom, it seems often to be the case that these incidents have involved older persons. But this impression is consistent both with the hypothesis that wisdom increases with age as well as with the view that wisdom decreases with age. It is consistent with the increase of wisdom with age if the framework for comparison – the typical or normal behavior or speech – includes persons of all ages. (In order to keep the discussion simple, the issue of possible cohort changes in wisdom is ignored.) That is, our conclusion that incidents of wisdom are less frequent for younger than for older persons would have to be based on observation of wise behavior or speech across a wide range of ages using the same criteria for wisdom at each age while remaining blind to the ages of the persons who are behaving or speaking. Yet it seems unlikely that our ad hoc observations have been this well controlled, for it is rare that we do not know or cannot make a reasonable guess as to the age of the person, and it is likely that our criteria for wise behavior or speech shift as we take the age of the person into account.

Instead, it is more likely that our ad hoc observations have been carried out within a framework for comparison that includes only one age group, namely, older persons (for reasons to be discussed later). We note that the behavior or speech of an older person is so remarkable – that is, it stands out from what seems to be typical behavior or speech for older persons – that we make the attribution of wisdom to this person. Whereas it is true that our observation of remarkable, wisdomlike behavior on the part of an older person is consistent with the hypothesis that wisdom increases with age, it is also quite consistent with the hypotheses that wisdom decreases with age or that wisdom is not age related. A search for wisdom within the limited group of older persons, rather than across all ages, does not provide an adequate data base for choosing among these alternative developmental hypotheses.

Nevertheless, one might argue, even if it is granted that our ad hoc observations of wisdom have been within-age observations rather than observations across ages, does not the fact that incidents of wisdom-related behavior and speech are remarkable – they stand out, they attract our attention – only among older persons but not among younger persons provide support for the hypothesis that wisdom increases with age? Not necessarily. One reason that the behavior or speech of older persons might sometimes be found remarkable stems from the ageist nature of our society. The commonplace but incorrect stereotype of old age is that it is a time of decreasing intellectual competence (Meacham, 1983a). Given this expectation of decline, young people are sometimes surprised when an older person engages in behavior or speech that may be merely competent at a normative level. Rather than reform their false stereotype of aging, it might be easier for younger people in our society to interpret this older person's behavior or speech as an isolated instance of wisdom. In short, there is good reason to be skeptical that apparently remarkable behavior and speech, that is, wisdomlike behaviors, are in fact remarkable. These behaviors might be no different from the typical behavior of most older people or indeed the typical behavior of people at any age.

### The data are not adequate to decide

There are some data that touch on this question of the developmental function for wisdom. Clayton and Birren (1980, p. 118) found, using their multidimensional scaling technique, that young and middle-aged persons placed the stimulus word *aged* closer to the stimulus *wise* than did older persons. This finding suggests that young and middle-aged persons hold the traditional view of an association between age and wisdom, whereas older persons who might be said to be in a better position to know hold the view that age and wisdom are not necessarily closely associated. So the Clayton and Birren finding provides no support for the traditional view that wisdom increases with age; furthermore, the finding is not inconsistent with the hypothesis that wisdom decreases with age.

Holliday and Chandler (1986) similarly asked young, middle-aged, and older persons to rate a large number of descriptors according to how good each descriptor was for describing the category of wisdom. Because no age differences were found, the data were pooled for all subsequent analyses. Nevertheless, the mean values at each age for each descriptor can be examined on the question of whether wisdom is believed to increase, decrease, or remain stable with age. Inspection of the means reveals that older people appear more likely than younger people to endorse the descriptor "may be any age" (p. 50), a trend consistent with the finding of Clayton and Birren (1980). In response to the descriptor "older," the ratings of the three age groups appear approximately the same.

Overall, there was relatively *low* endorsement both of the descriptor "may be any age" and of the descriptor "older" (pp. 50–51). This finding at first appears contradictory, at least from the traditional perspective that wisdom increases with age. Logically, the only resolution of low endorsement of both statements is that a good descriptor of wise people would be "younger." But it is probably more reasonable to interpret the data as meaning that age is not central to the notion of wisdom. This latter conclusion is supported by the fact that "may be any age" does not appear as a defining variable for any of the five factors or dimensions that emerged in Holliday and Chandler's analysis. "Older" appears as a defining variable for the general competencies factor but not for the two factors considered most central to wisdom, exceptional understanding and judgment and communication skills (p. 61).

In the preceding paragraphs I have drawn inferences about whether wisdom increases, decreases, or remains stable with age from what persons of different ages say about wisdom. This is, of course, not at all the same as having data that bear on whether people of different ages might in fact be termed wise on the basis of their speech or actions. Data bearing on the latter point are provided by Baltes et al. (in press), who asked young, middle-aged, and older persons to engage in life review and life-planning tasks. When performance on the life review tasks was compared on six different wisdom-related criteria, including good advice, rich knowledge, good life review, contextualistic thinking, and relativistic thinking, there were no differences between the three groups (with one exception). The lack of differences as a function of age serves to further undermine the traditional view that wisdom increases with age.

The one exception in the data of Baltes et al. (in press) was for the criterion termed "awareness of uncertainty": In response to life review tasks, older and middle-aged persons displayed a greater awareness of uncertainty than younger persons. The fact that it is this particular criterion having to do with uncertainty or doubting that emerges as differential is consistent with what I have proposed as the essence of wisdom. But the finding that older people are more aware of uncertainty than younger people would appear at first to be most consistent with the traditional view of wisdom as increasing with age rather than the hypotheses for which I am arguing, that wisdom can also decrease or remain stable with age. But here it is important to turn to the second task employed by Baltes et al. (in press), the planning task. On this task, both younger and older persons performed best when confronted with life problems specific to their own ages. If this conclusion from the second task is then employed in interpreting the data from the life review task, the apparent greater awareness of uncertainty by older people is readily interpretable as something other than wisdom, for life review is widely regarded as a task more typical of and appropriate for older than younger persons (Butler, 1963).

*Why has wisdom been thought to increase with age?*

Despite my argument based on the weakness of our ad hoc observations that wisdom might decrease or remain stable as well as increase with age, and despite the fact that the empirical data do not help in distinguishing between these three possible developmental hypotheses, it is nevertheless still true that by and large wisdom has been associated with development in late adulthood and old age. Why has wisdom been thought to increase with age? The answer, I will argue, is that the association of wisdom with aging reflects primarily the needs of younger people to attribute wisdom to older persons.

The association by young and middle-aged people of wisdom with being older is clear in the data of both Clayton and Birren (1980) and Holliday and Chandler (1986). Young adulthood brings a new awareness of the difficulties and responsibilities associated with the tasks of adulthood. It becomes necessary to make significant and irreversible decisions having to do with finding a meaningful and productive work role in one's society, with constructing intimate and lasting relationships with other people, with nurturing children so that they might be prepared as young adults to face these same challenges, and so forth. Yet at the very time these responsibilities must be assumed and these decisions made, young adults find themselves lacking in the knowledge and experience that could make such decisions more sound, that could provide some certainty that work and love will succeed and prevail. The difficulty in making such decisions rationally is that one would like to know now how society will be structured and what opportunities will emerge and recede in future years. Not only can young adults not know this, but they are relatively powerless, despite their idealism, to affect the course of society until through their own aging they have attained positions of power within society.

In the face of such uncertainty, it must be comforting and indeed necessary for young adults to believe that those older persons who are in positions of power have indeed learned from experience, see things within a larger context, use common sense, think carefully before making decisions, are knowledge-able, understand life, see the essence of situations, are reliable and moral – in short, that older persons are wise (the list is drawn from Holliday and Chandler's [1986, p. 59] descriptors for wise people). Rationally, I can argue that many decisions of my government have not been wise; yet emotionally, I need to believe that wisdom resides and will occasionally triumph within the institution of government. The issue here is not whether older people in fact have such attributes; the point is that it is reasonable that younger people would need to believe and trust that older people, particularly those in po-sitions of power in society and those to whom younger people might turn for advice, have such attributes.

Young adulthood and middle age are also times of hard work and sacrifice, of unfulfilled hopes and dreams, of risks taken and opportunities lost. To not work hard, to not sacrifice, yet to not prosper in the end creates no dissonance; but what can be the rationale for a life of hard work and sacrifice that appears to be directed toward the disaster of poor health, poverty, social isolation, and declining physical and mental abilities that, by the false yet commonplace stereotype, represents the reality of old age in our society (Meacham, 1983a; McTavish, 1971)? One hope to which young and middle-aged persons might cling is that, despite the fact that the efforts of adulthood do not appear to be paying off with wealth, recognition of achievements, or power and status, old age will bring a certain maturity, an awareness, an ability to say things that are worth listening to, an understanding of life, an understanding of other people, a philosophical attitude, respect, and so forth – in short, wisdom (again, the list is drawn from Holliday and Chandler [1986, p. 59]). The issue here is not whether as we grow older we will in fact attain these attributes; the point is that it is reasonable that young and middle-aged people would need to believe and trust that at least the reward of wisdom, if no other, will be theirs as they approach the end of a life of hard work and sacrifice. To be consistent with this belief, wisdom must be a quality that is not possessed by younger people – else why continue to work hard and sacrifice – but is possessed by at least a few older people, as proof that the promise of wisdom is one on which delivery is occasionally made. Furthermore, the gift of wisdom can be taken as part of the apology of a younger, ageist society toward its elders; when health, friends, and status are gone, at least wisdom remains.

It should not escape notice that many contemporary writers on the topic of wisdom, including myself and several of the contributors to the present volume, are still young or middle-aged, not old and, at least by the traditional perspective, not yet wise. One rather significant methodological issue that has not been faced directly within the traditional perspective is the epistemological one: How can researchers and writers who are not yet wise write credibly on the topic of wisdom? The epistemological problem is not quite the same as, for example, writing about mental illness or about life in another culture, for here we can assume that researchers and authors have at least an adequate level of intellectual competence as well as some minimal frame of reference held in common with the people about whom they are writing, so that they can put forth at least a fairly decent interpretation of mental illness, of life in another culture, and so forth. But suppose wisdom itself is of a higher order of intellectual competence or understanding, so that for middle-aged researchers to pontificate on the topic of wisdom is as absurd as for children considered concrete-operational within Piaget's structural-developmental theory to presume to describe and discuss the nature of formal operations. By the traditional perspective on wisdom and aging, on what grounds would middle-aged researchers be able to recognize instances of wise behavior and speech by older persons?

In short, there is a major epistemological problem here, and it is possible that many research programs on wisdom pursued by young or middle-aged researchers are ill-conceived; perhaps wisdom is a topic that should be reserved to researchers who are certifiably old and wise, or perhaps younger researchers should employ certifiably old and wise persons as their research aides, to be the assessment instruments for the identification of wise behavior and speech in the research population. I make these suggestions not in seriousness, however, but merely to indicate that the continued pursuit of wisdom by young and middle-aged researchers in the face of the epistemological problem must be motivated by other than the orthodox reasons for research programs. For example, recognizing as most social scientists do that in the course of our research and writing we have the potential to define our subject matter, and in view of the reality of our own individual aging, it is reasonable for researchers in gerontology to want to ascribe to their research participants those positive qualities they themselves might acquire in the course of their own aging. Gergen (1973) has presented good evidence to show that social scientists label the characteristics of their research participants so that there is an alignment of positive qualities with the qualities that might be assumed to inhere within the social scientists' own social, educational, and economic classes. Similarly, as middle-aged researchers we need to subscribe to the traditional perspective that wisdom increases with age because we expect that shortly our own wisdom, now budding, will inevitably come into full bloom.

Does wisdom come with old age? It is interesting that, according to the data of Clayton and Birren (1980) and of Holliday and Chandler (1986), older people appear to see somewhat more distance between themselves and wisdom than that which younger people see between older people and wisdom. Is the promise of wisdom not fulfilled? Still, as already noted, it is difficult to draw conclusions from these particular data, and so it is more prudent at this point to say merely that older people as well need to subscribe to the traditional perspective that wisdom increases with age. Why not? In an ageist society in which to grow old means to risk losing control over the resources in one's life, to lose power, respect, and status, it is reasonable to want to believe that there remain some special qualities that have been achieved in the course of life that cannot be stripped away by younger people. These special qualities are ones that cannot be acquired in any way other than to have lived, worked, and loved for six or seven decades, qualities such as having learned from experience, being mature, being a source of good advice, being interesting to talk with, knowing when to give or withhold advice, understanding other people, being philosophical, astute, discerning, respected, and so forth – in short, being wise (list from Holliday and Chandler [1986, p. 59]). The issue here is not whether older people in fact have such attributes; the point is that it is reasonable that older people in an ageist society would want to believe that they do have at least these special qualities of wisdom, special because these qualities can be achieved only by virtue of being old. To grant that younger people might also be wise would be to give away that special quality that comes with aging. Thus for older people as well as for younger people, the commonplace association of wisdom with aging reflects primarily a motivation or need to have such an association hold true.

## Wisdom decreases with age

### Consider this alternative

To summarize to this point, the traditional view of an association of wisdom with aging, that is, the hypothesis that wisdom increases with age, does not remain strong. It has been argued that our ad hoc observations of wisdomlike behavior and speech are consistent with not only increases but also decreases and stability of wisdom with age and that good empirical evidence to support the notion that wisdom increases with age is lacking. I would like, therefore, to direct our attention to one of the alternative hypotheses, and so consider in more detail the possibility that wisdom decreases with age. In doing so, I recognize that the arguments and evidence are just as scanty for this hypothesis as for the traditional one. Still, it would seem that at this early point in our investigation and understanding of the concept of wisdom all possible hypotheses ought to be entertained. As it turns out, the hypothesis that wisdom decreases with age eliminates some of the awkwardnesses noted with the traditional hypothesis.

Said starkly, my hypothesis is that all people are wise to begin with, as children, but that as we grow older most people lose their wisdom. Age or aging is not essential to wisdom. Wisdom needs to be understood not as a quality that can be achieved or attained by a select few in late adulthood or old age but instead as a quality that is maintained and preserved by only a select few over the course of life. Of course, I should anticipate some rebellion against the hypothesis that wisdom decreases with age. It is difficult to conjure images of young people engaged in wise behaviors or speech. But if it is the case that all younger people are wise, then wisdom-related behavior and speech on the part of one or a few young people would not strike us as remarkable. Wisdom-related behavior and speech become remarkable by virtue of their incidence being relatively low, which can be the case in late adulthood and old age regardless of whether wisdom is hypothesized to increase or decrease with age. According to the traditional hypothesis that wisdom increases with age, the incidence of wisdom is low in late adulthood and old age because only a few individuals have attained this rare quality as they have grown old; by the hypothesis that wisdom decreases with age, only a few have been able to retain their wisdom over the course of life.

The discovery by people who have grown old that there is not a turning point at which wisdom is bestowed, the acceptance by older people that they can be as foolish and as human as younger people, the remembrance with pride that as younger people they did and said things that even now, or perhaps only now, strike one as wise, are consistent with the trend within the data of Holliday and Chandler (1986, p. 50) for older people to be more likely than younger people to endorse the descriptor that a wise person "may be any age." Furthermore, the hypothesis that wisdom decreases with age solves, in some respects, the epistemological issue that is raised by the traditional perspective, that is, the problem of how unwise, middle-aged researchers could hope to recognize wisdom in their older, wiser research participants. If all researchers were wise as children, and we hope that not all have lost their wisdom by middle age, then there ought to be at least a few middle-aged researchers who have retained sufficient wisdom that they can recognize wisdom in children, in their peers, and in adults who are far older than they. Finally, the hypothesis that wisdom decreases with age is consistent with the finding within the data of Clayton and Birren (1980) that older people tend to perceive somewhat greater distance between wisdom and the stimulus word *aged* than younger people foresee for them.

If it is the case that wisdom decreases with age, then a further reason can be deduced (to add to those listed earlier) as to why people would need to attribute wisdom to older rather than younger people. If what is typical in the course of life is that the wisdom of one's youth is lost or given up, then – assuming that one can recognize when one is no longer wise – the recognition that wisdom has been lost could lead, as any loss, to grief or depression at the loss, especially if it is clear that one has traded away one's wisdom for more material but short-term rewards, for life in the fast lane, or in Riegel's (1978, p. xvi) words (referring to the discipline of psychology), "for a lentil soup." Denial of the loss and insistence that wisdom is yet to be, that wisdom increases with age, might be one way of coping with this recognition and the associated depression.

## Wisdom in youth

I would be delighted at this point to be able to produce some good empirical evidence for the existence of wisdom in childhood, adolescence, and young adulthood. Unfortunately, there is a great risk at this point of a hurling back and forth of ad hoc observations in support of one hypothesis or the other, along with disparaging remarks that the observations hurled in defense of the other hypothesis do not, after all, really represent paradigmatic instances of wisdom. Nevertheless, I will introduce two such observations of youthful wisdom, if for no other reason than to show that this is not how the issue of whether wisdom increases or decreases with age will likely be resolved.

Let me begin with the paradigmatic case of wisdom, Solomon, whose wisdom was such that there was none like it before nor will there be any like it after Solomon (I Kings 4:12). What was the essence of Solomon's wisdom? Solomon was confronted by two women, each of whom claimed to be the mother of the same child. The wisdom of Solomon consisted not in the knowledge he held, for he did not know who was in fact the mother of this child. The wisdom of Solomon was in his recognition that he did not know and that he could not act without first devising a procedure – the proposal to divide the child by sword and distribute the halves to the two women – so as to increase his knowledge (I Kings 4:16–28). But this wisdom of Solomon was a wisdom of his youth! In old age, Solomon became rich and powerful and "loved many strange women" who "turned his heart after other gods" so that "he kept not that which the Lord commanded" (I Kings 11). Certainly, according to the Old Testament, it is possible for young people to be wise: "A wise son makes a glad father" (Proverbs 10:1); "A wise son heareth his father's instruction" (Proverbs 13:1); "Great men are not always wise; neither do the aged understand judgment" (Job 32:9). Although a variety of meanings are associated with wisdom in the Bible, both young and old people were capable of being wise (McFayden, 1921; cited in Clayton and Birren, 1980, p. 107).

The diary of Anne Frank (1952) is introduced by Eleanor Roosevelt as "one of the wisest and most moving commentaries on war and its impact on human beings." Written while Anne was 13–15 years of age, her diary provides an opportunity to search through the ruminations and insights of an adolescent for instances of wisdom. In discussing the disagreements between her own family and the Van Daan family, Anne moves from a position of confident knowledge to a moderate and wise position in which she accepts the possibility that her own family has not always been in the right:

Until now I was immovable! I always thought the Van Daans were in the wrong, but we too are partly to blame. We have certainly been right over the subject matter; but handling of others from intelligent people (which we consider ourselves to be!) one expects more insight. (Frank, 1952, p. 126)*

Later, in reflecting upon her relationship with her father, there is a similar movement:

No, Anne, you still have a tremendous lot to learn, begin by doing that first, instead of looking down on others and accusing them. (p. 205)

And in contrasting her friend Peter with herself, she remarks that it is hard

to stand on your own feet as a conscious, living person. Because if you do, then it's twice as difficult to steer a right path through the sea of problems. . . . How can I make clear to [Peter] that what appears easy and attractive will drag him down into the depths. (p. 229)

I take these brief passages to be indicative of Anne's capacity to reject the easy extreme of dogmatic knowing. Her rejection of the opposite extreme of paralyzing doubt, and so her striving for the moderate, wise course between knowing and doubting, is revealed in the following:

That's the difficulty in these times: ideals, dreams, and cherished hopes rise within us, only to meet the horrible truth and be shattered. It's really a wonder that I haven't dropped all my ideals, because they seem so absurd and impossible to carry out. Yet I keep them, because in spite of everything I still believe that people are really good at heart. (p. 237)

---

*These excerpts are reprinted, with permission of Doubleday & Company, from *Anne Frank: The diary of a young girl.*

## A two-dimensional wisdom space

Even if it is granted that children, adolescents, and young adults display speech and behaviors that might be taken as instances of wisdom, certainly, it still might be argued that the experience and increased knowledge that come only with advanced age must impart to wisdom a quality that marks it as somehow different from the wisdom of youth. Yes, there can be differences in the quality with which wisdom is expressed, but these differences in quality do not touch directly upon the essence of wisdom. The essence of wisdom is in knowing that one does not know, in the appreciation that knowledge is fallible, in the balance between knowing and doubting. But this attitude toward knowledge can be expressed in many domains differing widely in their character.

I can expand upon this point by returning to the work of Hartshorne (1987), who argued for a philosophy of wisdom based on a search for the moderate course between extremes (or, as I argue, between knowing and doubting). There is more to Hartshorne's analysis, for he suggests in addition a second dimension ranging between the ultrasimple, too trivial to notice, on the one hand, and the ultracomplex, too profound to grasp, on the other. In other words, "the mean between the extremes can be achieved on different levels of intensity or complexity of experience" (Hartshorne, 1987, p. 52). By way of illustration, Hartshorne notes that a single flower and a simple musical chord have both variety and unity but on a superficial level, that is, our aesthetic capacities or intellectual resources are not challenged in our appreciation of a flower or a simple chord. But a natural forest and a symphony are, in contrast, far more diverse, profound, and challenging and can severely strain the resources of one individual to fully appreciate while not doing so for another: "Adults and children obviously differ in this respect, and education plays a role" (Hartshorne, 1987, p. 4).

By extension from Hartshorne's analysis I can now propose a two-dimensional model of wisdom. The first dimension, representing the essence of wisdom as an appreciation that knowledge is fallible and as a striving for balance between knowing and doubting, is not a developmental dimension (this dimension is not different from the confidence ordinate in the knowledge context model [Meacham, 1983b]). The attitude of wisdom is accessible to people of all ages, just as excessive confidence and lack of curiosity, on the one extreme, and excessive cautiousness and fear of acting, on the other, are states in which people of all ages can be found. The second dimension, concerned with whether the domain in which wisdom has been expressed is simple or profound, captures changes in the quality of wisdom. These changes reflect not a change in the essence of wisdom but rather the age-related accumulation of information, experiences, and insights (the abscissa in the knowledge context model).

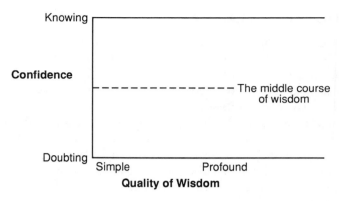

Figure 9.1. A two-dimensional wisdom space.

Both of these dimensions are shown in Figure 9.1. Any instance of wisdom can be located within this two-dimensional wisdom space

1. according to the extent to which it meets the definitional criterion of wisdom, namely, as an expression of both knowing and doubting, and
2. according to the quality of the instance of wisdom on a continuum from simple to profound.

Observing that the space is two-dimensional makes clear why there is disagreement in conversation and in the research literature over whether particular ad hoc observations of wisdom are in fact exemplary of wisdom or not. Because the space is two-dimensional, it is difficult to judge which is the more wise, an instance of apparently wisdom-related speech or behavior that suits the definitional criterion but is rather simple or an instance that is profound but is nevertheless somewhat removed from the definitional criterion. The first instance would be located along the median of Figure 9.1 but near the left side, the second near the right side but at a greater distance from the median. For example, Markman (1977) raised the question of whether young children could realize that they had not understood instructions on how to perform a task in a situation in which she had deleted critical information from the instructions. The sensitivity of young children to their own lack of knowing and their subsequent efforts to elicit further information as a necessary prelude to action is consistent with the definitional criterion of wisdom – that is, the children can be described as simultaneously knowing and doubting – but the wisdom of these children would have to be regarded as simple, not profound, in the view of most adults.

Although the information, experiences, and insights that come with maturity make it likely that instances of profound wisdom will be more evident among older than among younger people, the two-dimensional wisdom space does not impose a developmental proscription against younger people providing evidence of profound wisdom. Consider, for example, the wisdom of Martin Buber, who, at the age of 14, was confronted by his lack of understanding of the nature of time and space – whether finite or infinite – and consequently was also confronted with his vulnerability within the world, a confrontation sufficiently terrifying that he considered the possibility of suicide as a means of avoiding it (Friedman, 1981, p. 27). In terms of the two-dimensional wisdom space (and the knowledge context model), Buber was in the grip of extreme and paralyzing doubt. Relief came from reading Kant, through whom Buber realized that the concept of infinity of time and space as well as the concept of their finiteness are merely human ideas without any necessary correspondence to reality. Buber acknowledged near the end of life that he had continued to reflect on the problem of time without being able to come to a resolution of the issue of infinity (Friedman, 1981, p. 32), so it was not the case that Buber bounced, in his understanding of time and space, from the paralysis of doubt to dogmatic knowing. Instead, he constructed a moderate and wise position from which he was then able to move forward to other issues in his life and philosophy. The wisdom of the 14-year-old Buber not only fits the definitional criterion, of simultaneously knowing and doubting, but would be accepted by most adults as profound rather than simple.

I confess to not having understood for more than a few minutes each time he explained it Riegel's (1973, 1979, p. 51) proposal that a person at any developmental level could progress directly to a mature stage of dialectical thinking, so that a child might reach dialectical maturity without having progressed through, for example, Piaget's stages of concrete or formal operations. I would like to cautiously suggest, however, that there is a consistency between my current understanding of what Riegel proposed and the present concept of wisdom as simultaneously knowing and doubting, also accessible to persons of any age or developmental level. For Riegel, dialectical conflicts and contradiction are fundamental properties of thought at any age (see also Rychlak, 1976, p. 12). A person who is dialectically mature, as in the case of the young Buber, does not necessarily resolve "these conflicts but is ready to live with these contradictions; stronger yet, the individual accepts these contradictions as a basic property of thought and creativity" (Riegel, 1979, p. 53). In short, the concept of dialectical maturity can be understood as a wisdom that is available at all ages.

## Maintaining and restoring wisdom

### The risks to wisdom

In summary up to this point, I have rejected the notion that wisdom increases with age. More important, however, I have argued that wisdom, considered in its essence as an appreciation that knowledge is fallible, as a simultaneous knowing and doubting, is a potential for people at any age, including childhood. Finally, I have advanced the thesis that wisdom decreases with age, although the possibility that seemingly more profound manifestations of wisdom might be likely to emanate from older rather than younger persons has been admitted. Is there a contradiction between the notion that the achievement of wisdom is a potential reality for people at any age and the claim that wisdom decreases with age? No, not if the following descriptions of some of the ways in which people come to be less wise as they grow older are reasonable. The present chapter should not be taken as a pessimistic view of aging, that is, that we must inevitably become less wise. Instead, it is an optimistic view, that if we can recognize the reasons for the decline with age in the expression of our potential for wisdom, then we can guard against these threats to wisdom and so maintain our wisdom throughout the adult years.

If we assume that children are wise at the outset, then they can be located along the wise median of the wisdom space of Figure 9.1. In terms of the quality of their wisdom, perhaps children should be placed somewhat more toward the left, simpler expression of wisdom, than toward the right, more profound expression of wisdom. As one grows older, it is difficult to move within this space from simple to profound, for to do so requires capacities to recognize diversity and complexity as well as having a store of knowledge and insight or, in Hartshorne's (1987) terms, intellectual resources and education. Nevertheless, wisdom is neither gained nor lost, regardless of the efforts that might have gone into such movement along the median of wisdom; it is merely that the expressions of wisdom become more profound with the experience of age.

In contrast, the easier directions of movement are away from the median of wisdom – that is, the aforementioned type *a* and *b* movements (Meacham, 1983b):

  *a.*  One can rapidly accumulate information, moving directly toward the upper boundary of the wisdom space. At this extreme, one feels that one knows a great proportion of all that can be known and so acts with great confidence.
  *b.*  On the other hand, one can be overwhelmed by uncertainties, doubts, and questions, and so move directly toward the lower boundary of the wisdom space, so that in the extreme one becomes excessively cautious and unable to act.

What are some of the reasons that an individual might be propelled toward one or the other of these extremes and so no longer maintain and express the wisdom of youth?

*Accumulation.* One likely reason for the loss of wisdom with age is the emphasis within Anglo–American culture upon accumulation as the criterion for appropriate and successful development, so that to be successful is to accumulate more property, power, and wealth and, by extension to the psychological domain, more skills, expertise, information, and so forth (Lichtman, 1987; Looft, 1971; Riegel, 1972). In schools a premium is placed upon absorbing as much information as possible rather than raising questions about and critically evaluating what is already known. How often does a teacher enter the classroom intending to challenge the students' beliefs, not merely so that false information might be replaced with presumably more valid information but so that the students might leave the class feeling less confident about their knowledge (and so more wise)? Instead, the emphasis is upon knowing rather than doubting, and so the easy course of movement is away from wisdom toward the extreme of believing that one knows all, or at least enough – the course followed by the young stockbroker, Bud Fox, in the movie *Wall Street*. In Figure 9.1, the movement is upward and to the right, more sophisticated yet less wise (type *a*).

Yet, as Hartshorne (1987, p. 136) pithily reminds us, "Bigness and power do not guarantee goodness or wisdom," although they might provide us with a sense of importance. It is easy to mistake the accumulation of information, power, and importance for wisdom because the more power one has, the less likely are other people to challenge one's apparent wisdom. Yet on several counts it appears that success and wisdom are antithetical. Indeed, Marcel (1951, cited in Holliday & Chandler, 1986, p. 19) commented that one of the functions of wisdom was to guard against the excessive pride that can follow from successful mastery and control. In short, one reason why wisdom decreases as one grows older is that increasing age generally brings more information, more experience, more power, greater success, and so forth, and all of these carry with them the risk of loss of wisdom through excessive confidence in knowing.

*Stereotyping and intolerance.* One's confidence in knowing can also be increased, and wisdom lost, through immersion in an intellectual climate that forces a too early defense of one's views, a premature foreclosure of possible conceptual positions. Rather than being permitted to playfully entertain ambiguous or contradictory positions, we are often either forced to quickly abandon tentative notions or forced into a dogmatic defense of what are likely to be still untenable positions. In the course of defending such positions, we adopt a more extreme and hardened stance, moving further from the moderation of wisdom. Hartshorne (1987, p. 22) suggested that there was a conspiracy among extremists to ignore moderate positions; but the conspiracy is not only one of ignoring but also one of annihilating. For those who hold an extreme position of confident knowing, the raising of doubts by someone with a more moderate position can be threatening. The opposite, however, is not the case: For those in a wise, moderate position, already balancing both knowing and doubting, it is not threatening that others might appear to be confident in their knowledge. An intellectual climate hostile to ambiguity and contradiction is one that encourages easy solutions, such as stereotyping and intolerance (cf. Chandler, 1975, p. 175), to the legitimate questions that arise in the course of our daily experience. To adopt these easy solutions, to abandon ambiguity and contradiction for the sake of greater confidence in what one seems to know, is to abandon wisdom. In Figure 9.1, the course of movement is upward and to the left, simpler and less wise.[3]

*Cultural change.* The other easy direction of movement within the wisdom space of Figure 9.1 is away from the median of wisdom and toward the lower boundary, so that in the extreme one becomes excessively cautious and unable to act (type *b*). One condition that likely promotes such movement is rapid technological and cultural change in society. Although a few adults are able to learn about and adapt to such changes in the course of their careers, many older adults are not given the opportunity to keep up with new fashions, technical innovations, career opportunities, changing roles for men and women, and the like. Furthermore, learning that these new possibilities exist but not being able to master them can have as a by-product increasing doubts about the worth of what one has come to know and master in the past. The greater the extent of cultural change, the greater the impact on older adults who because of their prior investment as young adults in learning skills and in commitments made, for example, to particular belief or value systems, have the most to lose. The force of technological and cultural change, therefore, is to drive adults not toward becoming wiser as they grow older but toward having increased doubts about the extent and value of what they do know and toward becoming more cautious in their actions based on that knowledge. In Figure 9.1, the course of movement is downward and to the right, more complex but less wise.

*Tragedy.* More dramatic in its impact than experiencing technological and cultural changes can be the shrinking of intellectual and emotional space that too often follows as a result of major tragedies in life such as life-threatening and chronic illness, death of family and friends, divorce, and loss of a way of life, a community, an institution, or nation to which one has made a commitment. Such tragedies strike one at the personal level as irrational, incomprehensible, unjust. The intellectual frameworks to which one would ordinarily turn as tools for constructing meaning in such crises prove inadequate, and so one is forced, in terms of the wisdom space of Figure 9.1, from the sophisticated, complex, or profound toward the simpler, more basic, and perhaps more intuitive. The course of movement is from right to left as well as away from the median of wisdom toward the lower boundary, for one has lost the confidence in knowing that provides the standpoint for engaging in confident action. Children are relatively protected from such tragedies by their families; young adults have opportunities, particularly in terms of time, to struggle back from such tragedies; in late adulthood and old age there is less protection and less opportunity, and so the potential for tragedy to lead to loss of wisdom is greater.[4]

## The origin and maintenance of wisdom

If I have convinced the reader that despite the potential for wisdom at all ages there are substantial risks that the wisdom of youth will be lost as one progresses through late adulthood and old age, then some questions such as the following must arise: How can we strive to maintain wisdom in the face of such risks of losing it and falling into either dogmatism or skepticism? Once lost, can wisdom be regained and, if so, how? The answers to these questions follow from learning more about the origin of wisdom: Knowing how wisdom develops in children can suggest ways in which wisdom might be maintained or restored in adulthood and old age.

Much of the thinking about the notion of wisdom has considered wisdom to be an attribute located within the mind of individual persons, that is, some people have wisdom, others do not. This line of thinking is consistent with the accumulation metaphor of Anglo–American society and of its psychology, that is, psychological qualities are understood as traits located within individual minds. Instead, it might prove useful to consider wisdom as developing not within the mind of an isolated child but within the framework of interpersonal relations within which the child is immersed. This perspective is consistent with the perspectives of several theorists who have rejected individual cognition and consciousness as the basis for individual and societal development in favor of interpersonal relations, communication, and cooperation as that basis (Habermas, 1984; Harré, 1984; Meacham, 1984; Vygotsky, 1978). For example, Habermas (1984) rejects intrasubjectivity as a starting point in understanding the individual and society, arguing instead for basing these in intersubjectivity, in the community of persons in dialogue. A similar perspective is advanced by Harré (1984), who argues that the primary reality is the array of persons in conversation, with the psychological realities of human minds brought into being only as secondary realities.

To support the suggestion that the origin of wisdom is in interpersonal relations, let me turn to what Erikson (1963, 1982; Erikson, Erikson, & Kivnick, 1986; Meacham, 1989) has said. Erikson describes the mature faith or wisdom that can develop at the end of life as a reconciliation of "opposing old-age tendencies toward trust and assurance, on the one hand, and toward wariness and uncertainty, on the other" (Erikson et al., 1986, p. 219). The resemblance of Erikson's description of wisdom to the present conception of wisdom as a balance between knowing and doubting becomes more clear in

considering Erikson's suggestions regarding the *origins* of this mature faith
in the infant's struggles

to integrate a sense of confidence and belief in the universe, and the relative predictability of its laws, with a discriminating cautiousness and skepticism about the
same universe and its realistic unpredictabilities and unreliabilities. . . . Evolving from
lifelong experiences of hopeful confidence and cautious skepticism. . . . (Erickson et
al., 1986, pp. 218–238)

Thus Erikson grounds the wisdom of old age in the development in infancy
of trust in one's providers and in one's self (Erikson, 1963, p. 269); as the
infant comes to know and trust his or her providers, the infant must at the
same time face their possible loss, that is, the infant must doubt that which
he or she knows. To be securely attached to one's providers is the wisdom
of infancy; from this springs curiosity, creativity, and achievement.

The maintenance of wisdom throughout the life course and its restoration
if it has been lost depend upon the continued immersion of the individual
within a "wisdom atmosphere" that assists the individual in avoiding the
extremes of too confident knowing and of paralyzing doubt. In a wisdom
atmosphere, there is a supportive network of interpersonal relations in which
doubts, uncertainties, and questions can be openly expressed, in which ambiguities and contradictions can be tolerated, so that individuals are not forced
to adopt the defensive position of too confident knowing. Furthermore, the
recognition through expressing one's doubts that others share similar doubts
and yet have found a basis for confident action can keep individuals from
being forced into the position of paralyzing skepticism.

The maintenance of wisdom and its restoration also depend upon a willingness to cultivate a certain detachment from the knowledge, success, power,
and importance that represent threats or risks to wisdom. The fact that these
are among the presumed benefits of increasing age is consistent with the
decline of wisdom with age. In order to counter these risks, it becomes
essential that one strive to generate questions and doubts about the knowledge
one has acquired, to question the value of one's success, to challenge the
basis for one's own power and authority. Yet it is not easy for adults to
question their hard-won knowledge; as Krantz and Bacon (1977, p. 146) note,
the trick is to be "a sophisticated adult knower while simultaneously being a
naive child of wonder." And it is not easy to call into question one's own
authority. These challenges are both more easily carried out within a network
of supportive interpersonal relations, in which the challenges to our own
knowledge and authority come gently from those around us (Meacham &
Emont, 1989).

The notion of a wisdom atmosphere of supportive interpersonal relations
can be brought together with the individualistic wisdom space of Figure 9.1
by noting that the extreme of too confident, dogmatic knowing can also be
characterized by its social isolation, that is, the dogmatist fails to listen to or
respect what others have to say. Conversely, the extreme of paralyzing doubt

reflects a failure to enter into dialogue with others with whom one can share the burden of one's doubts and from whom one can gain the support required to engage in confident action. It is the middle course, the median of wisdom, that is associated with immersion in interpersonal relations, mutual understanding, and dialogue. When relationships with others are damaged or severed, then wisdom declines.

## Conclusion

I have argued that the essence of wisdom is to hold the attitude that knowledge is fallible and to strive for a balance between knowing and doubting. In this effort to set forth what is at the core of wisdom, I have endeavored to strip away some potentially confounding dimensions. Among these are dimensions such as reasoning ability, which might be common both to wisdom as well as to many other categories of cognitive and interpersonal functioning; dimensions such as being empathic and a good listener, which although perhaps strongly associated with wisdom are secondary to or derived from the fact of being wise; and dimensions such as experience and maturity, which come with advanced age. Experience and maturity change merely the quality of expression of wisdom, from simple to profound, without touching upon its essence.

It is commonly said that wisdom is derived from the experience that comes with growing older. In my view, the developmental course of wisdom is more complicated than this. Our experience presents the greatest threat to our wisdom, particularly when it leads merely to the accumulation of information, to success, and to power. Our experience also presents the greatest risks of losing our wisdom, particularly when we find ourselves in an atmosphere of stereotyping and intolerance, or when we are confronted by rapid technological and cultural change, or when we are touched by personal tragedy. The more experiences of these kinds, all of which accumulate as we grow older, the greater is our need to struggle to retain our wisdom. Much of our experience as we grow older changes merely the quality of what we say and do, so that it is more complex, sophisticated, or even profound, but these changes of quality are not of the essence of wisdom.

Only a rather limited and unique set of experiences can be helpful toward maintaining or restoring wisdom. These are the experiences that take place within a wisdom atmosphere, a framework of supportive interpersonal relations in which one may safely discover and reveal the limitations of and doubts regarding what one knows as well as be saved from extreme skepticism and paralysis of action through sharing the burden of one's doubts and receiving from others the confidence that comes with knowledge. It is through the supportive and sharing relationships within a wisdom atmosphere that one gains the courage to engage in confident and wise action even in the face of one's doubts.

## Notes

1 In Figure 1 in Meacham (1983b), the midpoint of the ordinate should be labeled 0.5, not 5.0.
2 Pushing further the analogy between climbing a hill and movement on the knowledge context matrix is unlikely to prove productive. Nevertheless, afficionados of the knowledge context matrix may find it of interest to consider what is analogous to "bovine wisdom," to grazing at a constant elevation around the hillside. With no increase or decrease in elevation, there is no change in acquired knowledge. Nevertheless, as one moves along such a contour of the matrix, the context within which one knows changes from extreme confidence – one feels that one knows all – to extreme doubt – one is extremely cautious or anxious due to the great amount that remains unknown. This seems to provide a rough description of cows, who might be said to have relatively little capacity for learning but whose behavior varies, depending on the context, from extreme stubbornness (dogmatism) to extreme skittishness (skepticism).
3 Stereotyping and intolerance are examples of movement of type *e* in the knowledge context matrix (Meacham, 1983b, p. 124). The outcome remains the same as that for type *a*, namely, overconfident knowing.
4 Type *d*. See Meacham (1983b) for types *c* and *f*.

## References

Baltes, P. B., Dittmann-Kohli, F., & Dixon, R. (1984). New perspectives on the development of intelligence in adulthood: toward a dual-process conception and a model of selective optimization with compensation. In P. B. Baltes and O. G. Brim, Jr. (Eds.), *Life-span development and behavior* (Vol. 6, pp. 33–76). New York: Academic Press.
Baltes, P. B., Smith, J., Staudinger, U. M., & Soworka, D. (in press). Wisdom: one facet of successful aging? In M. Perlmutter (Ed.), *Late-life potential*. Washington, DC: Gerontological Society of America.
Bronowski, J. (1973). *The ascent of man*. Boston: Little, Brown.
Brown, A. L. (1982). Learning and development: the problems of compatibility, access, and induction. *Human Development, 25,* 89–115.
Butler, R. N. (1963). The life review: an interpretation of reminiscence in the aged. *Psychiatry, 26,* 65–76.
Chandler, M. J. (1975). Relativism and the problem of epistemological loneliness. *Human Development, 18,* 171–180.
Chandler, M. J. (1987). The Othello effect: essay on the emergence and eclipse of skeptical doubt. *Human Development, 30,* 137–159.
Clayton, V. P., & Birren, J. E. (1980). The development of wisdom across the life span: a reexamination of an ancient topic. In P. B. Baltes and O. G. Brim, Jr. (Eds.), *Life-span development and behavior* (Vol. 3, pp. 104–135). New York: Academic Press.
Dixon, R. A., Kramer, D. A., & Baltes, P. B. (1985). Intelligence: a life-span developmental perspective. In B. B. Wolman (Ed.), *Handbook of intelligence: theories, measurements, and applications* (pp. 301–350). New York: Wiley.
Erikson, E. H. (1963). *Childhood and society* (2nd ed.). New York: Norton.
Erikson, E. H. (1982). *The life cycle completed*. New York: Norton.
Erikson, E. H., Erikson, J. M., & Kivnick, H. Q. (1986). *Vital involvement in old age: the experience of old age in our time*. New York: Norton.
Frank, A. (1952). *Anne Frank: The diary of a young girl*. (B. M. Mooyaart, Trans.). New York: Simon & Schuster.
Friedman, M. (1981). *Martin Buber's life and work: the early years 1878–1923*. New York: Dutton.
Gergen, K. (1973). Social psychology as history. *Journal of Personality and Social Psychology, 26,* 309–320.
Habermas, J. (1984). *The theory of communicative action*. Boston: Beacon Press.
Harré, R. (1984). *Personal being*. Cambridge, MA: Harvard University Press.

Hartshorne, C. (1987). *Wisdom as moderation: a philosophy of the middle way.* Albany: State University of New York Press.

Hilts, P. J. (1981, July 23). "Creationism" back in schools as new science. *The Washington Post,* p. A1.

Holliday, S. G., & Chandler, M. J. (1986). *Wisdom: explorations in adult competence.* Basel, Switzerland: Karger.

Krantz, D. L., & Bacon, P. (1977). On being a naive questioner. *Human Development, 20,* 141–159.

Lichtman, R. (1987). The illusion of maturation in an age of decline. In J. M. Broughton (Ed.), *Critical theories of psychological development* (pp. 127–148). New York: Plenum.

Looft, W. R. (1971). The psychology of more. *American Psychologist, 26,* 561–565.

McFayden, J. E. (1921). *The wisdom books.* London: J. Clarke. Cited in Clayton and Birren, 1980, p. 107.

McTavish, D. G. (1971). Perceptions of old people: a review of research findings and methodologies. *The Gerontologist, 11,* 90–101.

Marcel, G. (1951). *The decline of wisdom.* London: Harvill Press. Cited in Holliday and Chandler, 1986, p. 19.

Markman, E. M. (1977). Realizing that you don't understand: a preliminary investigation. *Child Development, 48,* 986–992.

Meacham, J. A. (1983a). Aging, work, and youth: new words for a new age of old age. In B. Bain (Ed.), *The sociogenesis of language and human conduct* (pp. 153–162). New York: Plenum.

Meacham, J. A. (1983b). Wisdom and the context of knowledge: knowing that one doesn't know. In D. Kuhn and J. A. Meacham (Eds.), *On the development of developmental psychology* (pp. 111–134). Basel, Switzerland: Karger.

Meacham, J. A. (1984). The social basis of intentional action. *Human Development, 27,* 119–124.

Meacham, J. A. (1989). Autonomy, despair, and generativity in Erikson's theory. In P. S. Fry (Ed.), *Psychology of helplessness and control in the aged.* Amsterdam: North-Holland.

Meacham, J. A., & Emont, N. C. (1989). The interpersonal basis of everyday problem solving. In J. D. Sinnott (Ed.), *Problem-solving: theory and application.* New York: Praeger.

Perlmutter, M., & Hall, E. (1985). *Adult development and aging.* New York: Wiley.

Riegel, K. F. (1972). The influence of economic and political ideologies upon the development of developmental psychology. *Psychological Bulletin, 78,* 129–144.

Riegel, K. F. (1973). Dialectical operations: the final period of cognitive development. *Human Development, 16,* 346–370.

Riegel, K. F. (1978). *Psychology, mon amour: a countertext.* Boston: Houghton Mifflin.

Riegel, K. F. (1979). *Foundations of dialectical psychology.* New York: Academic Press.

Rychlak, J. F. (1976). The multiple meanings of "dialectic." In J. F. Rychlak (Ed.), *Dialectic: humanistic rationale for behavior and development.* Basel, Switzerland: Karger.

Sternberg, R. J. (1985). Implicit theories of intelligence, creativity, and wisdom. *Journal of Personality and Social Psychology, 49,* 607–627.

Vygotsky, L. S. (1978). *Mind in society.* Cambridge, MA: Harvard University Press.

Waugh, E. (1945). *Brideshead revisited.* Boston: Little, Brown.

Wohlwill, J. F. (1973). *The study of behavioral development.* New York: Academic Press.

# 10 Wisdom and Reflective Judgment: knowing in the face of uncertainty

*Karen Strohm Kitchener and Helene G. Brenner*

> In youth and beauty wisdom is rare.
> – Chinese fortune cookie, 1988

This book attests to the fact that the concept of wisdom has received renewed attention in the legitimate literature of psychology after a long hiatus of being dismissed as an unscientific folk ccnstruct. Similarly, after years of neglect, investigators have been exploring the area of adult cognitive development, attempting to describe qualitative differences in the thinking of adults and adolescents or children and to trace and understand their genesis. Researchers such as Fischer and Kenny (1986), Kitchener and King (1981, in press), and Basseches (1986), to name a few, have suggested that the cognitive structures of adults continue to develop and differentiate beyond adolescence in critical ways.

It is the thesis of this chapter that the research on one model of adult cognitive development, the Reflective Judgment model, illuminates the development of many attributes associated with wisdom as well as the relationship between wisdom and intelligence. The model (Kitchener & King, 1981, in press) describes the development of epistemic cognition (Kitchener, 1983), or an individual's knowledge about the limits of knowing, the certainty of knowing, and the criteria for knowing. Further, it describes the developmental relationship between epistemic cognition and good judgment in the face of uncertainty. In other words, the model explicates how individuals move beyond understanding issues that can be known with certainty through the process of logical or formal reasoning to understanding issues of knowing in the face of uncertainty.

As we will argue in the subsequent paragraphs of this chapter, an awareness of the unknown and its implications for real-world problem solving and judgment have been identified as central characteristics of wisdom. Although we do not claim that the Reflective Judgment model provides an inclusive explanation of wisdom, we do suggest that some aspects of wisdom may, in fact, be explained by the development of Reflective Judgment.

212

The four aspects of wisdom on which we will focus and that seem most closely related to the development of Reflective Judgment are as follows:

1. the presence of unavoidably difficult, "thorny" problems inherent in the lives of adults (Dixon & Baltes, 1986; Kekes, 1983);
2. a comprehensive grasp of knowledge characterized by both breadth and depth (Clayton & Birren, 1980; Dixon & Baltes, 1986; Holliday & Chandler, 1986);
3. a recognition that knowledge is uncertain and that it is not possible for truth to be absolutely knowable at any given time (Clayton & Birren, 1980; Holliday & Chandler, 1986; Meacham, 1982); and
4. a willingness and exceptional ability to formulate sound, executable judgments in the face of this uncertainty (Baltes, Smith, Staudinger, & Sowarka, in press; Dixon & Baltes, 1986).

After describing these four issues we will turn to a discussion of the Reflective Judgment model and the research on it, which provide a foundation for understanding the development of these aspects of wisdom.

Several authors have suggested that wisdom operates in the face of difficult, real-life problems – often ones that involve pragmatic decisions (Baltes et al., in press; Clayton, 1982; Dixon and Baltes, 1986; Kekes, 1983). Specifically, Dixon and Baltes (1986) have argued that wisdom is activated in the presence of difficult problems that do not have clear-cut solutions. Clayton (1982) uses the ability to deal with paradoxes and contradictions in social situations to differentiate wisdom from intelligence. Kekes (1983) similarly states, "the context, therefore in which the sign of wisdom, good judgment, is to be sought is where a man must make decisions about hard cases." He further defines "hard cases" as those that " . . . occur when a decision is called for and it is unclear which ideals should guide one" (p. 283). Solomon's famous "child custody" judgment is a paradigm case of such a complex problem in which there appeared to be no way to judge with certainty the identity of the real mother. Solomon's wisdom was manifest in his ability to construct a solution that moved beyond the horns of the dilemma.

It should be noted that outside of the field of wisdom research, several investigators have been interested in defining problems that must be solved in the face of uncertainty and differentiating them from those that are not. Problems that cannot be solved with certainty have been variously labeled ill-defined, ill-structured, real-life, or wicked-decision problems (Churchman, 1971; Kitchener, 1983; Neisser, 1976; Simon, 1976). Whereas the definitions of such problems have varied (Wood, 1983), generally, they have been contrasted to well-structured problems or puzzles (Kitchener, 1983; Neisser, 1976; Simon, 1976). Although distinctions can be made between types of well-structured problems (Churchman, 1971; Wood, 1983), in general, within a well-structured problem all the elements necessary for a solution are available to the problem solver or known with a high degree of confidence. As Wood suggests, these include the acts open to the decision maker, states of nature, possible outcomes, and the utility of the outcome to the decision maker. In fact, this class of problems is quite circumscribed, limited to those that can be solved by a deductive algorithm or those for which a single solution can be agreed upon via a set of observations and a group of preestablished rules.

By contrast, Wood suggests that in wicked-decision problems, one or more of the elements necessary for a solution are unknown or not known with any degree of certainty. In addition, there are two or more complementary or antithetical conceptions of the issue that must be considered before a solution can be developed. Again, while others (Churchman, 1971; Wood, 1983) have differentiated between types of ill-structured problems, it is most important for this discussion to establish that there are limited sets of problems that can be solved with high degrees of certainty and many more that cannot. It is when individuals are faced with this second kind of problem, ill-structured or wicked-decision problems, that the presence or absence of wisdom is particularly apparent.

Breadth and depth of knowledge is recognized as a second important aspect of wisdom (Baltes et al., in press; Dixon & Baltes, 1986; Holliday & Chandler, 1986). The *Oxford English Dictionary* (1971) includes this concept of wisdom as one definition: "Knowledge (especially of a high or abstruse kind); enlightenment, learning, erudition." It was in this tradition that Aristotle articulated that the wise person "would know all things to the extent possible, be able to learn all difficult things, and be capable of teaching this knowledge to others" (Ross, 1908).

Furthermore, among the recent psychological explorations into the construct of wisdom, Dixon and Baltes (1986) and Baltes et al. (in press) have identified an extensive knowledge base, expertise, or an expert knowledge system as a prerequisite for wisdom. Similarly, studies investigating laypersons' conceptions of wisdom indicate that exceptional understanding and having a large store of information are one aspect of the good reasoning associated with wisdom (Holliday & Chandler, 1986; Sternberg, 1985). In fact, based on their investigation, Holliday and Chandler (1986, p. 80) concluded that "the emergence of a competency factor seems to imply that wisdom must rest on a sound foundation and that the superior abilities of wise people are rooted in a necessary prerequisite level of skill."

Exactly what types of experiences contribute to this expert knowledge base remains to be investigated. Aristotle believed that education in philosophy and the classics was essential for its acquisition. Others (Clayton, 1982; Holliday & Chandler, 1986) propose that a wide range of life experiences and the ability to learn from these experiences are necessary for the development of wisdom. Indeed, one explanation for attributing wisdom to increasing age lies in the assumption that life experience helps one acquire this breadth and depth of knowledge.

A third characteristic ascribed to wisdom is the understanding that human knowing is characterized by uncertainty (Kitchener, 1983; Meacham, 1983;

Taranto, 1989). Wisdom has been associated with an awareness of the limits of one's own personal knowledge, the general limits of human knowing, and the limited certainty with which ill-defined problems can be solved. Historically, both Socrates (Plato, 1956) and Aristotle (Ross, 1908) identified an awareness of the limits of personal knowledge as characteristic of the wise person. For Socrates, wisdom was identified with individuals aware of their own ignorance, and Aristotle (Ross, 1908) described wise people as aware of the limitations of their own wisdom. Erikson (1982) similarly associated wisdom with both an awareness of the unknown personal and world future as well as an awareness of the ultimate uncertainty – that of death.

For Meacham (1983), wisdom involves recognizing that what one knows is only part of what can be known. The remainder is unknown and represents both a challenge and direction for growth. Kekes (1983) also writes on the themes of human limitations and possibilities. Paradoxically, he suggests, one must be aware of one's limitations in coming to be aware of all the possible options. Wisdom necessitates recognizing the dialectical nature of knowing, yet having the discipline and humility to ponder and choose the best solution possible.

Kitchener (1983), Taranto (1989), and the group working on wisdom at the Max Planck Institute in Berlin (Baltes et al., in press; Dittmann-Kohli & Baltes, in press) have tied the awareness of the limits of human knowing to the types of problems that call for wise judgment. Taranto (1989), for example, suggests that "the problems on which wisdom operates appear to call for the kind of intelligence that can recognize, not only the limits of one's own knowing in problem solving, but the limits of knowing strategies available for solving problems" (p. 10). In other words, she suggests that wisdom is called for when adults are faced with ill-structured problems.

The fourth aspect of wisdom, which is particularly relevant to Reflective Judgment research, is the capacity to make sound judgments and decisions about life problems in the face of uncertainty. The *Oxford English Dictionary* (1971) reflects the paramount importance of making judgments to the definition of wisdom: "Capacity of judging rightly in matters relating to life and conduct; soundness of judgment in the choice of means and end." Paralleling this definition, the work at the Max Planck Institute in Berlin begins from what the investigators claim is the lay conception of wisdom: It involves good judgment and advice about life issues that are difficult and uncertain. Dittmann-Kohli & Baltes (in press) argue that "wisdom is understood to promote superior understanding demonstrated in the ability to exercise good judgment about important but uncertain matters and deriving solutions to these practical problems." In fact, their work involves a conception of wisdom that entails insight into life matters, good judgment, and advice about difficult life problems (Baltes et al., in press).

The concept of the wise person who is a good judge, capable of making astute decisions, is also prevalent among laypersons' descriptions of wisdom, as exhibited in both ancient folklore (e.g., the Bible, parables, proverbs) and in recent studies. In ancient tradition as well as in technologically primitive societies, wise people were made judges and trusted with social decision. Current studies suggest that contemporary laypersons continue to associate wisdom and exceptional judgment (Holliday, & Chandler, 1986; Sternberg, 1985).

In summary, wisdom has been described as a kind of intellectual ability that allows a few individuals to make particularly exceptional judgments about uncertain, problematic life issues (Dixon & Baltes, 1986; Clayton, 1975; Clayton & Birren, 1980; Dittmann-Kohli & Baltes, in press; Meacham, 1983). Such judgments are most typically exercised in relationship to problems for which no solution is readily available and are based on a deep and complex grasp of the issues involved.

## Wisdom and Reflective Judgment

First, we must acknowledge that our own research is not about wisdom per se. As we have argued in the opening section of this chapter, many (Baltes et al., in press; Clayton & Birren, 1980; Dixon & Baltes, 1986; Meacham, 1983) have included in their definitions of wisdom the capacity to understand the uncertainties involved in knowing and to make sound judgments in the face of them. To the extent that these are essential aspects of wisdom, and we believe they are, understanding the development of Reflective Judgment, which describes different forms of epistemic cognition and its relationship to judgment, has relevance for understanding the acquisition of wisdom.

Elsewhere, epistemic cognition has been distinguished from both cognition and metacognition (Kitchener, 1983). A brief overview of these three cognitive processes follows with an emphasis on the description of epistemic cognition.

Cognition refers to the premonitored acquisition processes on which knowledge of the world is built, such as reading, remembering, learning new words, and so on. Metacognition involves monitoring the effectiveness of these cognitive processes, for example, asking if one has effectively learned a spelling list, reviewing the list, and being aware of typical kinds of spelling errors. In other words, it involves knowing how to know and how effective one is at knowing something.

By contrast, epistemic cognition involves an individual's implicit theory of knowledge, that is, a theory of how certain one can be about what we know and the criteria for knowing. Whereas metacognition allows one to monitor the effectiveness of a particular strategy for solving a problem, epistemic cognition allows one to monitor whether a problem is solvable under any condition, for example, whether a solution to a problem can be had with certainty or whether it cannot. Such monitoring involves knowledge about the limitations of one's own knowing as well as the limitations of all knowing strategies.

It should be noted that individuals differ in their knowledge of the limits of knowing (Kitchener & King, 1987). For example, some believe that all things are knowable through direct observation and with a high degree of certainty. Others believe that not only is their own knowing limited by the vastness of what there is to know but also that human knowing is by its very nature limited and that, furthermore, many things can never be known with certainty. Both Meacham (1983) and Taranto (1989) have argued that it is the latter form of epistemic cognition that is central to the definition of wisdom.

As noted in the preceding section others have argued that wisdom involves not just an awareness of uncertainty but rather that wisdom is called for when a judgment must be made about important but uncertain matters (Baltes et al., in press; Dixon & Baltes, 1986). Kitchener (1983) has argued that epistemic cognition is necessary for understanding and explaining the differences in how people approach and make judgments about ill-structured, real-life problems; thus, it ought to be particularly important for distinguishing those whom we might consider wise from those we do not.

Many (Basseches, 1986; Broughton, 1978; Kitchener & King, 1981, in press; Perry, 1970) have argued that individuals' epistemic assumptions change between adolescence and adulthood; thus, they bring different forms of epistemic cognition to problem solving. Some, as Labouvie-Vief (1980) has noted, bring assumptions that preclude them from seeing the "inherent relativity of multiple intellectual perspectives" (p. 154). Sometimes such individuals assume that knowledge is objective and truth can be known directly. In other words, they do not acknowledge uncertainty. They may reduce all problems to puzzles, assuming they have single correct solutions and that their task is to apply the correct procedure to identify the right answer, for example, to find someone who knows the answer or how to determine it (Kitchener & King, 1981, in press; Perry, 1970). Clearly, such a decision maker would not fit with our conventional understanding of a wise person (Holliday & Chandler, 1986; Sternberg, 1985).

By contrast, others might assume that human knowing is characterized by uncertainty. For them, well-structured problems may be understood as limited exceptions to the typical nature of problems they face. Decision making about such wicked problems is not reducible to a mechanical process or an algorithm. Rather they recognize that solutions must be constructed. Included in their construction may be judgments about the credibility of evidence and opinion, evaluations of alternative perspectives, integrations of opposing models of the issue, and so on. Ultimately, they must develop what can be recognized as a reasonable solution. Although such individuals may not necessarily be

Table 10.1. *Reflective Judgment: changes in epistemic assumptions*

| Stage | View of knowledge | Concept of justification |
|---|---|---|
| 1 | Knowledge simply exists and, therefore, does not need justification. Knowledge is concrete, e.g., I know what I see. | Beliefs need no justification since there is an absolute correspondence between what is believed and what is true. |
| 2 | Knowledge is absolutely certain, or certain but not immediately available. We can know directly or via authorities. | Beliefs are unjustified, unexamined, or justified via authority (e.g., teacher, parent). Subjects assume there is a "right" answer to most issues. |
| 3 | Knowledge is absolutely certain or temporarily uncertain. In the areas of temporary uncertainty, we can know only via our intuitions or biases. | In areas in which answers exist, beliefs are justified via authorities. In areas in which answers do not exist, there is no rational way to justify beliefs. Beliefs are justified strictly intuitively. |
| 4 | Knowledge is idiosyncratic since situational variables (e.g., incorrect reporting of data, data lost over time) dictate that we cannot know with certainty. | Beliefs are justified by giving idiosyncratic reasons, e.g., choosing evidence that fits the beliefs. Decisions appear as partially reasoned and somewhat arbitrary. |
| 5 | Knowledge is contextual and subjective. Since what is known is known via perceptual filters, we cannot know directly. We may know only interpretations of the material world. | Beliefs are justified within a particular context via the rules of inquiry for that context. Justifications are assumed to be context specific; thus choosing between competing interpretations is often difficult and resisted. |
| 6 | Knowledge is personally constructed via evaluations of evidence, opinions of others, etc., across contexts; thus we may know our own and other's personal constructions of issues. | Beliefs are justified by comparing evidence and opinion on different sides of an issue or across contexts and then constructing solutions that are evaluated by personal criteria (e.g., values or the pragmatic need for action). |
| 7 | Knowledge is constructed via the process of reasonable inquiry into generalizable conjectures about the problem at hand, e.g., which interpretation seemed most probable based on the current evidence. | Beliefs are justified probabilistically via evidence and argument using generalizable criteria, e.g., which argument offers the most complete or compelling understanding of an issue. |

considered "wise," their decision making has many of the characteristics typically associated with wisdom.

*The development of Reflective Judgment: a theoretical model*

Kitchener and King (1981, in press; Kitchener, King, Wood, & Davison, 1989) have provided a model that describes the development of seven forms of epistemic cognition (Table 10.1). The model, called the Reflective Judgment model, describes an individual's assumptions about what can be known and what cannot (e.g., our knowledge of some things is ultimately uncertain), how we can know (e.g., by observing events directly, via authority), and how certain we can be in our knowing (e.g., absolutely, probabilistically). Following from each form of knowing is a description of how beliefs are justified in light of the certainty or lack of certainty of knowledge. Each form of justification appears to be a logical outgrowth of a set of epistemic assumptions. For example, as noted elsewhere (Kitchener et al., 1989), it would be inconsistent simultaneously to hold both the assumptions

1. that knowledge consists of what an authority says is true

and

2. that beliefs are justified through generalized rules of inquiry, evaluation of pertinent data, and the evaluated views of experts.

Authority-based beliefs would more consistently be justified by referring to an authority, which is what the model postulates.

The model also postulates that the seven forms of epistemic cognition are sequentially ordered. In other words, an individual who uses Stage 7 reasoning would typically have shown evidence of the other six forms of epistemic cognition at earlier ages.

As outlined in Table 10.1, the epistemic assumptions of the early stages (i.e., Stages 1–3) do not acknowledge that real uncertainty exists. Rather, they assume that, ultimately, uncertainty can be reduced to certainty, for example, by consulting an authority or by waiting until the truth is known sometime in the future. As a consequence, these stages are less central to an understanding of the concept of wisdom and will not be discussed further here. (For a more complete description, see Kitchener & King, in press, or Kitchener et al., 1989.)

By contrast, Stages 4–7 are more central for understanding of the concept of wisdom since each acknowledges the uncertainty of knowing. Although there are subtle differences in the understanding of the causes of uncertainty between Stages 4 and 7, what appears to mature in the later stages is the understanding of how judgments can be made in the face of this uncertainty.

To be more specific, in Stage 4 the uncertainty of knowing is acknowledged; however, it is believed to result from reasons that are quite specific to the events in question. For example, individuals may argue that we cannot know with total certainty about historical events because no one is still alive who experienced them or they may argue that we cannot know with certainty about scientific questions because there are too many variables to control. It is as if the individual is unable to draw generalizations about the limitations of human knowing.

Since in Stage 4 there is no way to know with certainty, individuals also conclude that there is no way to adjudicate between alternative points of view about an issue. Knowing is presumed to be idiosyncratic to the individual, for example, "I can know for myself and others can know for themselves, but there is no way to judge one set of claims as better than any other." They do not distinguish between considering evidence for a belief objectively and then evaluating that belief in light of evidence and choosing evidence that fits their prior beliefs while deliberately ignoring evidence that is not consistent with them. In other words, judgments are viewed as idiosyncratic and basically nonrational. Whereas almost any reason can be offered for judgments, the reasons themselves are not understood as being open to evaluation.

In Stage 5, the uncertainty of knowing is further generalized. Individuals infer that all knowing is subjective since what is known is known via perceptual filters, and they claim that we can only know within a context that takes into consideration the perceptual filter of the knower. Thus, they perceive multiple frameworks and perspectives on an issue, understanding them as examples of interpretations that result from different perceptual filters. Sometimes individuals will label their thinking as "relativistic" and seem to imply that this means that each perspective is encapsulated by the context in which it was generated.

Justifications are understood as similarly encapsulated by perspective; for example, a historian can offer an interpretation of an event, but since the event is always filtered through the historian's own perception and the perspective of all prior sources, there is no way to judge the interpretation as better or worse than another historian's, which is similarly limited. Further, individuals appear perplexed by the problem of choosing among alternative perspectives since, as Perry (1970) and Meacham (1983) have observed, choosing means rejecting possible avenues of choice. To choose means to face loss. As a consequence, individuals seem unable to offer interpretations that combine complementary perspectives, and they are unable to synthesize contradictory perspectives. They are more likely to assume that such differences in perspective are not amenable to a resolution. In fact, when forced to choose, they operate within a single perspective using the decision rules for that perspective and in some ways ignoring the multiplicity of perspectives they perceive. In other words, although they perceive the multiplicity of perspectives and the uncertainty of knowing when faced with ill-structured problems, they appear unable to form the objective synthetic judgments associated with wisdom.

In Stage 6, individuals similarly acknowledge that knowing is uncertain, that there are many perspectives on an issue, and that knowledge must be understood in relationship to the context within which it is generated. Nevertheless, individuals suggest that personal knowledge claims may be constructed via evaluating evidence, opinions of others, the relevance of arguments, and so on across perspectives. In other words, some perspectives may be judged to be more valid than others.

In this stage, there appears to be an initial recognition that all situations about which conflicting evidence and opinion exist require some kind of action by the knower to resolve them. In other words, judgments are necessary to complete the situation. They are made by comparing evidence and opinion or identifying shared meaning and common experience across multiple perspectives. Individuals claim that the outcome of the judgment, that is, their point of view, may be justified as better founded, more inclusive, or more reasonable. Despite the recognition that choices must be made to bring closure to a problem, individuals express some discomfort with their own evaluations of the validity of perspective, arguing that their evaluations are personal ones. In other words, as with those whom we consider to be wise, they are aware of the limits of their own personal knowledge, yet despite these limits, they are drawn to formulate a judgment based on good reasons.

As with the prior three stages, in Stage 7, individuals acknowledge the uncertainty of knowing, although this uncertainty generalizes beyond an understanding of the personal limits of knowing to an understanding about the nature of knowledge in general, that what can be known will always exceed what one knows, and that our tools for knowing are always imperfect. Sometimes, individuals will even acknowledge that well-structured problems are only certain within fairly specific parameters. They also recognize that many perspectives may be brought to bear on an issue and that many but not all of these perspectives may be potentially valid.

On the other hand, individuals clearly abandon the spectator view of the knower, which characterizes the earliest stages of development (Stages 1–3) as well as the ambivalence about the need to choose which characterizes the middle stages (Stages 4 and 5). It is not that they are unaware that to choose something means not to choose something else. It is rather that they appear to have accepted choice as one of the responsibilities of adult life. As a result, they suggest that evidence and interpretations of evidence can be constructed into evaluated knowledge claims about the nature of the problem under consideration. Knowledge, they argue, must be constructed via critical inquiry or through the synthesis of opposing views. Such constructions often go beyond the evaluations of others' perspectives. Rather, they are generative, offering, much like Solomon, a new, more complete way to view the issue under consideration.

Although individuals acknowledge the potential fallibility of their own judgments, they frequently suggest that these judgments are justifiable as offering the most complete or compelling conclusion for the issue or are the most workable alternative available. In other words, although they maintain objectivity about their own views and understand that their views reflect their own perceptions of the issue, nevertheless, they offer solutions for the problem at hand that show intelligent, reflective thought. Just as wisdom is characterized by the realization that one never has the final answer but that one must settle for a "good" answer, one that does the most good while doing the least harm, similarly, at Stage 7, individuals synthesize from the breadth and depth of the body of available knowledge the best possible judgment.

What is important about the description of the stages of epistemic cognition for understanding the construct of wisdom is that each of the latter four stages acknowledges the uncertainty of knowing, yet not all have the characteristics we commonly associate with wisdom. Although we would not claim that those who exhibit Stage 7 reasoning necessarily have the wisdom of Solomon, they do exhibit some of the characteristics typically associated with wise individuals. For example, individuals who score in Stage 7 exhibit an awareness of the context in which a problem is framed as well as an awareness that one's own judgment as well as the judgment of others reflect an interpretation of the issue, a characteristic labeled relativism by others (Baltes et al., in press; Labouvie-Vief, 1980). However, they do not succumb to the traps of Stage 5 relativism and are able to make judgments that consider several perspectives and offer a solution for the problem at hand.

In other words, the model suggests that it is not enough to recognize the contextual nature of events, nor is it enough to recognize the uncertainty of knowing in the face of ill-structured problems, nor is it enough to come to a judgment about such problems. Rather, it is how, at minimum, these three are interrelated that allows them to provide a foundation for wise judgment. Further, the model suggests that these aspects of thinking are developmentally related.

Assuming that the epistemic assumptions and nature of judgment described by Stage 7 of the model are foundational for wisdom, the data on the development of this form of reasoning should also be relevant to our understanding of how these attributes of the wise person develop. In the following section, the data on the development of Stage 7 epistemic cognition will be reviewed, particularly in relationship to age, education, and intelligence.

### The development of Reflective Judgment: the data

Several assumptions have guided the research on the development of Reflective Judgment. First, in order to observe the role that epistemic assumptions play in problem solving, we ask individuals to engage in ill-structured or wicked-decision problem solving. As has been noted elsewhere (Kitchener, 1983), whereas cognition and metacognition can be observed in both well- and ill-structured problem solving, epistemic assumptions cannot be observed unless there are potentially conflicting perspectives on an issue or unless there are potentially valid alternatives that can be brought to bear on it. Second, a researcher has the highest potential for identifying assumptions about knowledge and the nature of judgment when people are asked directly about how they know and the extent to which they can be sure about what they know and when they are asked to make a judgment about an issue. Third, we can only gauge the consistency with which people use similar epistemic assumptions in a variety of problem-solving situations if we ask them to engage in considering several ill-structured problems.

In the research that follows, epistemic assumptions were measured using the Reflective Judgment Interview (RJI) (Kitchener & King, 1981). On the RJI, individuals are questioned about four ill-structured problems that sample the dilemmas of knowing in historical, scientific, religious, and everyday contexts. An overall score for each subject is derived by weighting the most typical and second most typical stage score for each problem and then deriving a mean score over all problems. Scores on individual problems can also be evaluated for cross-problem consistency. The scoring system (Kitchener et al., 1989) and psychometric properties of the interview have been reviewed elsewhere (Kitchener & King, in press; Mines, 1982). In the following discussion, scores (e.g., 2.5, 3.0) refer to mean stage scores unless specified otherwise. For example, if a subject's score is reported as 2.5, the person was at the midpoint in the transition between Stages 2 and 3.

In general, the data suggest older, more highly educated subjects score at higher Reflective Judgment stages; however, even among highly educated groups, Stage 7 reasoning is rare prior to age 30. Specifically, in a recent review (Kitchener & King, in press) of the RJI scores of 800 traditionally aged high school and college students, mean scores ranged from 2.79 for high school freshmen to 3.99 for college seniors. The mean scores of advanced graduate students (5.04) were roughly one stage higher than those of the college seniors. This fact denotes that, on the average, although advanced graduate students recognize the uncertainty of knowing, they remain embedded in the subjectivity of particular contexts.

On the other hand, there is evidence that some adults who have at least a college education can and do use Stage 7 reasoning when tested on the RJI. In one study (Kitchener et al., 1989), about half of the subjects (47%) who were over age 32 had a mean score of Stage 7 on the RJI. By contrast, only 2 out of 150 individuals who were younger than age 28 had a mean Reflective Judgment score of Stage 7, and no individuals younger than age 22 had a mean Reflective Judgment score of Stage 7. In fact, prior to age 24, Stage 6 reasoning is almost equally as rare. It should be noted that all of the participants in these groups had at least a college education and all of those in the older group had some graduate education.

To summarize, reasoning characterized by an awareness of the uncertainty of knowing and an ability to make reasoned judgments despite this uncertainty is clearly not associated with youth or young adulthood. At minimum, in highly educated samples it is observed with some consistency only after the early thirties.

Although the RJI score (Kitchener et al., 1989) correlates highly ($r = .79$)

with age, at least in the samples tested, education also appears to play an important role in the development of later forms of epistemic cognition. This is not too surprising considering that colleges and universities are among the few socially sanctioned institutions whose role directly involves considering epistemological issues. They provide the individual with the explicit opportunity to consider what can be known and how it can be known. Further, social interactions among peers and with faculty challenge egocentric beliefs about knowing truth and lead to the decentration necessary to understand multiple perspectives. However, the lack of a higher education does not necessarily preclude attainment of the later Reflective Judgment stages. In fact, as many have argued, later adult experiences often direct people to consider the ambiguities in experience and the uncertainties in life. Clearly, there have been individuals who have understood the uncertainties of knowing without receiving advanced graduate education. On the other hand, such individuals may be identified more frequently in highly educated samples.

Data also support the sequentiality of the Reflective Judgment stages. Sequentiality has been tested several ways. Using Davison's (1979) test, we examined the hypothesis that subdominant stages would be adjacent to dominant stages, as they would be if stages were sequential. The alternative hypothesis was that they would not be adjacent. The hypothesis that the dominant and subdominant scores were independent was rejected even when a new method of scoring was introduced that corrected for the inherent biasing involved in having a single rater assign both dominant and subdominant scores (Kitchener et al., 1989); thus, the sequentiality hypothesis was supported.

Further, the scores of the individuals in three groups at three testing points have been examined for stage skipping and sequential change (Kitchener et al., 1989). At the first testing, the mean ages of individuals in the three groups were 16, 20, and 28. The individuals were subsequently tested after a 2- and then a 4-year interval. Using the criteria that the lower score could appear in the dominant or subdominant position at time $n$ before it appeared at time $n + 1$, no subjects skipped stages. Rather, in the two younger groups, the scores of 88% of the subjects increased sequentially and there were no reversals between the first and third testings. For the older group, fewer subjects' scores increased (23%) and reversals occurred in 8% of the cases. Since many of the subjects in the older group were scoring at Stages 6 and 7 at the first testing, the time-3 scores may have been influenced by a regression or ceiling effect on the RJI. Even so, taken together, these data also support the sequentiality of the Reflective Judgment stages.

Despite the strength of these data, it should be noted that in any single individual the sequence has been followed only between Stages 2–6 and 5–7. In other words, no subject has been followed through the entire sequence. Most of those who scored in Stage 7 at the third testing were already scoring at Stage 5 or 6 at the first testing. A fourth testing has recently been completed (King, pers. commun.) that may clarify the full sequence.

On the other hand, the data do not contradict the claim that the epistemic cognition characteristic of Stage 7 is an outgrowth of a developmental sequence. It does not appear that Stage 7 reasoning develops full blown, as Athena from Zeus' head. At least that has not been observed. Further, Kitchener and King (in press) have argued that the sequence reflects an increasing complex ability to differentiate and reintegrate abstract concepts. Assuming that Stage 7 reasoning does characterize several qualities associated with wisdom, these data would suggest that underlying wise judgment is the development of the ability to reason complexly with abstractions.

*Reflective Judgment and intelligence*

There are almost as many definitions of intelligence as there are psychologists, and there are certainly many who are more knowledgeable than we are about the scope of such definitions. Traditionally, intelligence, whether understood from the psychometric or the Piagetian tradition, has almost universally been measured in relationship to well-structured problems (King, 1986; Kitchener, 1986; Kitchener & King, in press). Although some (e.g., Wechsler [1958] and Terman [1973], who developed measures of intelligence) defined it more broadly, the items on most tests evaluate the amount of information the individual has available and how a person reasons inductively or deductively in well-structured problems. Even problems used to measure judgment (e.g., Horn, 1982) often reduce to puzzles since all of the parameters in the problem are specified with certainty.

Similarly, King (1986) and Kitchener and King (in press) have argued that Inhelder and Piaget (1958) measured formal operations in relationship to well-structured problems. Just as in the psychometric tradition, the parameters of the problems were either defined or could be generated with certainty. Further, they have suggested that whereas formal operations allow individuals to reason adequately about propositions in well-structured problems, they do not provide a basis for questioning the assumptions on which propositions are based or for justifying beliefs when evidence is incomplete and the parameters of problems are not defined clearly. Formal operations, when defined as the ability to operate on propositions inductively and deductively, do not account for differences in epistemic assumptions. In other words, epistemology and logic are different domains (Kitchener & Kitchener, 1981) even though they may both be important to problem solving.

Empirically, neither verbal measures of intelligence nor measures of formal operations have been able to account for later forms of Reflective Judgment stages (Kitchener, 1986; Kitchener & King, in press). Although the correlations between verbal intelligence scores and the RJI have ranged from a low of .14 to a high of .78, even in longitudinal studies where subjects act as their own controls, differences in RJI scores could not statistically be accounted for by changes in verbal intelligence score (see Kitchener, 1986, for a review). Similarly, subjects scoring between Stages 3 and 7 on the RJI have scored as fully formal operational on Piagetian tasks, suggesting that formal operations do not empirically differentiate between the middle and upper stages of the model (Kitchener & King, 1981).

Therefore, although it seems reasonable to assume that some minimal ability in well-structured problem solving may be necessary for ill-structured problem solving, the skills associated with puzzle solving simply do not account for the epistemic assumptions that allow individuals to recognize and come to grips with uncertainty.

**Conclusions**

We have suggested that many who have written on wisdom have identified it with the ability to develop and defend good judgments about the difficult, wicked-decision problems characteristic of adult life. Such judgments reflect a recognition of the limits of personal knowledge, an acknowledgment of the general uncertainty that characterizes human knowing, and a humility about one's own judgments in the face of such limitations. We have also suggested that these are the characteristics of Stage 7 Reflective Judgment reasoning.

Assuming that the Reflective Judgment model describes the sequence of steps leading to the ability to form judgments about ill-structured problems, it also illuminates the development of these aspects of wisdom. To summarize, the model would suggest that those who are wise can distinguish between well- and ill-structured problems. Although they recognize the uncertainty of knowing and the relativity of multiple perspectives, they can overcome this relativity, find the shared meaning, evaluate the alternative interpretations, and develop a synthetic view that offers, at least, a tentative solution for the difficult problem at hand. Further, it would suggest that these aspects of wisdom are the outcome of a developmental sequence and that, at least typically, as our Chinese fortune cookie alludes, they are not associated with the young. It also suggests that although these aspects of wisdom may be part of the intellectual domain, they are not the same as what is typically measured by intelligence tests or tests of formal operations. Wisdom is more than logic and is generally uncalled for when faced with well-structured problems.

As we acknowledged earlier, we do not claim, however, that the Reflective Judgment model accounts for all of what wisdom is understood to involve. Generally, wisdom has been associated with socially relevant, pragmatic intelligence (Baltes et al., in press; Holliday & Chandler, 1986) or good judgment about life issues. By contrast, Reflective Judgment has been focused on one aspect of intellectual problem solving and up to now has not been generalized to or measured with personally relevant life problems. Based on our arguments presented here, we would expect that those who are at the earlier or middle Reflective Judgment stages would not show wisdom when faced with such problems; however, those who score high in Reflective Judgment would be more likely to do so.

Further, other research on laypersons' definitions of wisdom (e.g., Holliday & Chandler, 1986) has emphasized the importance of good communication and interpersonal skills. Neither of these would be accounted for by the development of Stage 7 Reflective Judgment. As many have noted, we commonly observe many cognitively complex but socially inadequate individuals. Social sensitivity and interpersonal finesse may require the cognitive complexity to see multiple perspectives (Selman, 1980); however, it undoubtedly requires a great deal more. What this may suggest is that wisdom is a rare combination of attributes and that cognitive development is only one aspect of the array. Those aspects of wisdom characterized by the ability to make reasoned judgments in the face of uncertainty may, however, be illuminated by the Reflective Judgment model.

## References

Baltes, P. B., Smith, J., Staudinger, U. M., & Sowarka, D. (in press). Wisdom: one facet of successful aging? In M. Perlmutter (Ed.), *Later-life potential*. Washington. DC: Gerontological Society of America.

Basseches, M. (1986). Dialectical thinking and young adult cognitive development. In R. A. Mines and K. S. Kitchener (Eds.), *Adult cognitive development*. New York: Praeger.

Broughton, J. (1978). Development of concepts of self, mind, reality and knowledge. In W. Damon (Ed.), *New directions in child development: social cognition*. San Francisco: Jossey-Bass.

Churchman, C. W. (1971). *The design of inquiring systems; basic concepts of systems and organizations*. New York: Basic Books.

Clayton, V. (1975). Erickson's theory of human development as it applies to the aged: wisdom as contradictive cognition. *Human Development, 18*, 315–321.

Clayton, V. (1982). Wisdom and intelligence: the nature and function of knowledge in the later years. *International Journal of Aging and Human Development, 15*, 315–321.

Clayton, V., & Birren, J. E. (1980). The development of wisdom across the life span. In P. B. Baltes & O. G. Brim (Eds.), *Life span development and behavior* (Vol. 3, pp. 103–135). New York: Academic Press.

Davison, M. L. (1979). Testing a metric unidimensional, qualitative, unfolding model for attitudinal or developmental data. *Psychometrika, 44*, 179–194.

Dittmann-Kohli, F., & Baltes, P. B. (in press). Toward a neofunctionalist conception of adult intellectual development: wisdom as a prototypic case of intellectual growth. In C. Alexander and L. Langer (Eds.), *Beyond formal operations: alternative endpoints to human development*. New York: Oxford University Press.

Dixon, R. A., & Baltes, P. B. (1986). Toward life span research on the functions and pragmatics of intelligence. In R. J. Sternberg & R. K. Wagner (Eds.), *Practical intelligence* (pp. 203–235). New York: Cambridge University Press.

Erikson, E. (1982). *The life cycle completed.* New York: W. W. Norton.

Fischer, K. W., & Kenny, S. L. (1986). Environmental conditions for discontinuities in the development of abstractions. In R. A. Mines and K. S. Kitchener (Eds.), *Adult cognitive development.* New York: Praeger.

Holliday, S. G., & Chandler, M. J. (1986). *Wisdom: explorations in adult competence.* Basel, Switzerland: Karger.

Horn, J. L. (1982). The aging of human abilities. In B. B. Wolman (Ed.), *Handbook of developmental psychology.* Englewood Cliffs, NJ: Prentice-Hall.

Inhelder, B., & Piaget, J. (1958). *The growth of logical thinking from childhood to adolescence.* London: Routledge & Kegan Paul.

Kekes, J. (1983). Wisdom. *American Philosophical Quarterly, 20,* 277–286.

King, P. M. (1986). Formal reasoning in adults: a review and critique. In R. A. Mines and K. S. Kitchener (Eds.), *Adult cognitive development.* New York: Praeger.

Kitchener, K. S. (1983). Cognition, metacognition and epistemic cognition: a three-level model of cognitive processing. *Human Development, 4,* 222–232.

Kitchener, K. S. (1986). The Reflective Judgment model: characteristics, evidence, and measurement. In R. A. Mines & K. S. Kitchener (Eds.), *Adult cognitive development.* New York: Praeger.

Kitchener, K. S., & King, P. M. (1981). Reflective Judgment: concepts of justification and their relationship to age and education. *Journal of Applied Developmental Psychology, 2,* 89–116.

Kitchener, K. S., & King, P. M. (in press). The Reflective Judgment model: ten years of research. In M. L. Commons, C. Armon, L. Kohlberg, F. A. Richards, T. A. Grotzer, & J. D. Sinnott (Eds.), *Adult development. Models and methods in the study of adolescent and adult thought.* New York: Praeger.

Kitchener, K. S., King, P. M., Wood, P. K., & Davison, M. L. (1989). Consistency and sequentiality in the development of Reflective Judgment: a six year longitudinal study. *Journal of Applied Developmental Psychology, 10,* 73–95.

Kitchener, K. S., & Kitchener, R. F. (1981). The development of natural rationality: can formal operations account for it? In J. Meacham & N. R. Santilli (Eds.), *Social development in youth: structure and content.* Basel, Switzerland: Karger.

Lavouvie-Vief, G. (1980). Beyond formal operations: uses and limits of pure logic in life-span development. *Human Development, 25,* 141–161.

Meacham, J. A. (1983). Wisdom and the context of knowledge: knowing that one doesn't know. In D. Kuhn & J. A. Meacham (Eds.), *On the development of developmental psychology.* Basil, Switzerland: Karger.

Mines, R. A. (1982). Student development assessment techniques. In G. R. Hanson (Ed.), *New directions for student services: measuring student development* (Vol. 20, pp. 65–92). San Francisco: Jossey-Bass.

Neisser, U. (1976). General, academic and artificial intelligence. In L. B. Resnick (Ed.), *The nature of intelligence.* Hillsdale, NJ: Erlbaum.

Perry, W. G. (1970). *Forms of intellectual and ethical development in the college years.* New York: Holt, Rinehart & Winston.

Plato (1956). The apology (W. H. D. Rouse, Trans.). *Great dialogues of Plato.* New York: Mentor.

Ross, W. D. (Ed.) (1908). *The works of Aristotle* (Vol. 8). Oxford: Oxford University Press.

Selman, R. L. (1980). *The growth of interpersonal understanding.* New York: Academic Press.

Simon, H. A. (1976). Identifying basic abilities underlying intelligent performance of complex tasks. In L. B. Resnick (Ed.), *The nature of intelligence.* Hillsdale, NJ: Erlbaum.

Sternberg, R. J. (1985). Implicit theories of intelligence, creativity and wisdom. *Journal of Personality and Social Psychology, 49,* 607–627.

Taranto, M. A. (1989). Facets of wisdom: a theoretical synthesis. *International Journal of Aging and Human Development, 29,* 1–21.

Terman, L. M. (1973). *Concept mastery test: manual.* New York: Psychological Corporation.

Wechsler, D. (1958). *The measurement of adult intelligence.* Baltimore: Williams & Wilkins.

Wood, P. K. (1983). Inquiring systems and problem structure: implications for cognitive development. *Human Development, 26,* 249–265.

# 11    Wisdom: the art of problem finding

*Patricia Kennedy Arlin*

Whereas there can be wisdom in answers that are given or in problem solutions, wisdom is not simply defined by solutions or by answers. Wisdom may be more a matter of interrogatives rather than of declaratives. Answers and problems with their solutions are parts of a larger whole that include the formulation of the problem and the question(s) that drove that formulation. Wisdom is found more in particular questions that are posed than in the solutions that are given form by those questions.

Wertheimer (1945, p. 123) argued that the " . . . function of thinking is not just solving an actual problem but discovering, envisaging, going into deeper questions. Often, in great discovery the most important thing is that a certain question is found." The same may be said of wisdom. Wisdom may be recognized not so much by the problem solution but rather by the question or problem that is found. Wisdom may be the means by which one discovers, envisages, or goes into deeper questions.

Some of these deeper questions are the productive questions of Wertheimer (1945), the generic questions of Mackworth (1965), and the new problems of Piaget (1980): "Clearly though the modest facts assembled may have permitted us to answer a few minor outstanding questions, they continue to pose a host of problems. . . . [but] new problems are often more important than the accepted solutions" (Piaget, 1980, p. 304). Wisdom may be contained in the recognition of these new problems. It may be more in the art of the question than in the art of the question's answer that wisdom is found to be understood.

Wisdom understood in terms of questions rather than answers may contribute to the ever-changing ratio of potential knowledge to acquired knowledge, which for Meacham (1983) defines wisdom. Knowing what one does not know can be represented by the questions one asks, the doubts one has, and the ambiguities one tolerates. This type of knowing is the gift of one who has thought deeply in a domain and has a substantial knowledge based within that domain. It is not the gift of one who simply knows the surface features of a domain but does not suspect the deep structures that are to be found beneath.

230

The role of the question in both problem finding and in wisdom is only one of several features that problem finding and wisdom have in common. Wisdom and problem finding are not the same phenomenon. In some contexts it might be argued that problem finding is a necessary but not sufficient condition for wisdom. One can be a problem finder without being particularly wise, but it is difficult to conceive of a wise person who does not ask questions whose forms reflect the highest level of problem finding.

Problem finding has as its outcome "the discovery of many general questions from many ill-defined problems" (Mackworth, 1965, p. 52). The question is the central concern of problem finding. The answer is the central concern of problem solving. The solutions we derive are the direct result of the questions we ask when confronted with a problematic situation. Wisdom is grounded in those general or generic questions that result from optimal problem finding.

There are other features as well that are shared by problem finding and by wisdom. These include

1. the search for complementarity;
2. the detection of asymmetry in the face of that which appears symmetrical and in equilibrium;
3. openness to change: its possibility and its reality;
4. a pushing of the limits, which sometimes leads to a redefinition of those limits;
5. a sense of taste for problems that are of fundamental importance; and
6. the preference for certain conceptual moves.

These commonalities between wisdom and problem finding will be explored in this chapter in the context of the varying descriptions of problem finding, the few empirical studies of problem finding that exist, and the tentative cognitive-developmental model that emerges from these descriptions and studies. Within this model an attempt is made to describe some of the mental processes of the intellect that underlie problem finding. Certain developmental variables that potentially might contribute to or limit problem finding are introduced. Finally the discussion returns to a description of wisdom as the art of problem finding.

*1. The search for complementarity.* Problem finding is essentially the establishment of the need for a new and a highly complex mental program (Mackworth, 1965). *Program* is understood as an organized set of mental rules, principles, and operations. The most important feature of the new program is the discovery of overlap and agreement where formerly only isolation and difference were recognized (Bartlett, 1958). This discovery of overlap and agreement in the face of what appear to be unrelated or contradictory phenomena may be described as the psychological equivalent of the principle of complementarity in physics. It may also be an operative principle in problem finding (Arlin, 1975/76) as well as in wisdom. One means by which complementarity is achieved is the strategy of "emphasizing conceptual conflict as a necessary preparation for its resolution" (Holton, 1973, p. 130). Wisdom may be expressed both in the emphasis on conceptual conflict and in its resolution.

*2. The detection of asymmetry.* The problem finder detects a type of asymmetry or a lack of balance where the casual observer notes no differences or finds a conventional explanation to be satisfactory. It was the detection of a type of asymmetry that compelled Einstein toward the development of his theory of relativity (Holton, 1973). This ability to notice relevant and often subtle features is a characteristic of expertise (Bransford, Franks, Vye, & Sherwood, 1986). It is this noticing of features that Cassirer (1923, p. 29) argues must be explained, and it is the noticing of features that may well characterize the act of problem finding. The noticing of subtle features, the detection of asymmetry, characterizes wisdom as well. Genius is not a requirement for wisdom. Wisdom involves a sensitivity to both symmetry and asymmetry. Wisdom is present in the noticing of subtle features that make a difference in problem definitions and ultimately in problem solutions.

*3. Openness to change.* One of the earliest references to problem finding was in the work of the sociologist Merton (1945). It was within the context of a sociology of knowledge that he used the term *problem finding* to describe the contributions of scientists whose questions led to breakthroughs within their respective fields. In the same year (1945), Wertheimer, in his work on productive thinking, commented that "often in great discovery the most important thing is that a certain question is found" (p. 123). This comment in effect names the act of problem finding. Although Wertheimer did not use the term problem finding, he anticipated Mackworth's (1965) definition of success in problem finding: " . . . the discovery of many general questions from many ill-defined problems" (p. 52).

Mackworth (1965) used the construct of problem finding in his attempt to describe originality in science. He suggested that problem finding is the earmark of the true scientist, whereas complex problem solving is the work of the highly trained technician. Mackworth emphasized that ill-defined problems rather than well-structured problems are the stimuli for problem finding. In problem finding, "it is a rather exacting requirement to have to work back from an unknown point or to have to simplify the mismatch between present position and an unknown destination" (Mackworth, 1965, p. 60). A solution or decision often is called wise when it has reduced or simplified the mismatch between the present position and an unknown outcome.

The distinction between presented problems and discovered problems is a useful one proposed by Getzels (1964) in his studies of problem solving and creativity. Discovered problems are problems that exist but "remain to be identified or discovered, and no standard method for solving them is known to the problem-solver or to the others" (Getzels, 1964, p. 241).

This description of discovered problems led Getzels and Csikszentmihalyi (1965, 1970, 1976) to argue that the fundamental difference between a creative and noncreative process is that the former lacks a problem stated in terms of clear goals to achieve. In their studies of artists engaged in the discovery of problems that result in their artistic productions, the basic category of analysis of the creative process became the identification of the ability to "discover" a problem in the first place. This was accompanied by the willingness to remain open to the possibility of change throughout the experience.

Wisdom, like problem finding, has as one of its requirements this willingness to remain open to receive new information and on the basis of that information to be willing to change one's worldview. Bransford et al. (1986) consider the willingness to remain open to change to be part of a possible definition of wisdom: "Perhaps wisdom arises from the opportunity to experience changes in our own beliefs and assumptions – changes that help us realize that the ideas and priorities that seem so clear today will probably be modified as a function of new experiences" (p. 32).

Getzels and Csikszentmihalyi (1970) further described the discovered problem situation as a situation wherein "the problem does not have a known formulation; and there is, therefore, no known solution . . ." (p. 93). They further emphasize that the solution to the problem cannot be compared "against a predetermined standard of right or wrong but only, as in the case of a work of art" be considered critically (p. 93).

*4. Pushing the limits.* The wisdom of a solution, of a judgment, or of advice that is given is often recognized when it is considered critically. Wisdom is not attributed to judgments or solutions because of their close conformity to an acknowledged standard of right or wrong. Wise decisions, solutions, and judgments are often acknowledged as wise because they push these standards to their limits or create types of metastandards that redefine the acceptable.

This pushing of the limits is described by Getzels and Dillon (1973) in terms of the need for more "fertile theories, the new and more heuristic problems that will give direction and meaning to what will be done" (p. 722). Wisdom in the face of ill-defined problem situations in both one's occupational expertise and in one's life, like problem finding, requires the formulation of problems in ways that will give direction and meaning to the choices that are made. Wisdom requires one to admit the possibility of change at any point in the process. Change becomes the one constant in the process.

The relationship of wisdom to problem finding has been obscured because of the close association of problem finding with descriptions of originality and creativity in the doing of science and of art. As long as problem finding is seen to be congruent with originality, invention, artistry, and creativity, it lacks generativity as a construct for studies of basic cognitive processes.

Problem finding as a fundamental cognitive process did receive occasional acknowledgment. Little attention was paid, however, to the mental processes of the intellect that might underlie problem finding or to the potential developmental processes that might contribute to it. In this capacity, problem finding was viewed as one step in the problem-solving process that was described as "defining the problem" or "defining the givens." These acknowledgments, when they did occur, took the form of comments made in passing. Three examples of these acknowledgments are contained in the works of Osler and Weiss (1969), in a report of a conference on heuristic teaching (Stanford University, 1971), and in a review of problem finding by Dillon (1983).

In a study of concept attainment, Osler and Weiss (1969, p. 49) hypothesized that "under the conditions of nonspecific instructions the task presented to subjects has two components, namely, problem finding as well as problem solving, and the superior performance associated with high intelligence may be the result of greater proficiency at either or both of these components." Even in this context little effort was made to define problem finding.

One could infer that Osler and Weiss's (1969) concept of problem finding was that of problem definition or the identification of the givens in a problem situation. What is of interest is their description of problem finding in the context of the "conditions of nonspecific instructions," which suggests that problem finding is activated in ill-defined problem situations. Despite this, they seem to imply that both problem finding and problem solving are well-defined processes that are closely related to other factors of intelligence.

Similarly, in a report of a symposium on heuristic teaching (Stanford University, 1971), one finds the assumption that problem finding and problem solving are closely related: " . . . problem finding and divergent thinking are valued equally with problem solving and convergent thinking . . . " (p. 21). In this context, the psychometric definitions of creativity in terms of Guilford's (1967) "structure of the intellect model" are closely aligned with problem finding and problem solving.

Within these three works (Dillon, 1983; Osler & Weiss, 1969; Stanford University, 1971) there appears to be a direct equation between problem finding and divergent thinking, on the one hand, and problem solving and convergent thinking, on the other. Such equations provide too narrow an interpretation of problem finding. If problem finding is considered as one more instance of divergent thinking, the case cannot be made that problem finding is an important dimension of wisdom.

In an attempt to build on the relationship between problem finding and problem solving, Dillon (1983) drew upon both Mackworth's (1965) and Getzels and Csikszentmihalyi's (1976) earlier work. Although Dillon's (1983) efforts are laudable, he failed to separate the problem-finding process from the problem-solving process: "In its broadest sense, the term problem finding may be taken to refer to those activities, processes and events which precede the solving of a clearly posed problem" (p. 102).

*5. A sense of taste for problems that are of fundamental importance.* The sociologist Merton (1973) reports that Nobel laureates whom he has interviewed "uniformly express the strong conviction that what matters most in their work is a developing sense of taste, of judgment, in seizing upon problems that are of fundamental importance" (p. 452). Merton illustrates his point by citing one laureate's description of his mentor: "he led me to look for important things, whenever possible, rather than to work on endless detail or to work just to improve accuracy rather than making a basic new contribution" (Merton, 1973, p. 453).

This "sense of taste, of judgment, in seizing upon problems that are of fundamental importance" may be another aspect of problem finding that can be associated with wisdom. This is not to say that all laureates are wise, nor is it to claim that wisdom is to be found only in persons of outstanding accomplishment. The purpose of emphasizing these laureates' comments is to try to understand what is essential to problem finding and what is not.

Problem finding, understood in terms of creativity or originality or as a function of divergent-thinking factors, has made a small contribution to the study of wisdom. Problem finding understood in terms of fundamental developmental and mental processes provides a means of describing wisdom in both competence and performance terms that transcends its use in studies of creativity and problem solving.

*6. The preference for certain conceptual moves.* Several empirical studies of problem finding have contributed to its definition. These studies have been quite domain specific. The earliest studies were those of Getzels and Csikszentmihalyi (1965, 1970, 1976). The initial focus of these studies was on creative thinking in art students and on the "concern for discovery" as an attitudinal component of their creative production.

In a 10-year follow-up of the same subjects, discovered problems became for Getzels and Csikszentmihalyi (1976) the outcome of problem finding. This outcome was defined in terms of a set of behaviors and attitudes that the artists brought to their work. The artists painted because they were compelled by the questions they asked themselves, for which only their artistic products could approach the answers.

Getzels and Csikszentmihalyi quantified problem finding in three ways:

1. quantification at the problem formulation stage;
2. quantification at the problem solution stage; and
3. quantification of the concern for problem finding in general.

Their quantifications were based on observations of art students as they engaged in developing a still-life drawing on the basis of a set of stimulus objects.

At the problem formulation stage, they included the number of objects manipulated by the subjects as they chose the stimuli for their still-life drawings, the uniqueness of the objects chosen, and the exploratory behavior exhibited during selection and arrangement of the objects. Exploratory behavior included the observation of the objects and sensory feedback received from the objects. It included, as well, active experimentation with the objects.

Quantification at the problem solution stage included openness to problem structure, discovery-oriented behavior, and changes in problem structure and content. Quantification of concern for problem finding was determined on the basis of three questions that were asked of the artist:

1. Why did you arrange the objects as you did?
2. What were you thinking while you were drawing?
3. Could any of the elements in your drawing be eliminated or altered without destroying its character?

If problem finding is conceived of only as a set of variables that describes an artist's creative act, it has little to offer to discussions of wisdom. If, however, these quantifications of problem finding are removed from the situation of artistic production and are thought about as conceptual moves in the face of ill-defined problems, a case can be made for their relevance in the study of wisdom.

These conceptual moves would include the number of problem spaces or frames that are accessed, manipulated, or combined; the uniqueness of these combinations; and the active experimentation that occurs during this exploratory phase. The conceptual moves at the problem solution stage would include openness to the problem structure; discovery-oriented behavior wherein the problem spaces are changed, substitutions are made, and frames are altered; and changes in problem structure and content relative to the moves that have been made.

Perkins (1988) hints at problem finding as a basic process when he comments that certain results on problem finding " . . . at least suggest that having certain patterns of deployment prominent in their repertoires may make practitioners within a discipline more creative" (p. 379). The construct of "patterns of deployment" suggests that problem finding may have an important role to play in expertise. These patterns may describe the ordering of some of these conceptual moves in thought that result in problem finding and may represent a preparatory phase for wisdom.

"Patterns of deployment" may be the result of reflection and judgments of their appropriateness. Insofar as these patterns are the result of reflection and judgment, they may contribute to this discussion of wisdom. Concern for problem finding implies the introduction of some planning metacomponents (Sternberg, 1988); the utilization of selected knowledge acquisition components (Davidson & Sternberg, 1984; Sternberg & Davidson, 1982); and the acknowledgment that any solution is a relative one. If it is relative, new elements can be introduced and existing elements can be changed or eliminated in the light of new information.

Thus far, within this discussion of the six features that wisdom and problem finding have in common, a number of observations about wisdom have been made:

1. Wisdom may be the means by which one discovers, envisages, or goes into deeper questions.
2. Wisdom can be ascertained in knowing that what one does not know can be represented by the questions one asks, the doubts one has, and the ambiguities one can tolerate.
3. Wisdom may be expressed both in the emphasis on conceptual conflict and in its resolution.
4. Wisdom may have complementarity as its operative principle.
5. Wisdom may be recognized in the noticing of subtle features and in the detecting of asymmetry where none has been detected before.
6. Wisdom may be attributed to decisions, judgments, and practices that are made in the face of uncertainty, ambiguity, and complexity.
7. Wisdom has as one of its requirements the willingness to remain open to receive new information and on the basis of that information to be willing to change one's worldview.
8. Wisdom is often recognized when the solution to a problem is considered critically. Wise decisions, solutions, and judgments are often acknowledged as wise because they push standards to their limit or create types of meta-standards that redefine the acceptable.
9. Wisdom may be detected in certain patterns of deployment prominent in the repertoires of some practitioners within a discipline that may constitute a part of their expertise.
10. Wisdom requires a "sense of taste" or of judgment in seizing upon problems that are of fundamental importance; it is, in part, a sense of the important.
11. Wisdom can be represented as a set of conceptual moves that include the number of problem spaces or frames that are accessed, manipulated, or combined; the uniqueness of these combinations; and the active experimentation that occurs in exploration of these spaces. These moves also include openness to problem structure and discovery-oriented behavior wherein the problem spaces are changed, substitutions occur, frames are altered, and changes are made in problem structure and content relative to the moves that have been made.
12. Wisdom involves the utilization of some planning metacomponents, the partial utilization of knowledge acquisition components, and the acknowledgment that any solution is a relative one. It is relative because new elements can be introduced and existing elements can be changed or eliminated in the light of new information.

The proposition that all wise persons are problem finders is an easier one to entertain than is the proposition that all problem finders are wise. Even if these commonalities shared by wisdom and problem finding hint at the cognitive processes of the intellect that underlie wisdom, the developmental question of how wisdom is acquired remains unanswered.

The introduction of the developmental question is the basis for clarifying the possible relation between wisdom and problem finding. It is also the basis for the adaptation of a model of problem finding to a model of wisdom and its prerequisites.

The developmental question provides entree into one final set of studies that built upon the work of Getzels and Csikszentmihalyi (1965, 1970, 1976) but departed from their work in significant ways. The focus of these studies was the question of the cognitive processes and developmental prerequisites that could be associated with problem finding. This set of studies provides an alternative conception of problem finding. Ultimately, a model of wisdom that has some features in common with other developmental models emerges (Baltes & Smith, 1987; Dixon & Baltes, 1986; Holliday & Chandler, 1986).

### A developmental model of problem finding and wisdom

The work of Getzels and Csikszentmihalyi (1965, 1970, 1976) led to further investigations of problem finding. Three investigators attempted to study the process of problem finding and relate it to other non-domain-specific variables. Arlin (1974, 1975, 1975/76, 1977) attempted to show that problem finding was systematically related to other aspects of human thought. Schwartz (1977) explored problem finding in the social domain. He showed the individual transformations of the same interpersonal dilemmas into quite different problem formulations. Smilansky (1985) studied students' formulations of problems that they were having in school. He found that the form in which the problems were posed, even when the content was the same, showed wide individual variation. He reported that there was a tendency for measures of the quality of problem positing to be positively related to measures of problem solving. Smilansky (1985), having stated the relationship, went on to argue that one must be a very good problem solver before one can become a good problem finder. This suggestion echoed the stage proposition of Arlin (1975). This proposition suggests that problem solving and problem finding are two distinct processes. The stage proposition played an important role in the development and revision of a problem-finding model.

Beginning with an attempt to describe a cognitive process model of problem finding (Arlin, 1974, 1975/76), it became clear that one of the most important predictors of the quality of questions raised in a ill-defined problem situation was that of formal operational reasoning. Traditional measures of divergent thinking and conceptual complexity contributed little to the prediction equations.

Further studies (Arlin, 1975, 1977) sought more firmly to establish the links between formal reasoning and problem finding. It became clear that the measures of formal reasoning were, in effect, problem-solving measures. Well-defined problems were presented to the problem solver. Each problem had one correct answer. Though Piagetians place emphasis on the method of solution rather than on the solution itself, the problems cannot be considered ill-defined. Problem-finding situations are by definition ill-defined. They have no known method of solution, and when a solution is found, there are no criteria by which their correctness can be established.

Observations such as these led to a fifth-stage hypothesis that formal reasoning was a necessary but not sufficient condition for problem finding and that problem finding might constitute a more advanced stage in adult cognition. Several attempts at models of problem finding followed (Arlin, 1984, 1986, 1989).

Initially, problem finding was thought to be the fifth stage. Later, it became one of the important forms of reasoning associated with postformal or fifth-stage thought. Postformal reasoning is best characterized as reasoning that is metasystematic (Commons, Richards, & Kuhn, 1982), reflective (King, Kitchener, Davidson, Parker, & Wood, 1983), and dialectic (Basseches, 1980; Riegel, 1973). Structurally, the logic of postformal reasoning is a relativistic type of logic (Arlin, 1984; Kramer, 1983; Sinnott, 1981). It is reasoning that involves simultaneous expansions and contractions of thought. These expansions and contractions represented for Apostle (1979) a basis for proposing to the Geneveans a model of adult thought that did not violate their framework:

> I think something that has to happen after the formal stage has been reached is the combination of different spaces of possibilities . . . [This involves two simultaneous moves—] contractions and expansions. . . . [Both] consist in the comparison of different types of universal logical possibilities and these comparisons . . . would be the combination, the synthesis of very many INRC groups with each other. (p. 11)

Apostle's description of postformal reasoning in terms of "simultaneous moves" that are both "contractions" and "expansions" appears to be a restatement of the complementarity principle. Complementarity may be an operative principle in both problem finding and wisdom.

The model suggests the primacy of formal-operational thought in the emergence of the schemata, operations, and strategies associated with postformal thinking. The extension of this model to account for wisdom suggests the primacy of postformal thought in the emergence of the schemata, operations, and strategies associated with wisdom. What is stressed within the model and within this chapter is the role of problem finding in mediating between these descriptors of postformal reasoning and descriptors of wisdom.

The similarities between this model and life span conceptions of wisdom are numerous. Baltes and his colleagues (Baltes, Dittmann-Kohli, & Dixon, 1984; Dixon & Baltes, 1986; Baltes & Smith, 1987) start from an everyday definition of wisdom as entailing "good judgment and advice about difficult but uncertain matters of life" (Dixon & Baltes, 1986). From this definition comes an operational definition of wisdom as "expertise in the domain of fundamental pragmatics of life" (Dixon & Baltes, 1986). The concept of wisdom as expertise opens up the study of wisdom as an expert knowledge system and allows further specification of the nature of that knowledge system using criteria drawn from life span theory and cognitive psychology.

Baltes and Smith (1987) define this criterion set as

1. richness of factual knowledge about life;
2. richness in procedural knowledge about life;
3. life span contextualism;
4. awareness of relativism associated with variations in values and life priorities;

and

5. uncertainty of life, its recognition and management.

What is missing in large extent from life span research and particularly from this model of wisdom is a cognitive-developmental perspective. This perspective, particularly when interpreting young adult cognition, might explain the performance of some younger adults judged as wise when the life span work stresses the hypothesis that among the top performers in wisdom would be a disproportionately large number of older adults. Except for the criterion of uncertainty of life, this hypothesis receives little support.

A cognitive-developmental interpretation of adult intellectual functioning can establish the necessary links between formal reasoning, postformal reasoning, and wisdom. The cognitive-developmental perspective both theoretically and empirically emphasizes dialectical and relativistic thinking (Arlin, 1984, 1985; Cavanaugh, Kramer, Sinnott, Camp, & Markley, 1985; Commons & Richards, 1984), uncertainty (Meacham, 1983), and problem finding (Arlin, 1975, 1986). The latter entails the generation of generic questions from ill-defined, uncertain problems. These characteristics of postformal reasoning map directly on three of the life span wisdom criteria, namely, contextualism, relativism, and uncertainty.

These three criteria suggest a type of ill-definedness to the problems that are formulated and the solutions that are brought forth about the difficult but uncertain matters of life in general and of the areas of one's expertise in particular. The questions that one asks of one's life, one's experience, and one's discipline when one has thought deeply about such matters may be the single most powerful predictor of one's decisions and judgments and of the wisdom of those decisions and judgments.

Werthheimer states, "Often in great discoveries the most important thing is that a certain question is found" (1945, p. 123). Wisdom may guide the detection and selection of that question. Often, in wisdom, the most important thing may be that a certain question is asked. This is the art of problem finding, the asking of these generic questions in the face of ill-defined problems whether these problems are life problems or discipline-based problems. Although problem finding and wisdom share many features in common, their greatest commonality may be in the role of the question that is found under conditions of uncertainty and the relativity of the solutions that are offered in the face of these ill-defined problem situations.

## References

Apostle, L. (1979, June). *Construction and validation in contemporary epistemology.* Paper presented at the Archives de Jean Piaget, Geneva.

Arlin, P. K. (1974). *A cognitive process model of problem finding.* Unpublished Ph.D. dissertation, University of Chicago.

Arlin, P. K. (1975). Cognitive development in adulthood: a fifth stage? *Developmental Psychology, 11,* 602–606.

Arlin, P. K. (1975/76). A cognitive process model of problem finding. *Educational Horizons, 54,* 99–106.

Arlin, P. K. (1977). Piagetian operations in problem finding. *Developmental Psychology, 13,* 247–248.

Arlin, P. K. (1984). Adolescent and adult thought: a structural interpretation. In M. L. Commons, F. A. Richards, & C. Armon (Eds.), *Beyond formal operations: late adolescent and adult cognitive development* (pp. 258–271). New York: Praeger.

Arlin, P. K. (1986). Problem finding and young adult cognition. In R. A. Mines and K. Kitchener (Eds.), *Adult cognitive development: methods and models* (pp. 22–32). New York: Praeger.

Arlin, P. K. (1989). Problem finding and problem solving in young artists and young scientists. In M. L. Commons, J. D. Sinnott, F. A. Richards, & C. Armon (Eds.), *Beyond formal operations II: comparisons and applications of adolescent and adult developmental models.* New York: Praeger.

Baltes, P. B., Dittmann-Kohli, F., & Dixon, R. A. (1984). New perspectives on the development of intelligence in adulthood: toward a dual-process conception and a model of selective optimization with compensation. In P. B. Baltes & O.G. Brim, Jr. (Eds.), *Life-span development and behavior* (Vol. 6, pp. 33–76). New York: Academic Press.

Baltes, P. B., & Smith, J. (1987). *Toward a psychology of wisdom and its ontogenesis.* Unpublished manuscript based on an invited address by the first author at the annual meeting of the American Psychological Association.

Bartlett, F. C. (1958). Programme for experiments on thinking. *Quarterly Journal of Experimental Psychology, 8,* 145–162.

Basseches, M. (1980). Dialectical schemata: a framework for the empirical study of the development of dialectical thinking. *Human Development, 23,* 400–421.

Bransford, J. D., Franks, J. J., Vye, N. J., & Sherwood, R. D. (1986). *New approaches to instruction: because wisdom can't be told.* Paper presented at a conference on similarity and analogy, University of Illinois.

Cassirer, E. (1923). *Substance and function.* Chicago: Open Court.

Cavanaugh, J. C., Kramer, D. A., Sinnott, J. D., Camp, C. J., & Markley, R. P. (1985). On missing links and such: interfaces between cognitive research and everyday problem solving. *Human Development, 28,* 146–168.

Commons, M. L., & Richards, F. A. (1984). Systematic, metasystematic and cross-paradigmatic reasoning: a case for stages of reasoning beyond formal operations. In M. L. Commons, F. A. Richards, & C. Armon (Eds.), *Beyond formal operations: late adolescent and adult cognitive development* (pp. 92–119). New York: Praeger.

Commons, M. L., Richards, F. A., & Armon, C. (Eds.) (1984). *Beyond formal operations: late adolescent and adult cognitive development.* New York: Praeger.

Commons, M. L., Richards, F., & Kuhn, D. (1982). Metasystematic reasoning: a case for levels of reasoning beyond Piaget's stage of formal operations. *Child Development, 53,* 1058–1069.

Davidson, J. E., & Sternberg, R. J. (1984). The role of insight in intellectual giftedness. *Gifted Child Quarterly, 28,* 58–64.

Dillon, J. T. (1983). Problem finding and problem solving. *Journal of Creative Behavior, 16,* 97–111.

Dixon, R. A., & Baltes, P. B. (1986). Toward life-span research on the functions and pragmatics of intelligence. In R. J. Sternberg & R. K. Wagner (Eds.), *Practical intelligence: nature and origins of competence in the everyday world.* New York: Cambridge University Press.

Getzels, J. W. (1964). Creative thinking, problem-solving and instruction. In E. Hilgard (Ed.), *Learning and instruction: the Sixty-fifth Yearbook of the National Society for the Study of Education.* Chicago: The University of Chicago Press.

Getzels, J. W., & Csikszentmihalyi, M. (1965). Creative thinking in art students: an exploratory study. Cooperative Research Report No. S–080. Chicago.

Getzels, J. W., & Csikszentmihalyi, M. (1970). Concern for discovery: an attitudinal component of creative production. *Journal of Personality, 38,* 91–105.

Getzels, J. W., & Csikszentmihalyi, M. (1976). *The creative vision: problem finding in art.* Chicago: Van Nostrand.

Getzels, J. W., & Dillon, J. T. (1973). The nature of giftedness and the education of the gifted. In R. M. W. Travers (Ed.), *Second handbook of research on teaching.* Chicago: Rand McNally.

Guilford, J. P. (1967) *The nature of human intelligence.* New York: McGraw-Hill.

Holliday, S. G., & Chandler, M. J. (1986). *Wisdom: explorations in adult competence.* Basel: Karger.

Holton, G. (1973). *Thematic origins of scientific thought: Kepler to Einstein.* Cambridge: Harvard University Press.

Kramer, D. (1983). Post-formal operations? A need for further conceptualization. *Human Development, 26,* 91–105.

King, P. M., Kitchener, K. S., Davidson, M., Parker, C. A., & Wood, P. K. (1983). The justification of beliefs in young adults: a longitudinal study. *Human Development, 44,* 45–55.

Mackworth, N. H. (1965). Originality. *The American Psychologist, 20,* 51–66.

Meacham, J. A. (1983). Wisdom and the context of knowledge: knowing that one doesn't know. In D. Kuhn and J. A. Meacham (Eds.), *On the development of developmental psychology.* Basel, Switzerland: Karger.

Merton, R. K. (1945). Sociology of knowledge. In G. Gurviteh and W. E. Moore (Eds.), *Twentieth century sociology.* New York: Philosophical Library.

Merton, R. K. (1973). *The sociology of science.* Chicago: University of Chicago Press.

Osler, S. F., & Weiss, S. R. (1969). Studies in concept attainment: effect of instruction at two levels of intelligence. In L. E. Tyler (Ed.), *Intelligence: some recurring issues.* New York: Van Nostrand, 48–60.

Perkins, D. N. (1988). The possibility of invention. In R. J. Sternberg (Ed.), *The nature of creativity.* New York: Cambridge University Press.

Piaget, J. (1980). *Experiments in contradiction.* Chicago: University of Chicago Press.

Riegel, K. (1973). Dialectic operations: the final period of cognitive development. *Human Development, 16,* 346–370.

Schwartz, D. (1977). *The study of interpersonal problem posing.* Unpublished Ph.D. thesis, University of Chicago.

Sinnott, J. D. (1981). The theory of relativity: a metatheory for development? *Human Development, 24,* 293–311.

Sternberg, R. J. (1988) (Ed.). *The nature of creativity.* New York: Cambridge University Press.

Smilansky, J. (1985). Problem finding and creative problem solving. *Journal of Educational Psychology, 76,* 377–384.

Stanford University Symposium on Heuristic Teaching (1971). Palo Alto: Stanford University.

Sternberg, R. J., & Davidson, J. (1982). The mind of the puzzler. *Psychology Today, 16,* 37–44.

Wertheimer, M. (1945). *Productive thinking.* New York: Harper and Bros.

## 12 An essay on wisdom: toward organismic processes that make it possible

*Juan Pascual-Leone*

Why to call paths / the wakes of chance? / All travellers are walking, like Jesus, on the sea.
– Antonio Machado[1]

Since man is above all future-making, he is, above all, a swarm of hopes and fears.
– Ortega y Gasset[2]

I give you counsel for I am an old man: / never follow any counsel.
– Antonio Machado[3]

### Introduction

In *Philosophy of Symbolic Forms* (1929) and *An Essay on Man* (1944) Cassirer points to forms of symbolic processing that are mutually contradictory in appearance but jointly needed, as alternative forms of rationality (cf. Krois, 1987), to encode aspects of outer or inner reality. Cassirer lists myth and religion, language, art, history, and science as *some* of these symbolic forms. Each encodes a *different reality* found in the complex life of man or woman. A similar claim is made by Habermas (1970, 1984) when he describes alternative modes of science making (e.g., technical-analytic, historical-hermeneutic, critical-social, and reconstructive), each autonomously developed to serve a different kind of interest. As Zubiri (1986) describes it: The human is an *animal of realities*. Cassirer could have added wisdom as another form of symbolic processing.

As a form or mode of processing, wisdom is concerned with human life as a totality from the perspective of an intelligent and willful coping with it. Wisdom deals with *vital reason* (Ortega y Gasset, 1980), that is, insightful practical rationality about one's life *(vita* in Latin) and one's living in all its aspects/realities. Vital reason is concerned with the person as a concrete, evolving totality – a totality that extends into the future *and the possible* of a person. David Bakan (pers. commun., August 1988) illustrates this projection into the future with the example of *danger:* the assessment of an

244

impending possible (i.e., potentially real) harm, damage, or loss. An important part of wise living and wise life counseling is prevention of danger.

From a life span perspective (Jung and Erikson must be credited with this idea) wisdom can be regarded as the ultimate possible achievement of a normal person's growth. It is the *category* that describes the moment *(state* or stage) in development when the psychological system becomes fully coordinated across experiential contexts and across alternative forms/modes of processing. The following are psychological examples of alternative processing modes: experiential versus conceptual, thinking versus willing/acting versus feeling, remembering the past versus coping with the present versus planning for the future, cognitive versus affective versus existential processing, and so on. The wise individual, although anchored in the present, has dialectically integrated into a manifold totality the multiple aspects of his or her self-experience and has done so not just conceptually but experientially (as empirical self and as existence), historically (as unique historically conditioned evolving totality immersed in an evolving society), and culturally (Jaspers, 1970, 1971; Pascual-Leone, 1983, in press-a).

Holliday and Chandler (1986) might agree with this view, for they intimate that wisdom involves a coordination of multiple forms of knowledge accumulated by the subject throughout life. These forms of knowledge can be grouped within three types (cf. Habermas, 1970, 1984):

1. technical knowledge – related to what Jaspers (1970) would call *knowledge of the world;*
2. practical knowledge – human, interpersonal/social knowledge, which Jaspers and self-psychologists would call *knowledge of the Other;*
3. emancipatory knowledge – that increases the freedom of the self and opens possibilities of self-development, the kind that Jaspers and personality psychologists might call *knowledge of the self,* including ego extensions into the unconscious.

A newly acquired dialectical integration of the person as a totality has been documented in older people's self-reports (Johnson, 1982; Ryff, 1984). If and when this dialectical integration reaches sufficient breadth and cohesiveness over the person's control processes and over his or her storehouse of informational processes (cognitive, affective, inter- or intrapersonal, cultural, religious or existential, etc.), wisdom appears. Such is the main thesis of this chapter. This coordination takes place as a result of the efforts by the inner true self (the "actual" self; Higgins, in press-a, in press-b) to resolve dialectical contradictions that unavoidably emerge among/between various self-schemes (life projects, values, motives, self- and Other evaluations, self-ideals and actual conduct, ideals about the Other and his or her realities, ideals about the world and its realities, alternative bodies of knowledge, etc.). These self-schemes tend originally to be developed in different life contexts, but they clash as the person enters new situations that bring them into conflict. These conflicts are the yeast out of which wisdom emerges (Norman S. Endler, pers.

commun., December 1988; the same idea was first proposed and elaborated by Jaspers [1970] with his theory of "limit/boundary situations" and their role in human growth). The attempt to resolve these contradictions dialectically, common in adulthood (Basseches, 1984; Pascual-Leone, 1983, in press-a), produces new and encompassing self-structures, which constitute a new, more autonomous self; this is an *ultraself control center* (Kant's or Husserl's transcendental self; Jung's "Self"), which is a distant self-organization superordinate to the subject's own *interpersonal/empirical self* (the ordinary self of adults, which Jung and Jungians call the "ego"). This ultraself, which phenomenologically could be called a "nonself" because it is decentered from the self's perspective and can take a mental distance from it, makes it possible for the subject to examine his or her own "I" or I-self (the operative/affective self) as a *detailed* object of introspective knowledge (the "me," or figurative self, can be observed much earlier!). As a consequence, he or she becomes fully aware of self as an "agent" and as a feeling "soul" across different contexts; and this generates consciousness of the inevitable dialectical contradictions in human existence (Basseches, 1984; Pascual-Leone, 1983). These developments initiate growth toward wisdom, which is brought about by the *subject's continuously renewed acts of will,* that is his or her conscious existential choice not to surrender to the encountered life and/or inner contradictions and crises but to actively persist in the always renewed attempt to cope. These renewed acts of will toward inner (existential) clarity foster the growth of characteristics such as openness toward reality; empathic mental distancing from emotions, from the self, and from salient aspects of situations; cultivation of mental choice and freedom of judgment; and exertion of will and of external freedom.

Perhaps the origin of this movement toward wisdom – of this "growing into human maturity" (Pascual-Leone, 1983) – is the presence in the subject of what might be called a *will-to-be* disposition. In this expression I understand "to be" as meaning what existentialist philosophers (e.g., Heidegger, 1966; Jaspers, 1959, 1970, 1971; see also Arendt, 1981) and some psychologists (e.g., Maslow, 1968) mean by *being*: what psychologists call "true self" or "true nature" of the person. The will-to-be disposition is a motive that propels the person toward human growth. The origin of this disposition, derived from child-rearing patterns and mentor models that the subject has had, is not our concern now. If the person has a will-to-be disposition, he or she shall progress toward maturity and wisdom with life experience; if the person has instead a will-not-to-be (e.g., neurotic attitudes or an excess of anxiety/fear), he or she must change it into a "will to be" before life experiences can move him or her toward maturity and wisdom. If this will exists, when the person is old enough, in the "late formal" years (see p. 256), the process of growing toward wisdom might slowly begin. An analysis of this process in its self-structural highlights is the first objective of this chapter. The onset of this process of growth may be marked by the emergence of an *existential self,* as described in existential philosophy. With the advent of this existential self-consciousness the person begins to exhibit characteristics that are illustrated by the three quotes at the head of the chapter:

1. The self is aware that life offers no clear path to be followed (there are many uncertain vital matters).
2. The self is projected toward the future (the past is not a shelter but a springboard).
3. In matters of vital reason the person is ultimately on his or her own (no help or counsel can replace the personal choice).

In the first epigraph of this chapter Machado (1964) takes Jesus' walk on the waters as a symbol of human existence: "Traveller [he says elsewhere in the same book], there is no path, the path is made by your walking. . . . Traveller, there are no paths, only the wakes on the sea." (p. 203; translated by JPL). The image is of vital reason creating a person's life path out of choices made in the chancy here-and-now. This image echoes Duns Scotus as reported by Hanna Arendt (1981). Scotus's vision is that of a will that by its choices keeps converting the undefined *contingency* of the future into the irretrievable and permanently structured *necessity* of the past. Scotus's will and Machado's traveler (Ortega's vital reason) represent the situation of all humans: There is no authentic life – no life conducive to wisdom – unless the person lives by true convictions, using the will to control unwanted impulses or desires induced by circumstances (e.g., Jaspers, 1970). These conflicts of existential choice highlight the importance of vital reason's imagination: mentally going to the past, the future, and the possible by way of serene reflection (meditative thinking; see the section on "the will of wisdom: will-not-to-will"). The form of praxis – conscious goal-directed activity addressed to the environment – that this authentic living might take will greatly depend on personal/historical contingencies of the individual's life; for example, some find themselves privileged whereas many others are oppressed and/or experience the oppression of others; these contingencies condition the actual manifestation of authentic living (cf. Freire, 1973).

## The three heads (aspects) of wisdom

The theme introduced in the preceding section, *wisdom-as-will within vital reason,* is one of three themes about wisdom found, in various guises, in religious, philosophical, and psychological literature. A second consistent theme is *wisdom as valid existential counseling.* The wise person is a good and sensitive counselor in personal life matters. Based on his study of the Old Testament, Scott (1971, p. 184) writes: "Wisdom, as we have seen, is basically counsel about how life should be lived." A similar conclusion is found in other literatures from major religions and in the writings of leading psychologists. Baltes and his associates define wisdom as entailing "good judgment and advice about difficult but uncertain matters of life" (Baltes, Smith, Staudinger, & Sowarka, in press, p. 8; see also Baltes, Dittmann-Kohli, & Dixon, 1984; Dittmann Kohli & Baltes, in press). This definition is consistent with a dominant aspect of people's implicit theories about wisdom (Holliday & Chandler, 1986; Johnson, 1982; Sternberg, 1985a).

But the counsel provided by wisdom is unlike ordinary expert counsel in that *it aims to render itself unnecessary*. This paradox of wisdom-as-counsel is illustrated in the second Machado epigraph of the chapter. The poem (which unintentionally captures the flavor of Zen Buddhism) conveys the model of a person who carefully seeks and listens to advice, mentally accommodating to it, but takes free personal decisions about the vital matters at hand. The apprentice of wisdom should not be a "believer" but should challenge from within (using the mentor's own methods and teaching) the mentor's teachings or deeds. A dramatic illustration of this practice is found in the Old Testament's Book of Job. Job challenges God on account of the miseries of his human existence and does so against the advice of three conventional counselors (who in my view represent the "believer's" viewpoint); after the confrontation, God praises Job's conduct while condemning the attitude of the three counselors, who were only advising Job to accept God's will. Clearly wisdom's counsel is not to follow the advice of the counselors but to become one of them via intelligent and emancipated thinking, feeling, and willing.

The third theme of wisdom follows from the second: *wisdom's ability for empathic intuitive experiencing of the problems and issues of the Other or of nature* – from a decentered perspective corresponding to Other's and nature's as much as one's own. This empathic knowledge is well illustrated in Kierkegaard's dictum: "The majority of men are subjective towards themselves and objective towards all others – terribly objective sometimes – but the real task is in fact to be objective towards one's self and subjective towards all others" (quoted by Schrag, 1977, p. 11). A wise person seems to move effortlessly from an attitude of empathic communion with the Other's subjective experiencing to the mental-affective attitude of agency – analytical and detached awareness of the Other as a social object (Bakan, 1966; Buber, 1958, 1961). It is as if in wisdom the self's agency (that aspect of the interpersonal/empirical self called by Buber the "I-it" experiencing of a fellow person) and the self's communion (Buber's "I–thou" experiencing of a person) were intimately coordinated and functioning simultaneously (cf. Maslow, 1968). This empathic but fully decentered, analytic experiencing requires, in the view of Jaspers (1970), the blending of love and care with intelligence (analytical cognition). Many others have expressed similar views (e.g., Augustine – Bakan, 1966; Buber, 1961; Burnaby, 1955; Erikson, 1982; Scheler, 1973;

Jung – Jacobi, 1967; Maslow, 1968; Jungian and Freudian analysts – Holliday & Chandler, 1986; Johnson, 1982; Pascual-Leone, 1983, in press-a).

These three themes of wisdom in fact relate to three main aspects of our mind traced by Hanna Arendt (1981) in the history of philosophy. I refer to *thinking* (vital reason and knowledge-in-counseling), *willing* (self-monitoring using vital reason), and *judgment/feeling* (empathic but analytical appreciation and evaluation of life's contingencies, of Other and nature).

In the remainder of the chapter I will disregard the aspect of wisdom-as-counsel because it is already well recognized in the current psychological literature. Instead I shall focus, in the next four sections, on the study of wisdom-as-will and of will itself. This is a major process-analytical aspect that is largely absent from the current literature. Then I examine the theme of wisdom-as-feeling/judgment. I conclude with a concise definition of wisdom and a comparison of intelligence, creativity, and wisdom, suggesting possible ways of investigating their life span differences neurophysiologically.

## Wisdom-as-will: the existential self-monitoring of vital reason

Willful autonomy, although not found in the factor analyses of Holliday and Chandler (1986), appears in the phenomenological analysis of some of their most prototypical descriptors of wise people. This is the case of items "thinks for him or herself," "mature," "understands him or herself," "thinks carefully before making decisions," "weighs the consequences of actions," "plans things carefully," "self-actualized," "poised," and so on. Willful autonomy also appears in interviews about wisdom conducted by Johnson (1982) and in the pioneering work of Maslow (1968).

For the classics, the will had the function nowadays assigned to the self. It provided the steering function and the power of the mind to take a mental distance from misleading situations. Arendt describes Augustine's formulation as: "And this power of the mind is due not to the Intellect and not to Memory but only to the Will, that unites the mind's inwardness with the outer world" (1981, p. 101). According to Duns Scotus (Arendt, 1981), another great classic philosopher of the will, the power of imagination, which serves to anticipate future possibilities and the consequences of possible action (and to anticipate [Lewin, 1951] the motives and values related to them), is an achievement of the will; and this achievement opens up the possibility of mental choice and existential/personal freedom. For the classics, as for us, freedom is made possible by the will. Jaspers's modern view echoes that of Augustine (Burnaby, 1955): "Volition is a *relation to oneself*, a self-awareness in which I am the object of my active conduct rather than my contemplative scrutiny. . . . As Kierkegaard put it: 'The more will the more self' " (Jaspers, 1970, p. 135).

Thus conceived, the will appears as a sort of mental attention – "attention of the mind" it is called by Augustine (Arendt, 1981, p. 100). According to Augustine, this mental attention – the will – causes thinking by coordinating intelligence/memory with the self's intentional direction and the input from the sense organs: "It is the will that makes them function and eventually 'binds them together'" (Arendt, 1981, p. 100). Similar views are found in William James (1966): *"Effort of attention is thus the essential phenomenon of will"* (emphasis is his own, p. 317). Three pages later he adds: "To sum it all up in a word, *the terminus of the psychological process of volition, the point to which the will is directly applied, is always an idea."* Finally, regarding free will, he says (p. 323): *"The question of fact in the free will controversy is thus extremely simple. It relates solely to the amount of effort of attention which we can at any time put forth."*

Recent writers on the will or related conscious processes, phenomenologists (e.g., Ricoeur, 1967; Silber, 1960), and psychologists (e.g., Jung, 1959b; Lewin, 1951; Piaget, 1962) lead us to recognize three different aspects within this volitional attention of William James.[4] A first aspect is what Ricoeur calls Kant's antinomy. This is the fact that *in an act-of-will there usually occurs an implicit choice between two antinomic alternatives.* One alternative is the inner freedom of what James calls (see the preceding paragraph) the conscious "idea" of what must be done (cf. Ricoeur, 1967); this is what Kant (1951, 1960) calls the "noumenal" realm or "dispositional" imperative and Lewin (1951) calls a "quasi-need." The other alternative is constituted by initially unconscious, simpler, and more biological motives that push for an opposing behavior (these are the "needs" of Lewin, the unconscious forces of Jungians and Freudians, the "phenomenal" realm or "natural" desires of Kant).

The second aspect of the will (of volitional attention) is, as Ricoeur (1967) emphasizes, *motivational.* Motives and values from all levels of complexity intimately connected with the body's self-experience or with personal history confront one another in the act-of-will; the final outcome follows a principle of summation (Freud's *overdetermination*): Compatible forces add their strength, and the dominant alternative in terms of these sums ends up controlling consciousness and the will function; but still the two alternatives appear to combine (synthesize) in secondary aspects of the performance resolution. Kant (1951) and Luria (1973), among others, call this process of resolution *dynamic synthesis;* Jung (1960), in an interesting 1916 manuscript, calls it "the transcendent function," for it serves to combine in performance conscious with unconscious processes. This mechanism, hitherto mysterious, has nowadays become clearer with the advent of neuronal computation and parallel distributed processing; these *dialectical dynamic syntheses* are (unwittingly) being modeled in the new science by "relaxation" methods of computation (e.g., Rumelhart, McClelland, & The PDP Research Group, 1986).

The third aspect of the will appears when we consider the canonical case of voluntary attention: the will exerted in *motivationally misleading situations.* A situation is motivationally misleading when its most salient features actually cue the natural needs against which the idea (or rational quasi-need) attempts to assert itself. Under these conditions, a dynamic synthesis in the direction of the willful idea would only be possible if there are content-free brain resources capable of generating the *mental-attentional effort* – "effort" that James spoke about and current cognitive psychology has come to recognize. The third aspect of the will – which James and the classics call "attention" and Kant could have called "transcendental determinants of the will" – is the set of brain hardware resources that enable the will's idea to win.

A process model of attentional volition should therefore model the will as being a dynamic functional system, that is, *a complex function* of the self. The main processes might be of four kinds. The first kind, *affective goals,* provides the motivational aspect; self-controlled affective goals are the quasi-needs that motivate the willful idea. The second kind, *metaexecutives,* are intellective or intellectual plans for realizing in action the idea. These two kinds of function are *informational/subjective operators* because they provide the information that structures the person's subjective experience and his or her objective performance. The other two kinds of processes, *mental-attentional energy* and *mental interruption* (active, *central* inhibition), are by contrast noninformational (i.e., content-free, nonspecific) mechanisms provided by the brain's architecture; monitored by the dominant metaexecutives (see the points that follow), they are capable of boosting the activation of idea processes while inhibiting other processes that oppose the idea. Their function is that of *hidden hardware operators* controlled by the dominant metaexecutive. I discuss briefly, in four points, these operators of the will function; for more detail see Pascual-Leone (1983, 1984, 1987, in press-a, in press-b).

1. The first subjective operator (a set of components, in Sternberg's [1985b] terminology) is the person's set of "cool" (i.e., reflective, *self-controlled)* *affective goals* and his or her personal, more or less automatized *intentional dispositions* (e.g., enduring cognitive styles and controls) that together stipulate slow-changing and enduring *general intentional directions* to the mental processes, which are not necessarily conscious (cf. Higgins, in press-a, in press-b, in press-c; Markus & Wurf, 1987).

2. The second subjective operator is a set of metacognitive plans and knowledge structures. These are primarily high-order *executive processes:* intellective (Piaget's concrete operational) or intellectual (formal operational) processes. They are cued by automatized aspects of the situation, affective goals, and other executives. These are the sort of processes that Sternberg (1985b) calls metacomponents and neo-Piagetians call complex conscious executive schemes or *metaexecutives* (e.g., Pascual-Leone 1983, 1984; in these works I use the term *ultra-executive* instead of *metaexecutive,* the two being

synonymous). But the will is not always controlled by these conscious or preconscious schemes (i.e., *egoschemes*); it can also be monitored by the affective and personal schemes already mentioned as the will's subjective operator (1). The result is *conation,* a sort of unconscious volition.

3. The first hidden hardware operator is a content-free attentional capacity called *mental energy or M operator,* an activation-boosting mechanism. According to Luria (1973) and other neuropsychologists, this sort of mechanism is related to capacities subserved by the brain's prefrontal lobes. It also relates to what is often called *working memory* (but see Pascual-Leone [1987] for arguments against reducing mental attention to working memory). The executives and metaexecutives of operator 2 mobilize and allocate this mental energy.

4. The second hidden hardware operator is a central active-inhibition mechanism, that is, an *interrupt* function or interruption/disinterruption capacity, which may also be provided by the prefrontal lobes (cf. Damasio, 1985; Fuster, 1980; Luria, 1973; Stuss & Benson, 1984). Will executives mobilize and allocate the interrupt function.

Together these four will operators control the activation of *action schemes* (i.e., Sternberg's performance components); they produce a sequence of mental acts, leading to action, that constitutes the *act-of-will.* This model is claimed as the processing kernel of both will and mental attention (cf. Pascual-Leone, 1983, 1984, 1987, in press-a). Operators 1, 3, and 4 are obligatory constituents of mental attention; but operator 2 might often be absent in attention; mental attention could be steered solely by operator 1 or by nonconscious executives (an instance of this case is any act of attending aroused by curiosity, an affect; e.g., a car accident). Furthermore, acts-of-will always take place at the level of *executive processing* (planning and action monitoring, but not action itself). By contrast, acts of mental attention may be defined as well at other levels of processing such as *affective processing* or *pure action processing* (e.g., perception and scanning) where executive processing might not intervene at all. This dialectical-constructivist conception of levels of processing was presented in detail by Pascual-Leone (1984) and is summarized in Figure 12.1.

Monitored by operators 1 and 2, operators 3 and 4 of the *will function* apply themselves to the subject's repertoire of schemes to inhibit schemes inconvenient for implementing the current *mentally dominant executive* (schemes dominant at the level of executive processing). At the same time schemes congruent with this dominant executive are boosted in activation. As a result of this *act-of-will,* the field of highly activated (dominant) schemes in the subject – *the field of mental centration* – can radically change. It can change as abruptly as the state of a country suddenly suffering a successful coup d'état or military takeover (see Pascual-Leone [1983] for a detailed discussion of this analogy). The state of mind changes by the action of the will because the new "leaders" (i.e., the now mentally dominant affects and/

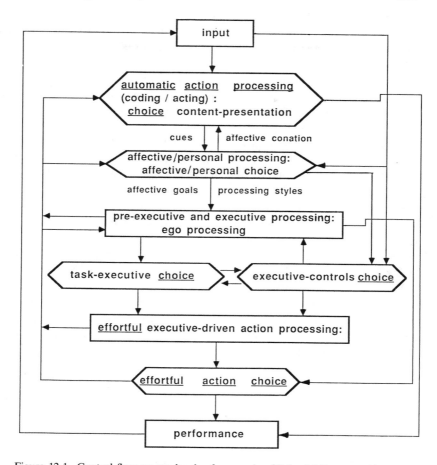

Figure 12.1. Control flow among levels of processing (dialectial "moments") during generative construction of here-and-now performances. *Note:* Personal processing is the activation and choice of personality stylistic schemes (automatized cognitive styles). Preexecutives are executive schemes that in the current task serve as exploratory procedures. Executive processes are the executive schemes that carry plans and controls of the task at hand. Controls are executives that monitor mobilization and allocation of hardware resources (e.g., mental capacity, interruption capacity). Allocation and use of hardware resources is called effortful processing/choice.

or metaexecutives) actively inhibit opposing forces via the interruption mechanism while boosting allied forces – relevant schemes – by allocating to them mental energy.

Phenomenologically, this mental revolution, when it is an *act-of-will*, often appears as one or more *dynamic/creative syntheses* that coordinate the four will operators to produce the act-of-will performance (for dynamic/creative syntheses see Pascual-Leone, 1980, 1983, 1984, 1987, in press-a, in press-b; Pascual-Leone & Goodman, 1979; Pascual-Leone, Goodman, Ammon, &

Subelman, 1978). *These syntheses anticipate and bring to the present events of the future (or the possible) by using either imagery* (this is Kant's "transcendental imagination"; e.g., Kant, 1960, 1965) *or mental/internal language.* This imagination and/or mental language provide cues to steer the organismic performance in the willed-for direction (e.g., a student or professional who decides to cancel a vacation with friends and instead stays home to work). *An act-of-will is therefore a series of executive syntheses projected into the future as a conscious anticipatory praxis.*[5]

Notice that by this definition an act-of-will controlled by metaexecutives is essentially different from mental choices purely driven by habits or by consolidated schemes (transfer of learning), by emotions ("hot" affective determinants), or by salient cues of situations. Mental choices induced by Freud's superego are not expressions of the will. Although superego processes may be sequences of dynamic/creative syntheses, *they are directed to the past* and their function is to accommodate performance to past interdictions and prescriptions. *Acts-of-will are directed to the future and deal with executive choice in a relative, or radical, autonomy from past prescriptions or interdictions.*

Known paradoxes of the will can be explained with this model. Before addressing the important issue of wisdom-as-will, I shall discuss two of these paradoxes since the will construct, dismissed by behaviorism, is still not well recognized in modern psychology. This historical dismissal may explain its absence in modern psychological discussions of wisdom (e.g., Baltes et al., in press; Erikson, 1982; Holliday & Chandler, 1986; Johnson, 1982; Sternberg, 1985a).

### Explaining two paradoxes of the will: Claparede's and Skinner's

Somewhere Piaget writes that his mentor Claparede proposed a paradox of the will. This is the paradox: The will works to overcome bad habits and to control the compelling pull of *motivationally misleading situations;*[6] yet it often turns out to be weak when it is most needed but strong when it is not (or no longer) needed. This paradox is explained by the character of "mental-revolution" of the will's application and the learning effect it brings about. When a subject finds him- or herself in motivationally misleading situations where he or she lacks well-developed metaexecutives, his or her will appears weak. Although during *executive processing* (see Figure 12.1) the willful resolution was firm, it often fails in the initial encounters with *action processing,* that is, with the hard, misleading reality of everyday experience. The best a subject can do under these conditions to avoid unwanted behavior is to escape the "tempting" situation. Negative affects (e.g., guilt) often ensue, and the subject engages in anticipatory planning and in after-the-fact reexaminations of his or her failure to achieve self-control. These reexaminations are actual *executive-learning situations,* where the subject, little by little, can acquire suitable metaexecutives for this sort of act-of-will. Techniques along these lines are currently used by cognitive therapists. By these and other executive-learning means the relevant metaexecutives and coping strategies develop, and these acts-of-will eventually succeed. Once the metaexecutives and coping strategies have been extended to other common will-demanding situations and automatized, the subject could exhibit a very strong will in the sense that he or she unflinchingly maintains the desired course. At this point, however, the *act-of-will* (i.e., dynamic/creative syntheses engineered with mental energy and interruption power) is much less needed since the new *automatized meta-executive strategies* can avoid or minimize the disrupting interference of misleading situations without expending much mental energy or interruption capacity.

Another paradox of the will has been tacitly brought up by Skinner (1953, 1971; Catania & Harnad, 1988). Skinner has expressed the view that since the human mind is so strongly conditioned by its learning history – and this is quite true – it cannot be free, and thus the will is an illusion. This is a paradox: The continuously evolving complexification of culture and the open character of human history, as well as empirical observations of human creativity and existential choices, show that freedom and will in fact exist. A solution to the paradox is possible within the model of *will syntheses* sketched in the preceding paragraphs. It is possible because Skinner's empirically grounded claim emphasizes only the great power of situations – the power of that "shallow" level of mental processing that deals with the choice of action schemes (i.e., the processing of Sternberg's performance components). This is the driving power of an automatic mental-processing level – Neisser's (1967) "preattentive processing" – that I have called *automatic-action processing* and contrasted with *affective processing, executive processing,* and *effortful action processing* (see Figure 12.1). According to this conception, situations (or rather their *automatic-action cues)* tend to induce subjects to act in ways that conform to past experience unless the subject effortfully (i.e., using mental energy and mental interruption) resists. This is the key to solving Skinner's will paradox. The solution is to recognize that subjects, using their metaexecutives and executive-level processing, decide to abandon the motivationally misleading situations and move to other environments that compel them to evolve in the direction they actually want to evolve.[7] This decision of the self to change environments, thus controlling the subject–environment interactions, is a possibility recognized by modern personality theory (e.g., Endler, 1983). To explain this decision – a new idea not facilitated by the situation – we need to endow the subjects with organismic mechanisms of the will.

### The self's organization in young adulthood

It is now recognized that development continues beyond late adolescence, through late adulthood, by way of a number of qualitative metamorphoses in affective–cognitive experiencing and thinking (Basseches, 1984; Commons, Kohlberg, Richards, & Sinnott, in press; Commons, Richard, & Armon, 1984; Commons, Sinnott, Richards, & Armon, 1989; Kramer, 1983; Labouvie-Vief, 1982, 1985). In two recent chapters (Pascual-Leone, 1983, in press-b) I proposed a conceptualization of this change. The person moves, after adolescence and prior to old age, through four different ego developmental stages (which space limitations prevent me from summarizing here). In each of these stages the will – "manager" of the conscious self – has a functional structure and evolves in ways that psychologists have generally ignored (but see Lewin, 1951; Piaget, 1962). The reflections of philosophers throughout history (e.g., Aristotle, Augustine, Scotus, Descartes, Kant, Husserl, Scheler, James, Jaspers, Heidegger, Ricoeur, Arendt) can help in this matter. I will now synthesize these views, giving them the form of a testable psychological model. I do not discuss in detail the evolution of the will through adult stages; I focus instead on the initial stage of ego adulthood, the "late formal" stage, to contrast it with the final optional stages of mature adulthood, the stages I have called "dialectical" and "transcendental" – transcendental in the Kantian, not in the religious/metaphysical, sense. For more detail readers should consult my recent chapters on adult self-development (Pascual-Leone, 1983, in press-b). The ideas that follow, although original, are consistent with the current trend toward a dynamic, developmental, and constructivist interpretation of the self/ego (e.g., Bearison & Zimiles, 1986; Case, 1988; Case, Hayward, Lewis, & Hurst, 1987; Fischer & Elmendorf, 1986; Fischer & Lamporn, in press; Higgins, in press-a, in press-b, in press-c; Markus & Wurf, 1987; Singer & Kolligian, 1987). The novelty of what follows with regard to current theories of self-organization is twofold:

1. I explicitly show the place and the role of the will function and its "acts-of-will" in the self-organization and thus suggest a more detailed analysis of the operative–affective self (the I-self of William James, 1966) than heretofore attempted in psychological models.
2. I explicitly relate these descriptive constructs to causal mechanisms discussed in detail elsewhere (e.g., Johnson, Fabian, & Pascual-Leone, in press; Pascual-Leone, 1980, 1983, 1984, 1987, in press-a, in press-b; Pascual-Leone & Goodman, 1979) that account for their development and effective functioning.

By the first adult stage (late formal stage, generally spanning from 17 to 25 years of age) the person may already have a well-formed mature repertoire of conscious or preconscious (i.e., *ego)* schemes and schemas (i.e., very complex schemes of schemes). This repertoire is that of a formal-reasoning thinker in the intended meaning of neo-Piagetians – a meaning that does not signify "logico-mathematically formal" but *intuitively formal,* in the sense that the person can now mentally entertain, or learn to entertain, processes from the perspective of *any* logical modality: past, present, imaginary, empirically possible/necessary, rationally possible/necessary, and so on. This intuitively for-

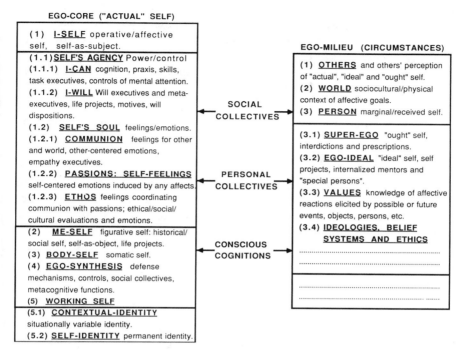

EGO-CORE ("ACTUAL" SELF)

(1) <u>I-SELF</u> operative/affective self, self-as-subject.

(1.1)<u>SELF'S AGENCY</u> Power/control
(1.1.1) <u>I-CAN</u> cognition, praxis, skills, task executives, controls of mental attention.
(1.1.2) <u>I-WILL</u> Will executives and meta-executives, life projects, motives, will dispositions.
(1.2) <u>SELF'S SOUL</u> feelings/emotions.
(1.2.1) <u>COMMUNION</u> feelings for other and world, other-centered emotions, empathy executives.
(1.2.2) <u>PASSIONS: SELF-FEELINGS</u> self-centered emotions induced by any affects.
(1.2.3) <u>ETHOS</u> feelings coordinating communion with passions; ethical/social/cultural evaluations and emotions.
(2) <u>ME-SELF</u> figurative self: historical/social self, self-as-object, life projects.
(3) <u>BODY-SELF</u> somatic self.
(4) <u>EGO-SYNTHESIS</u> defense mechanisms, controls, social collectives, metacognitive functions.
(5) <u>WORKING SELF</u>
(5.1) <u>CONTEXTUAL-IDENTITY</u> situationally variable identity.
(5.2) <u>SELF-IDENTITY</u> permanent identity.

← SOCIAL COLLECTIVES →

← PERSONAL COLLECTIVES →

← CONSCIOUS COGNITIONS →

EGO-MILIEU (CIRCUMSTANCES)

(1) <u>OTHERS</u> and others' perception of "actual", "ideal" and "ought" self.
(2) <u>WORLD</u> sociocultural/physical context of affective goals.
(3) <u>PERSON</u> marginal/received self.

(3.1) <u>SUPER-EGO</u> "ought" self, interdictions and prescriptions.
(3.2) <u>EGO-IDEAL</u> "ideal" self, self projects, internalized mentors and "special persons".
(3.3) <u>VALUES</u> knowledge of affective reactions elicited by possible or future events, objects, persons, etc.
(3.4) <u>IDEOLOGIES, BELIEF SYSTEMS AND ETHICS</u>

Figure 12.2. Categorical organization of the ego-schemes total repertoire.

mal, late formal, thinker also has, or can be taught to acquire, the full power of three ways of abstraction: reductive/generic abstraction, constructive/reflective abstraction, and causal abstraction.

At this point of development the *interpersonal self* (i.e., the ordinary, *empirical self,* called by Jungians and others the "ego") is fully constituted along with the adult repertoire of conscious or preconscious schemes – this is the adult *ego repertoire* (i.e., *the ego,* for short[8]). This ego contains two consciously distinct and irreducible supercategories of schemes: the ego-core *(true self* or "subject" of experience) and the ego-milieu *(self's context* or *circumstances,* i.e., the "object" of experience). As Ortega asserted, "I am myself and my circumstances" (Ortega y Gasset, 1914/1961, p. 45). That is, the Other (the fellow person) and our common world are experientially constructed (abstracted) using systems of schemes that come to belong to the subject's own ego (see Husserl, 1970, p. 183).

Figure 12.2 (taken with modifications from Pascual-Leone, in press-b) summarizes in a symbolic/linguistic manner, using labels that readers familiar with current ego/self theories should understand, the main qualitatively different subrepertoires (i.e., functional categories of schemes) of the ego. The *ego-core* is constituted by all the schemes that dynamically construct the self in its manifestations and capabilities. It contains a number of subordinate repertoires (i.e., "subdirectories"), each one having many different "files" and each file related to a different sort of situation. The main subrepertoires of the ego-core are five, but I shall only discuss here the *I-self*, or the operative/affective self. The *ego-milieu* also contains a number of subordinate repertoires, of which I mention three:

1. *Others,* that is, representations of other persons;
2. *world,* that is, representations of outer realities reflecting the self's physical/sociocultural environment;
3. *persona,* in Jung's sense of the ego's "external person" (Jacobi, 1962).

This is the subrepertoire of schemes corresponding to the Other-centered, *social* aspects of the self that often are *marginal* in the ego and *received* from external models. Two sorts of operative schemes functionally relate ego-core and ego-milieu and thus create our conscious structuring of the *intersubjective world of everyday experience,* of what philosophers often call, after Husserl, the *lifeworld* (cf. Husserl, 1970; Schutz & Luckmann, 1973). These sorts are cognitive/metacognitive structures and social-cognitive structures. The social-cognitive structures, which I have called *collectives* (Pascual-Leone, 1983, in press-b), coordinate two or more personal schemes (self or others) by means of procedural/operative schemes that stipulate the roles and operative intersubjective play patterns within the (more-or-less generalized) collective group. These structures define ethical/moral norms within a given collective (such as a society peer group, a workplace, or a family group), thus bringing social/ethical/moral constraints to the will.

The I-self is the subrepertoire where the will can be said to have its roots and where changes leading to wisdom might first begin. The I-self subcategory of schemes accounts for the subject's *conscious* cognitive, judgmental, and affective capabilities. These three modes of processing are characterized, respectively, by the evaluation modality of true–false (related to Kant's pure reason), which I shall denote by the commonsense *cognitive* expression *I-can;* the pragmatic evaluation modality good–bad (related to Kant's judgment), which I denote by the *affective–cognitive* expression *self's soul* and characterize as *feeling;* and the evaluation right–wrong (related to Kant's practical reason), which I denote by the *volitional/ethical* expression *I-will.* These three subrepertoires, like all other subrepertoires of the self, are interconnected by means of structural links induced by experience. In fact, the *working self,* that is, the *self "files"* (schemes or structures) *that the subject customarily uses across situations,* largely fulfills this function of dialectical integration of the self's many subrepertoires.

The subrepertoires of I-can (i.e., cognitive/pragmatic self) and I-will (i.e., executives of the will) represent what Bakan (1966) has called the agency of the person – the repertoire that gives him or her an assertive, analytical, and self-relying approach. Because this idea becomes important later in the chapter, I add that these I-can and I-will subrepertoires originate and develop induced by the affective goals of positive power affects: mastery, independence, pleasure of being cause, feeling of being in control, and so on. The self's soul/feelings subrepertoire is discussed later, and I shall skip it now.

## Position of the will in the self's organization

To begin the analysis of the will's complex function within the ego, it is desirable to discuss first the ideas of Kant (1960), a thinker who has deeply analyzed the will. In this discussion I interpret psychologically basic notions of Kant in light of Silber's (1960) excellent study. But there is much more in Silber's and in Kant's work of interest for psychologists than I can discuss here; for instance, the stages of will development as a function of experience. (It is worth comparing Kant with William James [1966] on this matter.) After studying the present chapter, readers of Silber and Kant might not find it difficult to extend the model discussed in what follows to individual/developmental differences of will.

Kant regards the will as jointly constituted by three constructs:

1. *Willkür*, which I interpret as *act-of-will;*
2. *Wille*, which I interpret as *judgment-of-will;* and
3. *Gesinnung*, which I interpret as *disposition-of-will.*

An *act-of-will (Willkür)* is a decision-producing sequence of (one or more) dynamic/creative syntheses generated by the person's content-free (i.e., "transcendental" in Kant's terminology) intrinsic powers. Such act-of-will ensures the person's "radical capacity of free choice" (Silber, 1960, pp. ciii, civ). The content-free intrinsic powers Kant is talking about are explicated by will operators 3 and 4 discussed previously: mental-attentional energy and mental interruption. The "radical capacity of free choice" is explicated by dynamic/creative syntheses. These dynamic/creative resolutions are given performance closure by the organismic Gestalt principles of "field" resolution (the *F* operator discussed elsewhere; e.g., Pascual-Leone, 1980, in press-a; Pascual-Leone & Goodman, 1979) and by an organismic principle of schematic overdetermination of performance (see Pascual-Leone, in press-a; Pascual-Leone & Goodman, 1979). In neurophysiological terms these two constructs correspond, respectively, to cortically located processes of lateral inhibition (which give *closure* to the fields, *F*, of activated neurons) and to Sherrington's well-known *principle of summation* of synaptic transmissions. Both factors can be called a priori and transcendental using Kant's terminology.

The *judgment-of-will (Wille)* is the repertoire of metaexecutive schemes and scheme-motives[9] related to the person's life project and to his or her moral/ethical conduct. Activated schemes from this repertoire can inform and give rational direction to the act-of-will. As Silber (1960, p. civ) puts it: "Kant makes room in the will for the presence of the moral law by introducing the concept of *Wille,* which refers to the purely rational aspect of the will. *Wille* is as much part of the will as *Willkür,* for without it there could be no rational structure for freedom, no experience of obligation, and hence no awareness of the power of volition." The judgment-of-will corresponds to my organismic will operator 2 – the metaexecutives of the will's complex function discussed in the preceding; it also corresponds to the *I-will* subrepertoire of the *I-self* repertoire, in the model outlined in Figure 12.2. This I-will subrepertoire contains will executives as well as information about the self relevant to the will's decisions, such as the subject's updated life projects and his or her subrepertoire of motives that inform the actual choices. From this material the judgment-as-will metacomponent is spontaneously constituted prior to each act-of-will and thus informs this act.

The processes involved in this constitution may be of different kinds: They may be directed by *purely affective* goals that mobilize mental attentional energy and mental interruption (will operators 1, 3, and 4) to produce a dynamic synthesis without the intervention of metaexecutives; and/or the processes may be directed by effortful metaexecutives (part of what Pascual-Leone & Goodman [1979] call LM-structures); finally they can also be directed by automatized metaexecutives (part of what Pascual-Leone and Goodman call LC-structures). This third kind corresponds to what Kant has called the disposition-of-will.

According to Kant, the *disposition-of-will* is the "underlying common ground" of all the acts-of-will of a person who is consistent in his or her "personality" (a term used by Kant in the sense of personhood, i.e., being a creature capable of free choice) and in the use, or misuse, of existential freedom. Kant's disposition-of-will corresponds mainly to *automatized* will-relevant executives and metaexecutives of the person (LC-structures of Pascual-Leone & Goodman, 1979), which I listed under operator 1 of the will's complex function, along with the affective goals; but it also reflects old (and thus strong) executive LM-structures that have become *operations* in the neo-Piagetian sense (i.e., that coordinate in themselves executive and action schemes needed to perform; Pascual-Leone, 1983). In the model of the self in Figure 12.2 schemes making up the disposition-of-will should be found in subrepertoire *I-will* along with judgment-of-will schemes.

The functional difference between disposition and judgment of the will (i.e., essentially, between will habits and will problem solving) becomes clear when we examine acts-of-will taking place at the different levels of processing – the levels discussed in the previous section (see Figure 12.1). The distinction I have made between the level of *executive processing* and the levels of *action processing* is already prefigured in Kant by his distinction between two sorts of acts-of-will:

1. noumenal (i.e., essentially, abstract conceptual) or dispositional acts, which result in an intention or plan to act in a certain manner ("dispositional intention"), and
2. phenomenal or specific acts, which produce the action in question.

Kant points out that when the judgment-of-will is weak, it may produce a morally right act-of-will at the level of intention (at the executive processing level) to be followed by a morally wrong act-of-will in actual performance (at the action-processing level). This is particularly true, Kant emphasizes, when the action situation in question is such that obedience to "moral law" (performing a morally right act) has bad consequences for the person's own comfort or welfare.

In these *motivationally misleading situations* the person may end up acting in ways that are contrary to his or her intended (i.e., executively anticipated) plans and/or against past self-integrations (life projects and working self's prescriptions). Such a conduct might lead to subsequent regrets (moral feelings, existential guilt) that show that the person's will, although weak (self-contradictory), is basically autonomous and free at least at the executive processing level (James, 1966; Jaspers, 1970; Kant, 1960). *Lasting negative moral feelings,* which may follow "bad" performance in motivationally misleading situations, tell us, Kant suggests, that the person's disposition-of-will (e.g., the automatized will executives) are still moral even if the performance is not. Kant, James, and Jaspers depict the person as divided, in motivationally misleading conflict situations, between two allegiances: the ethical/rational feelings and the natural/instinctual feelings, both found in the *self's soul* sub-repertoire of Figure 12.2, and both attempting to take over the self's here-and-now existential reactions (dynamic syntheses). In these motivationally misleading situations the direction of choice between these two kinds of *good feelings* (Kant, James, and Jaspers insist in the basic goodness of *both* motives) reflects their relative degree of dominance. Ethical/rational feelings are indicators of the strength of developmentally sophisticated and advanced (e.g., humanistically oriented or psychologically "spiritual"; see Pascual-Leone, in press-b) motives and values. Natural/instinctual feelings are indicators of the strength of equally good but developmentally more basic values.

*Existential conflicts of the will such as these occur between/among motives and values that are all good, albeit belonging to different levels of ontogenetic development.* As both Kant and Jaspers emphasize, the problem of existential will and free choice often originates in the fact that acts of choice are also necessarily acts of renunciation. Not to renounce is to remain at the mercy of "temptations" caused by a will easily swayed by circumstances (this state is called by Kant *heteronomous freedom)*. In contrast, an "unconditional volition in absolute choice" (Jaspers, 1970) – one that interrupts effectively what is not chosen by judgment-of-will in an act-of-will – produces *autonomous freedom.* As Jaspers says: "The man who lacks a proper will would like to do one thing and not leave the other undone; the man with a will is aware of willing only when he chooses" (Jaspers, 1970, p. 143). "It is as unconditional volition in absolute choice that *Existenz* [i.e., wisdom] becomes real" (Jaspers, 1970, p. 142).

Thus a developmental task on the way toward wisdom is to acquire efficient metaexecutives of the will and developmentally sophisticated structures of knowledge; another task is to learn to mobilize and allocate mental-attentional energy and mental interruption. Only in this manner can the will choose autonomously. This development of the will mechanisms, if it was not already fostered by parental upbringing, takes place with the many life tasks and vital-reason decisions the person has to solve during the postadolescence (17–25) years and young adulthood (25–35) (e.g., vocational/professional choice, personal beliefs and life projects, mate choice, life commitments, etc.)

### The will-to-will of young (or middle) adulthood

According to Arendt (1981), Heidegger calls "will-to-will" the phase of existential growing when the person, consciously or unconsciously, seeks opportunities to exert willful choices by interrupting/rejecting unchosen alternatives. This is a stage of will development commonly found during the late formal (17–25) and young adulthood (25–35) years but also found in middle adulthood (35–55). In this phase the style of willing and deciding is often too forceful, often dichotomic, and lacking nuance (too black vs. white), more or less depending on sociocultural and mentor models. There are examples of life contingencies that might be traceable to this style of willing; for instance, the all-too-common repeated divorces found during these years could be related, among other factors, to strong will-to-will disposition in at least one of the partners. A person in this phase of will development might fail the wise counsel given by Machado's poem (see third epigraph of this chapter) by the expedient method of refusing to listen or by thoughtlessly doing the contrary of what was suggested. Nietzsche (cf. Arendt, 1981) may be the philosopher of the will who illustrates this will-to-will phase in the most dramatic manner, as in a caricature. Unable to apply itself on the past (the past is fixed), the will-to-will often turns toward the future, seeking to be cause by bringing about change. Will-to-power emerges as a motive, which causes the growth of the *I-can* repertoire in new directions, weakening or strengthening (depending upon sociocultural factors) authority and tradition (which represent the past). This pleasure of being cause, of experiencing that "I can," motivates the practice of will-to-will, accelerating growth of the *I-will* repertoire.

Notice that expert life counselors still driven by this I-can motive may not be able to practice counseling in the spirit of Machado's poem. These otherwise excellent counselors might satisfy in their social intelligence the five criteria of advanced intelligent "pragmatics" that Baltes and his Berlin group have found (e.g., Baltes et al., 1984; Baltes et al., in press); but nothing exists in these *cognitive* criteria to protect the counselor from expecting and perhaps demanding (the expectation is induced by the counseling role and the counselor's will-to-power or I-can motives) that the client follow the counselor's advice.

One should expect greater detachment in the counselor, such as would fulfill Machado's requirement, only when the counselor has evolved beyond the interpersonal self by having developed a new self-control organization, which is higher than the interpersonal self and functionally detached from it. This higher center is the *ultraself* or *transcendental self* [also called by other names in the literature: Existenz, Self (with uppercase S), meditative existence, transcendental or cosmic consciousness, absolute consciousness, nonself, "void," etc.]. The transcendental self emerges after a developmental–structural transition in the self-organization (Edinger, 1973; Jacobi, 1967; Jaspers, 1959, 1970, 1971; Jung, 1968, Pascual-Leone, 1983, in press-b). In this qualitative–structural transition the empathic *affects* – love according to Augustine, Scotus, Buber, Scheler and Jaspers; care, according to Heidegger and Zen Buddhism – *come to blend inextricably with cognitions.* And thinking becomes so open to reality (the true concrete Others and the world) that in Heidegger's felicitous expression the nature of "thinking" becomes "thanking" (Arendt, 1981, p. 185; Heidegger, 1966, p. 85) – a grateful relaxed acknowledgment of reality as such and of the "letting-oneself-into its nearness" (Heidegger, 1966, p. 89). There is an intuition of the hidden reality concealed and also revealed by ordinary experience. This is a kind of *meditative thinking* (Heidegger, 1966; Pascual-Leone, in press-b) that can lead to encompassing, metasystematic, bold causal abstractions. I have elsewhere characterized this thinking as constituted by *dialectical* and *transcendental operations* (see Pascual-Leone, 1983, in press-b). This thinking requires a "waiting" attitude, where the person wills only when he or she really must do so on vital, ethical, or existential grounds; it is a pure resting-in-itself of willing, which, renouncing willing, has "released itself" (Heidegger, 1966, p. 85) to inner and outer reality. This kind of "uncommitted" but absorbing experiential thinking/thanking of reality has already been recognized by personality/clinical psychologists (e.g., Maslow, 1968; Tellegen, 1981).

### The will of wisdom: will-not-to-will (vital reason's open reading of reality and of self's unconditional life projects)

In the will-to-will phase the self is overly focused on the future to the detriment of the past (or vice versa if the will-of-power is suppressed by the self). It becomes specialized in experiencing change and/or seeking generic stabilities and invariances. Experiencing is focused on the external/objective/cognitive to the detriment of the intimate/subjective/affective or vice versa. Thinking-as-thanking (i.e., thinking as the unconstrained epistemic *impression* of reality upon the person) and willing as the operative *expression* upon reality of the person's self cannot be coordinated. Wherever one looks in the person's manifold repertoires of qualitatively different ways of processing experience (of receiving the "impression" of reality) and/or acting (praxis, the "expression" upon reality), one finds a certain lack of balance during the will-to-will phase. The self cannot coordinate effectively the different qualitative strands of his or her ways of experiencing and acting and focuses on some to the detriment of others, while perhaps attempting to explore many alleys in the outside world and the Other.

Sooner or later, the growth of experience and praxis brings about the emergence of unavoidable dialectical contradictions among different but equally important strands of processing in the subject's self. But contradictions are hard to tolerate within the self's organization, and they induce the psychological organism to problem-solve, to cognitively learn and reequilibrate. This cognitive learning factor and the biologically rooted functional decrease in availability of attentional hardware mechanisms such as mental energy and mental interruption (which spontaneously occurs in the late thirties or forties of most people; Pascual-Leone, 1983) force the self to rework his or her coping strategies, and sometimes to change the personal life project. This is what Piaget (e.g., 1962; Pascual-Leone, 1988) would have called *disequilibration,* which precipitates much, not always conscious, mental reworking of these different processing strands seeking reequilibration. In two recent chapters (Pascual-Leone, 1983, in press-b) I have provided a theoretical account of these processes and the developmental stages that they may generate.

At the end of this sequence of psychological metamorphoses the organization of the ego is different. Superordinate to the original self's control center (whose sketch I diagrammed in Figure 12.2) an *ultraself control center* has appeared. Unlike the original interpersonal self, this ultraself does not emerge directly from interactions with the Other; it is rather born from the inner efforts of the will-to-will self in resolving dialectical contradictions among the self's files within and across subrepertoires. This attempt to dialectically integrate the diverse files produces new and encompassing mental strategies, cognitions, values, and so on, detached from external experience and from the interpersonal self, which can "take a distance" from the old self. This is probably Kant's, Husserl's, and Hegel's "transcendental self" – which I call *ultraself* to emphasize its being a distinct superordinate self-organization. Experimental evidence in support of this ultraself notion is not available; but phenomenological/clinical evidence has been obtained by Jung and his followers (e.g., Edinger, 1973; Jacobi, 1967; Jung, 1959a, b; Stevens, 1982) and can also be found in the existential philosophy, meditation, spiritual, and history-of-religion literatures.

This ultraself has many paradoxical characteristics:

1. It is a self, since it is a self-control center of consciousness, but it has no self-representation in consciousness and volitionally can appear as truly detached from the self, subordinating it to a broader "cosmic" consciousness. As Jaspers (1959, 1970, 1971) has emphasized, this transcendental self is deeper than the separation between phenomenal subject and object: It cannot be subjectively inspected (it is neither part of the "me" nor of the inspectable "I"). But it appears at times as an *encompassing* self-knowing inner *presence* or as symbols in mystical experiences of all sorts (e.g., Jung, 1959a,b).
2. Like an invisible concert master or conductor, this transcendental self manages to coordinate voices and strands of being that heretofore were unreconcilable: affect with cognition, generic conceptualizations with empathic/experiential concreteness of detail, the will's focus on the future with memory's concern with the past or thinking/feeling's concern with the present.
3. It is open to reality, reality being experienced as an encompassing manifold process, the hidden causal texture of the lifeworld, which is both concealed and revealed by its lifeworld manifestations.
4. Functionally detached from the interpersonal self as well as from the Other and the world, it can will-not-to-will (will only *if it must* for vital, ethical, or existential reasons), concentrating instead in the continued attempt to bring into harmony and completion the possible concrete life relations emerging among the three necessary partners – self, Other, world – of the person's life.[10]

The ancient Greeks called this higher and more integrative mode of processing *reason.* Kant (1965) and constructivist thinkers ever since also call it "reason," contrasting it with simple "understanding." Following Ortega, on grounds that by now should be clear, I have called it *vital reason.* Anticipating existential phenomenology (e.g., Jaspers, Ortega, Heidegger, and Sartre), Scheler (1961, 1973) posited that a *heightened affective awareness* of life's *resistances,* when attentively experienced in an open yet *detached* manner (i.e., letting oneself into the nearness of reality by bridging with feeling the gap between contradictory aspects), is at the origin of spiritual (i.e., ultraself) growth and valid cognition. Husserl (1970) gave to this manner of experiencing the forbidding name of *transcendental phenomenological reduction.* Scheler describes it as the mental attitude whereby inferential and existential/affective aspects of objects or situations offering resistances to praxis are "suspended," suspended in the sense of being tuned down to mere actualities by an aware but detached "releasement" (Heidegger, 1966) toward a *pure* (uninvolved) *existential awareness* (blended cognition and affect) of the ongoing situations. Heidegger (1966) calls this qualitatively different mental attitude *meditative thinking,* and he contrasts it with "calculative thinking," the pragmatic thinking dominant in our technological culture (cf. Buber's [1958] I–thou vs. I–it experiencing; Maslow's [1968] B-cognition vs. D-cognition; see also Tellegen, 1981). The active open thinking (curiosity, care) and the will-not-to-will of this meditative mental processing (with its processing style of mobilizing mental energy without causing the mental interruption of ongoing memorial processes; see Pascual-Leone, 1983, 1984, 1987) facilitates sensitive reading of patterns and invariances across vast repertoires of acquired life knowledge and thus brings about wisdom-in-counseling. But to explain this growing into wisdom we must still discuss the changes that take place in affect.

## Wisdom as feeling/judging: the inner dialectical integration of agency and soul (communion)

Many pointers suggest that affective growth and affective integration are important to wisdom. As suggested, philosophers of the will have expressed in various ways the view that love (or other related positive affects – desire, interest, hope, etc.) may, in the face of misleading and/or difficult vital situations,[11] allow the will to mature, deepening vital reason and moving the person toward wisdom. The importance of love is also suggested by psychologists' recent work. Johnson (1982) often reports in his interviews of wise people who blend intelligent autonomy and adaptability with kindness, human caring, empathic communion, and compassion. Baltes et al. (in press), whose concern for wisdom is almost exclusively cognitive, are nonetheless compelled to admit that "excellent character" is another characteristic of wisdom. In Holliday and Chandler's (1986) rich analyses of wisdom's prototypical item descriptions, the category of "social/interpersonal caring" can be easily inferred from many typical item descriptions (e.g., "fair," "sensitive," "even-tempered," "kind," "discreet," "unselfish," "non-judgmental," etc.) even though their factor analyses, perhaps overloaded with cognitive items, do not show a separate human caring factor.

Finally, in the field of academic psychotherapy (which in this regard had lagged behind the therapies of the unconscious – Freudian, Jungian, etc.) there is now full awareness of the importance of emotions (i.e., overt or covert manifestations of affects) in the processes of human growth (e.g., Greenberg & Safran, 1987; Guidano, 1987; Malatesta & Izard, 1984). This new theorizing is important to us for another reason: Its theories of the self (e.g., Greenberg & Safran, 1987; Guidano, 1987; Higgins, in press-a, in press-b, in press-c; Horowitz, 1987; Horowitz & Zilberg, 1983; Markus & Wurf, 1987) are generally consistent with the neo-Piagetian dialectical-constructivist theory that informs this chapter. For instance, all these theories conceive the self as a manifold repertoire of executive and metaexecutive schemes (or schemelike discrete functional units), which generate consciousness as they apply. But current clinical/dynamic theories of the self are also important because they tacitly follow the pioneer work of Jung and Jungian analysts (Edinger, 1973; Jacobi, 1962, 1967; Stevens, 1982) in regarding the truly mature self – the terminal, ideal growth point of human development – to be the subject's state of wisdom.

In the models of the will and the self presented here, the role of affect was also intimated. I spoke, following Kant, of ethical/moral feelings, of motives and of values, intervening in the judgment-of-will and the acts-of-will. Let us examine more closely the person's operative self, that is, the I-self, to see the role of affect in the self and how affect conditions the development of wisdom. Figure 12.2 divides the I-self broadly into self's agency and self's soul. The *I-can* (i.e., cognitive/pragmatic self) and the *I-will* (i.e., judgment-of-will and disposition-of-will) fall under agency because they contain the conscious executives and metaexecutives producing the self's cognitive (i.e., true–false) evaluations and his or her praxis. The feelings of the self are in the scheme directory that I call *organismic soul*.[12] The self's soul is constituted by three subrepertoires, very important for wisdom, which contain preconscious/conscious evaluations of the subject's own effective reactions to experience:

1. Feelings vis-à-vis the Other, that is, *communion* of the self – communion (Bakan, 1966) because it contains affective evaluations of the Other (and also of the world) done with such a mental attitude that, motivationally, subject and object of affective experience become one, and thus the subject easily adopts the perspective of the Other. This subrepertoire owes its origin to processing and performances that were under the control of affective goals dominated by love (attachment) and other related "altruistic" affects.
2. The second subrepertoire corresponds to what the classics called the *passions* of the self and its *feelings*. This is where self-produced affective evaluations of the self (e.g., good–bad) are stored and where self-represented *affective goals,* including "good" or "bad" instinctual and hedonistic goals as well as conscious self-accepted *values*[13] of any kind, exist. This subrepertoire owes its origin to processing and performances induced by any kind of affects, from power affects (mastery, incompetence, dependence, independence, etc.) to love affects, curiosity affects, fear-related affects, and so on.
3. The final self's soul subrepertoire represents the coordination of the other two soul repertoires. This is the ethical self, or *ethos*.[14] The *ethos* subrepertoire is the site of moral feelings and ethical evaluations (right–wrong or bad–good judgments) of motives and possible acts (e.g., morality); it is also the site of experiential feelings (e.g., aesthetic judgments).

Paraphrasing Kant within the present theory, the organismic soul (i.e., schemes from this repertoire) reacts negatively, with self-originating moral or ethical feelings, whenever the subject's agency (i.e., schemes from the I-will subrepertoire) initiates an action (action-processing level, see Figure 12.1) that is dissonant with the soul – with the communion and/or *ethos* subrepertoires. This state of affairs causes what Piaget (1962) could have called an *affective/personal disequilibration* – a conflict between the agency and the communion/*ethos* subrepertoires.

This conflict provokes the activation of affective and personal schemes that might be cued by it and thus begins an organismic choice process at the affective processing level (see Figure 12.1). Along with it, perhaps cued by new affective goals created by the affective-processing output, there are new executive schemes and metaexecutives, perhaps from the I-will and I-can subrepertoires, that become activated. And these new executives enter in competition with the activated executives whose conversion in possible action (action processing) led initially to the affective conflict. The competition among these various strands of executive schemes is settled at the executive processing level. This level of processing is where acts-of-will (acts of voluntary mental attention; see Pascual-Leone, 1980, 1983, 1984, 1987, in press-a) actually take place. The outcome of this executive processing might be "a change of heart": The soul subrepertoire, or more precisely the communion and *ethos,* might reverse a course of action (such as a fraud, seduction of a young person, escape from a line of duty, etc.) that, cued by "tempting" circumstances, the passion (self-feelings) subrepertoire of the soul might have previously initiated. This passion subrepertoire could have brought about an affective-processing outcome that made dominant, at the executive processing level, some executives that were "bad" in terms of the *ethos* and communion subrepertoires; and these executives would have used mental attentional energy and interruption capacity to initiate the bad action – the action that caused the affective disequilibration (e.g., guilt feelings). The new act-of-will causing the change of heart should mobilize again the interruption mechanism and mental energy to defeat its opposition (just like in a military takeover) and redirect, in a direction acceptable to the communion/*ethos* subrepertoires, the course of current action via a new action processing that eliminates the bad feelings and restores affective equilibrium.

Notice that, as described, the motivationally misleading situations that impose the use of will often represent a conflict between two different strands of soul and/or of affective schemes. Generally the opponents are self-schemes first developed to fulfill needs of power-related affective goals (as is often the case with the I-can, I-will, and passion/self-feeling subrepertoires) *versus* schemes developed to serve love-related affective goals (as commonly happens with communion and ethos). The notion that power and love affects are main determinants of self and/or personality has a long history in both philosophy and psychology. Bakan (1966) was the first academic psychologist to explicitly formulate, as agency and communion, the categories that in the self stand for these two functional sorts of schemes. In the categories of Bakan, which I have differentiated and made more restricted, agency would have to include passion/self-feeling, whereas communion might also include the *ethos* subrepertoire. Using momentarily, for the sake of simplicity, this broader formulation, one could conclude that the processes of the self-determination in the ordinary person are the silent struggle between his or her agency and communion.

Thus formulated, one can simply state the nature of wisdom-as-feeling/

judgment. It is the asymptotic level of the personal learning process that this struggle brings about: the state when agency and communion have become perfectly coordinated into a single totality (dialectically integrated) and jointly determine in a harmonious way every performance. Indeed, practice in these affective/personal disequilibration and reequilibration sequences must progressively make the schemes of the various subrepertoires mutually inconsistent. All theories of learning would make this prediction. Wisdom is the point when this slow and often painful learning process has come to an end, and the development of the ultraself (transcendental self) organization is completed. At this point the person's *true* ("actual") *self* and his or her *persona* (external person) are well coordinated (see Figure 12.2). Although the individual's style still reflects his or her historical determinations (mentors, models, etc.), the substance of *persona's* communication is relatively free from this history; it serves the current purpose of true/"actual" self.

### On differences between intelligence, creativity, and wisdom, and their possible neuropsychological projections

Sternberg's (1985a) excellent work interrelating people's implicit theories of intelligence, creativity, and wisdom and relating the first two with their corresponding explicit (psychometric) theories has clearly shown the reality of these intuitive notions. He concludes that "in general, intelligence, creativity and wisdom are positively correlated attributes in people, although intelligence and wisdom are more closely related than is either of these two constructs to creativity" (Sternberg, 1985a, p. 621). The purpose of this final section is to address the issues of their interrelation and their process-analytical organismic definition in terms of the theory and model suggested in the preceding sections.

From a dialectical constructivist perspective intelligence, as currently understood by people or in psychometrics, appears as a complex *functional* category, a category describing the organism's complex ability to discover relations or to resolve conflicts and contradictions *occurring within the cognitive domain,* so as to increase the consistency and scope of knowledge. In particular, intelligence is concerned with discovering relations, or solving cognitive conflicts, that can be found in mental processing between different mental *levels of constructive abstraction:* from sensorial/perceptual information that deals with the present to inferential/representational processes dealing as well with the past, the future, and the possible in a progressively broader scope.

From this perspective, creativity appears as the complex *functional* category dealing with the organism's complex abilities for moving from a *truly novel* (cf. Pascual-Leone, 1980) *abstract idea* to the truly novel explicit *formulation or formalization* of it and/or to the truly novel concrete object that properly constitutes the idea's *realization or concretization or vice versa.* Creativity is concerned with the inventive construction of forms of any kind that epistemologically reflect (I call it *epireflect* for short) patterns extracted from another distant, much higher or much lower level of constructive abstraction. In the arts, this invention of epireflective forms across different levels of constructive abstraction is often called *expression* when it moves from the mind's ideas or feelings to external objects, words, or sensorial/motor forms; it is called *impression* when it moves in the opposite direction (cf. Cassirer 1944, 1957). Thus defined, creativity is the common element of science and art emphasized by constructivist thinkers like Leonardo, Goethe, and Cassirer (1972).

Wisdom, we saw before, is a complex *state or trait* (cf. Endler & Edwards, 1985) category of the domain of vital reason. It is the state reached by the person when the interrelations and dialectical integrations (the resolution of contradictions) across all and any of the vital domains of his or her *manifold totality* have attained a "critical-mass" point where new qualitative principles of integration and functioning across domains (cognitive, affective, social/interpersonal, existential, etc.) have emerged. These new principles can be illustrated in three points:

1. Regarding wisdom-as-counsel, wisdom causes the expert counselor to adopt the paradoxical attitude expressed by Machado's poem: It fosters freedom while stressing authority of reason and reasonable tradition.
2. In wisdom-as-will, very much in the spirit of ancient Taoism, its principle is an active "will-not-to-will" – restricting interventions on the Other, world, or self to those needed to restore harmonious relations among them. With wisdom the totality over which dialectical coordinations are sought expands from the person's own world, as it is in ordinary states of intelligence, to encompass the wholeness of human reality.
3. In wisdom-as-feeling/judgment, wisdom appears as the state of dialectical integration where the person's own agency and communion are fully coordinated.

Intelligence as a functional category is clearly involved in the emergence and the use of wisdom, as the definitions just given should show. Creativity as a functional category is more involved in intelligence than in wisdom under these definitions because when the person reaches the state category of wisdom, truly novel (creative) intelligent operations have become secondary: The person has already accumulated so much experience that products of past creativity can now replace a creative function that at this point might not be at its best.

All three categories of human competence share the mechanisms of mental attention and acts-of-will that I have described, in particular, the use of mental attentional capacity and interruption/disinterruption capacity to ensure executive control in the total repertoire (the brain cortex!) of the ongoing strands of scheme activity. They differ, however, in the types of situations and mental attitudes *(in the structural types of dynamic syntheses)* that each of them more often requires. According to its definition, intelligence should require dynamic syntheses locally utilizing mental attentional energy and interruption capacity in all sorts of mental contexts. Creativity should require them locally within a more restricted type: in the context of cognitively misleading situations where the subject must move from concretenesses to new and encompassing abstract ideas or vice versa. Wisdom should necessitate encompassing dynamic syntheses applying on manifold structures of great brain scope, structures that integrate the analytical/formalized (left hemisphere!) with holistic/experiential (right hemisphere!) knowledge, blending affective, personal, and cognitive domains: syntheses that might simultaneously engage vastly different areas of the cortex (cf. Benson & Zaidel, 1985; Eccles, 1980; Hellige, 1983; Luria, 1973).

Taking a monist interactionist (i.e., constructivist) position with regard to mind–body relations, as exemplified by Sperry and others (e.g., Natsoulas, 1987; Sperry, 1976, 1980, 1985), it is possible to make some inferences. What we know or can infer from modern neuropsychology regarding possible brain manifestations of these three categories of human competence might serve to illustrate, in an intuitive fashion, differences and interrelations among the three categories and suggest new ways of testing these theoretical analyses. It is known in the literature on brain electrophysiology, regarding evoked potentials (EPs), that some so-called endogenous EPs relate to mental attentional effort, and the location and pattern of EPs obtained is affected by the structural (not the content) characteristics of the task at hand (e.g., Gaillard & Ritter, 1983; Regan, 1989). Since intelligence appears, as efficient and well-adjusted performance, across structurally different tasks that require mental attentional effort, it can be expected that measures of *"neural adaptability" all over the cortex,* reflecting the EP wave change as a function of the tasks' structural conditions, might be related to intelligence. This kind of result has been obtained repeatedly by a number of experimenters (e.g., Eysenck & Barrett, 1985; Hendrickson, 1982; Jensen, Schafer, & Crinella, 1981; Schafer, 1982, 1984; Schafer & Markus, 1973).

It also appears that the functional structure of problem situations thought to require creativity, in the sense defined in this section, relate to that of activities where the prefrontal lobes intensively intervene (Damasio, 1985; Fuster, 1980; Luria, 1973; Shallice, 1982; Stuss & Benson, 1984). One could predict, although I do not know of direct empirical results to this effect, that highly creative persons would tend to exhibit, in creativity situations, greater activity *in the prefrontal lobes of the brain* than less creative persons, relative to the activity exhibited by the same persons in situations where creativity is not required. With modern technology this prediction can easily be tested.

Finally, there is an electroencephalographic (EEG) measure that is a sensitive indicator of the degree of long-range order, that is, coordination across the cortex, of the EEG frequency signals. This is the "coherence" measure, a mathematical EEG variable related to the consistency of phase relationships within specific frequency bands between different points of the scalp (Dillbeck & Bronson, 1981; Orme-Johnson, 1977). Coherence should appear in the EEG under proper *meditation* conditions whenever the person has developed numerous manifold structures spanning over the brain: whenever the cortex is sufficiently integrated as a totality. This is, I believe, a distinct structural mark of wisdom. Thus, wise persons *placed under proper meditation conditions and after some meditation training* should exhibit high-coherence spread over the cortex, particularly in prefrontal and vertex areas (areas corresponding to regions where high-level executive, metaexecutive, and knowledge processing takes place). This pattern of coherence has been repeatedly found in advanced meditators (e.g., Alexander, Boyer, & Jacoby, in press; Alexander, Cranson, Boyer, & Orme-Johnson, 1986; Nidich, Ryncarz, Abrams, Orme-Johnson, & Wallace, 1983). I suggest that wise persons might exhibit this coherence pattern after just a few hours of meditation practice, much sooner than ordinary – nonwise – meditators.

## Concluding remarks

This essay has been my attempt, informed by philosophical and psychological literature, to analyze developmental aspects that make wisdom unique. The last section compared creativity, intelligence, and wisdom. The overall conclusion was that these are three distinct products of the mind: Wisdom differs from the other two in involving not just cognition but affect and personality as a whole. Driven by the development of will, wisdom appears with the emergence of progressively higher levels of affect/self-control, which as they advance, bring about a better dialectical integration of personality. In turn this integration produces – this might be the descriptive core of wisdom – a weakening of ego-centered characteristics, which leads to greater intuition and empathic understanding of Other, self, world, and nature as equally strong concerns. From this perspective, wisdom is the rarely attained, *asymptotic* state of normal human growth toward maturity.

## Notes

1 Para que llamar caminos / a los surcos del azar? / Todo el que camina anda, como Jesus, sobre el mar (Machado, 1964, p. 198).
2 Y como el hombre es, ante todo, futuricion; es, ante todo, un enjambre de esperanzas y temores (Ortega y Gasset, 1980, p. 96).
3 Doy consejo a fuer de viejo: / nunca sigas un consejo (Machado, 1964, p. 269).
4 Not every recent writer agrees with a modular decomposition of the will. See Westcott (1988) for an opposing humanistic view. Westcott argues that volition should be studied nonreductionistically, as an independent human capacity like perception or cognition. But a functional modular decomposition need not be reductionistic. My attempt will be to model the *developmental emergence* of the will from a number of simpler processes, to show its evolution, that bring about wisdom.

5 Praxis is the more or less conscious, goal-directed activity – action processing – addressed to distal objects in a situation in order to satisfy some need or desire, including spiritual ones. A situation is an ecological system constituted by (1) a context or immediate environment; (2) a subject–1, who has a mental set providing a construal of the context; (3) optionally, other subjects; (4) optionally, within the mental set of subject–1 and perhaps of other subjects, affective goals and possibly a plan to act in the context in order to achieve the goals. When condition 4 exists, the situation is called a task. Only tasks lead to praxis.

6 A situation is misleading when it cues schemes incompatible with the chosen relevant praxis; it is strongly misleading if the cues in question are shared with relevant schemes, so that the initial application of the misleading schemes will lower the probability of subsequent application of relevant schemes (Pascual-Leone & Goodman, 1979). Misleading schemes are often activated and apply first (i.e., rapidly) because they require a low level of processing, being facilitated by salient cues and habits.

7 This possibility is entertained by Skinner, but he fails to see its process-analytical implications: "We do control ourselves, but not as initiating agents. We control ourselves as we control the behavior of others (by changing our environment), but we do so because we have been exposed to contingencies arranged by the social environment we call culture" (from Skinner's reply in Catania & Harnad, 1988 p. 32). Skinner does not see that the conscious decision to change environments and its implementation cannot be explained in terms of habits; these acts of will require an organismic mechanism or "initiating agent."

8 I am calling ego, explicating the use introduced by psychoanalytical ego psychology, the total repertoire of conscious or preconscious schemes. Notice that this use is at variance with that of the Jungians, who call "ego" what I am here calling self and call Self – with uppercase S – what I call ultraself or transcendental self.

9 A scheme-motive, or motive for short, is a personal scheme (i.e., a scheme coordinating affects with cognitions – Pascual-Leone, 1983, in press-b) that connects a mental operation, or a possible personal act in the lifeworld, to the set of positive/negative affects that are rewarded or penalized when the act in question is carried out (cf. McClelland, 1985).

10 Now the nature of will has changed, but its strength has not diminished. The capacities of mental energy and interruption may have decreased (Pascual-Leone, 1983), but this is compensated by the powerful I-will repertoire of executives and metaexecutives and the I-can repertoire of structures that a lifelong history of willful experiencing have afforded. Further, because strong affects have now mellowed and the salience of situational cues has decreased, situations are weakened in their misleadingness.

11 For instance, in the face of limit/boundary situations and striving to cope (see Jaspers, 1970; Latzel, 1981; Pascual-Leone, 1983, in press-b).

12 I retain the old word *soul* to emphasize individual-difference characteristics, which are essential in this subrepertoire – something that terms like *psyche* or *feelings system* do not convey.

13 Values are schemes connecting affective goals with their corresponding objects, actions, or situations.

14 *Ethos,* a term introduced by Scheler (1973), is the set of tacit or explicit values, sentiments, and self-accepted rules of conduct that characterize a person (or a human group) from the perspective of human relations, existential projects, belief systems, and life-style.

# References

Alexander, C. N., Boyer, R. W., & Jacoby, R. (in press). In R. Forman (Ed.), *The problem of pure consciousness.* New York: Oxford University Press.

Alexander, C. N., Cranson, R. W., Boyer, R. W., & Orme-Johnson, D. W. (1986). Transcendental consciousness: a fourth state of consciousness beyond sleep, dreaming and waking. In J. Gackenbach (Ed.), *Sleep and dreams: a source book* (pp. 282–315). New York: Garland.

Arendt, H. (1981). *The life of the mind.* New York: Harcourt, Brace, Jovanovich.

Bakan, D. (1966). *The duality of human existence.* Chicago: Rand McNally.

Baltes, P. B., Dittmann-Kohli, F., & Dixon, R. A. (1984). New perspectives on the development of intelligence in adulthood: toward a dual-process conception and a model of selective optimization with compensation. In P. B. Baltes & O. G. Brim, Jr. (Eds.), *Life-span development and behavior* (Vol. 6, pp. 33–76). New York: Academic Press.

Baltes, P. B., Smith, J., Staudinger, U. M., & Sowarka, D. (in press). Wisdom: one facet of successful aging. In M. Perlmutter (Ed.), *Late-life potential.* Washington, DC: Gerontological Society of America.

Basseches, M. (1984). *Dialectical thinking and adult development.* Norwood, NJ: Ablex.

Bearison, D. J., & Zimiles, H. (Eds.) (1986). *Thought and emotion.* Hillsdale, NJ: Lawrence Erlbaum.

Benson, D. F., & Zaidel, E. (Eds.) (1985). *The dual brain.* New York: Guilford.

Buber, M. (1958). *I and thou.* New York: Charles Scribner's Sons. (Original work published in 1923.)

Buber, M. (1961). *Between man and man.* London: Collins.

Burnaby, J. (Ed.) (1955). *Augustine: later work.* Philadelphia: Westminster Press.

Case, R. (1988). The whole child: toward an integrated view of young children's cognitive, social, and emotional development. In A. D. Pellegrini (Ed.), *Psychological bases for early education* (pp. 155–184). Chichester, England: Wiley.

Case, R., Hayward, S., Lewis, M., & Hurst, P. (1987). Toward a neo-Piagetian theory of cognitive and emotional development. *Developmental Review, 8,* 1–51.

Cassirer, E. (1944). *An essay on man.* New Haven, CT: Yale University Press.

Cassirer, E. (1957). *The philosophy of symbolic forms, (Vol. 3), The phenomenology of knowledge.* New Haven: Yale University Press.

Cassirer, E. (1972). *The individual and the cosmos in renaissance philosophy.* Philadelphia: University of Pennsylvania Press.

Catania, A. Ch., & Harnap, S. (Eds.) (1988). *The selection of behavior.* New York: Cambridge University Press.

Catania, A. C., & Harnad, S. (1988). *The selection of behavior: the operant behaviorism of B.F. Skinner – Comments and consequences.* Cambridge: Cambridge University Press.

Commons, M. L., Kohlberg, L., Richards, F. A., & Sinnott, J. D. (Eds.) (in press). *Adult Development,* Vol. 2, *Models and methods in the study of adolescent and adult thought.* New York: Praeger.

Commons, M. L., Richards, F. A., & Armon, C. (Eds.) (1984). *Beyond formal operations: late adolescence and adult cognitive development.* New York: Praeger.

Commons, M. L., Sinnott, J. D., Richards, F. A., & Armon, C. (Eds.) (1989). *Beyond formal operations II: comparisons and applications of adolescent and adult developmental models.* New York: Praeger.

Damasio, A. R. (1985). The frontal lobe. In K. M. Heilman & E. Valenstein (Eds.), *Clinical neuropsychology* (pp. 339–377). New York: Oxford University Press.

Dillbeck, M. C., & Bronson, E. C. (1981). Short-form longitudinal effects of the transcendental meditation technique on the EEG power and coherence. *International Journal of Neuroscience, 14,* 147–151.

Dittmann-Kohli, F., & Baltes, P. B. (in press). Towards a neofunctionalist conception of adult intellectual development: wisdom as a proto-typical case of intellectual growth. In C. Alexander & E. Langer (Eds.), *Beyond formal operations: alternative endpoints to human development.* New York: Oxford University Press.

Eccles, J. C. (1980). *The human psyche.* New York: Springer International.

Edinger, E. F. (1973). *Ego and archetype.* Baltimore, MD: Penguin Books.

Endler, N. S. (1983). Interactionism: a personality model, but not yet a theory. In M. M. Page (Ed.), *Nebraska Symposium in Motivation 1982: personality-current theory and research* (pp. 155–200). Lincoln, NB: University of Nebraska Press.

Endler, N. S., & Edwards, J. M. (1985). Evaluation of the state-trait anxiety concept within an interactionist model. *The Southern Psychologist, 2,* 63–71.

Erikson, E. H. (1982). *The life cycle completed.* New York: W. W. Norton.

Eysenck, H. J., & Barrett, P. (1985). Psychophysiology and the measurement of intelligence. In C. R. Reynolds & V. Willson (Eds.), *Methodological and statistical advances in the study of individual differences.* New York: Plenum Press.

Fischer, K. W., & Elmendorf, D. (1986). Becoming a different person: transformations in personality and social behavior. In M. Perlmutter (Ed.), *Minnesota symposium on child psychology* (Vol. 18, pp. 137–178). Hillsdale, NJ: Lawrence Erlbaum.

Fischer, K. W., & Lamporn, S. (in press). Sources of variations in development levels: cognitive and emotional transitions during adolescence. In A. de Ribaupierre (Ed.), *Mechanisms of transition in cognitive and emotional development.* New York: Cambridge University Press.

Freire, P. (1973). *Pedagogy of the oppressed.* New York: Seabury Press.

Fuster, J. M. (1980). *The prefrontal cortex.* New York: Raven Press.

Gaillard, A. W. K., & Ritter, W. (Eds.) (1983). *Tutorials in event related potential research: endogenous components.* New York: Elsevier.

Greenberg, L. S., & Safran, J. P. (1987). *Emotion in psychotherapy.* New York: Guilford Press.

Guidano, V. F. (1987). *Complexity of the self: a developmental approach to psychopathology and psychotherapy.* New York: Guilford Press.

Habermas, J. (1970). *Knowledge and human interests.* Boston: Beacon Press.

Habermas, J. (1984). *The theory of communicative action,* Vol. 1, *Reason and the rationalization of society.* Boston: Beacon Press.

Heidegger, M. (1966). *Discourse on thinking.* New York: Harper & Row.

Hellige, J. B. (Ed.) (1983). *Cerebral hemisphere asymmetry: method, theory, and application.* New York: Praeger.

Hendrickson, A. E. (1982). The biological basis of intelligence. Part 1: Theory. In H. J. Eysenck (Ed.), *A model for intelligence* (pp. 151–196). New York: Springer.

Higgins, E. T. (in press-a). Development of self-regulatory and self-evaluative processes: costs, benefits, and trade-offs. *Self processes in development: Twenty-third Minnesota Symposium on child psychology.*

Higgins, E. T. (in press-b). Patterns of self-beliefs: the psychological significance of relations among the actual, ideal, ought, can, and future selves. *Processes in self-perception: the Ontario Symposium.* Hillsdale, NJ: Erlbaum.

Higgins, E. T. (in press-c). Knowledge accessibility and activation: subjectivity and suffering from unconscious sources. *Unintended thought: the limits of awareness, intention, and control.* New York: Guilford Press.

Holliday, S. G., & Chandler, M. J. (1986). Wisdom: explorations in adult competence. In J. A. Meacham (Ed.), *Contributions to human development* (Vol. 17). Basel, Switzerland: Karger.

Horowitz, M. J. (1987). *States of mind: a configurational analysis of individual psychology* (2nd ed.). New York: Plenum Medical Books.

Horowitz, M. J., & Zilberg, N. (1983). Regressive alterations of the self-concept. *American Journal of Psychiatry, 140* (3), 284–289.

Husserl, E. (1970). *The crisis of European sciences and transcendental phenomenology.* Evanston, IL: Northwestern University Press.

Jacobi, J. (1962). *The psychology of C. G. Jung.* New Haven: Yale University Press. (Originally published in 1942.)

Jacobi, J. (1967). *The way of individuation* (R. F. C. Hull, Trans.). New York: Meridian.

James, W. (1966). In G. Allport (Ed.), *Psychology: the briefer course.* New York: Harper & Row.

Jaspers, K. (1959). *Truth and symbol.* New Haven, CT: College and University Press.

Jaspers, K. (1970). *Philosophy* (Vol. 2). Chicago: University of Chicago Press.

Jaspers, K. (1971). *Philosophy of existence.* Philadelphia: University of Pennsylvania Press.

Jensen, A. R., Schafer, E. W. P., & Crinella, F. M. (1981). Reaction time, evoked brain potentials, and psychometric *g* in the severely retarded. *Intelligence, 5,* 179–197.

Johnson, J., Fabian, V., & Pascual-Leone, J. (in press). Quantitative hardware-stages that constrain language development. *Human Development.*

Johnson, R. E. (1982). *A study of wisdom as reported by older adults in America.* Ann Arbor, MI: University Microfilms International.

Jung, C. G. (1959a). The archetypes and collective unconscious. In H. Read, M. Fordham, & G. Adler (Eds.), *The collected works of C. G. Jung* (Bollinger Series XX, Vol. 9, Pt. 1). Princeton, NJ: Princeton University Press.

Jung, C. G. (1959b). The aion: researches into the phenomenology of the self. In H. Read, M. Fordham, & G. Adler (Eds.), *The collected works of C. G. Jung* (Bollinger Series XX, Vol. 9, Pt. 2). Princeton, NJ: Princeton University Press.

Jung, C. G. (1960). *The structure and dynamics of the psyche* (Bollinger Series XX, Vol. 8). Princeton, NJ: Princeton University Press.

Jung, C. G. (1968). *Man and his symbols.* New York: Doubleday Press.

Kant, I. (1951). *Critique of judgement* (J. H. Bernard, Trans.). New York: Hafner Press.

Kant, I. (1960). *Religion within the limits of reason alone.* New York: Harper & Row.

Kant, I. (1965). *Critique of pure reason* (N. Kemp Smith, Trans.). Toronto: Macmillan.

Kramer, D. A. (1983). Postformal operations? A need for further conceptualization. *Human Development, 26,* 91–105.

Krois, J. M. (1987). *Cassirer: symbolic forms and history.* New Haven: Yale University Press.

Labouvie-Vief, G. (1982). Dynamic development and mature autonomy: a theoretical prologue. *Human Development, 25,* 161–191.

Labouvie-Vief, G. (1985). Intelligence and cognition. In J. E. Birren & K. W. Schaie (Eds.), *Handbook of the psychology of aging* (Vol. 2, pp. 500–530). New York: Van Nostrand Reinhold.

Latzel, E. (1981). The concept of "ultimate situation" in Jaspers' philosophy. In P. A. Schlipp (Ed.), *The philosophy of Karl Jaspers* (pp. 177–208). LaSalle, IL: Open Court.

Lewin, K. (1951). Intention, will, and need. In K. Rapaport (Ed.), *Organization and pathology of thought* (pp. 95–150). New York: Columbia University Press.

Luria, A. R. (1973). *The working brain.* Middlesex: Penguin Books.

Machado, A. (1964). *Obras: poesia y prosa.* Buenos Aires: Losada.

McClelland, D. C. (1985). *Human motivation.* Glenview, IL: Scott, Foresman.

Malatesta, C. Z., & Izard, C. E. (Eds.) (1984). *Emotion in adult development.* Beverly Hills, CA: Sage.

Markus, H., & Wurf, E. (1987). The dynamic self-concept: a social psychological perspective. *Annual Review of Psychology, 38,* 299–337.

Maslow, A. H. (1968). *Toward a psychology of being* (2nd ed.). Princeton, NJ: Van Nostrand.

Natsoulas, T. (1987, Summer). Consciousness and commissurotomy: I, spheres and streams of consciousness. *The Journal of Mind and Behavior, 8*(3), 435–468.

Neisser, U. (1967). *Cognitive psychology.* New York: Appleton-Century-Crofts.

Nidich, S. I., Ryncarz, R. A., Abrams, A. I., Orme-Johnson, D., & Wallace, R. K. (1983). Kohlbergian cosmic perspective responses, EEG coherence, and the TM and TM-sidhi programme. *Journal of Moral Education, 12*(3), 166–173.

Orme-Johnson, D. (1977). EEG coherence during transcendental consciousness. *Electroencephalography and Clinical Neuropsychology, 43*(4), 581–582.

Ortega y Gasset, J. (1961). *Meditations on Quixote* (E. Rugg & D. Marin, Trans.). New York: W. W. Norton. (Originally published in 1914.)

Ortega y Gasset, J. (1980). *Sobre la razon historica.* Madrid: Alianza Editorial.

Pascual-Leone, J. (1980). Constructive problems for constructive theories: the current relevance of Piaget's work and a critique of information-processing simulation psychology. In R. Kluwe & H. Spada (Eds.), *Development models of thinking* (pp. 263–296). New York: Academic Press.

Pascual-Leone, J. (1983). Growing into human maturity: towards a metasubjective theory of adulthood stages. In P. B. Baltes & O. G. Brim (Eds.), *Life span development and behavior* (Vol. 5, pp. 117–156). New York: Academic Press.

Pascual-Leone, J. (1984). Attention, dialectic and mental effort: toward an organismic theory of life stages. In M. Commons, F. Richards, & C. Armon (Eds.), *Beyond formal operation: late adolescence and adult cognitive development* (pp. 182–215). New York: Praeger.

Pascual-Leone, J. (1987). Organismic processes for neo-Piagetian theories. A dialectical causal account of cognitive development. *International Journal of Psychology, 22,* 531–570.

Pascual-Leone, J. (1988). Affirmations and negations, disturbances and contradictions, in understanding Piaget: Is his later theory causal? *Contemporary Psychology, 33,* 420–421.

Pascual-Leone, J. (in press-a). An organismic process model of Witkin's field-dependence-independence. In T. Globerson & T. Zelniker (Eds.), *Cognitive style and cognitive development.* Norwood, NJ: Ablex.

Pascual-Leone, J. (in press-b). Reflections on life-span intelligence, consciousness and ego development. In C. N. Alexander & E. J. Langer (Eds.), *Higher stages of human development: perspectives on adult growth.* New York: Oxford University Press.

Pascual-Leone, J., & Goodman, D. R. (1979). Intelligence and experience: a neo-Piagetian approach. *Instructional Science, 8,* 301–367.

Pascual-Leone, J., Goodman, D. R., Ammon, P., & Subelman, I. (1978). Piagetian theory and neo-Piagetian analysis as psychological guides in education. In J. M. Gallagher & J. Easley (Eds.), *Knowledge and development* (Vol. 2, pp. 243–289). New York: Plenum.

Piaget, J. (1962). Will and action. *Bulletin of the Menninger Clinic, 26,* 138–145.

Regan, D. M. (1989). *Human brain electrophysiology: evoked potentials and evoked magnetic fields in science and medicine.* New York: Elsevier.

Ricoeur, P. (1967). Philosophy of will and action. In E. W. Straus & R. M. Griffith (Eds.), *Phenomenology of will and action* (pp. 8–25). Pittsburgh, PA: Duquesne University Press.

Rumelhart, D. E., McClelland, J. L., & the PDP Research Group (1986). *Parallel distributed processing* (Vol. 1). Cambridge, MA: MIT Press.

Ryff, C. D. (1984). Personality development from the inside: the subjective experience of change in adulthood and aging. In P. B. Baltes & O. G. Brim (Eds.), *Life span development and behavior* (Vol. 6, pp. 243–279). New York: Academic Press.

Schafer, E. W. P. (1982). Neural adaptability: a biological determinant of behavioral intelligence. *International Journal of Neuroscience, 17,* 183–191.

Schafer, E. W. P. (1984). Habituation of evoked cortical potentials correlates with intelligence. *Psychophysiology, 21,* 597.

Schafer, E. W. P., & Markus, M. (1973). Self-stimulation alters human memory brain responses. *Science, 181,* 175–177.

Scheler, M. (1961). *Man's place in nature* (H. Meyerhoff, Trans.). Boston: Beacon Press.

Scheler, M. (1973). *Selected philosophical essays* (D. Lachterman, Trans.). Evanston, IL: Northwestern University Press.

Schrag, C. O. (1977). *Existence and freedom.* Evanston, IL: Northwestern University Press.

Schutz, A., & Luckmann, T. (1973). *The structures of the life-world.* Evanston, IL: Northwestern University Press.

Scott, R. B. Y. (1971). *The way of wisdom.* New York: Macmillan.

Shallice, T. (1982). Specific impairments of planning. In D. E. Broadbent & L. Weickrantz (Eds.), *The neurobiology of cognitive functions* (pp. 199–209). London: The Royal Society.

Silber, J. R. (1960). The ethical significance of Kant's religion. In I. Kant, *Religion within the limits of reason alone* (pp. LXXIX–CXXVII). New York: Harper & Row.

Singer, J. L., & Kolligian, J., Jr. (1987). Personality: developments in the study of private experience. *Annual Review of Psychology, 38,* 533–574.

Skinner, B. F. (1953). *Science and human behavior.* New York: Free Press.

Skinner, B. F. (1971). *Beyond freedom and dignity.* New York: Bantam Books.

Sperry, R. W. (1976). Changing concepts of consciousness and free will. *Perspectives in Biology and Medicine, 20,* 9–19.

Sperry, R. W. (1980). Mind–brain interaction: mentalism, yes; dualism, no. *Neuroscience, 5,* 195–206.

Sperry, R. W. (1985). Consciousness, personal identity, and the divided brain. In D. F. Benson & E. Zaidel (Eds.), *The dual brain* (pp. 11–26). New York: Guilford. (Originally presented in 1977.)

Sternberg, R. J. (1985a). Implicit theories of intelligence, creativity and wisdom. *Journal of Personality and Social Psychology, 49* (3), 607–627.

Sternberg, R. J. (1985b). *Beyond IQ: a triarchic theory of human intelligence.* New York: Cambridge University Press.

Stevens, A. (1982). *Archetypes*. New York: William Morrow.

Stuss, D. T., & Benson, D. F. (1984). Neuropsychological studies of the frontal lobes. *Psychological Bulletin, 95*, 3–28.

Tellegen, A. (1981). Practicing the two disciplines for relaxation and enlightenment: comment on "Role of the feedback signal in electromyograph biofeedback: the relevance of attention," by Qualls and Sheehan. *Journal of Experimental Psychology: General, 110*(2), 217–226.

Westcott, M. (1988). *The psychology of human freedom: a human science perspective and critique*. New York: Springer-Verlag.

Zubiri, X. (1986). *Sobre el hombre*. Madrid: Alianza Editorial.

# 13    Conceptualizing wisdom: the primacy of affect–cognition relations

*Deirdre A. Kramer*

The past decade has ushered in enormous changes in the way in which adult development is construed, particularly in the area of adult cognitive development (e.g., Baltes, Dittmann-Kohli, & Dixon, 1984; Berg & Sternberg, 1985; Cavanaugh & Morton, 1989; Labouvie-Vief, 1981; Labouvie-Vief & Chandler, 1977; Poon, 1985; Sinnott, 1989). Traditional models of aging, which were derived from child-centered conceptions, often stress, at best, stability or, more often, regression in developmental trajectories and have failed to take into account adaptive forms of intelligence in later life. Some of the models that challenge tradition favor contextualism (e.g., Baltes et al., 1984; Berg & Sternberg, 1985; Cavanaugh & Morton, 1989; Poon, 1985), whereas others favor organicism (Kramer, 1989a; Labouvie-Vief, 1981).

The issues surrounding the controversy about whether organicism or contextualism is the preferable model are many and lie beyond the scope of the present chapter (see Dixon, Kramer, & Baltes, 1985; Kahlbaugh, 1989; Kramer, 1987a; Kramer & Bopp, 1989; Labouvie-Vief, 1981; Lerner & Kauffman, 1985; Meacham, 1989; Overton, 1984). However, these models share a united concern that traditional, mechanistic models have failed to take into account the varied and multiple contexts in which development occurs, including the sociohistorical context, the individual's meaning-making activities and goals, the relationship context, or the developmental context (Kramer & Bopp, 1989). Not surprisingly, then, mechanistic models have traditionally resulted in decline or, at best, stability representations of cognitive aging processes. Contextualist and organismic models are more likely to foster growth conceptions (Kramer, 1987b). The increasing interest in wisdom, as indicated by the present volume, reflects this emergent concern with forms of adaptation that continue to develop over the course of the life span (Holliday & Chandler, 1986; Meacham, 1983).

The present chapter adopts an organismic framework. Organicism, as defined by Pepper (1942), relies on the root metaphor of integration. It assumes

The author would like to thank Michael J. Bopp, Patricia E. Kahlbaugh, Robert J. Sternberg, and Maria A. Taranto for their comments on an earlier draft of this chapter.

279

the primary interdependence of variables as they evolve over time. This root metaphor is based on dialectical theories, which posit that all knowledge evolves toward states of increased integration via the interplay of contradiction (within and between systems) and its resolution.

In an organismic framework, everything is dynamic, or moving. One cannot fully understand a phenomenon by studying it in stagnant form. Rather, any moment, element, or event takes on new meaning in the context of the whole, which is seen not as a fixed "entity" but rather as a process unfolding over time. All phenomena are also inherently integrated, but this integration may not be apparent at earlier points in time. Rather, it is realized in ongoing, concrete experience. Integration occurs via the interplay of conflict and its resolution, where elements find their "nexuses," that is, become unified with their apparent antitheses in the context of an emergent, unified whole, which then forms the basis for a new thesis. Thus, the process continues indefinitely until the interdependence of all "elements" is achieved in consciousness (a goal never actually attained).

Throughout this process, the organism is an active constructor of experience, not merely a machine passively reacting to it. As active organisms, people construct interpretations of environmental events and continually act on and interact with the environment in order to construct and reconstruct their experience. In doing so, they may be seen as operating like lay theorists where, if psychologically healthy, they continually adapt their lay theories to fit the ever-changing events of their world, altering that world in the process or, conversely, if psychologically unhealthy, they actively work to maintain existing constructions of reality, no matter how unsatisfying these are. The wise person may be seen as a lay theorist who maintains a certain set of assumptions about social reality and is able to effectively apply these to a variety of domains in order to resolve problems arising in his or her own experience, advise others in resolving their problems, shape social institutions, and seek meaning and continuity in experience.

It is not to be assumed that such lay theorizing is purely cognitive in nature though. A central tenet of organicism – *the* central tenet – is integration. All phenomena are inherently interdependent. Any attempt to separate variables creates an artificial conceptualization of them, a "snapshot" that isolates one moment from its dynamic, evolving whole, distorting it in the process. Analogously, any attempt to isolate "pure" cognitive processes from affect is arbitrary. Cognition and affect are interdependent and attain their meaning in the praxis, or activity, of the organism. Wisdom has often been seen as a form of intelligence, involving cognitive processes. However, such processes cannot be separated from affect, which serves to motivate and sustain cognitive processing (Haviland & Kramer, 1989; Kramer & Haviland, 1989). Along these lines, Rybash, Hoyer, and Roodin (1986) proposed that real-life events result in the simultaneous activation of both affective and cognitive schemata, which requires that both be integrated in an effective problem solution. They argued against the notion of primacy of either domain.

In summary, in an organismic framework, psychological adaptation cannot be seen as separate from the functional contexts in which it occurs. Meaning-making activities in these contexts may lead to growth; wisdom is one form of this growth. Thus, wisdom, or any psychological process, should enable the individual to adapt to the tasks of adult life. Such tasks include choice of a career, development of an intimate relationship (usually ending in marriage), adjustment to the many stressors of adult life, including raising children (Aldous, 1978) and assuming increasingly complex social roles (Labouvie-Vief, 1980; Sinnott, 1984), adjustment to the disillusionment that often sets in on the job (Bray & Howard, 1983) and in marriage (Aldous, 1978), developing new priorities for dealing with this disillusionment (Bray & Howard, 1983; Levinson, 1978), including ones related to generativity (Erikson, 1968), dealing with conflicting roles and dreams (particularly among females) (Roberts & Newton, 1987), the reenrichment of the marital bond in later life (Aldous, 1978), adjustment to retirement, coping with chronic illness, and ultimately, facing and accepting the ultimate separation – death (Erikson, 1968). These are just some of the tasks facing adults; there are countless others. Wisdom, whatever its essence, should serve to foster the resolution of such tasks. However, they will evoke both emotional and cognitive reactions, so wisdom cannot be separated from either cognition or affect. It should serve to foster the resolution of these various issues, conflicts, crises, and tasks.

In this chapter, a model of wisdom will be presented using an organismic perspective. This model is depicted in Figure 13.1. It will be argued that cognitive and affective development reciprocally interact to produce a number of wisdom-related skills or processes that enable wisdom to operate through the individual in a variety of ways (e.g., in making life decisions, advising others, and engaging in spiritual reflection). These serve the function of enabling the person to resolve the many and ongoing tasks and stressors of adult life, which in turn fosters continued cognitive and affective development. The endless source of stress and opportunities for growth in one's life will provide the person with ongoing possibilities for maintenance and development of wisdom-related capacities.

Thus, wisdom is an area in which continued growth across the life span is possible. This model was derived from a number of sources. These include historical and contemporary conceptions of wisdom, research and theory on cognitive and effective development, and the metatheoretical tenets of organicism. Themes and issues from these three areas were integrated to formulate the model presented in Figure 13.1. The components of these models will be described in ensuing sections. In the next section, an overview of the construct of wisdom will be provided, followed by a discussion of the functions

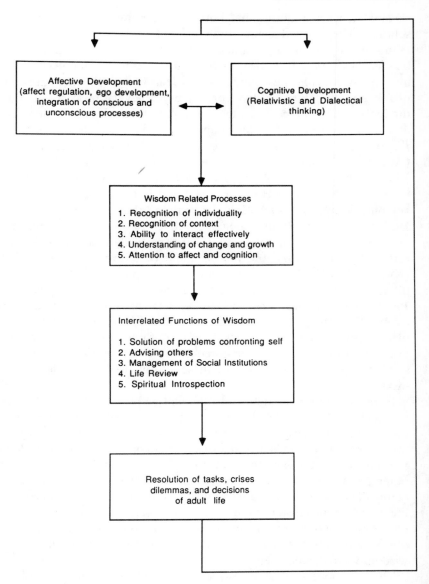

Figure 13.1. A model of wisdom.

of wisdom and the cognitive processes that serve these functions. In the section following that, a discussion of the ways in which cognitive and affective development interact to produce wisdom will be provided. In the fourth section, it will be shown how cognition and affect interact to produce wisdom-related processes via each of the functions of wisdom. In the final section, conclusions, implications, and unresolved issues will be discussed.

## Wisdom: an overview

The concept of wisdom has captured the imagination of life span developmentalists interested in progressive cognitive change in adulthood for over a decade now (e.g., Brent & Watson, 1980; Clayton, 1982; Clayton & Birren, 1980; Dittmann-Kohli & Baltes, in press; Holliday & Chandler, 1986; Meacham, 1983; Moody, 1983; Sowarka & Heckhausen, 1985; Sternberg, 1985). Yet there is to date no standard definition of the term. The concept "wisdom" is a rather broad, if elusive, one with diverse connotations. This can be seen in the following two definitions of the word *wisdom* taken from two dictionaries:

1. The quality or state of being wise; knowledge of what is true or right coupled with good judgment; 2. scholarly knowledge or learning; 3. wise sayings or teaching; 4. wisdom of Solomon
Synonyms: discrimination, judgment, understanding, sagacity; Antonyms: stupidity, foolishness, and ignorance
*(Random House College Dictionary,* Revised Edition, 1980)
1. a. accumulated philosophic or scientific learning: KNOWLEDGE; b. ability to discern inner qualities and relationships: INSIGHT; c. good sense: JUDGMENT; 2. a wise attitude or course of action; 3. the teachings of the ancient wise men. Syn: SENSE
*(Webster's Seventh New Collegiate Dictionary,* 1972)

From these definitions, it is clear that wisdom is a broadly defined concept, ranging from the mere *possession* of knowledge to *moral judgment.* The word *wise* meets with an even greater diversity of meanings in these dictionaries than the word *wisdom.* Not surprisingly, this diversity carries over to the conceptualization of wisdom in the psychological literature, both with respect to the processes involved and the domains to which these processes are applied.

Each of the models of wisdom specifies a given domain of problems in which wisdom-type judgments occur. They all seem to converge on the point that wisdom pertains to *human affairs.* However, "human affairs" are more or less broadly defined from model to model. Moody (1983) noted that, historically, practical wisdom was originally associated with philosophy but became increasingly differentiated from philosophical or theoretical wisdom over time as it became associated with such fields as "administration, law, or the management of human affairs" (Moody, 1983, p. 2). Thus, to Moody, practical wisdom would most closely serve the function of governing society, whereas theoretical wisdom, which was associated increasingly with religion and theology over time, would serve the function of questioning the nature of human existence and providing meaning to life.

Clayton (1982) defines the domain of wisdom as that of "human nature," which includes social, interpersonal, and intrapersonal problems. She distinguishes between intelligence and wisdom and specifically operationalizes wisdom as representing thought about human nature and hence as requiring certain kinds of processing (i.e., those based on contradiction and paradox). Somewhat similarly, Dittmann-Kohli (1984a) identifies the wisdom domain as comprising self-knowledge and interpersonal knowledge, which contains parallels to the intra- and interpersonal domains.

Brent and Watson also define the domain of wisdom as that of "human nature and human relationships." The kinds of processes described, such as the ability to perceive others' intentions, through sensitivity to, for example, nonverbal and other emotional cues, suggest the kinds of skills associated with the social-cognitive and social-intelligence literatures.

These models do not differentiate problem solving about human affairs from social or practical intelligence. It is not clear whether they imply that "intelligence" cannot be extended to include processing about social information. Some theorists have argued that social intelligence requires qualitatively different operations than intelligence about the physical world (e.g., Damon, 1979). However, Murray (1983) analyzed the similarities and presumed differences between processing of social and physical content and concluded that the boundaries between the two domains are not clear-cut. Brent and Watson (1980) and Clayton (1982) do not elaborate on this issue. Thus, it is not entirely clear how they differentiate wisdom from social intelligence or existing conceptions of social cognition. Along these lines, the prototypical conceptions of wisdom generated in a series of studies by Sternberg (1985) were significantly correlated with those for intelligence, and self-ratings on the wisdom characteristics were significantly related to measures of social intelligence. As Sternberg notes, people (which included both professional and lay theorists) have a difficult time distinguishing intelligence from wisdom. This appears to carry over to contemporary models of wisdom, and perhaps this is due to the plurality of conceptions of wisdom that have characterized our (intellectual) heritage.

Holliday and Chandler (1986) have made strides with such differentiation. They isolated five factors, including two that appeared unique to wisdom:

1. exceptional understanding of ordinary experience (e.g., the ability to see essences, understand contexts, and be in touch with the self); and
2. judgment and communication skills (i.e., perceptiveness, the ability to weigh consequences and consider multiple points of view, and the ability to analyze and communicate about life).

Intellectual skills and interpersonal skills played a less central role in the conceptualization of wisdom, although they were included among its components and were seen as necessary conditions for its development.

Dittmann-Kohli and Baltes (in press; see also Baltes, Smith, Staudinger, & Sowarka, in press; Dittmann-Kohli, 1984b) have also made strides in differentiating wisdom from practical and social intelligence. Like Moody (1983), they distinguish between practical and philosophical (theoretical) wisdom and narrow the scope of the practical wisdom domain to that of the "pragmatics of life." The pragmatics of life refer to "extrapersonal, intrapersonal, and interpersonal" situations that are personally meaningful to the individual. They distinguish practical wisdom from social and practical intelligence, primarily in that practical wisdom judgments would specifically center on issues and goals that have long-term relevance in the context of an individual's life (or the lives of those around him or her) – that is, life decisions. Therefore, although practical wisdom might involve social intelligence, it represents a very specific type of social intelligence – one geared toward the solution of personally meaningful life decisions – and it involves an understanding of societal, not just interpersonal, issues since age-graded and nonnormative sociohistorical events have an impact on individual life decisions.

Thus, within the general domain of human affairs, there is a diversity of subdomains within which wisdom has been posited. Furthermore, wisdom has been associated with several roles, including that of making decisions in one's own life, offering counsel to others, managing the affairs of society, and posing questions about the fundamental meaning of existence. In the present author's view, these are all functions of wisdom and need not compete for consideration in models of wisdom. The next section will address these functions in greater detail.

## Functions of wisdom in adult life

In assessing a psychological competence in adulthood such as wisdom, an organismic perspective would require an analysis of its function in the lives of adults – that is, how it helps them assume the tasks of adult life (i.e., commitments, raising children, coping with illness, etc.) described in the preceding section. There are at least five possible functions of wisdom in adult life, which can capture the variety of domains represented within the general designation of human affairs without sacrificing the coherence or integrity of the wisdom construct. It has the further advantage of integrating practical and spiritual (i.e., theoretical and philosophical) wisdom, which the present author does not see as separate domains (see also Moody, 1983; Taranto, 1989) and allowing for wisdom to serve the dual roles of enabling one to solve one's own dilemmas and advising others in theirs.

One function of wisdom is the role it plays in enabling the individual to resolve dilemmas and make decisions in his or her life – "life planning," according to Dittmann-Kohli and Baltes (in press). These choices would involve both intra- and interpersonal knowledge and skills. In making important decisions, one might have to negotiate age-graded, history-graded, and nonnormative events (Dittmann-Kohli & Baltes, in press), be in touch with one's feelings, needs, and expectations (Dittmann-Kohli, 1984a; Holliday & Chandler, 1986; Sternberg, 1985), differentiate the needs of the self from the expectations of others (Kramer & Haviland, 1989; Rybash et al., 1986) and societal conventions (e.g., see Labouvie-Vief, Hakim-Larson, DeVoe, & Schoeberlein, 1989), conduct adequate interpersonal relationships, including the use of cooperative, tolerant modes of conflict resolution (Kramer, 1989a), be open to advice from others (Sternberg, 1985), and weather the often difficult processes of change and development (Kramer, 1989a).

A second function of wisdom is that of advising others, which would be particularly useful for the generativity tasks of middle-aged adults, according to Erikson's theory. Wisdom has often been associated with its advisory role, for example, in the common citation of Solomon's wisdom in advising two women who claimed one baby as their own (e.g., Clayton, 1982; Clayton & Birren, 1980; Holliday & Chandler, 1986; Sternberg, 1985; Taranto, 1989), and emerges as an important factor in prototypical conceptions of wisdom (Holliday & Chandler, 1986; Sowarka & Heckhausen, 1985; Sternberg, 1985).

A third function of wisdom is that of management and guidance of society. Moody (1983) noted that historically wisdom was associated with the management of the practical affairs of society. According to some theorizing, mature adults should be most equipped to handle the tasks of managing society. Thus, Schaie (1977–1978) hypothesized that the cognitive functions most suited to middle and old age are those associated with the integration and application of already acquired knowledge, in contrast to the acquisition of new knowledge, which is appropriate to youth. During middle age, such knowledge would be geared toward executive skills in guiding future generations. In the present author's conception, this aspect of wisdom can take a variety of forms, ranging from the raising of a family to community service to ministry to managing a business (or any subdivision thereof) to international politics. Middle age, in particular, may be a time where this aspect of wisdom is most operative, which is adaptive since it also serves the function of generativity, and might offset some of the disillusionment that occurs in middle age with unfulfilled career and marital dreams and fulfilled ones that did not bring expected promises (Aldous, 1978; Bray & Howard, 1983; Levinson, 1978). However, there still are many elder statesmen and older adults who serve in a nurturant capacity as parents, grandparents, spouses, friends, and siblings. Thus, this aspect of wisdom will undoubtedly continue to play a central role in the lives of aging people as well and occurs earlier in life too; however, it may be more central to the tasks of middle age.

A fourth function of wisdom is that of life review. According to Erikson (1968), the aging individual evaluates his or her life in order to provide meaning and continuity. Thus, in Schaie's (1977–1978) model, cognitive processes in later life are geared toward self-reflection in the evaluation of one's life. Regardless of whether the emphasis is on evaluating experience for the purpose of guiding future generations or for the purpose of life review, it is nevertheless on the evaluative function of cognition as adaptive to later-life intellectual functioning. However, such processes have been largely overlooked in the cognitive aging literature.

Finally, a fifth function of wisdom is that of questioning the meaning of life. This function typically is subsumed under philosophical and theoretical conceptions of wisdom (Dittmann-Kohli & Baltes, in press; Moody, 1983) and in the present author's view is spiritual in nature (see also Moody, 1983). It has received the least attention in the literature, perhaps owing to, as Moody (1983) noted, the unpopularity of spiritual quests in contemporary society. Simply questioning the meaning of life is to make oneself a potential pariah in our culture. However, as Moody also notes, this is not feasible because without it, one cannot grasp the larger context in which all other events take place or resolve existential dilemmas. Like Moody, the present author will argue that other aspects of wisdom cannot be separated from spiritual wisdom if only because the intrapersonal development necessary for wisdom and spiritual development often go hand in hand (Hodges, 1986). Furthermore, it will be argued that spiritual wisdom involves many of the same processes as the other functions of wisdom, which will be shown in greater detail in a later section.

None of these five functions of wisdom is independent of the others; they are highly interrelated, and as such, development in one area is likely to facilitate and perhaps be necessary for development in another. For example, it would in all likelihood be impossible to advise another person adequately (i.e., the second function) without first having an adequate enough understanding of oneself, which is a component of the first function, because one would have to separate his or her own needs from those of the advisee. Thus, self-knowledge, which is crucial to making adequate decisions about one's own life, is also necessary for advising others.

In addition, life review and management of societal institutions can be seen as related. Theorists have suggested societal advantages that might accrue from the life review and evaluation processing that may come with age (e.g., Brent & Watson, 1980; Camp & McKitrick, 1989; Labouvie-Vief, 1980). Older adults may be suited as oral transmitters of experience, and those most successful at doing so may be those able to interpret and draw lessons from their experiences. Mergler and Goldstein (1983) presented a model that suggests that older adults do indeed serve such a function and cite a limited body of research that thus far tentatively supports this hypothesis.

Similarly, greater experience in making one's own life decisions and advising others will lead to a richer cognitive framework for interpreting and drawing lessons from past experience, that is, allow for a richer life review. Likewise, those best able to look back on and draw lessons from past experience will be those most capable of making decisions for themselves and guiding others to do so.

Finally, meaningful reflective activities in any of these areas are likely to raise questions about the nature of existence (i.e., spiritual wisdom). Conversely, those who are capable of posing questions about the nature of existence when it is in opposition to normative pressures might be those who can best put one's own and others' problems into broader perspective in order to make unclouded judgments. Furthermore, spiritual nourishment may provide one with the energy, the self-knowledge, and the capacities to engage in the psychological processes comprising wisdom in order to serve in the various functions of wisdom (e.g., see Hodges, 1986). These are just some of the ways that different functions of wisdom interact (e.g., see Moody, 1983). There is probably an infinite variety of possibilities for interaction.

In summary, there are at least five possible functions of wisdom that could aid in the tasks of adult development, and these are not to be seen as independent processes. Rather, keeping in line with the organismic tenet of the present chapter, they are seen as interdependent, reciprocal processes. What will be argued instead is (1) that there are certain psychological (i.e., cognitive and affective) processes that facilitate the development of wisdom in all of its functions and (2) that cognition and affect are both essential to the development of these processes.

*Cognitive processes*

Each of the models of wisdom offer a number of cognitive processes that are deemed to be involved in wisdom-type judgments. A broad array of cognitive processes have been proposed, raising questions about the differentiation of wisdom from practical and social intelligence. Of particular interest to the present author, however, are the ones that might be termed *relativistic* or *dialectical* and that foster an understanding of change, uncertainty, and contradiction. They may be well suited to the definition of wisdom because

1. at least some relativistic or dialectical beliefs appear in virtually all models of wisdom as constituting wise judgments and
2. they are not typically represented in psychological conceptions of practical and social intelligence and so provide an opportunity for distinguishing wisdom from other forms of adaptation.

Relativistic and dialectical thinking can be seen in historical conceptions of wisdom. For example, Holliday and Chandler (1986) summarized major Western philosophical approaches to the study of wisdom, and a number of these approaches emphasized the ability to reflect on uncertainty and paradox. Included are the earliest Western writings on wisdom, which date back to pre–2500 B.C. Egypt and stress the "difficulty in maintaining faith when confronted with the injustices and paradoxes of life" (Holliday & Chandler, 1986, p. 11). Similarly, the Mesopotamian literature deals with "the dilemma of death and the unjust suffering of good people" (p. 12) and as such focuses on the contradictions of human experience. The pre-Socratic tradition, particularly that of Heraclitus, stressed the ability to understand the contextual nature of existence and to understand interrelationships among elements within a given context. More recently, existential philosophers stress the relativistic and dialectical "search for personal meaning in a seemingly arbitrary world" (Holliday & Chandler, 1986, p. 18). Thus, relativistic and dialectical thinking are strands present throughout historical conceptions of wisdom.

Relativistic thinking, according to the present author's framework, involves the awareness of the subjective, arbitrary nature of knowledge (Kramer, 1983, 1989c). Knowledge is a function of the standpoint of the observer, and since different observers do not share exactly the same standpoint, contradiction is inherent in knowledge. Furthermore, such contradictions are irreconcilable, as one cannot say that a given context produces more valid knowledge than another. Knowledge is also seen as being in a continual state of flux since contexts are constantly changing, thus altering one's standpoint, and there is no necessary relationship between past and present contexts. Therefore, relativistic thinking would foster an awareness of the ill-structured, unpredictable nature of events.

Relativistic thinking has been hypothesized to develop during adolescence and/or early adulthood (Chandler, 1987; Kramer, 1983; Labouvie-Vief, 1980) and reflects the extreme multiplicity that Perry found to characterize college students who were in the process of questioning the meaning of "truth." The advantage of relativistic thinking to making wise decisions is that it allows one to take into consideration individual needs and priorities even when they conflict with one's own and to consider the circumstances surrounding the problematic event – in other words, to allow for multiplicity. The limitations of relativistic thinking, however, are that it makes it difficult to construct continuity and to make choices and commitments that might render solution impossible (Chandler, 1987; Kramer, 1989a; Perry, 1970). Thus, evolving a form of thinking that provides an integration of contradiction would be adaptive. Dialectical thinking offers such a solution.

Dialectical thinking, according to the present author's framework, derives from the root metaphor of organicism and involves an awareness of the integratedness of all knowledge (Kramer, 1983, 1989c). It is proposed developmentally to succeed relativistic thought. In a dialectical "lay theory," knowledge is seen as evolving through increasingly integrated forms via the interplay of conflict and its resolution. An individual thinking dialectically would realize the interactive nature of all events and thus would hold the interdependence, rather than independence, of variables to be a primary feature of reality. Precursors of this mode of thinking might be found in Perry's (1970) college students, who had achieved commitment within relativism, and it is similar to Labouvie-Vief's (1982) autonomous level of thinking. It has been hypothesized to develop at around middle age (Basseches, 1980; Kramer, 1983; Labouvie-Vief, 1982; Pascual-Leone, 1983), and there is evidence for such a progression, although there are individual differences as well (Basseches, 1980; Kramer, Goldston, & Kahlbaugh, 1988; Kramer, Melchoir, & Levine, 1989; Kramer & Woodruff, 1986).

Both relativistic and dialectical thinking lead one to question the view that knowledge is absolute and unchanging, and thus both are suited to problem solving of an ill-structured nature. Wisdom-type judgments are generally seen as ill-structured, prompting Meacham (1983) to propose that wisdom involves an awareness of how little one knows – as knowledge grows, so too may one's feelings of ignorance. Most modern psychological theorizing has emphasized some aspect of relativistic and/or dialectical thinking in conceptualizations of wisdom.

Clayton's (1982) and Moody's (1983) models both represent wisdom as involving judgments of a qualitatively different nature from other forms of intelligence, one necessitating a logic based on *contradiction and paradox* – a dialectical logic.[1] This is due in part to the complex and ambiguous nature of social reality and to the epistemological assumptions and biases inherent in human judgment. Clayton also proposes other processes that are associated with relativistic and dialectical thinking. These include an awareness of the changing, fluid nature of reality, the awareness of the embeddedness of problems in the concrete human situation, and hence the inability to separate form from content and focus on the here and now. Moody (1983) likewise notes the inseparability of wisdom from real-life, concrete situations and the importance of being aware of such inseparability.

Dittmann-Kohli and Baltes (in press) also propose that wisdom involves an awareness of the complexity and ambiguity inherent in social reality and the need to take into consideration the relativity of values, life-styles, and so on. Consequently, an ability to entertain contradiction is a necessary component of wisdom since contradictory judgments could ensue from different sets of criteria for evaluation. They subsume such concepts within two of their criteria, that is, uncertainty in problem definition and reflective relativism in problem solution. The former involves an awareness of the ambiguity and complexity inherent in wisdom-related situations and the ill-defined and multidetermined nature of wisdom-type tasks. The latter involves an awareness of the subjectivity involved in individuals' epistemological assumptions, priorities, and definitions of what constitutes a successful lifestyle and hence an ability to make conditional judgments and to reconcile contradiction.

Thus according to contemporary and many historical models, wisdom is a form of judgment pertaining to some domain of human affairs that involves an awareness of the ill-structured, contextual, and often contradictory nature of experience. As stated in the introduction to this chapter, in the present author's view, within the general domain of human affairs, the functions of wisdom are manifested in making decisions about one's own life, advising others in making decisions, management of societal affairs, life review, and spiritual questioning, all of which are interrelated. Relativistic and dialectical thinking are likely to aid the individual in each of these ways, in that they are well suited to the resolution of ill-structured problems, by taking into account indeterminism, contradiction, and change. However, the major assumption of this chapter is that these forms of thinking are not purely cognitive in nature but involve a great deal of affective involvement, as they are invoked in affectively laden situations and require conscious–unconscious integration for their development. In order to engage in them, it will be argued that one must have an incisive understanding of oneself and one's interactions with others, the functioning of social systems, and the nature of change. Without an awareness of one's inner emotional life, such understanding is unlikely to ensue.

## Cognition–affect integration

The bulk of scientific inquiry operates as though affect is irrelevant to cognition, most likely due to the widespread use of mechanistic models. The central tenet of organicism, however, is that all phenomena are interdependent; one cannot have cognition without affect or affect without cognition. The two systems of psychological functioning are inherently interrelated. Thus, this section will outline some of the ways that affect and cognition interact in relativistic and dialectical thinking. In this vein, relativistic and dialectical thinking are construed as lay theories, much like Kelly's (1955) "personal constructs," which provide the person with a scheme for organizing, interpreting, and guiding one's experience. As such, the lay theories are seen as incorporating both affective and cognitive dimensions of experience and sometimes as highly resistant to change – thus, many people resist becoming wise.

### Affective component of wisdom

Both Brent and Watson (1980) and Clayton and Birren (1980) hypothesized that wisdom incorporates affective as well as cognitive dimensions of experience. In Brent and Watson's work, wise individuals are described as concerned, compassionate, empathetic, and in possession of excellent senses of humor in the face of adversity. Similarly, in Clayton's (1976) work, wise individuals are seen as empathetic, understanding, gentle, and peaceful. Furthermore, Clayton and Birren propose that an integration of cognitive, affective, and reflective processes characterizes wisdom.

Holliday and Chandler (1986) adopt a similar position on the role of affect. They argue that wisdom is

defined by characteristics from cognitive, interpersonal, and experiential domains. To be considered wise, one must be both competent and interpersonally skilled and have judgement and communication skills that are exercised in a framework which includes substantial knowledge of human social concerns. (Holliday & Chandler, 1986, p. 82)

In this context, they argue for

a more modest or reduced role for cognitive factors in the definition of wisdom . . . purely cognitive aspects of wisdom do not serve to distinguish wise individuals from other competent people. Instead, the data indicate that basic cognitive skills represent necessary, but not sufficient, conditions for being recognized as wise. (Holliday & Chandler, 1986, p. 83)

Clayton and Birren (1980) emphasized the *integration of cognition, affect, and reflection* as a central defining feature of wisdom, a view with which the present author is in agreement. However, they, along with Holliday and Chandler (1986), provide little elaboration of how cognitive and affective processes are related in wise functioning. Roodin, Rybash, and Hoyer (1984) argued that the coordination of cognition and affect is the central locus of continued adult cognitive development. In particular, such an integration might involve the ability to reflect in the face of actual, sometimes adverse experiences in order to form impressions based on principles such as justice, equality, and so on, yet without simultaneously losing the experience to the intellect or ignoring the emotional reactions that may arise in response to the situation. In support of this view, Labouvie-Vief et al. (1989) have argued for a reemergence of the importance of considering subjective, affective experience with maturity and an integration of such experience with cognitive functioning. Furthermore, they found evidence for such a progression. The present section will provide greater elaboration of the reciprocal roles of affect and cognition in facilitating wisdom. It will be argued that the defense mechanism of projection exerts a key influence on whether one is able to achieve wisdom.

*Mechanisms of projection in development*

The issue of projection may be seen as a central one regarding the development of relativistic and dialectical thinking and hence of wisdomlike judgments. Projection is a defense mechanism whereby threatening or unacceptable impulses or emotions in the self are dissociated from one's conscious awareness, or one's representation of self, and "observed" in others. Thus, it lends itself to forming strong distinctions between self and other (though paradoxically the person using it is highly enmeshed with others). Chinen's (1985) analysis of elder tales provides a fascinating source for illustrating the relationship between projection and wisdom. Whereas fairy tales feature youthful characters, elder tales, in contrast, feature elderly protagonists and differ systematically from fairy tales in their treatment of the affairs of human life. Most significantly for the present discussion, fairy tales dichotomize good and evil, with good embodied in the protagonist and evil projected into an external source and with good triumphing over evil. In contrast, elder tales contain no such clean-cut heroes or foes. Rather, they represent good and evil as both inherent in the self rather than projecting them onto an external entity, and through spiritual illumination, the evil within the self is transcended. However, the evil within the self must first be accepted before it can be transcended.

Fairy tales reflect the immaturity of the main characters, for they have not yet accepted the evil within the self but rather engage in the defense mechanism of projection in order to dissociate the evil characteristics of the self from conscious awareness. The acceptance of both good and evil within the self in the elder tales marks a milestone of maturity that is reflected in personality transitions in the midlife and beyond (Gould, 1978; Jaques, 1970; Levinson, 1978) and involves a dialectical acceptance of the interrelationship between contradictory aspects of experience – for example, that good and evil represent different aspects of a single, unified whole.

*Socialization and the repression of emotion.* Suppression and repression are necessary features of growing up, at least in Western society. Haviland and Walker-Andrews (1987) note the necessity of modulating emotional expressivity from infancy on due to the strong empathic contagion effect to which humans are susceptible. Were people not to mask their emotions, others, empathically responding to these (as we do to infants), would be in a continual state of distress. Thus, from the earliest moments of life on, we engage in the ongoing effort to mask our emotions via both of these defense mechanisms. Unfortunately, since infants lack the necessary cognitive and linguistic skills to label their early experiences, some of this emotional masking is apt to be lost from conscious awareness, thus entering the realm of repressed emotional material (e.g., see Basseches, 1989a). Research shows that negative emotion-related memories are less extensively organized in our cognitive networks, that is, with fewer pathways to other memories, which results in poorer accessibility of such memories in conscious awareness (Isen, 1989). Perhaps the early masking of negative emotions contributes to their less extensive representation in memory.

Furthermore, socialization involves an ongoing struggle between child and caretaker to establish boundaries, to negotiate between the egocentric needs of the self and those of others. Given that the child is in a position of inferior power, early childhood is likely to involve frequent feelings of frustration, embarrassment, shame, and rage, emotions that are largely considered un-

desirable and/or unacceptable in our society (Miller, 1981). Thus, many of
the affective experiences of childhood are likely to become repressed during
socialization, especially those unacceptable ones that are not given labels by
surrounding adults (Basseches, 1989b). In other words, many of the emotions
we subsume under the label "negative emotions" are dissociated from the
conscious self during development. This is particularly so in the case of narcissistic disturbance (Miller, 1981).

Narcissistic disturbance, according to Miller (1981), is characterized by the
inability to differentiate the needs of the self from those of others. It results
from having received inadequate attention to one's own needs as an infant
and young child. Due to their own unhealthy narcissistic preoccupations, the
parents required – often unconsciously – that the child accommodate his or
her own needs to that of their own and failed to provide unconditional acceptance of the child's narcissistic strivings, egocentric longings, emotional
intensity, and so on. The person who develops a narcissistic disturbance seeks
out substitutes for the parental figures in his or her adult life, via accomplishments, love relationships, promiscuity, drugs, and so forth. All of these serve
the function of continually fighting off depression (e.g., with attempts at
grandiosity) and require rigid ego controls to attempt to live up to an overly
rigid ideal self. In fact, the narcissistically disturbed person, lacking empathy
with his or her feelings and needs (Kramer & Haviland, 1989), is said to have
created a false self (Miller, 1981). At the core of narcissistic disturbance is
the repression of myriad affective responses and as such the inability to recognize and experience one's emotional reactions, such as anger, directly. This
results in cognitive stunting as well (Kramer & Haviland, 1989). To some
extent, all children experience such repression with development (Haviland
& Walker-Andrews, 1987; Miller, 1981), but for many, this does not severely
impair their ability to form satisfying attachments and to set and achieve
realistic life goals.

Human beings, therefore, are likely to emerge from childhood with more-
or-less fragmented selves, often in the form of a good self and a bad self,
which are polarized. The fairy tales that Chinen documents are testimony to
this early developmental process, involving an externalization of evil, of the
bad self, in various projective forms, that is, in the praxis of the individual
rather than consciously reflected on. The first of these forms in simple *projection,* whereby the repressed emotions are attributed to other people, who
represent a mirror for one's lost (i.e., dissociated) emotions. The person
cannot see repressed emotion in the self but can see it in others. Thus, a
person's knowledge of the self is enacted not via reflective abstractions on
the self but via his or her perceptions of others. In order to become aware
of these projections, one would have to evolve relativistic ways of thinking,
that is, be aware of the subjective construction of knowledge, that what one
sees in other people is strongly influenced by one's own projections. The

inability to separate one's own needs from those of others would make it difficult to take the perspective of others, thus impeding the development of relativistic thinking. Paradoxically, however, the difficulties in affective, interpersonal experience that result from such projections would likely serve as the impetus for developing relativistic thought if the person is willing to take the risk to confront his or her own projections and grow (see Bopp, 1989; Kramer, 1989a). In turn, relativistic thinking would facilitate the resolution of these projections. The two (i.e., affect and cognition) would interact in a reciprocal manner.

A second form of projection is that of *projective identification,* a concept developed by object-relations theorists. Object-relations theory is an offshoot of psychoanalysis. In contrast to psychoanalysis, however, it sees our basic human conflicts as interpersonal rather than intrapersonal in nature, stemming from a basic need for human relatedness or attachment rather than motivated simply by sexual longings (Nichols, 1987). Object-relations theory, particularly when combined with systems theory, expands our traditional notions of self. No longer seen as contained within the boundaries of a single organism, personality is seen as expressed conjointly by two or more people in relationship (Nichols, 1987; Scarf, 1987). Object-relations theory focuses on the dyad, whereas family-systems theory focuses on relationships among two or more dyads to form a system (Bopp, 1985). This model of human behavior represents personality characteristics as extending outside of the traditional boundaries of the physical self to be expressed collectively by the system (see Bateson, 1972).

For example, Scarf (1987) argued that people often unconsciously (or consciously) seek out partners who are mirror images of their own psyche. If one has repressed anger, one might seek out a partner who openly expresses such anger. In contrast, that partner may have difficulty expressing tenderness, in which case he or she has sought one out because of the ability to express these feelings. The couple has entered into an unconscious pact, whereby the one has "agreed" to express the tender feelings for both people, and the other has agreed to express the anger for both partners. Both anger and tenderness are expressed within the dyad, but in a polarized, projected manner. Sometimes one partner may elicit the repressed emotional response in the other – that is, induce the other to experience one's own repressed emotion. This is the process of projection identification. However, this "contract" can and often does go awry over time as one begins to fight with the other over these repressed emotions. Thus, the person repressing her anger begins fighting with the partner over his anger, unaware that she is really projecting her own internal battle with herself onto the partner.

*Development beyond forms of projection.* Development – both intrapsychic and dyadic – would require becoming aware of these repressed emotions and

"owning" the internal battle being waged against them in order to stop projecting this battle onto other people (e.g., one's children, one's spouse, one's
friends, and one's "enemies"), which is both conflict engendering and limiting
of the growth of that other and also capable of preventing mature love (see
Person, 1988; Scarf, 1987). The ability to become aware of projective identification would be facilitated by dialectical thinking, as it would involve an
awareness of the inherent interdependence and inseparability of all phenomena (even personalities) (Kramer, 1989a). This would allow for a development
of the type of wisdom defined by Dittmann-Kohli's (1984a) older subjects,
who stated that wisdom about interpersonal interactions involves a genuine
interest in and ability to listen to (empathize) with the concerns of others.
Empathy, which was included in other models of wisdom as well, involves
the ability to be aware of one's projections so that one might also accommodate to the unique feelings and thoughts being expressed by another.

Thus, the thought processes described by Chinen and other theorists as
constituting wisdom, which involve awareness of relativistic and dialectical
principles, could not develop apart from affect. One must be able to first
become aware of and then transcend one's projections before one can develop
both the empathic skills and the cognitive processes associated with wisdom.
Chances are then that wisdom will develop out of emotionally problematic
situations, relationships, and experiences, in line with Brent and Watson's
(1980) view that pain can be a source of wisdom. Such situations will foster
the development of relativistic and dialectical thinking. A high degree of
affective and affective–cognitive integration is necessary in order to develop,
so that these ways of thinking can be enacted in one's life and one's relationships with others without simply imposing one's own needs onto others.

In other words, wisdom involves the emotional and cognitive ability both
to recognize one's own subjectivity and the interdependence of boundaries
between self and other and to transcend these limitations by trying to separate
one's own needs from others'. Labouvie-Vief (1982) describes this awareness
as involving the highest level of "cognitive" development, that of autonomous
thinking. Paradoxically, it is the awareness of one's subjectivity – or one's
projections – that allows one to begin the task of overcoming that subjectivity
(Labouvie-Vief, 1982; Scarf, 1987). One can never completely overcome his
or her subjective biases, but can continually work to make them conscious.
Without such a high level of integration, it would be difficult to separate one's
own needs from those of others and from societal conventions in order to
make wise judgments. Conversely, without adequate ego strength, one would
not be able to entertain such relativistic and dialectical assumptions about
the self; they would be too threatening.

*Relationship to age.* Wisdom has enjoyed an association with age throughout
history (Clayton & Birren, 1980), and thus it is not surprising that the affective

correlates of relativistic and dialectical thinking would also show a positive relationship to age. Personality stage theorists have stressed the acceptance and subsequent integration of conflicting parts of the self, such as good and evil, masculine and feminine, into a unified conception of self (Gould, 1978; Levinson, 1978). This process appears to gain ascendancy during the midlife crisis and is also reflected in the creative works of eminent artists throughout the centuries, where there is an acceptance of the inherent presence of both good and evil and creative and destructive forces within the self and the world (Jaques, 1970).

Jung (1958) argued that such processes spring from the need to integrate unexpressed parts of the self over time, resulting in development toward greater balance in the expression of one's personality. Thus, it could be deduced that there is development away from reliance on projection as a defense mechanism toward other, more mature defenses. Indeed, there is evidence to support this contention, with older adults engaged in less externalizing and more internalizing of their emotions and with greater use of such defense mechanisms as humor, sublimation, and suppression (Irion & Blanchard-Fields, 1987; Labouvie-Vief, Hakim-Larson, & Hobart, 1987; Vaillant, 1977). Kramer (1989a,b) presented a model in which relativistic and dialectical thinking were proposed to facilitate the process of overcoming externalization of blame for conflict resolution in others. Specifically, these modes of thinking allow for an appreciation of the interactive nature of conflict, in turn facilitating cooperative conflict resolution. Kramer's model will be described in greater detail in a later section.

### Research on affect–cognition relations in these modes of thought

Thus, the development of relativistic and dialectical thinking is intricately linked to the development of affect regulation. Like their affective correlates, relativistic and dialectical thinking are also related to age (Basseches, 1980; Blanchard-Fields, 1986; Kramer et al., 1989; Kramer, Melchior, & Levine, 1989; Kramer & Woodruff, 1986). However, research in the author's laboratory suggests that dialectical thinking is still found in only a minority of people. When it is found in prototypical form, however, it is in middle-aged and older adults (Kramer et al., 1989). Kramer (1987c) has suggested that our efforts be directed away from simply establishing a relationship to age and focused, rather, on individual differences in openness to growth.

Many of the older adults in the samples studied seem to have come to reject pure relativity (Kramer, Goldston, & Kahlbaugh, 1989; Kramer, Melchior, & Levine, 1989). Some people appeared to regress to the absolute level, whereas others maintained an inconsistent stance fluctuating between relativism and absolutism, and only a few seemed to integrate absolute and relativistic modes of thinking to reorganize at a more integrated, dialectical level (Kramer, 1987c). Part of embracing growth is accepting pain (Kramer, 1989a; Marris, 1974). Thus, it is important to study the affective processes, such as ego development, that enable one to take the risks of further development (Kramer, 1989a; Labouvie-Vief et al., 1987). With this view in mind, a project was undertaken to explore affect–cognition relations in two adolescent diaries.

The analysis focused on the diaries of Anne Frank and "Vivienne" (a girl who committed suicide) (Haviland & Kramer, 1989; Kramer & Haviland, 1989). The analysis of affect involved coding all of the emotion words in the diary, whereas the analysis of cognition involved coding all instances of absolute, relativistic, and dialectical thinking. The results revealed a close interdependence of cognition and affect in Anne Frank's diary. When the affective and cognitive developmental plots were superimposed on one another, enhanced affectivity was followed directly by increased cognitive processing, and the emergence of new forms of thinking (i.e., relativistic and early level dialectical thinking described by Kramer [1989c] as static systems) occurred in the context of these enhanced affectivity–cognitive phases.

For example, Anne frequently and unabashedly experienced myriad reactions, both positive and negative, to her interactions with others in the annex. Her relationship with her mother was particularly problematic for her, and early in the diary she takes a highly absolute view of her own correctness and her mother's incorrectness. However, these interactions and the distressing emotions they elicit in her prod her to think more deeply about their relationship, and toward the middle of the diary she begins to see it in more relativistic terms. This allows her to take her mother's perspective and to recognize her own contributions to their strained interactions. Thus, cognition and affect stand neither in a neutral nor in an antagonistic relationship to one another in Anne's diary but rather are integrated to produce continued cognitive (and emotional) growth.

In contrast, Vivienne showed no such integration as she became increasingly suicidal. Integration existed early in her diary but disintegrated as her pathology progressed. In particular, she became increasingly unable to access her emotions, and thus, instead of using cognition to resolve the emotional experience, she appeared to use it to defend against these emotions via strong reliance on the defense mechanisms of intellectualization, projection, and projective identification. In fact, her poetry revealed a strong implicit awareness of the repressive processes she experienced. However, she would have had to evolve a nonlinear mode of thinking, such as dialectical thinking, to make these more accessible to her everyday cognitive awareness. Unfortunately, she did not progress much beyond absolute – that is, nonrelativistic, nondialectical – modes of thinking. The consequence was that all development, both cognitive and affective, ceased. These results suggest the importance of coordinated affective and cognitive functioning in furthering the development of relativistic and dialectical forms of thinking.

These results receive further support in a study exploring the relationship between cognitive development and a decrease in self-reported affect intensity with age. Kramer, Goldston, and Kahlbaugh (1989) found that dialectical thinking was positively and linearly related to age, but upon closer examination it was only among those who maintained a high degree of affect intensity that this relationship held. Thus, an ability to respond affectively to the experiences of adult life and to stay affectively attuned later in life (when many people report a decline in affect intensity) may be necessary for continued development of dialectical thinking.

Labouvie-Vief et al. (1989) provide further evidence for a relationship between cognition and affect. In her system, there are four levels of cognitive development, including the presystemic, intrasystemic, intersystemic, and integrated (autonomous) levels. The latter three levels are similar to absolute, relativistic, and dialectical thinking, respectively (Kramer, 1989c). Intrasystemic thinking fosters an absolute conception of reality characterized by dualistic, dichotomized versions of right versus wrong, rationality versus emotionality, truth versus falsity, and so on. Intersystemic thinking fosters an awareness of the contextual nature of knowledge and the subjectivity inherent in all judgments. Finally, autonomous thinking allows one to begin to disembed one's thinking from societal conventions, to make decisions based on consideration of personal needs as well as existing conventions.

Labouvie-Vief et al. (1989) found evidence for a relationship between ego level and cognitive development such that those at lower levels of development were more likely to use immature defense mechanisms such as intellectualization and projection whereas those at higher levels use more mature mechanisms. Furthermore, cognitive development continued into later life among those who were of a high ego development level, mirroring the continued "development" (the data from both studies is cross-sectional) of those in the Kramer, Goldston, and Kahlbaugh (1989) study who were high in affect intensity. Thus, an important task for later-life development may be to maintain a degree of openness to one's affective experience, which may require the discarding of projection and other repressive coping mechanisms in favor of more mature defense mechanisms that do not involve repression.

Thus, projection and projective identification, on the one hand, and relativistic and dialectical modes of thinking, on the other, are highly interrelated. The problems posed in our relationships and experiences as a result of our projections provide the impetus for growth in modes of thinking that, paradoxically, allow us to become aware of these projections, that is, relativistic and dialectical modes of thinking. These, in turn, although serving the function of aiding in working through these defense mechanisms, cannot be fully developed until one is sufficiently aware of his or her projections and projective identifications, that is, until they no longer plague one's interactions to a great extent. In other words, these processes are inherently inseparable. Once these developmental tasks have been achieved, the person would be highly capable of wisdom (with the assumption that there are varying degrees of wisdomlike capabilities and that no one ever achieves complete or perfect wisdom).

## The role of cognition and affect in fostering wise judgments

Relativistic and dialectical thinking (and corresponding reduction in projection) would facilitate the five functions of wisdom (i.e., solving problems in one's own life, advising others, management of social institutions, life review, and spiritual introspection) in at least five ways:

1. through the recognition of individuality;
2. by taking into account context;
3. by fostering cooperative, empathetic strategies for interpersonal interaction;
4. through the recognition of possibilities for change; and
5. through recognition of the necessity of integrating cognition and affect.

### Recognition of individuality

The recognition of individuality is necessary both for making adequate decisions about the self and for advising others. As noted in most models of wisdom, there are no prescribed solutions that will be effective for all individuals at all times, but rather, the solution must take into account the individual needs and priorities of the person with the problem. When the problem pertains to the self, one must be aware of and be able to assert these needs despite possible opposition from others and from societal conventions. When the problem is confronting another, the advising person must be able to differentiate his or her own needs, priorities, and expectations from those of the other. To do so requires being able to overcome projection and recognize boundaries between self and other, requiring a high degree of integration of conscious and unconscious processes.

Similarly, with spiritual development, one needs to pose questions and express spirituality in a way that is comfortable to the self even though it might differ from prevailing conventions. Each person would experience his or her religious beliefs in a unique way, in accordance with his or her own style, goals, priorities, beliefs, and needs. A person, having gone through the process of reflection, might decide that traditional beliefs are not an appropriate avenue for finding his or her personal meaning. Furthermore, spiritual development, at least in the Christian tradition – involves being able to recognize one's repressed emotions and overcome the propensity to project these onto others and find fault with them (Hodges, 1986).

These processes would extend to the management of society and various institutions within it as well, where one in authority should be able to recognize the conflicting needs of his or her constituents, subordinates, co-workers, family members, and so on, of subgroups, and in the case of international politics, of other cultures and to separate these from one's own needs and priorities. In other words, one would recognize multiplicity, a feature of both relativistic and dialectical thinking. Finally, to the extent that one has been able to recognize one's own needs and make decisions accordingly – in effect, take responsibility for his or her actions – he or she will be able to look back on his or her life without great regret (Erikson, 1968). Part of this involves recognizing that what would satisfy an adequate life review for one person might not for another.

## Recognition of contextual embeddedness

Related to the recognition of individuality is the ability to place judgments in a broader context, including, for example, the developmental context (maturity of the person with the problem, life tasks, the sociohistorical context, ethnic groups, gender, etc.), and to take into consideration the ways that the judgment can facilitate adaptation to his context (or change the context, if that is the desired goal). Regarding individual development and advising others, wisdom would involve taking into account the developmental level of the person with the problem, the circumstances of his or her life, and/or the opportunities afforded by the culture at that time in history, accepted ways of acting, and so on, in appraising possibilities for action. Regarding spiritual development, many people choose to believe in a way that suits the religious background of their cultural or ethnic group; however, if unable to do so, or in advising others, those who are wise would accept the validity of a plurality of choices for religious worship for themselves and others, due to differing sociocultural constructions as well as individual choice. Furthermore, a high degree of spiritual development should go hand in hand with tolerance of cultural differences in expressing spirituality. Mature spiritual development would involve some reflection on the cultural foundations of those beliefs.

Regarding management of society, to be an effective manager, one would need to be able to represent the conflicting perspectives that arise from dealing with individuals and peoples of different ethnic and sociocultural backgrounds in order to solve problems and resolve disputes effectively.

## Effective interaction with others

Recognition of multiplicity and of the interdependence of all phenomena – for which a prerequisite is the ability to recognize distinctions between subject and object (i.e., to be aware of one's projections) – is a necessary prerequisite for wisdom. In order to *act* on such recognition, however, to make effective intrapersonal and interpersonal decisions in one's own life, to adequately advise others, and to manage the affairs of society, one must be able to successfully negotiate and/or resolve the conflicts that arise between the perspectives of self and other.

Kramer (1989a) presented a model of how dialectical thinking could facilitate the development of healthy interpersonal interaction patterns using the area of marital interaction as an illustration. The processes could be generalized to other interpersonal relationships, however, and are pertinent to interpersonal development. Dialectical thinking may facilitate the development of healthy interaction patterns in at least four ways:

1. by fostering an awareness and understanding of multiple levels of communication and their interrelationships;
2. by fostering flexible (i.e., nonpolarized) role prescriptions;
3. by fostering cooperative conflict resolution strategies; and
4. by fostering a recognition of and ability to negotiate the often difficult processes of change and development.

An awareness of any or all of these processes would facilitate solving problems in one's own life or advising and guiding others. Here, the author will focus on the conflict resolution model, which was proposed by Kramer (1989b).

Kramer (1989b) argued that those reasoning absolutely – that is, nonrelativistically and nondialectically – are likely to isolate the cause of conflict in one individual, either the self or other, that is, to dichotomize blame. Depending on whether the attributions are coupled with a high or low sense of efficacy, such an attribution could result in either submission or coercion, both of which have deleterious effects on the resolution of conflict: submission because it fosters repression of feelings, which might erupt in volatile behavior, and coercion because it typically results in escalation of conflict.

Thus, neither of these strategies allows for constructive interaction and subsequent growth. In contrast, the person thinking relativistically is likely to make attributions to opposing points of view or to unpredictable circumstances. He or she might, however, have low efficacy expectations due to the belief in unpredictability and chance and to the belief that each person has an inherent right to his or her own point of view without infringement by others. The conflict resolution strategy that is likely to ensue is one of detachment, or laissez-faire. The problem with this strategy is that it limits possibilities for interaction or growth. It is constructive in that it may be accepting of the other's perspective (and fosters wisdom in this sense) but limiting in that it does not provide a vehicle for resolving differences of opinion and to develop a mutually agreed-on perspective.

Dialectical reasoning is likely to result in attributions based upon organismic, systems perspectives; that is, the conflict is due to the interaction, or relationship among the members, or to tensions between or among internal and/or external sources. Efficacy expectations are likely to be high due to the belief that conflict acts as the impetus for growth through a synthesis of contradiction. Thus, the conflict resolution strategy likely to be chosen is that of *cooperation*. The person thinking in this way would not only be able to make more effective decisions in his or her own life but could more effectively provide guidance to others who are trying to do so and would more effectively serve in positions of authority or leadership.

## Change

A fourth skill involved in wisdom is the recognition of possibilities for change in subject and object and the evolution of social systems. At least within the bounds of an organismic framework, the whole point of resolving problems is to move the person, relationship, or group forward – to produce development, or at least change. Forms of thinking that allow for the possibility of change will better equip the person to do so. Relativistic and dialectical thinking allow for the recognition that one can transcend the rigid characterization of other people and groups as fitting into traits and recognize the primacy of change over stability. Relativistic and dialectical thinking both foster the view that one is in a constant state of change, although dialectical thinking goes a step further to propose that contradiction and conflicts inherent in all people, interactions, and events provide the impetus for growth as one resolves conflicts (via synthesis of contradiction) (Kramer, 1989c). Thus, the person thinking in this manner will be better equipped to recognize and nurture the potential for change in the self, others, and groups.

## Attention to both cognition and affect

Finally, for *any* of these processes to come about, one must be able to consider both cognitive and affective dimensions of experience. Regarding the self, one must be able to recognize the affective conflicts that motivate one's decisions, one's actions, and one's interactions with others and to integrate these with rational considerations. It is important to recognize these conflicts and motivations (i.e., one's projections) before advising others. Regarding the management of societal institutions, the recognition of affective conflicts may be particularly relevant in today's nuclear age in relationship to international politics. An example by Bopp (1989) is illustrative. His analysis of why the world sits on the brink of disaster suggests that it is a by-product of the failure of the superpowers to attain "wisdom." He showed how dissociation of affect from conscious awareness and corresponding projection has influenced the current state of international affairs, where our very existence is threatened with nuclear holocaust. According to Bopp, our leaders are engaged in a battle against their projected selves – in the form of the competing superpower (i.e., the "Evil" Empire) – as are theirs against us. Since it would require a transcendence of such polarization and the development of dialectical modes of thinking to alleviate this specter, the ability to prevent nuclear holocaust will certainly require nothing less than "wisdom."

Bopp presented a rationale for how the intimate relationship and its effect on intrapsychic development can form the prototype for understanding international affairs and even suggests ways in which the two superpowers, the Soviet Union and the United States, stand in intimate relationship with one another. Awareness of this "intimacy" would be a first step toward a truce. The beauty of wisdom would lie in the awareness that all human systems, all phenomena, are "intimately" related. As one elderly woman interviewed in a study conducted by the author noted: "We are all interlaced; we are all gonna sink or swim together" (Kramer, 1987b, p. 127). Intimacy involves threats to one's boundaries, it makes us sometimes painfully aware (through its mirror) of rejected parts of the self, it challenges us to grow, and gives us pain as well as joy. Thus, it helps us become wiser. As such, wisdom involves the ability to experience and participate in the broad spectrum of normal human experiences, good and bad, cognitive and affective – and to accept the uncertainties, imperfections, and limitations that lie therein. In addition, perhaps there is nothing more intimate than spirituality, if "God" (however construed) is viewed as love and as such never ceases to be with and love the individual – whether good or bad, beautiful or ugly, healthy or sick, proud or shameful, arrogant or humiliated – and, many would argue, is the source of all other love, compassion, and intimacy (Hodges, 1986).

### Conclusions, implications, and unresolved issues

The changes that have issued forth from the past decade of inquiry in the area of adult "cognitive" development have altered the ways in which we go about studying aging – the questions posed, the methods used, and what is considered admissible evidence influence the conclusions drawn. As we have altered our models of aging in the last 10 years, we are finding increasing evidence of progressive psychological adaptation in the second half of life. Consequently, we have been able to shift attention away from cognitive models based on the accumulation of abstract information and modes of knowing toward those that are integrated with real-life, affectively imbued experience. It is not surprising, then, that we are finding significant relationships between age and such wisdom-related processes as relativistic and dialectical reasoning, awareness of contradictory affective experiences within the self, supplantation of immature coping mechanisms such as projection and intellectualization with more mature ones that allow the integration of polarities within the self, thereby enabling one to more effectively perceive, tolerate, and empathically respond to the affective expressions of others as well. These are precisely the areas in which life experience will provide opportunities for growth. In sum, we are finding that there are, indeed, wise old people.

In this chapter, wisdom was seen as operating in five functional capacities and involves the application of relativistic and dialectical modes of thinking. Relativistic and dialectical thinking serves to facilitate these functions through the recognition of individuality, context, possibilities for change and growth, and both cognition and affect and by allowing for effective interpersonal skills. Wisdom, whether it functions to facilitate the resolution of dilemmas in one's own life, advise others, manage social institutions, or engage in life review and spiritual growth, appears to involve, at its core, an integration of cognition and affect. All of the models place wisdom in the domain of human affairs and relationships, which clearly cannot be considered affectively neutral domains. Not surprisingly, then, most of the models of wisdom incorporate an affective dimension, including such characteristics as compassion and empathy, and some specifically cite the integration of cognition and affect as being at the heart of wisdom (Clayton & Birren, 1980; Holliday & Chandler, 1986). The present chapter elucidated some of the ways in which "cognitive" processes associated with wisdom are reciprocally related to affective processes.

Research on the relation between cognition and affect supports this view. In order for genuine compassion or empathy, both of which are associated with wisdom, to occur, one must be able to recognize one's own projections and attempt to move beyond these in order to be receptive to the unique emotions of others. Relativistic and dialectical reasoning would likely evolve as the result of the obstacles caused by one's projections in order to become aware of and resolve them. At the same time, relativistic and dialectical thinking cannot flourish until one can be aware of and attempt to lay aside one's projections. Thus, these modes of thinking would also be necessary for the development of mature empathy and compassion, and vice versa. In order for either the cognitive or affective processes that are associated with wisdom to develop, it appears to be essential that cognition and affect are coordinated.

The story of Solomon is often cited as an example of a wise judgment. Many consider him wise because of his use of paradoxical "logic" in suggesting that the coveted infant be cut in half and each half given to one of the women who claimed him as her own. The present author does not dispute this. However, it is her view that the wisdom of his solution goes beyond that and beyond the solution itself – because the solution assumed that there is one correct way for a mother to react and that only the biological mother would react that way, both questionable assumptions that counter the relativism attributed to wisdom – rather Solomon's wisdom lies in his recognition that emotion must be taken into account in the solution of the problem, a recognition that escapes all too many researchers and laypeople alike.

Taranto (1989) concluded that a characteristic shared by all models of wisdom is the "acceptance of limitation," including the limitations of knowledge, of finitude, of self, and so on. Yet, according to Taranto, such awareness of limitation does not alone produce wisdom. In addition, wisdom involves a "response to limitation." In the present view, one could cite as one such limitation the affective constraints placed on experience via our human natures (although these "constraints" also produce advantages). Awareness of these affective constraints would enable us to attend to our emotions, thus fostering affect–cognition integration. Yet, as Taranto stated, it is important not just to be aware of such limitations, for one must respond to these as well. For example, one might decide to exploit the limitations of another. Few would classify such exploitation under the heading of wisdom. Rather, the awareness of limitation would be coupled with the ability to act compassionately and empathically, requiring a high degree of cognitive–affective integration.

There are certain issues as yet to be resolved, however, particularly concerning wisdom's relationship to other forms of psychological adaptation, such as ego development. If one of the unique facets of wisdom – that which separates it from other forms of intelligence – is the ability to perceive essences, to be in touch with the self (Holliday and Chandler, 1986), then these require a good deal of personality integration. How do these processes differ from ego development?

The ability to coordinate cognition, affect, and reflection might be seen as a synthesizing function of the ego. Someone at Loevinger's (1976) higher stages of ego development would likely manifest wisdom because such a person has been able to reflect on societal conventions, accept the polarities within the self, and make realistic decisions that foster both individuality and social responsibility. Furthermore, it is unlikely that such development would take place in the absence of integrated conscious and unconscious functioning. Current conceptions of wisdom – the present one included – although having identified wisdom-related processes that are distinct from conceptions of social and practical intelligence, have yet to differentiate clearly this construct from integrated personality functioning.

Perhaps ego development would represent a necessary condition for the development of wisdom, whereas wisdom itself represents an ability to perceive particular kinds of social realities and make particular kinds of judgments, such as those described in Holliday and Chandler's (1986) unique wisdom dimensions. There may be people who have well-integrated personalities who are not particularly attuned to such facets of human behavior. Furthermore, the same person might be considered wise by one person and unwise by another, depending on *that particular person's needs and the fit between his or her needs and the sensitivities of the "wise" (or unwise) person in question.* Thus, whether one can function in the advisory role of wisdom would be relative to the situation. A wise person would in all likelihood recognize that he or she cannot be of benefit to everyone – a further recognition of "limitations." Recognition of this would be adaptive in relinquishing control.

Furthermore, if wisdom involves an integration of cognition, affect, and reflectivity – and requires good personality integration for its development – then it is indeed a *highly developed* form of functioning, to which few may aspire, let alone achieve, which may account for the relatively small proportion of people at the dialectical level of thinking. Individual differences in such development, as well as the processes fostering such development (such as high affect intensity), represent an important concern for future work. These issues are debatable and hopefully will generate much debate. They are issues that, in the present author's opinion, will have to be addressed. At minimum, integrated personality functioning would be added to the list of capacities necessary for wisdom to take place.

Furthermore, each of the characteristics associated with wisdom, such as the ability to tolerate multiple viewpoints, attend to context, and respond empathically and compassionately, most likely represents a dynamic system of functions in and of itself with a complex developmental history of its own. Since the field of wisdom is in its infancy, it is premature to expect that the intricacies of wisdom's developmental trajectory will have been worked out. However, traditions in the areas of social-cognitive, personality, and affective development have generated numerous controversies centering on the development of any one of the hypothesized component processes of wisdom, including ego and personality development (Kegan, 1979; Levinson, 1978; Loevinger, 1979; McCrae & Costa, 1984), relativistic and/or dialectical thinking (Baltes et al., in press; Basseches, 1989b; Irwin & Sheese, 1989; Kramer, 1983, 1989c; Pascual-Leone, 1983; Rybash et al., 1986), and affective development (see Malatesta, 1981). The enormously complex task of charting out how these developing functions interact to produce wisdom is a task that will undoubtedly generate further controversy, and which awaits us.

Congruent with the organismic view adopted in the present chapter, the author sees both cognitive and affective systems as evolving over time via the interplay of contradiction (i.e., obstacles countered in one's experience) and its resolution (Kramer, 1989c; Kramer & Haviland, 1989). In terms of the relationship of cognitive and affective systems to one another, they would be relatively undifferentiated in infancy and would become differentiated over time to become increasingly hierarchically integrated. Their integrated, coordinated functioning would become particularly crucial to development from adolescence on (Haviland & Kramer, 1989; Kramer & Haviland, 1989).

This chapter has focused primarily on wisdom as an individual development.

However, individual development cannot be separated from the sociohistorical context in which it evolves (Baltes et al., 1984; Meacham, 1989). First, since wisdom enables one to act in self-related, interpersonal, and advisory functions, wisdom is a capacity that is shared among individuals. Second, Clayton (1982) argued that wisdom should be geared toward the solution of problems confronting society. In this vein, the present author would like to suggest that wisdom might be a characteristic of societies as well as individuals. One might conceive of societies as being more or less wise. In this sense, one might even question whether older societies, including so-called primitive ones, might be characterized by a wisdom that is lacking in younger societies such as our own. An analysis of the mourning processes involved in separation by Marris (1974) is a telling example.

Marris identified common mourning processes found in bereavement, urban renewal projections and relocation, and loss of traditional social structures. Interestingly, although some of the more technologically advanced Western cultures revealed an ignorance of the importance of mourning, sadness, and depression to continued growth (via their belief that technology can and should alleviate all suffering), the primitive cultures had highly conventionalized rituals and traditions for incorporating such grief processes into concrete experience, with no added guilt placed on the mourner by others for expressing his or her grief. In order for a society to conventionalize such processes as mourning, it must have an astute understanding of the importance of attending to affective experience. Otherwise, development cannot proceed. One would expect less dissociation of affect from cognition in such cultures and, therefore, greater possibility for the development of wisdom among its members.

In contrast, one might ask whether our own young culture – adolescent in years at most – may have internalized the dictates of absolute and intrasystemic thinking that characterizes adolescent thought and counters the thought processes that are considered wise. In doing so, it may have failed to evolve wisdom as a culture, thus making it harder to impart wisdom to those individuals socialized within its bounds. Bopp's (1989) analysis of how our leaders project their disowned hostility onto leaders of the competing superpower – and vice versa – supports this view. Some other Western cultures, which are much older than our own, also appear to have adopted a polarized mode of thinking, which again points to the issue that age alone is not sufficient to bring about maturity. Rather, it is the ability to reflect on accumulated experience, to confront obstacles, and to integrate cognition and affect – to make unconscious emotional material conscious and become aware of one's projections – that brings about maturity and hence wisdom.

In conclusion, research indicates that cognitive processes such as those described in the literature on wisdom cannot be neatly separated from affective processes. Thus, if any one conclusion could be drawn from the present chapter, it is that wisdom is not simply a form of intelligence, or cognition. It is a perspective on reality that can be developed in a meaningful sense (i.e., enacted in the real relationships with self, with other, with society, and with a spiritual power) only if one has evolved a relatively well-balanced personality, where conscious and unconscious processes do not stand in powerful opposition and where one has an understanding of relationship. An implication of this conclusion is that the preoccupation in our field with mechanistic models – models that separate cognition from affect, attempt to study "pure" cognitive processes apart from real-life motivations, intentions, and experiences, and rely heavily on computer models of intelligence – results in a distorted view of human cognition that for decades prevented us from seeing wise old people (see also Holliday & Chandler, 1986; Meacham, 1983). If wisdom involves an integration of cognition and affect, then it also represents a useful arena for exploring our assumptions about the relationship between cognition and affect in human adaptation and questioning the models and metaphors that have dominated psychological thought about human behavior for the past century.

### Note

1 The issue of whether the dialectic constitutes a unique logic is debatable, and the use of the term here reflects that of Clayton's, not the present author's. For a discussion of this issue, the reader is referred elsewhere (e.g., Basseches, 1989b; Kosok, 1976; Kramer, 1989b; Piaget, 1980; Popper, 1963).

### References

Aldous, J. (1978). *Family careers: developmental change in families.* New York: John Wiley & Sons.

Baltes, P. B., Dittmann-Kohli, F., & Dixon, R. A. (1984). New perspectives on the development of intelligence in adulthood: toward a dual-process conception and a model of selective optimization with compensation. In P. B. Baltes & O. G. Brim, Jr. (Eds.), *Life-span development and behavior* (Vol. 6, pp. 33–76). New York: Academic Press

Baltes, P. B., Smith, J., Staudinger, U. M., & Sowarka, D. (in press). Wisdom: one facet of successful aging? In M. Perlmutter (Ed.), *Later life potential.* Washington, DC: Gerontological Society of America.

Basseches, M. (1980). Dialectical schemata: a framework for the empirical study of the development of dialectical thinking. *Human Development, 23,* 400–421.

Basseches, M. (1989a). Toward a constructive–developmental understanding of the dialectics of individuality and irrationality. In D. A. Kramer & M. J. Bopp (Eds.), *Transformation in clinical and developmental psychology* (pp. 188–209). New York: Springer-Verlag.

Basseches, M. (1989b). A response to Irwin and Kramer. In M. L. Commons, J. D. Sinnott, F. A. Richards, & C. Armon (Eds.), *Beyond formal operations II: comparisons and applications of adolescent and adult developmental models* (pp. 161–178). New York: Praeger.

Bateson, G. (1972). Double bind, 1969. In G. Bateson (Ed.), *Steps to an ecology of mind.* New York: Ballantine Books.

Berg, S. A., & Sternberg, R. J. (1985). A triarchic theory of intellectual development during adulthood. *Developmental Review, 5,* 334–370.

Blanchard-Fields, F. (1986). Reasoning on social dilemmas varying in emotional saliency: an adult developmental perspective. *Psychology and Aging, 1,* 323–333.

Bopp, M. J. (1985). Contradiction and its resolution among the psychotherapies: results of a preliminary investigation. In G. R. Weeks (Ed.), *Promoting change to a paradoxical therapy* (pp. 271–301). Homewood, IL: Dow Jones-Irwin.

Bopp, M. J. (1989). The nuclear crisis: insights from metatheory and clinical change theories. In D. A. Kramer & M. J. Bopp (Eds.), *Transformation in clinical and developmental psychology* (pp. 234–250). New York: Springer-Verlag.

Bray, D. W., & Howard, A. (1983). The AT&T longitudinal studies of managers. In K. W. Schaie (Ed.), *Longitudinal studies of adult psychological development* (pp. 266–312). New York: The Guilford Press.

Brent, S. B., & Watson, D. (1980, November). *Aging and wisdom: individual and collective aspects.* Paper presented at the Third Annual Meeting of the Gerontological Society, in San Diego.

Camp, C. J., & McKitrick, L. A. (1989). The dialectics of forgetting and remembering across the adult lifespan. In D. A. Kramer & M. J. Bopp (Eds.), *Transformation in clinical and developmental psychology* (pp. 169–187). New York: Springer-Verlag.

Cavanaugh, J. C., & Morton, K. R. (1989). Contextualism, naturalistic inquiry, and the need for new science: a rethinking of everyday memory aging and childhood sexual abuse. In D. A. Kramer & M. J. Bopp (Eds.), *Transformation in clinical and developmental psychology* (pp. 89–114). New York: Springer-Verlag.

Chandler, M. (1987). The Othello effect. Essay on the emergence and eclipse of skeptical doubt. *Human Development, 30,* 137–159.

Chinen, A. B. (1985). Fairy tales and transpersonal development in later life. *Journal of Transpersonal Psychology, 17,* 99–122.

Clayton, V. (1976). *A multidimensional scaling analysis of the concept of wisdom.* Unpublished doctoral dissertation, the University of Southern California.

Clayton, V. (1982). Wisdom and intelligence: the nature and function of knowledge in the later years. *International Journal of Aging and Human Development, 15,* 315–321.

Clayton, V., & Birren, J. E. (1980). The development of wisdom across the life-span: a reexamination of an ancient topic. In P. B. Baltes & O. G. Brim, Jr. (Eds.), *Life-span development and behavior* (Vol. 3, pp. 103–135). New York: Academic Press.

Damon, W. (1979). Why study social cognitive development? *Human Development, 22,* 206–211.

Dittmann-Kohli, F. (1984a, September). Interpersonal and self-related knowledge as domains of adult intelligence: aspects of practical wisdom. Paper presented in *Intellectual functioning, social structure and aging,* at the National Institute on Aging, Bethesda, Maryland.

Dittmann-Kohli, F. (1984b). Weisheit als moegliches Ergebnis der Intelligenzwicklung im Erwachsenenalter. *Sprache und Kognition, 2,* 112–132.

Dittmann-Kohli, F., & Baltes, P. B. (in press). Toward a neofunctionalist conception of adult intellectual development: wisdom as a prototypical case of intellectual growth. In C. Alexander & E. Langer (Eds.), *Beyond formal operations: alternative endpoints to human development.* New York: Oxford University Press.

Dixon, R. A., Kramer, D. A., & Baltes, P. B. (1985). Intelligence: its life-span development. In B. B. Wolman (Ed.), *Handbook of intelligence: theories, measurements, and applications* (pp. 301–350). New York: John Wiley & Sons.

Erikson, E. H. (1968). *Identity: youth and crisis.* New York: W. W. Norton.

Gould, R. L. (1978). *Transformation: growth and change in adult life.* New York: Simon & Schuster.

Haviland, J. M., & Kramer, D. A. (1989). Affect–cognition relations in an adolescent diary I: the case of Anne Frank. *Human Development,* accepted with revisions.

Haviland, J. M., & Walker-Andrews, A. (1987). *The origins of affect.* Unpublished manuscript, Rutgers University.

Hodges, A. G. (1986). *Jesus: an interview across time.* New York: Bantam Books.

Holliday, S. G., & Chandler, M. J. (1986). *Wisdom: explorations in adult competence.* Basel, Switzerland: Karger.

Irion, J. C., & Blanchard-Fields, F. (1987). A cross-sectional comparison of adaptive coping in adulthood. *Journal of Gerontology, 42,* 502–504.

Irwin, R. R., & Sheese, R. L. (1989). Problems in the proposal for a "stage" of dialectical thinking. In M. L. Commons, J. D. Sinnott, F. A. Richards, & C. Armon (Eds.), *Beyond formal operations II: comparisons and applications of adolescent and adult developmental models* (pp. 113–132). New York: Praeger.

Isen, A. M. (1989). Affect and automaticity. In J. Uleman & J. Bargh (Eds.), *Unintended thoughts* (pp. 124–152). New York: Guilford Press.

Jaques, E. (1970). *Work, creativity, and social justice.* London: Heinemann.

Jung, C. G. (1958). Commentary on "The secret of the golden flower." In V. S. de Laszlo (Ed.), *Psyche and symbol: a selection from the writings of C. G. Jung* (pp. 302–351). Garden City, NY: Doubleday.

Kahlbaugh, P. E. (1989). William James's pragmatism: A clarification of the contextual world view. In D. A. Kramer & M. J. Bopp (Eds.), *Transformation in clinical and developmental psychology* (pp. 73–88). New York: Springer-Verlag.

Kegan, R. G. (1979). The evolving self: a process conception for ego psychology. *The Counseling Psychologist, 8,* 5–33.

Kelly, G. A. (1955). *The psychology of personal constructs.* New York: W. W. Norton.

Kosok, M. (1976). The systematization of dialectical logic for the study of development and change. *Human Development, 19,* 325–350.

Kramer, D. A. (1983). Post-formal operations? A need for further conceptualization. *Human Development, 26,* 91–105.

Kramer, D. A. (1987a, May). *Toward an organismic conception of the lifespan.* Paper presented at the Seventeenth Annual Meetings of the Jean Piaget Society, in Philadelphia.

Kramer, D. A. (1987b). Cognition and aging: the emergence of a new tradition. In P. Silverman (Ed.), *Modern pioneers: an interdisciplinary view of the aged* (pp. 114–132). Bloomington, IN: Indiana University Press.

Kramer, D. A. (1987c). *Relativistic and dialectical reasoning: consistencies and inconsistencies in development.* Paper presented at the annual Entwicklungspsychologie Kongress, September, in Bern, Switzerland.

Kramer, D. A. (1989a). Change and stability in marital interaction patterns: a developmental model. In D. A. Kramer & M. J. Bopp (Eds.), *Transformation in clinical and developmental psychology* (pp. 210–233). New York: Springer-Verlag.

Kramer, D. A. (1989b). A developmental framework for understanding conflict resolution processes. In J. D. Sinnott (Ed.), *Everyday problem solving in adulthood* (pp. 133–152). New York: Praeger.

Kramer, D. A. (1989c). Development of an awareness of contradiction across the lifespan and the question of post formal operations. In M. L. Commons, J. D. Sinnott, F. A. Richards, & C. Armon (Eds.), *Beyond formal operations II: comparisons and applications of adolescent and adult developmental models* (pp. 133–159). New York: Praeger.

Kramer, D. A., & Bopp, M. J. (1989). Introduction. In D. A. Kramer & M. J. Bopp (Eds.), *Transformation in clinical and developmental psychology* (pp. 1–22). New York: Springer-Verlag.

Kramer, D. A., Goldston, R. B., & Kahlbaugh, P. E. (1989). *Age, affect intensity, and dialectical beliefs.* Submitted manuscript.

Kramer, D. A., & Haviland, J. M. (1989). *Affect–cognition relations in an adolescent diary II: the case of Vivienne.* Submitted manuscript.

Kramer, D. A., Melchior, J., & Levine, C. (1989). *Age-relevance of content material and reasoning about interpersonal dilemmas.* Submitted manuscript.

Kramer, D. A., & Woodruff, D. S. (1986). Relativistic and dialectical thought in three adult age groups. *Human Development, 29,* 280–290.

Labouvie-Vief, G. (1980). Beyond formal operations: uses and limits of pure logic in life-span development. *Human Development, 23,* 141–161.

Labouvie-Vief, G. (1981). Proactive and reactive aspects of constructivism: growth and aging in life-span perspective. In R. M. Lerner & N. A. Busch-Rossnagel (Eds.), *Individuals as producers of their development: a life-span perspective* (pp. 197–230). New York: Academic Press.

Labouvie-Vief, G. (1982). Dynamic development and mature autonomy. A theoretical prologue. *Human Development, 25,* 161–196.

Labouvie-Vief, G., & Chandler, M. J. (1977). Cognitive development and life-span developmental theory: idealistic versus contextual perspectives. In P. B. Baltes (Ed.), *Life-span development and behavior.* New York: Academic Press.

Labouvie-Vief, G., Hakim-Larson, J., Devoe, M., & Schoeberlein, S. (1989). Emotions and self-regulation: a life-span view. *Human Development, 32,* 279–299.

Labouvie-Vief, G., Hakim-Larson, J., & Hobart, C. J. (1987). Age, ego level, and the life-span development of coping and defense processes. *Psychology and Aging, 2,* 286–293.

Lerner, R. M., & Kauffman, M. B. (1985). The concept of development in contextualism. *Developmental Review, 5,* 309–333.

Levinson, D. J. (1978). *The seasons of a man's life.* New York: Ballantine Books.

Loevinger, J. (1976). *Ego development: conceptions and theories.* San Francisco: Jossey-Bass.

Loevinger, J. (1979). Reply to Kegan. *The Counseling Psychologist, 8,* 39–40.

McCrae, R. R., & Costa, P. T., Jr. (1984). *Emerging lives, enduring dispositions: personality in adulthood.* Boston: Little, Brown.

Malatesta, C. Z. (1981). Affective development over the lifespan: involution or growth? *Merrill-Palmer Quarterly, 27,* 145–173.

Marris, P. (1974). *Loss and change.* New York: Pantheon Books.

Meacham, J. A. (1983). Wisdom and the context of knowledge: knowing that one doesn't know. In D. Kuhn & J. A. Meacham (Eds.), *On the development of developmental psychology* (pp. 111–134). Basel, Switzerland: Karger.

Meacham, J. A. (1989). Discovering the social-cultural context of research: listening to and learning from research participants. In D. A. Kramer & M. J. Bopp (Eds.), *Transformation in clinical and developmental psychology* (pp. 136–153). New York: Springer-Verlag.

Mergler, N. L., & Goldstein, M. D. (1983). Why are there old people? *Human Development, 26,* 72–90.

Miller, A. (1981). *Prisoners of childhood: the drama of the gifted child and the search for the true self.* New York: Basic Books.

Moody, H. R. (1983, November). *Wisdom and the search for meaning.* Paper presented at the 36th Annual Meetings of the Gerontological Society of America, in San Francisco.

Murray, F. B. (1983). Cognition of physical and social events. In W. F. Overton (Ed.), *The relationship between social and cognitive development* (pp. 91–101). Hillsdale, NJ: Erlbaum.

Nichols, M. P. (1987). *The self in the system: expanding the limits of family therapy.* New York: Brunner/Mazel.

Overton, W. F. (1984). World views and their influence on psychological theory and research: Kuhn–Lakatos–Laudan. In H. W. Reese (Ed.), *Advances in child development and behavior* (Vol. 18, pp. 191–226). New York: Academic Press.

Pascual-Leone, J. (1983). Growing into human maturity: toward a metasubjective theory of adult stages. In P. B. Baltes & O. Brim (Eds.), *Life-span development and behavior* (Vol. 5, pp. 117–156). New York: Academic Press.

Pepper, S. C. (1942). *World hypotheses.* Berkeley, CA: University of California Press.

Perry, W. G. (1970). *Forms of intellectual and ethical development in the college years: a scheme.* New York: Rinehart & Winston.

Person, E. S. (1988). *Dreams of love and fateful encounters: the power of romantic passion.* New York: W. W. Norton.

Piaget, J. (1980). *Experiments in contradiction.* Chicago: University of Chicago Press.

Poon, L. W. (1985). Differences in human memory with aging: nature, causes, and clinical implications. In J. E. Birren & K. W. Schaie (Eds.), *Handbook of the psychology of aging* (2nd ed., pp. 427–462). New York: Van Nostrand Reinhold.

Popper, K. R. (1963). What is dialectic? In K. R. Popper (Ed.), *Conjectures and refutations: the growth of scientific knowledge* (pp. 312–335). London: Routledge & Kegan Paul.

Roberts, P., & Newton, P. M. (1987). Levinsonian studies of women's adult development. *Psychology and Aging, 2,* 154–163.

Roodin, P. A., Rybash, J., & Hoyer, W. J. (1984). Affect in adult cognition: a constructivist view of moral thought and action. In C. Z. Malatesta & C. E. Izard (Eds.), *Emotion in adult development* (pp. 297–316). Beverly Hills, CA: Sage Publishers.

Rybash, J. M., Hoyer, W. J., & Roodin, P. A. (1986). *Adult cognition and aging: developmental changes in processing, knowing and thinking.* New York: Pergamon Press.

Scarf, M. (1987). *Intimate partners: patterns in love and marriage.* New York: Random House.

Schaie, K. W. (1977–1978). Toward a stage theory of adult cognitive development. *International Journal of Aging and Human Development, 25,* 423–429.

Sinnott, J. D. (1984). Postformal reasoning: the relativistic stage. In M. L. Commons, F. A. Richards, & C. Armon (Eds.), *Beyond formal operations: late adolescent and adult cognitive development* (pp. 298–325). New York: Praeger.

Sinnott, J. D. (1989). Changing the known; knowing the changing: the General Systems Theory metatheory as a conceptual framework to study complex change and complex thoughts. In D. A. Kramer & M. J. Bopp (Eds.), *Transformation in clinical and developmental psychology* (pp. 51–69). New York: Springer-Verlag.

Sowarka, D., & Heckhausen, J. (1985, November). *Laypersons's knowledge and beliefs about life-span development: wisdom as a guidepost for developmental directionality.* Paper presented at the Thirty-Eighth Annual Meetings of the Gerontological Society, in New Orleans.

Sternberg, R. J. (1985). Implicit theories of intelligence, creativity, and wisdom. *Journal of Personality and Social Psychology, 49,* 607–627.

Taranto, M. A. (1989). Facets of wisdom: a theoretical synthesis. *International Journal of Aging and Human Development, 29,* 1–21.

Vaillant, G. E. (1977). *Adaptation to life: how the best and brightest came of age.* Boston: Little, Brown.

*Part V*

**Integration of approaches and viewpoints**

14    The elements of wisdom:
      overview and integration

*James E. Birren and Laurel M. Fisher*

The purpose of this chapter is to provide an overview of the present volume
and to begin to explore and integrate the use and concept of the term *wisdom*.
In reviewing the preceding chapters, I find it refreshing to see a collection of
analyses about wisdom. The long neglect by psychologists of the subject matter
of wisdom is a curious fact that itself warrants attention, and it is here that
we will begin.

The present authors reviewed histories of psychology, handbooks, overviews
of psychology as a science, major textbooks, and selected works (e.g., Kantor,
1959; Koch, 1959) and determined that, indeed, the topic of wisdom was long
neglected in psychology. For example, the massive handbook of general psychology edited by Wolman (1973) does not index the subject of wisdom: There is
no mention of wisdom in the 45 chapters and over a thousand pages of text that
describe the content of psychology. On the other hand, one of the elements of
wisdom, reasoning, is well represented in selections of materials on experimental psychology (e.g., Stevens, 1951; Woodworth, 1938).

Among the factors that are likely to have contributed to psychology's neglect of the study of wisdom was the association of the subject to philosophy.
This association placed it off limits to the 19th- and early 20th-century empirically minded psychologists. Behaviorism, which dominated the mid-20th
century of psychological investigation, abhorred the "mentalistic" connotations inherent in the study of wisdom. Perhaps wisdom loomed as too large
a unit or phenomenon to invite attention by self-consciously scientific psychologists. Late in the 20th century, psychology appears to be more relaxed,
and the movements or schools of thought within psychology have diminished
in their dominance over what is an acceptable or unacceptable research matter. In this new climate, wisdom appears to be attracting attention, and investigators are moving into what was once off-limits territory.

### Definition of wisdom

It should not be assumed that the treatment of wisdom in the current volume
implies that psychology has introduced a new concept into human discourse.

317

The *Oxford English Dictionary,* which traces the evolution of word usage, indicates that the word *wisdom* was commonly used in Old English. The term appeared before the year 1000, and its roots appear to lie in the Teutonic languages. The summary definition of *wisdom* is as follows:

capacity of judging rightly in matters relating to life and conduct; soundness of judgement in the choice of means and ends; sometimes, less strictly, sound sense, especially in practical affairs: opposed to folly. (*OED,* 1933, pp. 191–192)

Historically, wisdom has been personified, almost always, as female in character. Yet it also has been viewed as a characteristic of divine nature, as in "the wisdom of the Father." Historical use of the term *wisdom* links it with knowledge, enlightenment, learning, philosophy, and science. Wisdom gives rise to wise habits and modes of action. Being *wise* implies that the individual is capable of exercising sound judgment:

capable of judging truly concerning what is right or fitting and disposed to acting accordingly; having the ability to perceive and adopt the best means for accomplishing an end; characterized by good sense and prudence. (*OED,* 1933, p. 193)

There is little doubt that the use of the English terms *wisdom* and *wise* has a rich tradition, as evidenced by the three pages devoted to this history in the *Oxford English Dictionary.*

## History of the term

The etymology of the words *wisdom* and *wise* suggests that they have always denoted or connoted high or elevated forms of behavior. Thus, being wise and displaying wisdom reflects forms of behavior that are admired, condoned, and encouraged. This fact suggests that wisdom is at the top of a hierarchically organized system in which wisdom is a complex compound of elements blended with experience. Over time, this blend results in superior human qualities. Later in this chapter we will attempt to examine the implicit or explicit definitions of wisdom as used by the various chapter authors. Because wisdom is a concept deeply rooted in our culture, it seems desirable first to consider the uses of the term *wisdom* in our society in comparison to those found in the scholarly analyses that comprise this book.

As noted earlier, one of the deep roots of the concept of wisdom lies in theology, which attributes wisdom to an all-powerful and all-knowing deity. The Bible contains a collection of writings known as the "wisdom literature." Not only is the "wisdom of the almighty God" expected to prevail, but the individual is expected to invite insight into God's plan insofar as he may choose to reveal and give access to the underlying wisdom of the universe. In this view, assuming that God has a pervasive plan for the universe and knows what is good for us, individuals humble themselves before God in an attempt to understand why "bad things happen to good people." Job's endurance of the calamities that befell him accompanied his conviction that an all-wise sovereign God had a plan. Thus, it is possible that these theological overtones contributed to psychologists' neglect of the study of wisdom in addition to their reluctance to deal with nonobservables and mentalistic concepts.

Just as the belief in an all-knowing deity is widespread, there is implicit in our culture a conviction that something like wisdom exists. One of the tasks of psychology is to probe, by means of research, to see if there is a phenomenon or a set of phenomena that to some degree corresponds to the cultural view of wisdom.

According to the *Encyclopedia Britannica,* we first discover the concept of wisdom in writings done in Egypt soon after 3000 B.C.; then, about 600 years later, we find writings of a vizier by the name of Ptah-hotep who attained high repute for his wisdom. His precepts were preserved in the form of a collection of proverbial sayings, which are claimed to comprise the oldest book in the world. They are a sort of ethical treatise: They discuss the nature of the good life and undertake to explain how this can be realized by the special group for whom they were written. Through the following 15 or more centuries, many other wise men arose in Egypt. Some of them left bodies of proverbs, but others were led by circumstances to consider more deeply the worth and meaning of human life. In other words, they were "compelled to think about metaphysical problems" (*Encyclopedia Britannica,* 1959, pp. 683–684) and, in that context, were thought to be wise.

## Wisdom and age

The concept wisdom contains within it a dimension that ranges, at one end, from religion and the belief that God alone possesses the ultimate wisdom to a more mundane view that practically minded administrators, leaders, business persons, and others can acquire the necessary experience and shrewdness in the conduct of daily affairs to be termed wise. In other words, people can become wise as they ripen in a particular culture. In particular, there is the notion in our culture that wisdom must ripen, and it is therefore attributed most often to older persons.

Another dimension of wisdom relevant to its attribution to older persons is the fact that it involves a changing balance between acting and reflecting. Young men are not regarded as likely persons to display wisdom because they are prone to act rather than to reflect upon the consequences of their actions. Thus, youth may have capacity to be wise but are too impelled to action to demonstrate this capacity. There is little doubt from the literature on criminal behavior and deviance that a youth is likely to act precipitously in pursuit of property and passion. The antithesis lies in wise behavior. This avenue of thought opens a door to attempts to distinguish wise and unwise behavior and between individuals regarded as wise and unwise.

Clayton (1975) defined wisdom as a construct that describes a way of thinking and an approach to life typical of the aged (see also Clayton & Birren, 1980). A pilot study by Birren (1969) examined the strategies used by successful middle-aged executives. The results indicated that as the executives matured, they noticed an increasing ability to generalize and to deal in a more detached manner or more abstractly with information in order to reach the most effective solution. Erikson, Erikson, and Kivnick (1986) also noted the element of detachment displayed in wisdom and its role in transcending limits: "Wisdom is detached concern with life itself in the face of experience, in spite of the decline of bodily and mental functions" (pp. 37–38). This research begins to link the concept of wisdom as it may be displayed in daily life to the kinds of decision strategies gained over time.

If individuals employ effective decision strategies and their reputation spreads, then as they grow older, they will be increasingly sought for advice. Thus, one avenue to the study of wisdom lies in the identification of persons who are sought for advice and presumably display the behavioral patterns that are characteristic of wisdom or wise people.

### The elements of wisdom

Setting aside the theological question of whether one can seek wisdom through prayer and searching for God's will, the everyday world offers the opportunity to examine whether and how some elders obtain the admirable quality of being wise. Our cultural background encourages us to believe that there is a ripening of qualities, a maturing and flowering in the later years that is good for the self and others. As noted earlier, the ability to be wise is often related to the ability to remain detached. However, the essence of wisdom may be a question of degree. If young men are too impulsive, cannot old men be too reticent? If young men can be foolhardy, are not the old too cautious? In addition to the ability to consider information more effectively, wisdom also requires an ability to act effectively on this information. This dimension of wisdom, the proneness to act, embraces the elements of one of the traditional fields of psychological investigation, that of drive and motivation. It can be subsumed under the older concept of *conation*.

The writings on wisdom also invariably reflect the necessity to have experience. Thus, the growth of knowledge is related to the attainment of wisdom. Knowledge in itself, however, is not enough, and one must add reasoning ability or how one uses this knowledge, to the criteria for wisdom. Thus, cognition and cognitive style, along with conation, are important and necessary elements in the attainment of wisdom.

The remaining element of behavioral processes is the emotional or affective

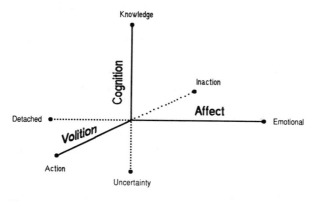

Figure 14.1. Throughout life, wisdom develops as a balance of cognition, volition (conation), and affect. The process of wisdom results in wise products, such as planning, decisions, and advice.

component. The wise person is thought to show emotional mastery such that his or her decisions are not likely to be dominated by such passions as anger or fear. However, the wise person is not entirely detached from the situation. This person will be able to maintain a reflective state of mind that generates alternative, if not novel, solutions to problems.

This excursion into the connotations and denotations of the term *wisdom* suggests that wisdom is an optimum form of behavior that humans can exhibit and that it represents a balance of elements compounded in such a way that, as individuals age, they may increasingly show behavior judged to reflect wisdom and may be thought of as wise persons.

This line of reasoning supports the idea that wisdom is a multidimensional construct, a blending of cognitive, affective, and conative elements (Figure 14.1). These are familiar domains for behavioral research, and research techniques are available for assaying such traits. Not all of the contributions in this book, however, are necessarily organized around the concept of trait. The state of the individual is also relevant as individuals pursue an optimum or wise course of action. To this should be added the context of the problem.

## The context of wisdom

Not only is the complex makeup of the traits and states of the individual who is presumed to be wise of relevance to decisions, but the context must be judged as well. Naturally occurring emergencies and crises may dictate time limits within which a solution has to be made. In addition to what the individual brings to the situation, there is also a matter of surveying what is required. Thus, although there may be elements in common between a wise general, soldier, judge, trial lawyer, teacher, and policeman, the complex set of simultaneous equations needed to be solved has different parameters. The multiple regression equation, which expresses the qualities of the individual, has to be weighted differently depending upon the context of the problem and the time constraints.

The approval of President Harry Truman to use the atomic bomb in a military operation over Japan was a weighted decision in terms of the consequences, but it had to be arrived at in a particular period of time. Whether one regards it as a wise or unwise decision depends upon the outcomes or products of the decision and the values of the persons viewing the decision. Whereas many persons may judge Truman's act to be wise and appropriate, there will be many others who regard it as being unwise and not in the best interest of humankind.

The foregoing example of President Truman's decision implies that long-standing values surround and color our evaluations of what wisdom is and who is wise. For example, we are perhaps least likely to attribute wisdom to persons of an opposite political party. Decisions to deregulate society will be thought wise by laissez-faire opponents but be ridiculed by opponents of strong governments. Particularly in a contemporary context, it is rare for persons to be termed "wise" if they are from different value orientations. These thoughts give rise to the fact that the area of value research should be coupled with that of wisdom.

In this regard, time again plays a role. One may struggle for the best long-range solution in which consequences may flow many years to the future or one may concentrate on a contemporary solution. Generally, wise persons are thought to project the consequences of their solutions far into the future: "I will plant seeds to grow in springs I will not see." Thus, what is good for the greatest number of people for the long run is presumably the most wise decision. The demand on the decision maker is to have an orientation in time that examines the past for relevant knowledge, experience, and precedent; that examines the present context of the problem to be solved; and that projects into the future the long-range effects.

It is here perhaps that we consider the products of decisions as another avenue to the study of wisdom. One may compare the products of wise judges with those of the decisions of unwise judges. This gives rise to the research question of what distinguishes or characterizes the products of wise decisions, providing that one can agree upon a class of individuals who are regarded as possessing the quality of wisdom.

**Pathways to understanding wisdom**

The foregoing suggests that individuals must have exposure to experience that will progressively accumulate in producing a wise person. In addition to the heavy value component, socialization in a particular facet of a culture may also facilitate the appearance of wisdom. Wisdom is obviously an admired, though somewhat vague, trait. It seems to have a hierarchical nature: that is, it is the optimum, ultimate expression of a blend of human qualities. This is in contrast to other elements of psychological research that often concern isolated properties, for example, of perception, memory, psychophysiological responsiveness. Wisdom seems to bring together separate components in a hierarchical manner so that we can study the highest rather than the most elemental forms of behavior. Since elementalism has not necessarily contributed to rapid advances in the last 100 years of psychological research, perhaps the study of wisdom may become a contemporary "hot" topic that can lead to accelerated insight into how behavior is organized and the conditions under which behavior becomes developed and/or disorganized.

To reach this end, many questions must be asked, including why there is the tendency to attribute wisdom to the old rather than to the young. Furthermore, there remains the question of whether there are not crucial experiences in life and critical periods that further the development of wisdom. This alludes to the often expressed view that tragedy is a substrate of experience from which wisdom can arise.

One of the tasks in refining our understanding of wisdom is identifying underlying dimensions. This is only partly embraced in the present definition of wisdom as a complex process referring to a way of thinking, feeling, and acting (cognition, affect, and conation). Given the fact that the concept of wisdom has a long history in our culture in connection with concepts in philosophy, religion, and literature, psychological research needs to come to terms with these implications. An alternative would be to replace wisdom with a more empirically tied concept, as has been done in the past with terms that connote mythical or spiritual forces. It seems, however, that psychology might profit from dealing with the cultural attributes of wisdom, much like biology might from dealing with suspected medicinal properties of natural substances.

A contradictory hypothesis is that there is no human trait that corresponds to the cultural concept of wisdom. A corollary to this hypothesis would be that wisdom is the reification of a mythical quality attributed to selected older persons in the service of an outlook on life that can be characterized as optimistic and hopeful.

Nonetheless, wisdom remains a complex concept in our terminology. Clayton (1975) attempted to explore the reference to wisdom in terms used by adults. She collected 165 descriptive words that are commonly applied to a wise person. Commonalities were not impressive, with three factors accounting for only 19% of the common variance. Conceivably, the individuals may attribute different qualities to wisdom in relation to age, sex, social class, and other characteristics. If wisdom exists like a Greek goddess on top of a mountain, there are clearly many methodological avenues to the top, with vague and shifting descriptions at the base – descriptions by villagers, who pass on the folklore of earlier generations that claim to have sighted her. Taranto points out that "wisdom as a concept appears as . . . rarified air, and while it is deemed so positive that we are inspired by it, it is a notion that is obviously difficult to grasp, let alone to hold on to" (Taranto, 1989, p. 3). Taranto concludes her excellent survey of alternative definitions of wisdom in the research literature with a linking of wisdom to personality characteristics such as patience, understanding, acceptance, interpersonal skills, and a sense of humor. More importantly, she links wisdom with the thought that wise persons recognize their own limitations and the limitations of life. This is quite different from regarding it as a sublime transcendent quality. Here wisdom is regarded as deeply rooted in the possibilities of daily life. Taranto suggests that, for some, personality style might preclude the development of wisdom, that is, if they cannot accept their limitations and the limitations of the context of problems. She expresses this view in a reference to a poem by Sara Teasdale (1945) entitled "Wisdom" (which follows). The opening suggests that wisdom arises when we cease to "beat [our] wings against the faultiness of things." This may suggest that youth throws itself against the unyielding to test its strength. With age we learn not to believe in the omniscience of self and to come to terms with our limitations.

> WISDOM
> When I have ceased to beat my wings
> Against the faultiness of things,
> And learned that compromises wait
> Behind each partly opened gate,
> When I can look life in the eyes,
> Grown, calm and very coldly wise,
> Life will have given me the truth,
> And taken in exchange my youth.*

To the present authors, wisdom seems to emerge as a dialectic that, on one pole, is bounded by the transcendence of limitations and, on the other, by their acceptance. Wisdom is tested by circumstances in which we have to decide what is changeable and what is not.

### Content analysis of the foregoing chapters

The implicit and explicit definitions of wisdom used in the present volume have been extracted and are presented in Table 14.1. In general, wisdom is seen as an integrative aspect of human life. Wisdom brings together experience, cognitive abilities, and affect in order to make good decisions at an individual and societal level. These conceptualizations of wisdom can be

*Reprinted with permission of Macmillan Publishing Company from *Collected Poems of Sara Teasdale.* © 1917, Macmillan Publishing Company, renewed 1945 by Mamie T. Wheless.

## Table 14.1. *Definitions of wisdom*

| Author (chap.) | Definition |
| --- | --- |
| Robinson (2) | *Three historical definitions*<br>*Greek:* an intellectual, moral, practical life; a life lived in conformity with truth, beauty.<br>*Christian:* a life lived in pursuit of divine, absolute truth.<br>*Contemporary:* a scientific understanding of laws governing matter in motion. |
| Csikszentmihalyi and Rathunde (3) | An evolutionary hermeneutical approach to the study of wisdom suggests that wisdom is a *holistic cognitive process*, a virtue or compelling guide for action, and a good, desirable state of being. |
| Labouvie-Vief (4) | A smooth and balanced dialogue between two sets of attributes; outer, objective, logical forms of processing (*logos*) and inner, subjective, organismic forms (*mythos*). |
| Baltes and Smith (5) | Wisdom is *expertise* in the domain of *fundamental life pragmatics*, such as, life planning or life review. It requires a rich factual knowledge about life matters, rich procedural knowledge about life problems, knowledge of different life contexts and values or priorities, and knowledge about the unpredictabilty of life. |
| Chandler and Holliday (6) | Contemporary philosophy of science limits conceptualization of wisdom to a technologic type of knowing. A more accurate description of wisdom may need well-defined, *multidimensional, prototypically organized competency descriptors*. It involves recovering age-old types of knowledge that have been forgotten. |
| Sternberg (7) | Wisdom is a *metacognitive style* plus sagacity, knowing that one does not know everything, seeking the truth to the extent that it is knowable. |
| Orwoll and Perlmutter (8) | A personologic study of wisdom suggests that wisdom is a multidimensional balance or *integration of cognition with affect*, affiliation, and social concerns. An advanced development of personality together with cognitive skills is the essence of wisdom. |
| Meacham (9) | Wisdom is an *awareness of the fallibility of knowing* and is a striving for a balance between knowing and doubting. Age is explicitly not a component of wisdom; in fact, one may lose it with age. Age is associated with changes in wisdom, from simple to profound manifestations. |
| Kitchener and Brenner (10) | Wisdom is an intellectual ability to be aware of the limitations of knowing and how it impacts solving ill-defined problems and making judgments, characteristics of *reflective judgment*. |
| Arlin (11) | Wisdom is closely associated with *problem-finding ability*, a fundamental cognitive process of reflection and judgment. |

Table 14.1. (*continued*)

| Author (chap.) | Definition |
| --- | --- |
| Pascual-Leone (12) | Wisdom is a *mode of symbolic processing* by a highly developed will. It is a dialectical integration of all aspects of the personality, including affect, will, cognition, and life experiences. |
| Kramer (13) | Wisdom is the organismic integration of relativistic and dialectical modes of thinking, affect, and reflection; a *perspective on reality* developed within interrelationships. |
| Birren and Fisher (14) | Wisdom is the *integration of the affective, conative, and cognitive aspects* of human abilities in response to life's tasks and problems. Wisdom is a balance between the opposing valences of intense emotion and detachment, action and inaction, and knowledge and doubts. It tends to increase with experience and therefore age but is not exclusively found in old age. |

placed on a continuum, with wisdom as solely a cognitive ability at one end (Baltes and Smith) and some higher integration of cognition with affect (Kramer) or other subjective forms of knowing (Labouvie-Vief) at the other. Cognitive abilities, action, and affect each appear to be a necessary but not sufficient component of wisdom for most authors in this volume.

How the authors viewed the various aspects of wisdom can be seen in Table 14.2. Most authors viewed the processes underlying wisdom as an integration or a balancing of two opposing aspects of personality – usually cognitive and emotional processes. Wisdom brings together previously separated processes of logical knowing with uncertainty and reflection. Pascual-Leone is unique in viewing the processes of wisdom as existential counsel, action of the will, and empathic feeling for others. Wisdom for Pascual-Leone can be seen through the act of giving others counsel in such a way as to impart autonomy and in the ability to feel for another person's concerns.

Generally, it is accepted that wisdom develops over time, that older people are wiser than younger people. The development of wisdom takes time to come about. The integration of cognition, affect, and action does not occur in the blink of an eye. Meacham's chapter is a notable exception to this generalization. Meacham explicitly states that wisdom does not come with age. Indeed, it is more likely that one *loses* wisdom with age. He suggests that the ability to balance facts with questions grows out of relationships with others. Meacham does, however, allow age to affect how wisdom is manifested, with simple wisdom a part of youth and profound wisdom found in later life.

Wisdom cannot be viewed apart from humans; it does not exist in a vacuum.

Examples of wisdom and definitional aspects of wisdom are set in the context of the "wise person." The wise person is empathic, exceptionally understanding, and open to change. Orwoll and Perlmutter extensively discuss wise persons and their personality traits. Their research suggests that a wise person has a highly developed personality, can transcend narcissism, and is aware of his or her limitations. Sternberg also focuses on the personality of wise people. He finds that a wise person intellectually accepts ambiguous situations while probing for the truth and avoids rigidity. Clearly, the wise person is an extraordinary person.

Few chapters deal with the products of wisdom. Csikzentmihalyi and Rathunde emphasize assessing how the environment will be affected when planning for the future. They suggest that long-term global criteria be used to guide and evaluate decisions. Kramer, on the other hand, sees the products of wisdom as related more to the individual. Wisdom leads to resolving life tasks, to an ability to conduct a life review, and to incorporating spiritual aspects of life on a daily basis.

About one-half of the authors lay out a program of research into aspects of wisdom. Several researchers approach wisdom through surveys of words and wise persons. As Sternberg points out, this is exploration into implicit or culturally defined aspects of wisdom. Others, such as Baltes and Smith, seek to uncover the processes of wisdom by setting up problems or ambiguous prose passages for young and older adults to solve or interpret. Baltes and Smith use think-aloud protocols from subjects of various age groups to infer levels of expertise in life tasks.

The analysis presented in Table 14.2 shows that there is a wide array of research that may be conducted on the topic of wisdom. The authors may disagree with our characterization of their efforts, but there can hardly be disagreement over the fact that a wide diversity exists. Specification of the lines of research that will be most profitable awaits future evaluation. However, there appears to be strength in the alternatives of studying wisdom in relation to its products, processes, development, and expression as well as the different ways in which one may gather data on wisdom.

As a result of the present analysis of the content of the chapters in this volume, the authors believe that wisdom is best conceptualized as being the result of an interaction between three main systems of behavior: cognition, affect, and conation. The matter cannot rest there, however, since time plays a role. That is, today's judgments may look wiser or less wise with tomorrow's benefit of hindsight. In this manner, the wise leaders of one century may be judged less kindly in the future as the long-range consequences of decisions become apparent. This aspect of wisdom is perhaps best developed by historians, who may be better placed to judge the context of decisions as well as their long-range consequences.

In this volume, wisdom is primarily regarded as an attribute of behavior,

Table 14.2. *Facets of wisdom*

| Author (chap.) | Processes of wisdom | Development of wisdom | Traits of a wise person | Products of wisdom | Research methodology |
|---|---|---|---|---|---|
| Robinson (2) | *Contemporary:* understanding the empirical laws of nature | — | *Greek:* love truth, beauty *Christian:* follow divine wisdom | — | — |
| Csikszentmihalyi and Rathunde (3) | a growth-oriented way to mediate between conflicting types of information | — | empathic, intelligent, reflectve | choosing between environmental options and our needs | — |
| Labouvie-Vief (4) | integration of reflection (*mythos*) and critical thinking (*logos*) | progress from single way of knowing to integration of affect | — | — | young and old interpret ambiguous text, events, and emotional processes |
| Baltes and Smith (5) | factual and procedural knowledge integrated with contextualism, relativism, uncertainty | outgrowth of extensive experience and rich knowledge base | — | peak performance, exceptional insight, advice giving | analyze think-aloud protocols of adults engaged in life planning, review, management tasks |
| Chandler and Holliday (6) | — | — | overall competence, good judgment, communication skills, see things in large framework, exceptional understanding | — | survey people on the common meaning of wisdom, catalogue older literature for concepts of wisdom |
| Sternberg (7) | good reasoning ability, sagacity, perspicacity | — | probes knowledge, seeks truth, welcomes ambiguity, resists automatization | — | survey people on the words defining wisdom and psychometric tests of cognitive processes |

| | | | | | |
|---|---|---|---|---|---|
| Orwoll and Perlmutter (8) | integrate cognition with affect | integration gained with age | highly developed personality, know limits of self, transcend narcissism | understands and is insightful about self and others, intuitive sense | measure adults who are nominated as wise on affective, cognitive abiliies, life history |
| Meacham (9) | maintain balance between accumulation of facts (*knowing*) and questions (*doubting*) | develops in context of interpersonal relations, *not age* | — | — | — |
| Kitchener and Brenner (10) | synthesize knowledge from opposing views | age-related progress through seven stages of knowing acceptance of uncertainty | good judge, realize knowing is uncertain, sensitive to context | — | longitudinal study of reflective judgment |
| Arlin (11) | search for complementarity, asking questions, push limits | postformal operations allow emergence of wisdom schemata | open to change, sense of basics, has much knowledge, problem finder | good decisions | young and old given undefined life events and are to determine problem and solve it |
| Pascual-Leone (12) | wisdom-as-counsel, wisdom-as-will, wisdom-as-feeling or judgment | resolution of contradictions among self-schemes during adulthood | person who can will-not-to-will | freedom | — |
| Kramer (13) | recognition of individuality, context, understand change, integrate affect and cognition | requires integration of cognitive and affective development | solves own problems, advises others, manages social institutions | resolution of life's tasks, life review, spiritual introspection | — |

but one might also add the prospects for considering the "wise society," a society that encourages processes of wise decision making. Even the wise society, however, has values that would lie behind judgments as to what constitutes wise behavior. It seems, therefore, that in addition to the study of the individual, there is also room for the development of a collective social psychological approach or perhaps political science approach to complement the present thoughts by psychologists.

### Discussion

The chapters in this volume are an introduction to a refreshing topic, wisdom. The descriptive term *introduction* is used because the explorations of the topic of wisdom are in an early stage. The subject is complex and elusive, but one that clearly seems to be worthwhile to pursue. The discussions of the nature of wisdom seem to promote integration of our knowledge about specific aspects of behavior, the forte of experimental and developmental psychologists. For this reason, the pursuit of wisdom would seem to be a useful research task for psychologists to undertake.

The historical reviews in the chapters indicate that wisdom was a topic much discussed by philosophers and theologians long before the growth of empirical psychology at the end of the 19th century. The early 20th century further neglected the topic of wisdom and did away with any reference to the subject as a consequence of the dominance of psychology by behaviorism, which eschewed such "mentalistic" terms as *wisdom*. Being intellectually free to do research on wisdom does not mean that the subject easily will be made tractable for purposes of research. There are many ways to study wisdom. The different definitions of wisdom in the chapters illustrate the wide range of opinions about how the subject might be approached. Perhaps we are entering a period of enthusiastic speculation about an old topic of human behavior that can now become a new frontier of research.

It is not usual to question the motives of researchers – why they devote their energies to particular topics. Evaluation is best reserved for the qualities of the research rather than the motives. However, psychologists are self-conscious about studying deficits in the aged and in some instances appear to be looking for some positive feature of life in the later years. Perhaps the thought is: If older persons cannot be quick, they can at least be wise. In part, this may be a result of the projection of a young person's attitudes into the attributions about late-life qualities. But the research on wisdom should be carried out, in our opinion, in a manner designed not to flatter or depreciate the aged but to describe the natural circumstances of a long life.

As we read the chapters, the authors appeared to be more discursive than empirically oriented. Those who described research of their own described "soft" research in which no variable was manipulated. This may only be reflecting an early phase in the sophistication of research on wisdom, although some authors came close to suggesting that since scientific methodology to date has not encouraged the study of wisdom, perhaps empirical research inside of a laboratory will *never* answer questions about wisdom. Perhaps, before real progress can be made toward understanding wisdom, more thought must be given to the application of scientific methods to the study of wisdom and deliberate encouragement of different conceptualizations and study designs.

It is ironic that scholars (e.g., Robinson) note that the end of the "Dark Ages" came when science began to put away phenomenalistic forms of knowing. Just so, it may be that the "dark age of wisdom" is coming to an end with the acknowledgment that there is room for evidence from outside laboratory approaches.

## Summary

Generally, the authors agree that the concept of wisdom pulls together many different elements of behavior as well as disparate parts of the scientific enterprise. In the attempt to make research on wisdom operational, this integration begins to fade. Some authors see wisdom as wholly a cognitive expertise about life. Others give equal weight to affect and subjective types of knowledge in the development of wisdom.

To complicate matters further, a closer examination of the many uses of the word *wisdom* shows that it is tied to many other issues. A wise decision implies a "best" solution – a value-laden judgment. In turn, values are, to a large extent, culturally determined. Science has never been comfortable with discussions or research on values. Some authors pointed out that psychologists need to be careful that the methodology chosen to study wisdom captures its multidimensional aspects and does not artificially constrict the investigation.

This friendly disarray is not cause for alarm. The chapters suggest that wisdom research is in the process of problem finding, the most exciting and exacting part of the process of knowing. The stage is set, ready for innovative methodologies to enter, beginning a scientific mapping of wisdom.

Wisdom may be dissected into its component processes: the development of wisdom, the traits of a wise person, and the products of the processes. Each part of the whole, in turn, can be segmented further. As wisdom is quite a practical, down-to-earth phenomenon, investigators are forced to bring their theoretical musings and empirical research to scrutinize everyday life. The various aspects of wisdom must apply to real people in real situations in real time.

The present authors view wisdom as an emergent property of an individual's inward and external response to life experiences. A wise person has learned to balance the opposing valences of the three aspects of behavior: cognition, affect, and volition. A wise person weighs the knowns and unknowns, resists overwhelming emotion while maintaining interest, and carefully chooses when and where to take action.

It is hoped that research on wisdom will help to develop useful tools to assist world and national leaders in the increasingly complex problems facing humanity. Many crucial decisions, from nuclear waste to water use, face leaders and policy makers each day. Thus, wisdom is not simply for wise people or curious psychologists; it is for all people and the future of the world.

## References

Birren, J. E. (1969). Age and decision strategies. In A. T. Welford and J. E. Birren (Eds.), *Decision making and age* (pp. 23–36). Basel, Switzerland: Karger.

Clayton, V. P. (1975). *The meaning of wisdom to young and old in contemporary society.* Paper presented at the meetings of the Gerontological Society, Louisville.

Clayton, V. P., & Birren, J. E. (1980). The development of wisdom across the life-span: a reexamination of an ancient topic. In P. B. Baltes and O. G. Brim, Jr. (Eds.), *Life-span development and behavior* (pp. 103–135). New York: Academic Press.

Erikson, E. H., Erikson, J. M., & Kivnick, H. Q. (1986). *Vital involvement in old age: the experience of old age in our time.* New York: Norton.

*Encyclopedia Britannica* (1959). Chicago: William Benton.

Kantor, J. R. (1959). *Interbehavioral psychology.* Bloomington, IN: Principia Press.

Koch, S. (Ed.) (1959). *Psychology: a study of a science.* New York: McGraw-Hill.

*Oxford English Dictionary* (1933). Vol. XII. Oxford: The Clarendon Press.

Stevens, S. S. (Ed.) (1951). *Handbook of experimental psychology.* New York: John Wiley.

Taranto, M. A. (1989). *The wisdom in autobiography.* Paper presented at the Nineteenth Annual Symposium of the Jean Piaget Society, Philadelphia.

Teasdale, S. (1945). *Collected poems.* New York: Macmillan.

Wolman, B. B. (Ed.) (1973). *Handbook of general psychology.* Englewood Cliffs, NJ: Prentice-Hall.

Woodworth, R. S. (1938). *Experimental psychology.* New York: Henry Holt.

# Name index

Abelson, R., 100
Anderson, J. R., 101
Apostle, L., 239
Aquinas, T., 20, 29, 33, 37
Arendt, H., 249–50, 262
Aristotle, 15–19, 33, 37, 38, 214, 215
Arlin, P. K., 7, 325, 329
Augustine, 249–50

Bakan, D., 244–5, 258, 268
Baltes, P. B., 5, 107, 109–11, 124, 129–36,
    139, 143, 188–9, 194, 213, 214, 215, 240,
    263, 284, 285, 290, 325, 327, 328
Birren, J. E., 6, 8, 30, 35, 45, 46, 130, 131,
    143, 150, 168, 190–1, 193, 197, 199, 291,
    292, 320, 326
Blanchard-Fields, F., 71
Bloom, B., 105
Bopp, M. J., 303, 304, 308
Bransford, J. D., 233
Brenner, H. G., 7, 325, 329
Brent, S. B., 130, 284, 291
Bronowski, J., 186
Broughton, J., 73
Brown, A. L., 183
Bruner, J., 55
Brunswik, E., 126
Buber, M., 203
Burhoe, R. W., 27, 37

Campbell, D. T., 26, 43
Campbell, J., 75
Cassirer, E., 56, 63, 232, 244
Chandler, M. J., 5, 6, 29, 30, 34, 35, 38, 45,
    46, 106, 107, 124, 125, 130, 131, 136,
    143, 169–70, 186, 189–91, 193, 195, 197–
    8, 214, 245, 284, 288, 292, 325, 328
Cheng, P. W., 101
Chinen, A. B., 45, 46, 75, 292–3, 294, 296
Clayton, V. P., 6, 30, 35, 45, 46, 130, 131,
    143, 150, 168, 190–1, 193, 197, 199, 213,
    283–4, 290, 291, 292, 308, 320, 323
Clinchy, B., 68

Csikszentmihalyi, M., 4, 233, 235–6, 238,
    325, 328

DeLong, H., 61
Devoe, M., 292
Dillon, J. T., 233, 234–5
Dittmann-Kohli, F., 188–9, 215, 263, 284,
    285, 290, 296
Dixon, R., 107, 124, 129–36, 139, 188–9,
    213, 214, 263

Einstein, A., 142
Elias, N., 57
Emerson, R. W., 31
Epicurus, 18
Erikson, E., 47, 76, 160–2, 181, 207–8, 215,
    286, 320
Erikson, J. M., 320

Fisher, L. M., 8, 326
Frank, A., 200, 298
Franks, J. J., 233
Freeman, M., 135
Freud, S., 66

Gergen, K., 197
Getzels, J. W., 232–3, 235–6, 238
Goldstein, M. D., 287
Goldston, R. B., 299
Gutmann, D., 75

Habermas, J., 29, 34, 35, 39, 41, 45, 64, 122,
    123, 131, 136, 139–40, 207, 244, 245
Hakim-Larson, J., 292
Harré, R., 207
Hartshorne, C., 186–7, 201, 204, 205
Haviland, J. M., 293
Heckhausen, J., 107
Heidegger, M., 263, 265
Helson, R., 166
Holliday, S. G., 5, 6, 29, 30, 34, 35, 38, 45,
    46, 106, 107, 124, 125, 130, 131, 136,
    143, 169–70, 189–91, 193, 195, 197, 198,
    214, 245, 284, 288, 292, 325, 328

333

# Subject index

act-of-will, 252–4
adaptation, 281
adult development, 67–8, 69–72; and emotional processes, 73–4; of self-concept, 74; *see also* postformal reasoning stage
affect, 291–2; and cognition, 292, 296, 298–9, 300–4; regulation, 295–6
age: decline of wisdom with, 197–9; myth of wisdom and old, 194–7; and Reflective Judgment Interview score, 223–5, 226; and wisdom, 79, 91–3, 106, 112–14, 128, 135, 168, 170–3, 191–7, 245, 266–7, 296–7, 319–20, 326
ambiguity, coping with, 155, 237
anger, 16, 70–1
asymmetry, 232
attributes of wise persons, 107–8, 328–9; behavioral, 327; societal, 330; *see also* characteristics of wisdom

causation, 17
changes: in adulthood, 256–9; cultural, 206; openness to, 232–3; recognition of possibilities of, 303
characteristics of wisdom, 326–9; empathy, 248–9; existential counseling, 247–8; feeling/judging, 266–9, 270–1; multidimensional, 320–1; wisdom-as-will, 244–7, 249; *see also* attributes of wise persons
Christianity, 19–20
cognition, epistemic, 216–17; stages of, 218–22
cognitive development: and affect intensity, 299; levels of, 299; and *logos*, 65–7
communication of wisdom, 46–8; and self-discovery, 46–7; *see also* counseling, wise
complementarity, 231–2
complexity, cognitive, 163–4
conation, 252, 320
concept attainment, *see* problem finding
conceptions, *see* definitions
conflict resolution: and dialectical thinking, 302–2; modes of thinking in, 297

context: environmental, 156–7; matrix, and knowledge, 184–7; of wisdom, 321–2
contextualism, 101–2
counseling, wise, 247–8, 262–3, 286
creativity, 6, 269–70, 271; factors of, 146; in problem finding, 232–4, 235–6; and pushing the limits, 233–5; and wisdom, 145–6, 149

dangers of wisdom, 41–4; as accumulation of knowledge, 42; as presumption, 43–4
development of wisdom, 44–8, 104–6, 207–9, 322–3, 327–8; through dialectical thinking, 300–4; and metaawareness of motivation, 45–6
dialectical thinking, 289–90, 300–4; and problem finding, 239
domains of wisdom, 96–7, 283–5
doubting, 185–7, 188–90; *see also* knowledge, context matrix

education, 172–3
ego development, 306–7
emotions, expression of, 73–4; *see also* affect
empathy, 296; and feeling/judging, 248–9
empiricism, 21–2
epic poetry and folk theories of wisdom, 13–14
Epicureanism, 18
*episteme*, 14, 22
epistemology: evolutionary, 26; vs. logic, 225–6
ethics, modern, 33–5; and decision making, 34–6
*eudaimonia*, 16, 17
evolutionary views of wisdom, 4, 26–49; as cognitive process, 28–32, 48; as personal good, 36–41, 49; as virtue, 32–6, 48–9
experience, contradictory aspects of, 293
expertise, 5, 132–4; and breadth and depth of knowledge, 213–14; vs. expert knowledge system, 96, 98–9; and problem finding, 236
expert knowledge, research on, 108–14; and

337

0(

# СОДЕРЖАНИЕ

Литературно-художественное издание

**Асламова Дарья Михайловна**
**НОВЫЕ ПРИКЛЮЧЕНИЯ ДРЯННОЙ ДЕВЧОНКИ**


*Издано в авторской редакции*
Художественный редактор *Е. Савченко*
Технические редакторы *Н. Носова, А. Щербакова*
Корректор *Е. Дорохова*


Изд. лиц. № 065377 от 22.08.97.

Налоговая льгота — общероссийский классификатор
продукции ОК-005-93, том 2; 953000 — книги, брошюры.


Подписано в печать с готовых монтажей 07.08.2001.
Формат 84 × 108 $^1/_{32}$. Гарнитура «Таймс». Печать офсетная.
Усл. печ. л. 23,5. Уч.-изд. л. 17,3.
Доп. тираж VIII 5100 экз. Заказ 197

ЗАО «Издательство «ЭКСМО-ПРЕСС»,
125190, Москва, Ленинградский проспект,
д. 80, корп. 16, подъезд 3.

Отпечатано в полном соответствии
с качеством предоставленных диапозитивов
в ОАО «Можайский полиграфический комбинат».
143200, г. Можайск, ул. Мира, 93.